An Introduction to Programming and Computer Science

Maria Litvin
Phillips Academy, Andover, Massachusetts

Gary Litvin
Skylight Software, Inc.

Skylight Publishing
Andover, Massachusetts

Skylight Publishing
9 Bartlet Street, Suite 70
Andover, MA 01810
(978) 475-1431
e-mail: support@skylit.com
web: http://www.skylit.com

Library of Congress Catalog Card Number: 97–091209

ISBN 0-9654853-9-0

5 6 7 8 9 10 ML 01 00

Printed in the United States of America

To Marg and Aaron

Brief Contents

Part Two. **Classes and Data Structures**

Contents

Part Two.   Classes and Data Structures

Chapter 17.   Linked Lists   289

Chapter 18.   Stacks   313

Chapter 19.   Recursion   327

Chapter 20.   Queues   345

Preface

C++ is becoming the language of choice for introducing college students across the country to computer science and programming. In high schools, the Advanced Placement* (AP) examination in Computer Science will be administered in C++ for the first time at the end of the 1998-99 academic year. While Maria was teaching an experimental year-long AP computer science course in C++ in 1995-96, we both saw the need for a manageable and concise textbook that would cover programming, algorithms, and data structures in a style indigenous to C++. Maria's students at Phillips Academy embraced the opportunity to take the AP course in C++ (even though they had to switch to Pascal in the final weeks before the AP exam) and, with their support, *C++ for You++* was born.

We have designed this book for a two- or three-semester high school or college introductory course in programming and data structures, with the choice of topics guided by a typical first-year college course as described in the College Board's Advanced Placement curriculum. Part 1 covers C++ programming (excluding classes), with the emphasis on effective programming practices and good style. Part 2 introduces C++ classes and covers the usual data structures as well as searching and sorting algorithms.

This *Special AP Edition* introduces the five AP classes, *apvector*, *apmatrix*, *apstring*, *apstack*, and *apqueue*, and explains how to use them. These classes were developed by the College Board's C++ AP Development Committee and are required for the APCS exam. This book follows the Committee's recommendations that students always use the *apvector* and *apmatrix* classes instead of built-in one- and two-dimensional arrays, and that the *apstring* class always be used instead of null-terminated strings. The *apstack* and *apqueue* classes provide standard implementations of the stack and queue data structures.

---

*Advanced Placement is a registered trademark of the College Entrance Examination Board which is not responsible for the contents of this text.

Students who take the A- or AB- level AP exam are expected to know how to use the *apvector*, *apmatrix*, and *apstring* classes in programs. Students who take the AB-level exam are also expected to use and re-implement the *apstack* and *apqueue* classes.

Computer science is an applied discipline, not just a set of academic theories. Therefore, the main thrust of *C++ for You++* is to teach students to write effective programs. Combining our experience as a teacher and a professional software engineer, we have sought to include modern, realistic examples and present them in a format teachers and their students will find accessible. Our labs and case studies aim to demonstrate the most appropriate uses of the programming techniques and data structures we cover.

We assume that at least one or two classes each week will be spent in a computer lab with students working independently or in small groups. The accompanying disk contains all the labs and case studies, and the teacher's edition disk provides complete solutions to all labs. To simplify some of the lab exercises, teachers can share "hints" or fragments of code from their solution disk. Meanwhile, "extra credit" tasks can make the lab exercises more challenging for more advanced students. The book also proposes several independent programming projects that can stretch over a couple of weeks. The *Workbook to Accompany C++ for You++* provides many additional questions, exercises, and projects.

C++ for You++ does not require prior knowledge of programming. For beginners seeking a primer on C++ programming, our book includes many code fragments and "cookbook" recipes (in the text and on the accompanying disk) for writing reliable programs. Our lab exercises ask students to modify or enhance existing code before having them write programs from scratch—a "training wheels" approach that turns out confident, competent programmers.

For those already familiar with C++ (including structures, but not necessarily classes), Part 2 can serve as an independent introduction to data structures. After a brief discussion of how to create modular programs, we introduce C++ classes and templates and learn how to implement and use them. Then we begin a serious discussion of some software development topics and techniques not specific to C++ that are important to any computer programmer. We discuss data structures (linked lists, stacks, queues, trees) and their uses, recursion, and common algorithms for searching, hashing, and sorting. We also describe the *apstack* and *apqueue* classes and their use.

C++ for You++ seeks to accommodate different learning styles and aptitudes. In general, we have tried to reveal the underlying concepts of C++, where possible, and emphasize the programming choices that have become part of the C++ culture. Straightforward "cookbook" examples are followed by more detailed explanations of how and why they work. Throughout the book, less important technical details are grouped in sections that can be skipped on a first reading. For instance, Chapter 10, "Monte Carlo Methods," is optional; Chapter 11, "Pointers, References, Dynamic Memory Allocation," can be skipped almost entirely (with the exception of Section 11.3, which explains how to pass arguments to functions by reference). Some more advanced topics, in particular friends, iterators, static class members (Sections 21.6 - 21.8) and inheritance (Chapter 28) are not part of the AP subset required for the AP exam and can be skipped or covered partially, as time permits. Stream input and output classes are summarized in more detail in an appendix.

Without further delay, let us begin learning to program in C++!

Acknowledgments

Our sincere thanks to Doug Kuhlmann, the chairman of the Mathematics Department at Phillips Academy, for suggesting that Maria switch her Advanced Placement computer science course to C++ three years ahead of the national requirement; his support was most valuable in this effort. We thank George Best for encouraging us to write this book. Thanks to Bill Adams of Concord Academy and Kathy Larson of Kingston High School who read a preliminary draft of the book and suggested some important improvements. We are very grateful to Deborah Roudebush of Potomac Falls High School for inspiring this *AP Edition*, encouragement, and help with converting programs from built-in arrays to *apstring*, *apvector*, and *apmatrix* classes. And our special thanks to Margaret Litvin for her thoughtful and thorough editing.

About the Authors

Maria Litvin has taught computer science and mathematics at Phillips Academy in Andover, Massachusetts, since 1987. She is an Advanced Placement Computer Science exam reader and, as a consultant for The College Board, provides C++ training for high school computer science teachers. Prior to joining Phillips Academy, Maria taught computer science at Boston University.

Gary Litvin has worked in many areas of software development including artificial intelligence, pattern recognition, computer graphics, and neural networks. As founder of Skylight Software, Inc., he developed SKYLIGHTS/GX, one of the first visual programming tools for C and C++ programmers. Gary led in the development of several state-of-the-art software products including interactive touch screen development tools, OCR and handwritten character recognition systems, and credit card fraud detection software.

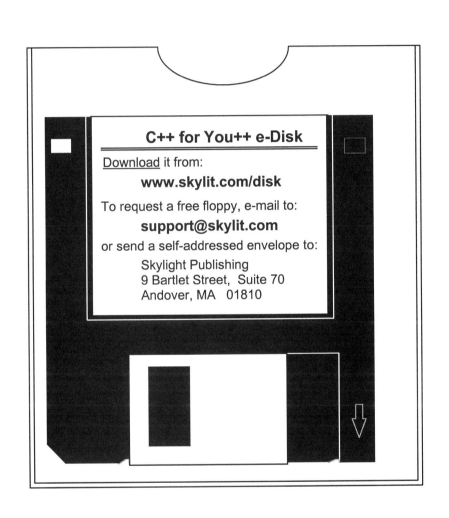

Part One

Programs:
Syntax and Style

1

Introduction to Hardware and Software

1.1.   Discussion

Spectacular achievements in computer technology in the past 50 years have reshaped our lives in many ways, and will continue to do so, to the delight of some and the chagrin of others. The proliferation of computers has not only changed our everyday circumstances but has also profoundly affected the ways we think, speak, "process information," learn, solve problems, and communicate. At the same time, paradoxically, the fundamental principles underlying the design of digital computers have changed little since UNIVAC, the first "general-purpose, programmable, digital, stored-program" computer, was installed in the Bureau of the Census in 1951.

A typical modern computer, like its ancient ancestors, is built around a ***CPU*** (Central Processing Unit) that reads "bits" of data from ***memory***, performs calculations or logical operations, and writes the resulting data back into memory. A computer system also includes ***peripheral devices*** that provide input and output and secondary mass storage. Only instead of the UNIVAC's CPU, which took up a cabinet the size of two vending machines and could perform 2000 additions or 450 multiplications per second with its vacuum tubes, Intel's Pentium microprocessor has 3.1 million transistors etched into a square slice of silicon wafer smaller than three quarters of an inch wide. It can run at over 300 ***MIPS*** (million instructions per second) and includes a "floating-point coprocessor" on the same chip for doing real-number arithmetic. Instead of UNIVAC's 1000 "words" of memory, a typical personal computer of the late 1990s has 8 to 64 "Megs of ***RAM***" (Megabytes, i.e. millions of bytes, of Random-Access Memory) packed in a few SIMMs (Single In-Line Memory Modules). And "peripheral" devices no longer seem quite so peripheral when a keyboard, a display, a hard drive, a floppy drive, a fax/modem, a trackball, a microphone, and a speaker can all be built into one "notebook" unit that weighs less than a hard-cover college textbook on computer architecture.

By now the progress in computer hardware has been celebrated enough in colorful graphs and charts that grow (or decrease, when appropriate) exponentially. The speed of microprocessors has been doubling roughly every two to three years since the introduction of Intel's 8086 microprocessor in 1978; the cost of one megabyte of RAM has halved at approximately the same rate.

A computer is a universal ***programmable*** device. It can model nearly any task that involves logical and arithmetic operations. Of course, it will not know how to go about a particular task without the appropriate program. But the idea that computers should have "software" has not always been as obvious as it seems today. UNIVAC's ancestor, ENIAC, developed in 1942-1946 primarily for military applications, was programmed by people actually connecting hundreds of wires to sockets — hardly a "software development" activity as we know it. (ENIAC occupied a huge room, had 18,000 vacuum tubes, could perform 300 multiplications per second, and used more than 180 kilowatts of electricity.) The breakthrough came in 1946 when John von Neumann (1903-1957), a brilliant mathematician working in Princeton's Institute for Advanced Study, came up with and developed the idea that a computer program can actually be stored in the computer memory itself in the form of encoded CPU instructions, together with the data on which that program operates. Hence the term "program-stored" computers. Virtually all modern computers are based on this ***von Neumann architecture***.

Digital program-stored computers quickly won out over their early competition, the analog computers. Analog computers represented information as different shapes of continuous electrical signals. They could solve differential equations and similar problems by transforming the shapes of the signals when they passed through analog electrical devices. The "programmers" could rearrange the electrical components and connections, but "software" programming was impossible.

By contrast, digital computers represent and handle all information in discrete binary bits: "on" or "off," "high" or "low," "1" or "0." The information is stored in memory by switching between the two ***binary*** states of memory "bits": each bit can be set to "1" or "0", "on" or "off." The CPU is essentially one very complex electrical circuit with many "digital" switches where one electrical current may switch another current on or off. When chained together, such switches can emulate logical operations. For example, a current A may be turned on only when current B <u>and</u> current C are both on. A current D may be on if the current E is <u>not</u> on. In modern microchips, the logical switches are microscopic semiconductor devices called transistors. Von Neumann proved that all arithmetic operations can be reduced to three simple logical operations: "and," "or," and "not."

Von Neumann computers are inherently <u>sequential</u>: the CPU fetches and processes one instruction at a time. Breathtaking progress in computer technology has left little time to seriously re-examine the basic "one CPU + memory" paradigm of computer architecture. Nevertheless, <u>parallel</u> computers and "supercomputers" with multiple CPUs have been built and used for time-critical applications. SIMD (<u>S</u>ingle <u>I</u>nstruction <u>M</u>ultiple <u>D</u>ata) machines work as ***array processors*** — the same CPU instruction is executed for many data elements at once. MISD (<u>M</u>ultiple <u>I</u>nstructions <u>S</u>ingle <u>D</u>ata) machines work as a pipeline (or a conveyer belt): each

CPU performs one operation on a data element and passes it on to the next CPU in the pipeline. These computers basically build on von Neumann architecture.

A few computer scientists are working on radically new computer architectures based on highly parallel computational models. For example, in a **data-driven** computer architecture, operations can be performed asynchronously, in a highly parallel manner. An operation is executed as soon as all its required operands "arrive," and the result of the operation is passed on or broadcast concurrently to all the waiting operations that might need it. Not long ago, a solution to a classical computer science problem too time-consuming for the fastest sequential computers was demonstrated in an experimental computation on a parallel "biocomputer." The solution was produced in the form of the mix of specific DNA molecules in a test tube.

In the remaining sections of this chapter we will get familiar with common computer terms, make a brief overview of the computer hardware components, and discuss software environment and development tools. We will also discuss how numbers and text are represented in computer memory.

1.2.   Hardware Overview

1.2.1.   The CPU

The functionality of a CPU is characterized by its instruction set and internal *registers*. The registers are specialized built-in memory cells that are used for holding operands, memory addresses, and intermediate results. Some of the registers are accessible to the programmer. The instruction set includes instructions for loading CPU registers from memory and storing their values into memory, for logical and arithmetic operations, and for altering the sequence of operations. The CPU fetches the next instruction from memory, interprets its operation code, and performs the appropriate operation. The instructions are executed in sequence unless a particular instruction tells the CPU to "jump" to another place in the program. Conditional branching instructions tell the CPU to continue with the next instruction or to jump to another place depending on the result of the previous operation.

Some CPUs can interpret hundreds of different instructions. Another approach is used in RISC (Reduced Instructions Set Chip) microprocessors, which have few basic instructions but can perform them very quickly. Computers with RISC microprocessors implement more complex operations through combinations of basic instructions in software.

Every computer has an internal "clock" that generates electrical pulses at a fixed frequency. All CPU operations and their component steps are synchronized with the clock's pulses; their duration is measured in *clock cycles*. The CPU's speed depends on the frequency of the clock. The Intel 8088 microprocessor in the original IBM Personal Computer, for example, ran at 4.77 MHz (megahertz, or million pulses per second). Seventeen years and five generations later, Intel's Pentium microprocessors run at 200 MHz; some instructions have also been optimized to take fewer cycles.

A microprocessor CPU connects to memory and other devices through a set of parallel lines controlled by digital electronics, called a *bus*. A CPU may use a separate *address bus* for specifying memory addresses and a *data bus* for reading and writing memory values. Besides the internal clock speed, the computer's overall performance depends on the speed of the bus transfers and the width of the bus. The 8086 microprocessor in the PC XT, for example, had a 16-bit bus, which means it could carry 16 bits of data concurrently from memory to the CPU. It also used 16-bit CPU registers. The Pentium has a 32-bit bus and 32-bit registers.

In a personal computer, the CPU is mounted on a PC (Printed Circuit) board, called the "motherboard," together with memory chips, the bus, and supporting electronics.

1.2.2. Memory

The computer memory can be viewed as a uniform linear array of *bits* for storing information. Each bit can have a value of 0 or 1. Most modern computers arrange bits in groups of eight, called *bytes*. Each byte has a unique address that can be used in CPU instructions to fetch the value stored in the byte or write a new value into it. A CPU does not have to read or write memory bytes sequentially: bytes can be accessed in any arbitrary sequence. This is why computer memory is called *random-access memory* or *RAM*. The size of RAM is measured in *kilobytes* (KB, or simply K) or *megabytes* (MB). A kilobyte is 1024 (2^{10}) bytes; a megabyte is 1024 x 1024 = 2^{20} = 1,048,576 bytes. (Powers of 2 have a special significance in computer technology for a reason that will become clear shortly.)

In the early days, designers of personal computers thought that 64K of RAM would be sufficient for the foreseeable future. An additional hardware mechanism, the *segment registers*, had to be added to the later versions of Intel's microprocessors to address a larger memory space, up to 1MB, while maintaining compatibility with the old programs. But the 1MB limit very quickly proved to be inadequate too. Eventually the Intel's 386 microprocessor came out with the 32-bit memory address bus, which allows programs to directly address four *gigabytes* (GB) of memory. One gigabyte is equal to $2^{30} = 1,073,741,824$ bytes. This should suffice for a while, but no one knows how long. (1 GB can hold roughly 250,000 pages of a text like this one.)

A small part of the computer memory is permanent non-erasable memory, known as *read-only memory* or *ROM*. A personal computer's ROM contains, among other things, the initialization code that *boots up* the *operating system* (that is, loads into memory the *boot record* or initialization code from the disk and passes control to it). Any computer program has to be loaded into memory before it can run. ROM solves the "first-program" dilemma — some program must already be in memory to load any other program into memory. The *operating system* has the job of loading and executing other programs. In a personal computer, ROM also contains the computer configuration program and hardware diagnostic programs that check various computer components. The ROM BIOS (Basic Input Output System) contains programs for controlling the keyboard, display, floppy disk drives, and other devices.

1.2.3.   Secondary Storage Devices

A computer's RAM has only limited space, and its contents are wiped out when the power is turned off. All the programs and data in a computer system have to be stored in secondary mass storage. The auxiliary storage devices include hard disks, floppy disk drives, tape drives, optical disks, and other devices. Access to data on these devices is much slower than access to RAM. An executable program has to be loaded from a disk, a floppy, or a tape into RAM before it can run. When a program is running, it can read and write data directly to and from secondary storage devices.

A hard or floppy disk has to be formatted by a special program before it can be used to store data. The formatting program splits the disk into *sectors* by placing special sector delimiter marks on it. The disk BIOS in ROM knows how to read or write a specified sector on a specified *track* and *cylinder* on the disk's magnetic surface under one of its read/write *heads.*

There are also WORM (Write Once, Read Many [times]) devices, which are used for data archiving purposes. CD-ROM (Compact Disk Read Only Memory) optical disks are used for publishing large programs and texts. A CD-ROM can hold more than 600MB (or up to 2 or 3 GB with data compression).

The operating system software organizes the data in secondary storage into *files*. A file may contain a related set of data, a program, a document, an image, and so on; it has a unique name. The operating system maintains a *directory* of file names, locations, sizes, date and time of the last update and other attributes. Thus a "file" is a <u>software</u> rather than a hardware concept.

1.2.4. Input and Output Devices

A personal computer receives user input through the keyboard and displays the output on the computer screen. In many programs the input is echoed on the screen as you type, creating the illusion that the keyboard is directly connected to the display. In fact, these are two entirely different devices that are connected only indirectly through the CPU and the currently running program. The keyboard sends the program digital codes that represent the pressed keys. The screen is controlled by a **video adapter** and displays the contents of special video memory in the adapter, called VRAM. VRAM is addressable by the CPU and may contain codes, colors and attributes of characters (when running in the so-called "text" modes) or colors or intensities of individual **pixels** ("picture elements") in graphics modes.

A mainframe computer (a very large multi-user computer) may have hundreds of terminals attached to it. The terminals send keystrokes and receive commands and display codes from the computer via digital transmission lines.

Printers, plotters, digitizing tablets, scanners and other devices receive commands and data from the computer in digital form and may send data or control codes back to the computer according to a specific communications protocol. Network adapters and cables are used to connect several computers into a LAN (<u>L</u>ocal <u>A</u>rea <u>N</u>etwork).

Modems transmit digital information through telephone lines. A sending modem encodes bits of information into a sequence of electrical pulses that emulate signals obtained from different acoustic tones in a telephone. A receiving modem decodes the signal back into digital form.   A modem communicates to the computer through a **serial port**, which is a connector to a standard hardware interface between a computer and some peripheral device.

Special data acquisition devices equipped with **A/D (analog-to-digital)** converters allow computers to convert an electrical signal into digital form by frequently sampling the amplitude of the signal and storing the digitized values in memory. **D/A (digital-to-analog)** converters perform the reverse transformation: they generate electrical currents from the digitized amplitudes stored in the computer. These devices allow the computer to receive data from instruments of all kinds and to serve as a universal control device in industrial applications and scientific experiments.

Input and output devices are connected to the computer via hardware *interface* modules that implement specific data transfer protocols. In a personal computer, the interfaces may be built into the motherboard or take the form of special adapter cards that plug into the bus. Devices connected to the computer are usually controlled by special programs called *drivers* that handle all the details and peculiarities of the device and the data transfer protocol.

1.3. Representation of Information in Computer Memory

Computer memory is a uniform array of bytes that does not privilege any particular type of information. The memory may contain CPU instructions, numbers and text characters, and any other information that can be represented in digital form. Since a suitable A/D converter can more or less accurately convert any electrical signal to digital form, any information that can be carried over a wire can be represented in computer memory. This includes sounds, images, motion, and so on (but, so far, excludes taste and smell).

The CPU instructions are represented in the computer memory in a manner specific to each particular brand of CPU. The first byte or two represent the operation code that identifies the instruction and the total number of bytes in that instruction; the following bytes may represent the values or memory addresses of the operands. The representation of memory addresses depends on the CPU architecture, but they are basically numbers that indicate the absolute sequential number of the byte in memory. The address of an instruction may be given in terms of the relative displacement from the current instruction. A CPU may have special *segment* registers and *index* registers that help calculate the actual address in memory for a specified instruction or operand.

The format for numbers is mostly dictated by the CPU, too, because the CPU has instructions for arithmetic operations that expect numbers to be represented in a certain way. Characters (letters, digits, etc.) are represented using one of the several character code systems that have become standard not only for representing text inside computers but also in computer terminals, printers, and other devices. The code assigns each character a number, which usually takes one byte (but may take two bytes if the character set is very large as, for example, in Japanese computers).

Fortunately, high-level programming languages such as C++ shield computer programmers from the intricacies of how to represent CPU instructions, memory addresses, numbers, and characters.

Representing other types of information is often a matter of a specific application's design. A black and white image, for example, may be represented as a sequence of bytes where each bit represents a pixel of the image: 0 for white and 1 for black. The sequence of pixels typically goes from left to right along each horizontal line of the image and then from top to bottom by row.

1.3.1. Numbers

Integers from 0 to 255 can be represented in one byte using the binary (base-2) system as follows:

Decimal	Binary
0	00000000
1	00000001
2	00000010
3	00000011
4	00000100
5	00000101
6	00000110
7	00000111
8	00001000
. . .	. . .
252	11111100
253	11111101
254	11111110
255	11111111

If we use 2 bytes (16 bits), we can represent integers from 0 to $2^{16}-1 = 65535$:

Decimal	Binary
0	00000000 00000000
1	00000000 00000001
2	00000000 00000010
. . .	. . .
65534	11111111 11111110
65535	11111111 11111111

In general, k bits can produce 2^k different combinations of 0's and 1's. k binary digits can represent non-negative integers in the range from 0 to 2^k-1. (A 16-bit memory address can identify $2^{16} = 65536$ different memory locations. Therefore, if we want to be able to address each individual byte, 16-bit addresses cover 64K bytes of memory space.)

CPUs perform all arithmetic operations on binary numbers. A CPU may have instructions that perform 8-bit, 16-bit, or 32-bit arithmetic, for instance. If the operand includes multiple bytes, the order of bytes in memory may depend on the CPU: in Intel's architecture, for example, the <u>least significant</u> byte is stored first, while in the 68000 family of microprocessors the <u>most significant</u> byte is stored first.

⌘ ⌘ ⌘

Since it is difficult for a human brain to grasp long sequences of 0's and 1's, programmers who have to deal with binary data often use the **_hexadecimal_** (or simply "**_hex_**") representation in their documentation and programs. The hex system is the base-16 system, which uses 16 digits. The first ten digits are the usual 0 through 9, with the eleventh through sixteenth digits represented by the letters 'A' through 'F'. A byte can be split into two four-bit **_quads;_** each quad represents one hex digit, as follows:

Decimal	Binary	Hex
0	0000	0
1	0001	1
2	0010	2
3	0011	3
4	0100	4
5	0101	5
6	0110	6
7	0111	7
8	1000	8
9	1001	9
10	1010	A
11	1011	B
12	1100	C
13	1101	D
14	1110	E
15	1111	F

Experienced programmers remember the bit patterns for the sixteen hex digits and can easily convert a binary number into hex and back. The following examples show a few numbers represented in the decimal, 16-bit binary, and hex systems:

Decimal	Binary	Hex
0	00000000 00000000	0000
1	00000000 00000001	0001
12	00000000 00001100	000C
32	00000000 00100000	0020
128	00000000 10000000	0080
255	00000000 11111111	00FF
256	00000001 00000000	0100
32767	01111111 11111111	7FFF
32768	10000000 00000000	8000
65535	11111111 11111111	FFFF

⌘   ⌘   ⌘

What about negative numbers? The same bit pattern may represent an unsigned (positive) integer and a negative integer, depending on how a particular instruction interprets it. Suppose we use 16-bit binary numbers, but now we decide that they represent <u>signed</u> integers. Positive integers from 0 to $2^{15}-1 = 32767$ can be represented as before. These use only 15 least-significant bits. As to negative integers, their representation may be *machine-dependent,* varying from CPU to CPU. Many CPUs, including the Intel family, use a method called two's-complement arithmetic. In this method, a negative integer x in the range from -1 to $-2^{15} = -32768$ is represented the same way as the unsigned binary number $2^{16} - |x| = 65536 - |x|$, where $|x|$ is the absolute value of x. For example:

Decimal signed	Decimal unsigned	Binary	Hex
-32768	32768	10000000 00000000	8000
-2	65534	11111111 11111110	FFFE
-1	65535	11111111 11111111	FFFF
0	0	00000000 00000000	0000
1	1	00000000 00000001	0001
32767	32767	01111111 11111111	7FFF

Unsigned numbers greater than or equal to 32768 would be interpreted as negative numbers. Note that in these numbers the leftmost bit is always 1, so this bit can serve as a sign indicator. −1 is represented as hex FFFF.

When you add two unsigned numbers and the result overflows the 16-bit value, the most significant (carry) bit is thrown away. For example:

```
        Decimal              Binary
        unsigned

          65530       11111111 11111010
   +          8       00000000 00001000
        -------------------------------
          65538       1 00000000 00000010


        Take away the lost carry bit:

   -     65536       1 00000000 00000000
        -------------------------------
              2       00000000 00000010
```

You obtain exactly the same result if you interpret the same binary values as signed numbers in the two's-complement form:

```
        Decimal              Binary
        unsigned

             -6       11111111 11111010
   +          8       00000000 00001000
        -------------------------------
              2       00000000 00000010
```

That is what makes the two's-complement representation of negative integers convenient.

⌘　⌘　⌘

Real numbers are represented using one of the standard formats expected by the CPU (or a separate floating-point arithmetic unit). Like scientific notation, this representation consists of a fractional part (mantissa) and an exponent part, but here both parts are represented as binary numbers. The IEEE (Institute of Electrical and Electronics Engineers) standard for a 4-byte (32-bit) representation uses 1 bit for the sign, 8 bits for the exponent and 23 bits for the mantissa. 127 is added to the exponent to ensure that negative exponents are still represented by non-negative numbers.

The mantissa represents a number x greater than or equal to 1 and less than 2. Its high-order binary digit (leftmost bit) is always equal to 1; this bit is implicit and not included in the binary representation. Figure 1-1 gives a few examples. This format allows programmers to represent numbers in the range from approximately -3.4×10^{38} to 3.4×10^{38} with at least seven digits of precision.

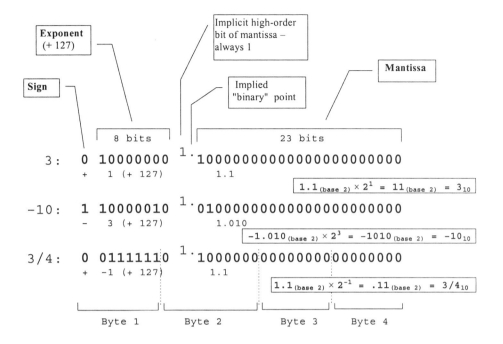

Figure 1-1.   IEEE standard representation of 32-bit floating-point numbers.

1.3.2.   Characters

Characters are represented by numeric codes. In most computers the numeric codes range from 0 to 255 and fit into one byte. The two most common character codes are EBCDIC (Extended Binary Coded Decimal Interchange Code), used in IBM mainframes, and ASCII (American Standard Code for Information Interchange), used in personal computers, printers and other devices. In the PC world, the term ASCII file refers to a text file (in which characters are represented in ASCII code), as opposed to a *binary file* that may contain numbers, images or any other digitized information. Normally you won't find EBCDIC-encoded data on a PC unless the file originated on a mainframe.

ASCII code proper defines 128 characters with codes from 0 to 127 and uses only seven bits in a byte. The second half of the code, from 128 to 255, is called *extended ASCII* and may vary from machine to machine. Codes from 33 to 127 represent "printable" characters: digits, upper- and lowercase letters, punctuation marks and so on. 32 (hex 20) is a space.

Hex	0_	1_	2_	3_	4_	5_	6_	7_
_0	0 NUL	16 DEL	32 (SPACE)	48 0	64 @	80 P	96 `	112 p
_1	1 SOH	17 DC1	33 !	49 1	65 A	81 Q	97 a	113 q
_2	2 STX	18 DC2	34 "	50 2	66 B	82 R	98 b	114 r
_3	3 ETX	19 DC3	35 #	51 3	67 C	83 S	99 c	115 s
_4	4 EOT	20 DC4	36 $	52 4	68 D	84 T	100 d	116 t
_5	5 ENQ	21 NAK	37 %	53 5	69 E	85 U	101 e	117 u
_6	6 ACK	22 SYN	38 &	54 6	70 F	86 V	102 f	118 v
_7	7 BEL	23 ETB	39 '	55 7	71 G	87 W	103 g	119 w
_8	8 BS	24 CAN	40 (	56 8	72 H	88 X	104 h	120 x
_9	9 HT	25 EM	41)	57 9	73 I	89 Y	105 i	121 y
_A	10 LF	26 SUB	42 *	58 :	74 J	90 Z	106 j	122 z
_B	11 VT	27 ESC	43 +	59 ;	75 K	91 [	107 k	123 {
_C	12 FF	28 FS	44 ,	60 <	76 L	92 \	108 l	124 |
_D	13 CR	29 GS	45 -	61 =	77 M	93]	109 m	125 }
_E	14 SO	30 RS	46 .	62 >	78 N	94 ^	110 n	126 ~
_F	15 SI	31 US	47 /	63 ?	79 O	95 _	111 o	127 (NUL)

Figure 1-2. ASCII code used in personal computers, printers and other devices.

The first 32 ASCII codes (0-31) are reserved for special *control* codes.   For example, code 13 (hex 0D) is "carriage return" (CR), 10 (hex 0A) is "line feed" (LF), 12 (hex 0C) is "form feed" (FF) and 9 (hex 09) is "horizontal tab" (HT).   The use of control codes may depend to some extent on the program or device that processes them.   A standard ASCII table, including more obscure control codes, is presented in Figure 1-2.

1.4.   Software Overview

The term *software* may refer not only to computer programs but also to implementations of tasks or functions through programs or data files, as in "software interface," "software fonts," and so on.   The line between hardware and software is not always clear.   In the modern world microprocessors are embedded in many objects, from microwave ovens and VCRs to satellites.   Their programs are developed using simulation tools on normal computers; when a program is finalized, it is permanently wired into ROMs.   Such programs are referred to as *firmware*.

A modern computer not only runs individual programs but also maintains a "software environment."   The bottom layer in this environment comprises BIOS, device drivers, interrupt handlers — programs that directly support hardware devices and functions.   The next layer is the *operating system,* a software program that provides convenient and efficient computer access services to users and standard support functions to other programs.

The operating system loads programs into RAM from secondary storage and runs them.   On mainframes, operating systems provide *time-sharing* that allows multiple users to work on the computer concurrently.   In such a multi-user system, one user may be slowly editing a file or entering data on a terminal using only a small fraction of available CPU time.   At the same time another program may be doing a lot of "number-crunching."   A multi-user operating system allocates "time slices" to each program and automatically switches between them.   The operating system prioritizes the "jobs" and swaps segments of programs in and out of memory as needed.   A personal computer assumes one user, but contemporary users often enjoy a *multi-tasking* operating system that lets them keep several programs active concurrently.

The operating system also establishes and maintains a file system in secondary storage.   Part of the operating system is a set of routines (sets of instructions, callable from other programs) that provide standard service functions to programs.   These include functions for creating, reading, and writing files.   The operating system *shell* provides a set of user commands, including commands for displaying, copying, deleting and printing files, executing programs, and so on. More modern operating systems use *GUI* (Graphical User Interface), where commands can be entered by selecting items in menus or by clicking a mouse on an *icon* that represents a command or an object graphically.

On personal computers, files are organized into a branching structure of directories and subdirectories. The operating system provides commands for navigating through the directory tree.

The top layer of software consists of *application* programs that make computers useful to people.

1.5.   Software Development

In the early days programs were written on paper in numeric code, then punched on cards or paper tape, read into computer memory from optical readers and tested by comparing the test results with the expected results. The current software development environment is much friendlier. A programmer is equipped with a number of software tools that make the process much more efficient.

Computer programmers very quickly realized that a computer itself is a perfect tool for assisting them in writing programs. The first step towards automation was made when programmers began to use *assembly languages* instead of numerically coded CPU instructions. In an assembly language every CPU instruction has a short mnemonic name. A programmer can give symbolic names to memory locations and can refer to these locations by name. For example, a programmer using Intel's 8088 assembly code can write:

```
index   dw     0           ; "Define word" -- reserve 2 bytes
                            ;  for an integer and call it "index".
        . . .
        mov    si,index     ; Move the value of index into
                            ;   the SI register.
        . . .
```

A special program, called the *assembler*, converts the program written in assembly language into the *machine code* expected by the CPU.

Obviously, assembly language is totally dependent on a particular CPU; "porting" a program to a different machine would require rewriting the code. As the power of computers increased, several *high-level* programming languages were developed for writing programs in a more abstract, machine-independent way. FORTRAN (<u>For</u>mula <u>Tran</u>slation Language) was defined in 1956, COBOL

(Common Business-Oriented Language) in 1960, and Pascal and C in the 1970s. C++ gradually evolved by adding *classes* to C in the 1980s.

A programmer writes the text of the program using a software tool, a program *editor*. Unlike general-purpose word-processing programs, programming editors have special features useful for writing programs. The text of a program in a particular programming language is referred to as *source code*, or simply the *source*. The source code is stored in a file, called the *source file* or the *source module*.

A program written in a high-level language obeys the very formal syntax rules of the language. This syntax produces statements so unambiguous that even a computer can interpret them correctly. A special program, called a *compiler*, analyzes the source code and translates it into *machine language* by generating appropriate CPU instructions. The result is saved in another file, called the *object module*. A large program may include several source modules that are compiled into object modules separately. Another program, a *linker*, combines all the object modules into one *executable* program and saves it in an executable file. Figure 1-3 illustrates the process of converting source code into an executable program.

With a large project, especially one that involves several developers, it may be difficult to keep track of different versions and changes to the source code. *Version-control* software imposes a discipline for changing code among the developers. It prevents two developers from modifying the same module at the same time and automatically saves previous versions of files. A *make* utility program processes a project description that specifies file dependencies and the commands necessary to build a particular file. *Make* examines the date and time labels on files; it will recompile a source file, for example, if its date is later than on the corresponding object file. *Make* can automatically build a number of specified executable programs.

Few programs are written right away without errors or, as programmers call them, *bugs*. Some errors violate the syntax rules of the language and are caught by the compiler. Other bugs come from a programmer's logical errors or failures to handle certain data or conditions properly. It is not always easy to correct bugs just by looking at the source code or by testing the program on different data. To help with this, there are special *debugger* programs that allow the programmer to trace the execution of a program "in slow motion." A debugger can suspend a program at a specified break point or step through the program statements or CPU instructions one at a time. With the help of a debugger, the programmer can examine the sequence of operations and the contents of registers and memory locations while the program is running.

In modern systems, software development tools are combined into one **_Integrated Development Environment_** (**_IDE_**). The IDE provides a convenient GUI (graphical user interface) — one mouse click on an icon will compile, link, and execute your program.

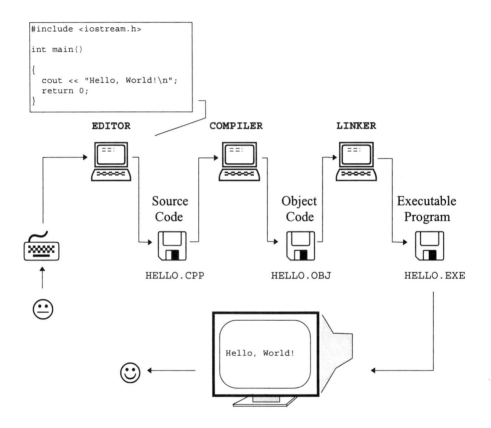

Figure 1-3.   Software development cycle: edit-compile-link-run.

1.6.   Suggested Reading

Portraits in Silicon, by Robert Slater, The MIT Press, 1987 (ISBN 0-262-19262-4).

> An informative history of computer concepts, technology, and software based on interviews with and profiles of key contributors.

History of Programming Languages II, edited by Thomas J. Bergin, Jr. and Richard G. Gibson, Jr., ACM Press and Addison-Wesley, 1996 (ISBN 0-201-89502-1).

> The volume is based on the Second ACM SIGPLAN History of Programming Languages Conference that took place on April 20-23 1993 in Cambridge, Massachusetts. Chapters on individual programming languages include a paper by each author of the language and biographies of the authors. The book includes chapters on C, C++, Pascal, Smalltalk, Lisp and other languages. A volume from the first conference (*History of Programming Languages,* edited by Richard L Wexelblat, Academic Press, 1981) covers ALGOL, BASIC, COBOL, FORTRAN, PL/I.

Hackers: Heroes of the Computer revolution, by Steven Levy.   Anchor Press/Doubleday, 1984 (ISBN 0-385-19195-2).

Practical Parallel Processing, by Alan Chalmers and Jonathan Fidmus, International Thompson Computer Press, 1996 (ISBN 1-85032-135-3).

> A survey of parallel computer architectures and applications.

Peter Norton's Inside the PC, by Peter Norton, Lewis C. Eggbrecht and Scott H.A. Clark, Sixth Edition, Sams Publishing, 1995 (ISBN 0-672-30624-7).

Inside Macintosh CD-ROM, Apple Computer, Inc., 1995 (ISBN 0-201-40674-8).

> Twenty-five *Inside Macintosh* books on a CD-ROM.

2

A First Look at a C++ Program

2.1.   Discussion

In this chapter we take our first look at a C++ program. We will identify some elements of the program, learn commonly used terms, and start to understand the general rules of "writing code" (an informal way of referring to programming).

The complexity of a program (or the amount of work performed by a programmer) is often measured in terms of *lines of code*: that is, the number of lines in the program source file.

2.2.   *Case Study:* Dictionary Program

For our first encounter we have chosen a program that is neither too large nor too trivial: about 120 lines of code. The program sets up a miniature on-line foreign language dictionary: you enter a word, and the program gives its translation in another language.   We have called this program Dictionary and named the program source file DICT.CPP. The "CPP" extension indicates that the program is written in C++ (C Plus Plus).

First, let's see how this program behaves after it is compiled and allowed to interact with a user:

```
ENGLISH-ITALIAN DICTIONARY
  (7 words)

Enter a word or 'q' to quit ==> I
io

Enter a word or 'q' to quit ==> this
questo

Enter a word or 'q' to quit ==> program
programma

Enter a word or 'q' to quit ==> hate
hate -- not in the dictionary.

Enter a word or 'q' to quit ==> love
amare

Enter a word or 'q' to quit ==> q
```

The dictionary itself is not a part of the program but is kept in a separate data file. We have named this file DICT.DAT and put in some English words and their Italian translations. Our toy dictionary contains only seven words. The first line in the data file holds the name of the dictionary.

Throughout the book, the 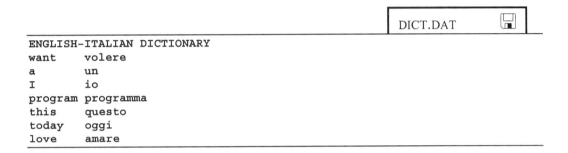 icon, preceded by the name of a file, indicates that the file is available on the accompanying disk.

DICT.DAT	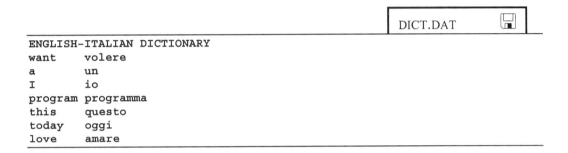

```
ENGLISH-ITALIAN DICTIONARY
want    volere
a       un
I       io
program programma
this    questo
today   oggi
love    amare
```

By separating the data file from the program we have made our program more general: the same program will work with different dictionary files and can therefore be used for different languages. We can also add or change words and translations easily without changing our program.

When we run our program, it initially reads the dictionary file and loads the words and their translations into the computer memory. The format of the dictionary data file has nothing to do with C++ and has been defined ahead of time by the programmer or system designer. The programmer then made sure that the program could read and use the DICT.DAT file. For example, the program "knows" that the first line in DICT.DAT is a title line that identifies the dictionary, and the program displays the title on the computer screen at the beginning of the session. The program also counts the entries in the dictionary and displays that number on the screen.

⌘   ⌘   ⌘

Figure 2-1 shows the source code for the program. To the uninitiated it looks quite cryptic. Fortunately, our intentions at this point are quite modest: we just want to get a glimpse of how C++ code looks and identify some of its elements and structures. By looking at various elements in the program, we also get an idea of what we need to know to be proficient with C++.

Take a quick look at this code and try to discern some structure in it. Then read the explanations that follow the code. If you do not understand some of the terms used in the explanations, be patient. We will define them in later chapters.

DICT.CPP

```
/* DICT.CPP

    This program works as an on-line dictionary. It reads a word
    and shows its translation.  The program loads the dictionary
    data from the DICT.DAT file.

    Author: M. Webster
    Rev. 1.0ap  09/20/98
*/

#include <iostream.h>
#include <fstream.h>
#include "apvector.h"
#include "apstring.h"

struct ENTRY {
    apstring word;
    apstring translation;
};

const int MAXWORDS = 1000;   // Max number of words in the dictionary

// Function prototypes:
bool LoadDictionary(apstring fileName, apvector<ENTRY> &dict);
bool FoundWord(const apvector<ENTRY> &dict,
               const apstring &word, apstring &translation);

/******************************************************************/
/**************          Main Program           ***************/
/******************************************************************/

int main()

{
    apvector<ENTRY> dict(MAXWORDS);
    apstring word, translation;
    bool ok, quit;

    // Load the dictionary from the file

    ok = LoadDictionary("DICT.DAT", dict);
    if (!ok) {
        cout << "*** Cannot load dictionary ***\n";
        return 1;
    }

    // Translate words

    quit = false;
    while (!quit) {
        cout << "Enter a word or 'q' to quit ==> ";
        cin >> word;
        cin.ignore(80, '\n');    // Read one word and
                                 //    skip the rest of the line
        if (word == "q")
            quit = true;
        else if (FoundWord(dict, word, translation))
            cout << translation << "\n\n";
        else
            cout << word << " -- not in the dictionary.\n\n";
    }
```

Comments

Preprocessor
#include *directives*

Function prototypes

"Main" function

Comments

```
        return 0;
}

/****************************************************************/
/*************              Functions              *************/
/****************************************************************/

bool LoadDictionary(apstring fileName, apvector<ENTRY> &dict)

// Reads dictionary entries from a file.
// Returns true if successful, false if cannot open the file.

{
    int cnt = 0;
    apstring line;

    // Open dictionary file:
    ifstream inpFile(fileName.c_str());
    if (!inpFile)
        return false;

    // Read and display the header line:
    getline(inpFile, line);
    cout << line << endl;

    // Read words and translations into the dictionary array:
    while (cnt < MAXWORDS &&
            inpFile >> dict[cnt].word >> dict[cnt].translation) {
        inpFile.ignore(80, '\n'); // Skip the rest of the line
        cnt++;
    }

    // Report the number of entries:
    cout << " (" << cnt << " words)\n\n";
    dict.resize(cnt);

    return true;
}

/****************************************************************/

bool FoundWord(const apvector<ENTRY> &dict,
               const apstring &word, apstring &translation)

// Finds a word in the dictionary.
//   dict -- the dictionary array
//   word -- word to translate
//   translation -- returned translation from the dictionary.
// Returns true if the word has been found, false otherwise.

{
    bool found = false;
    int i, len = dict.length();

    for (i = 0;   !found && i < len;   i++) {
        if (dict[i].word == word) {
            translation = dict[i].translation;
            found = true;
        }
    }
    return found;
}
```

Function header

Function body

Function header

Function body

Figure 2-1.   The source code of the Dictionary program.

2.3. Use of Comments

The first thing we notice is that the code contains some phrases in plain English. These are **comments** inserted by the programmer to explain and document the program's features. It is a good idea to start any program with a comment explaining what the program does, who wrote it and when, and how to use it. The comment may also include the history of any revisions: who made changes to the program, when, and why. The author must assume that his program will be read, understood, and perhaps modified by other people.

In C++, the comments may be set apart from the rest of the code in two ways. The first method is to place a comment between /* and */ marks:

```
/* Maximum number of words
          in the dictionary */
const int MAXWORDS = 1000;
```

In this method, the comment may be placed <u>anywhere</u> in the code, even within expressions. For example:

```
/* This is allowed, but bad style: */
const int MAXWORDS /* Max number of words in the dictionary */ = 1000;
```

The only exception is that **nested comments** (i.e. one set of /*...*/ within another) are normally not allowed:

```
/* /* This nested comment */  will NOT be processed
   correctly, unless your compiler has
   a special option enabled for handling nested comments. */
```

The second method is to place a comment after a double slash mark on one line. All the text from the first double slash to the end of the line is treated as comment. For example, we can write:

```
const int MAXWORDS = 1000;  // Max number of words in the dictionary
```

or

```
// Maximum number of words in the dictionary:
const int MAXWORDS = 1000;
```

Judicious use of comments is one of the tools in the constant struggle to improve the readability of programs. Comments document the role and structure of major code sections, mark important procedural steps, and explain obscure or unusual twists in the code.

On the other hand, excessive or redundant comments may clutter the code and become a nuisance. A novice may be tempted to comment each statement in the program even if the meaning is quite clear from the code itself. Experienced programmers use comments to explain the parts of their code that are less obvious.

Comment marks are also useful for ***commenting out*** (temporarily disabling) some statements in the source code. By putting a set of /*...*/ around a fragment of code or a double slash at the beginning of a line, we can make the compiler skip it on a particular compilation. This can be useful for making tentative changes to the code.

2.4. Functions

The Dictionary program exemplifies the traditional ***procedural*** approach to programming. In this approach, a program is viewed as a set of procedures or functions that operate on some data. Theoretically, it is possible to write any program as one continuous list of statements. But it is much easier to design, develop, and test a program if the program is split into smaller pieces, with each piece responsible for a particular procedure. In C++, fragments of code that perform a certain task or calculate and return a certain value are called ***functions***. (Other languages, such as Pascal, distinguish <u>functions</u>, which perform a calculation and return an answer, from <u>procedures</u>, which manipulate data but do not explicitly return a value. In C++ the term "procedure" is not used — everything is a "function.")

> **Every C++ program must have one special function, called `main()`, which receives control first when the program is executed.**

The C++ compiler (or, more precisely, the linker) builds into your executable program a small initialization module that makes some system-specific preparations and then passes control to `main()`. When your program is finished with `main()`, the initialization module takes over and does some cleaning up before it returns control back to the operating system. `main()` is often informally referred to as the ***main program*** (even though it is only a function and the program may have other functions). In our Dictionary program, `main()` is declared `int`, which indicates that this function returns an integer value:

```
  ...
int main()
  ...
```

int is a **reserved word** in C++, because it has a specific purpose in the language and cannot be used for other purposes. main is traditionally used only as the name of the main function.

In addition to main(), our Dictionary program contains two functions: LoadDictionary(...), and FoundWord(...). LoadDictionary(...) reads the DICT.DAT file and loads the dictionary into the computer memory. The FoundWord(...) function looks up a given word in the dictionary and retrieves its translation.

Functions may take **arguments** and may **return** a value. For example, the function

```
bool FoundWord(const apvector<ENTRY> &dict,
               const apstring &word, apstring &translation);
```

takes three arguments, written in parentheses after its name: dict, an array of dictionary entries; word, a character string that contains the original word; and translation, a string to which the translation is copied if the word has been found. The FoundWord(...) function <u>returns</u> a bool (short for **Boolean**, i.e., true/false) value that can be true if the word has been found and false otherwise.

In giving names to functions and their arguments, the programmer tries to choose names that will make the code more readable.

Whenever a statement in the program mentions a function name with some arguments in parentheses, the program carries out that function. We say that the function is **called** with certain arguments. A function can be called from main() or other functions.

For example, the first executable statement in the main program is

```
ok = LoadDictionary("DICT.DAT", dict);
```

This statement calls the LoadDictionary(...) function with two arguments, the name of the dictionary file and the dictionary array. The function reads the dictionary data from the file into memory and returns true if successful, and false if it could not find the file. The returned value is saved in a **variable** called ok.

A function uses the `return` statement to return a value:

```
return expression;
```

A `void` function cannot return any value, but it can use a `return` statement without a return value:

```
if (...)
    return;
```

The value returned by `main()` is usually interpreted by the operating system as an indicator of a successful run of the program or an error.

What actually happens in the computer when a function is called? This is explained in detail in Part 2. Basically, the program places the arguments where the function can get them, saves the place the function is called from, and passes control to the first instruction in the function code. When the function has finished its work, it places the return value where the calling statement can get it and goes back to the point where the calling function left off. A program can call a function as many times as it needs a certain task carried out.

The order of functions in source code is largely a matter of taste. Sometimes programmers put the main program first, followed by the functions; that is what we have done in the Dictionary program. Others may put the main program at the end. In any case, all functions have to be *declared* before we can call them: the compiler has to know what type of arguments they take and what type of values they return. This is accomplished by using *function prototypes,* which are usually placed somewhere near the top of the program. In our Dictionary program we put the prototypes for the `LoadDictionary(...)` and `FoundWord(...)` functions above `main()` so that when we call these functions from `main()`, the compiler will know what to expect:

```
...
// Function prototypes:
bool LoadDictionary(apstring fileName, apvector<ENTRY> &dict);
bool FoundWord(const apvector<ENTRY> &dict,
               const apstring &word, apstring &translation);

/*****************************************************************/
/*************         Main Program         *************/
/*****************************************************************/

int main()

{
    ...
```

Function prototypes *declare* functions and are also known as *function declarations*. Later in the program come the *function definitions*, which contain the actual function code. The code, placed between opening and closing braces, is called the *body* of the function. Function definitions must agree with their prototypes: they must take the types of arguments and return the types of values that their prototypes say they do. If a function is defined above its first use, no prototype is necessary (see Figure 2-2).

Usually, each function definition is accompanied by a comment that briefly describes what that function does, its arguments, and its return value, if any. The following is the complete definition of the `FoundWord(…)` function from our Dictionary program:

```
bool FoundWord(const apvector<ENTRY> &dict,
               const apstring &word, apstring &translation)

// Finds a word in the dictionary.
//   dict -- the dictionary array
//   word -- word to translate
//   translation -- returned translation from the dictionary.
// Returns true if the word has been found, false otherwise.

{
    bool found = false;
    int i, len = dict.length();

    for (i = 0;   !found && i < len;   i++) {
        if (dict[i].word == word) {
            translation = dict[i].translation;
            found = true;
        }
    }
    return found;
}
```

⌘   ⌘   ⌘

Sometimes it is convenient to view a function as a procedural abstraction, somewhat like the ice machine in a refrigerator. We know what goes in, we know what comes out, but until we are ready to build the machine, we are not too concerned about exactly what happens inside. Likewise, when we begin to write a program, we can (at some level of abstraction) assume that we will need functions to handle certain tasks — without worrying too much about the details of their code. We can create the prototypes for them, on the assumption that the functions will be coded later. When we have grasped the big picture and are ready to work out all the details, we can go back and write the code for all our functions.

To summarize, there are three main reasons for using functions. One is to split the code into manageable smaller pieces that can be conceptualized, programmed, and even tested separately. Another is to be able to perform the same task in the program several times without duplicating the same code, simply by calling the same function from different places in the program. Finally, thinking about functions keeps a programmer from getting bogged down in the nitty-gritty of a program before he has worked out the overall design.

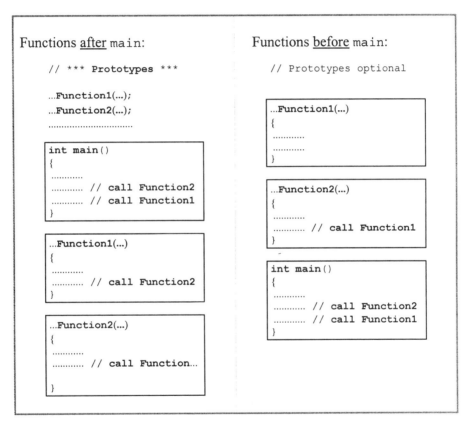

Figure 2-2. Placement of functions and function prototypes in the source code.

2.5.   Class Libraries and Header Files

If we look again at the `LoadDictionary(...)` function, we can see that it contains the lines:

```
    . . .
    // Read and display the header line:
    getline(inpFile, line);
```

This looks as if it might contain a call to the function `getline(...)`. But if this is indeed the case, where does this function come from, and where is it declared and defined? The answer is that `getline(...)` is indeed a function, and it comes with the `apstring` ***class***. A class is an important concept in C++, one that we will keep returning to again and again. At this point, all we need to know is that a class provides specific functionality in some prepackaged form. For example, the `apstring` class handles strings of text.

A modern C++ development environment supplies a vast collection of preprogrammed functions and classes for use in your programs. Like prefabricated construction blocks, these functions and classes can save you a lot of time.

Libraries of classes come with your C++ compiler and from independent software vendors. For instance, input and output in C++ programs is handled by the standard input and output classes provided with any C++ compiler. Other class libraries are available in the public domain. A few fundamental classes are combined in a library called the Standard Template Library (STL). The `apstring` and `apvector` classes used in the Dictionary program are two of the five "AP" classes provided by The College Board's AP C++ Development Committee for use in Advanced Placement examinations. These classes implement a subset of the STL.

Many functions in separate, already compiled modules are also collected in the *standard C library*. Strictly speaking, these library functions are not a part of the C++ programming language, but over the years of evolution of C and C++, they have become "standard." The standard library contains hundreds of functions that do all kinds of things: return the current time and date, convert numbers into character strings and vice versa, calculate mathematical functions, and so on. The actual libraries may differ slightly among suppliers of C++ compilers, but you can expect a vast majority of core functions to come with any compiler.

The compiler needs the definitions of classes and prototypes for the library functions; for your convenience, these are provided in the so-called ***include*** or ***header*** files that come with your compiler or with a class library. Instead of copying the required prototypes and definitions into your program, you can simply include the appropriate header file by using the `#include` directive. "Includes" are usually placed at the very top of a program. The Dictionary program, for example, has four "includes":

```
...
#include <iostream.h>
#include <fstream.h>
#include "apvector.h"
#include "apstring.h"
...
```

`iostream.h` and `fstream.h` contain definitions of classes for C++ standard input/output and file I/O; `apvector.h` and `apstring.h` contain the definitions of the `apvector` and `apstring` classes. The names for the system header files are not a part of the C++ language, but they, too, have become standard over time. A compiler's library documentation will tell you which header file to include with each function.

A header file is essentially a file of source code. The `#include` directive instructs the compiler to replace the "#include" line with the full text of the specified file. `#include` works with any source file, not just standard header files. Eventually you will write your own header files.

2.6.   The Preprocessor

`#include` is an example of a ***preprocessor*** directive. The preprocessor is a component of the compiler that does some preliminary work with your code before the actual compilation. The preprocessor strips comments from the code and expands `#include` directives into the actual text of the included file. There are other preprocessor directives. The most common two are `#define` for defining a constant or a ***macro*** and `#ifdef-#else-#endif` for ***conditional compilation***.

The `#define` directive has the general form of

```
#define someName expression
```

The preprocessor goes through your code, substituting *expression* for `someName` everywhere it appears. For example, we might say:

```
#define MAXWORDS 1000   /* Max number of words in the dictionary */
```

Defining a constant and referring to it in your program by name, rather than using its specific value, makes your code more general and easier to change.

For example, if we want to change the maximum size of the dictionary from 1000 to 3000, all we have to do is change one line in the program. Otherwise, we would have to go through and change every relevant occurrence of "1000" by hand.

`#define` was more useful in C. In C++ the preferred method of naming a constant is a constant declaration:

```
const int MAXWORDS = 1000;   // Max number of words in the dictionary
```

⌘   ⌘   ⌘

Conditional compilation allows you to include or exclude fragments of code from the program based on additional conditions. It takes the form:

```
#ifdef someName

... // some code (A)

#else

... // other code (B)

#endif
```

This means that if `someName` is defined, the first fragment (A) is compiled and included in the program; otherwise, the second fragment (B) is included. (The second part of the statement is optional. Without the `#else` and the second fragment, the compiler would simply skip fragment (A).) `someName` can be `#define`'d, defined through a special compilation option, or predefined under certain compilation conditions. The preprocessor includes the appropriate fragment into your program prior to compilation.

There is also an `#ifndef` directive — "if <u>not</u> defined." It instructs the compiler to include a particular fragment only if the name is <u>not</u> defined.

One use of conditional compilation is to include special "debugging" statements that assist in testing the program but are left out of the final version. For example:

```
// Comment out the following line for compiling without DEBUG:
#define DEBUG 1
        ...

        inpFile >> dict[i].word >> dict[i].translation;

#ifdef DEBUG
        cout << dict[i].word << dict[i].translation;
#endif
```

Another use is for handling code that is written for a specific system or compiler. For example:

```
#ifdef  _Windows

...// MS Windows-specific code

#else

... // MS DOS code

#endif
```

⌘ ⌘ ⌘

**The preprocessor directives stand out from the rest of the program.
Each directive is written on a separate line and starts with the #
character. Preprocessing is a separate step that precedes the actual
compilation.**

In the early versions of C compilers, the preprocessor was a separate program that read the source file, prepared it for compilation, and saved the result in a temporary file. Some modern compilers allow you to run just the preprocessor without compilation and save the result in a file.

2.7. Reserved Words and Programmer-Defined Names

In the C++ language, a number of words are reserved for some special purpose while other words are arbitrary names given by the programmer. A partial list of the C++ reserved words is shown below:

```
char        sizeof      if          default
int         typedef     else        goto
float       const       for         return
double      static      while       extern
short       void        do          class
long        enum        switch      private
unsigned    struct      continue    public
signed      union       break       protected
```

Reserved words are used only in a strictly prescribed way.

The C++ compiler is case-sensitive: changing one letter in a word from lowercase to uppercase makes it a different word. All reserved words use only lowercase letters.

Figure 2-3 shows a fragment from the Dictionary program with all reserved words highlighted.

In addition to reserved words, there are other standard names and words whose meaning normally does not vary. These include all library function names, names of predefined input and output classes, and some other words. Our Dictionary program uses the following standard names:

        cin, cout — stream I/O classes.
        ifstream, endl — stream I/O types and manipulators.
        apstring, apvector — AP classes.

Other names in the Dictionary program:

        ignore —

are names of *member functions* from the input/output class library. These names can be reused by the programmer for other purposes without conflict.

```
/* DICT.CPP
   ...
*/

#include <iostream.h>
#include <fstream.h>
#include "apvector.h"
#include "apstring.h"

struct ENTRY {
    apstring word;
    apstring translation;
};

const int MAXWORDS = 1000;   // Max number of words in the dictionary

// Function prototypes:
bool LoadDictionary(apstring fileName, apvector<ENTRY> &dict);
bool FoundWord(const apvector<ENTRY> &dict,
               const apstring &word, apstring &translation);

/****************************************************************/
/*************         Main Program          ************/
/****************************************************************/

int main()

{
    apvector<ENTRY> dict(MAXWORDS);
    apstring word, translation;
    bool ok, quit;

    // Load the dictionary from the file

    ok = LoadDictionary("DICT.DAT", dict);
    if (!ok) {
        cout << "*** Cannot load dictionary ***\n";
        return 1;
    }

    // Translate words

    quit = false;
    while (!quit) {
        cout << "Enter a word or 'q' to quit ==> ";
        cin >> word;                // Read one word and
        cin.ignore(80, '\n');       //   skip the rest of the line
        if (word == "q")
            quit = true;
        else if (FoundWord(dict, word, translation))
            cout << translation << "\n\n";
        else
            cout << word << " -- not in the dictionary.\n\n";
    }
    return 0;
}
```

Figure 2-3.   Reserved words in a fragment of the Dictionary program.

A programmer gives names to structures, functions, and variables. These names can use upper- and lowercase letters, digits, and the '_' (underscore) character. No name may start with a digit.

It is very important to chose names that are somewhat self-explanatory and improve the readability of the program. It is also desirable to follow a convention — for yourself or within a group or organization. For example, you could make all function names start with a capital letter, all names of variables start with a lowercase letter, all names of constants and structures uppercase, and so on.

C++ compilers allow very long names — up to at least 30 characters. But names that are too long clutter the code and actually make it harder to read.

2.8. Syntax and Style

Normally, you have to keep preprocessor directives, double-slash comments, and text within quotes on the same line. Aside from that, the compiler uses line breaks, spaces and tabs only to separate consecutive words, and one space works the same way as 100 spaces. The redundant white space (spaces, tabs and line breaks) is ignored. So our Dictionary program might have been written as follows:

```
#include <iostream.h>
#include <fstream.h>
#include "apvector.h"
#include "apstring.h"
struct ENTRY{apstring word; apstring translation;};const int MAXWORDS
=1000;bool LoadDictionary(apstring fileName,apvector<ENTRY> &dict); bool
FoundWord(const apvector<ENTRY> &dict,const apstring &word,
apstring &translation);int main(){apvector<ENTRY> dict(MAXWORDS);
apstring word,translation;bool ok,quit;ok=LoadDictionary
("DICT.DAT",dict);if(!ok){cout <<"*** Cannot load dictionary ***\n";
return 1;}quit=false;while(!quit){cout<<
"Enter a word or 'q' to quit ==> ";cin>>word ; cin.ignore(
80,'\n');if (word == "q")quit=true;else if(FoundWord(dict,word,
translation))cout << translation << "\n\n";else cout<<word<<
" -- not in the dictionary.\n\n";}return 0;}

            // End of main program
```

...

It would still compile and execute correctly. But although some people may insist that it makes as much sense as before, most would agree that it becomes somewhat less readable.

Arranging your code on separate lines, inserting blank lines, and indenting fragments of code is not required by the compiler — it is a matter of stylistic convention.

More or less rigid stylistic conventions have evolved among software professionals, and they must be followed to make programs readable and acceptable to the practitioners of the trade.

As we have mentioned above, programmers also have freedom in using comments and in choosing names for their structures, functions and variables. This is, pretty much, the limit of their stylistic freedom. The rest of the program text is governed by a set of very strict rules — the *syntax* rules of the programming language.

As opposed to English or any other natural language, programming languages have virtually no *redundancy*. Redundancy is a term from information theory that refers to less-than-optimal expression or transmission of information; redundancy in language or code allows the reader to interpret a message correctly even if it has been somewhat garbled. Forgetting a parenthesis or putting a semicolon in the wrong place in an English paragraph may hinder reading for a moment, but it does not usually affect the overall meaning. Anyone who has read a text written by a six-year-old can appreciate the tremendous redundancy in natural languages, which is so great that we can read a text with no punctuation and most words misspelled.

Not so in C++ or any other programming language, where almost every character is essential. We have already mentioned that in C++ all names and reserved words have to be spelled exactly right with the correct rendition of the upper- and lowercase letters. In addition, every punctuation mark or symbol in the program has a precise purpose; omitting or misplacing one symbol leads to an error. At the beginning, it is hard to get used to this rigidity of syntax.

The compiler catches most syntax errors, but in some cases it has trouble diagnosing the problem precisely. For example, braces in a C++ program are logical marks that set blocks of code apart from each other. Suppose we have accidentally omitted one closing brace on line 45 in the Dictionary program:

```
int main()

{
    apvector<ENTRY> dict(MAXWORDS);
    apstring word, translation;
    bool ok, quit;

    // Load the dictionary from the file

    ok = LoadDictionary("DICT.DAT", dict);
    if (!ok) {
        cout << "*** Cannot load dictionary ***\n";
        return 1;
    }

    ...
```

This closing brace has been accidentally omitted.

When we compile the program, the compiler can tell that something is not right but cannot figure out where the missing brace was supposed to be. Indentation could help a programmer to locate and fix the missing brace, but the compiler zooms right by. As a result, the compiler generates the following output:

```
Warning dict.cpp 49: Unreachable code in function main()
Error dict.cpp 68: Improper use of typedef 'bool' in function main()
Error dict.cpp 68: Statement missing ; in function main()
Error dict.cpp 124: Compound statement missing } in function main()
Warning dict.cpp 124: Function should return a value in function main()
```

As you can see, the compiler finally detected a missing brace — on line 124! (The numbers refer to the line numbers in the source code.)

Notwithstanding the compiler's somewhat limited capacity to diagnose your syntax errors precisely, you can never blame the compiler for errors. You may be sure that there is <u>something wrong</u> with your code if it does not compile correctly.

Unfortunately, the converse is not always true: the program may compile correctly but still contain errors — "bugs." The compiler certainly won't spot logical mistakes in your program. And just as a spell-check program will not notice if you type "wad" instead of "was" or "you" instead of "your," a compiler will not find errors that it can mistake for something else. So it is easy to make a minor "syntax" error that conforms to all the syntax rules but happens to change the meaning of your code.

Let's take an example from the FoundWord(...) code. Suppose we inadvertently slip an extra semicolon into our code:

```
bool FoundWord(const apvector<ENTRY> &dict,
               const apstring &word, apstring &translation)

// Finds a word in the dictionary.

{
    bool found = false;
    int i, len = dict.length();

    for (i = 0;    !found && i < len;    i++);  {
        if (dict[i].word == word) {
            translation = dict[i].translation;
            found = true;
        }
    }
    return found;
}
```

An unintended
semicolon

The program still compiles correctly because the syntax allows a semicolon after a for (...) statement. (We will cover the for loop in Section 7.2. For now, just keep in mind that a semicolon after a statement generally marks the end of that statement.) But the meaning of the program has changed. Our true intention is to repeat all the statements inside the braces until we find a word or finish scanning through the whole dictionary. We have indented these statements to remind ourselves that they are <u>inside</u> the for loop. Instead, the semicolon after for (...) is interpreted as an "empty" statement — nothing to repeat, except the for statement itself. As a result, the program compiles and runs, but cannot find any words in the dictionary.

⌘   ⌘   ⌘

C++ syntax is not very forgiving and may frustrate a novice. The proper response is attention to detail. Beginners can usually save time by carefully reading their code a couple of times before running it through the compiler. Get in the habit of checking that semicolons, braces, equal signs and other punctuation marks are where they should be.

2.9.   Statements, Blocks, Indentation

C++ code consists mainly of declarations, definitions, and statements. Declarations and definitions describe and define objects; statements describe actions.

> **Declarations and statements in C++ are usually terminated with a
> semicolon; statements are grouped into blocks using braces { }.
> Semicolons should not be omitted before a closing brace.**

Semicolons are only required <u>after</u> the closing brace in a few situations, which we will learn later.

Braces divide the code into ***nested blocks***. Statements within a block are usually indented by a fixed number of spaces or one tab. In this book we indent nested blocks by four spaces. The blocks are used to indicate that a number of statements form one ***compound*** statement that belongs in the same control structure, for example an ***iteration*** (for, while, etc.) loop or a ***conditional*** (if) statement. The outer block is always the body of a function. Figure 2-4 shows two nested blocks within a function.

```
bool FoundWord(const apvector<ENTRY> &dict,
               const apstring &word, apstring &translation)
{
    bool found = false;
    int i;

    for (i = 0;    !found && i < dict.length();    i++) {
        if (dict[i].word == word) {
            translation = dict[i].translation;
            found = true;
        }
    }
    return found;
}
```

Figure 2-4.   Nested blocks in the body of a function.

There are different styles of placing braces. Some programmers prefer placing both opening and closing braces on separate lines, as follows:

```
...
for (i = 0;    !found && i < dict.length();    i++)
{
    if (dict[i].word == word)
    {
        translation = dict[i].translation;
        found = true;
    }
}
...
```

This way it is easier to see the opening brace but easy to put, by mistake, an extra semicolon before it.

Another important way to improve the readability of your code is by spacing lines vertically. Use special comment lines and blank lines to separate sections, blocks, and procedural steps in your code.

2.10. Input and Output

In C++ input and output is implemented by means of *stream I/O classes*. A *class* is a key C++ concept and many elements of the C++ syntax are associated with defining and using classes. Classes are introduced in Part 2. Like standard library functions, stream I/O classes are not, strictly speaking, a part of the C++ syntax; they are built on top of it and form an attachment that has become standard.

The term *stream* has its origins in operating systems, such as UNIX and MS DOS. It refers to the abstract model of an input or output device in which an input device produces a stream of characters and an output device receives a stream of characters. Some input/output devices, such as a keyboard or a printer, are rather close to this abstract model. Ignoring the technical details we can say that a keyboard produces an input stream of characters and a printer receives and prints an output stream. Other devices, such as a personal computer screen or a hard disk, are actually random-access devices, not "stream" devices: software can write a character or even an individual pixel to any location on the screen or transfer a whole block of bytes to or from any sector on disk. Still, output to the screen or input/output to an ASCII disk file can be implemented as a logical stream with the help of the operating system software. For example, when we read from a disk file, the input is buffered so that characters are read into the program not directly from a disk but from an intermediate buffer in memory.

The C++ stream I/O class library provides two ready-to-use classes: one for input, called *standard input*, and one for output, called *standard output*. We can think of standard input as the keyboard and standard output as the computer screen. The name of the standard input in programs is cin and the name of the standard output is cout.

cin and cout are defined in the header file iostream.h which is normally included at the top of the program:

```
#include <iostream.h>
```

Until you learn the C++ syntax for classes, you can simply imitate available examples for using `cin` and `cout`.

C++ programmers say that the output operation *inserts* data into an output stream. The *stream insertion* operator is denoted by the `<<` symbol, as in:

```
cout << ...
```

The input operation *extracts* data from an input stream. The *stream extraction* operator is denoted by the `>>` symbol:

```
cin >> ...
```

We can extract numbers as well as characters from an input stream because the software routines that implement the class can convert a string of decimal digits into a binary number. Likewise, we can insert a number into the output stream. Then the class routines convert the internal binary representation of the number into a string of digits.

In the following fragment from the Dictionary program, the first statement shows a *prompt* on the screen and the second statement reads a word entered by the user:

```
cout << "Enter a word or 'q' to quit ==> ";
cin >> word;              // Read one word
```

A prompt is a message or symbol that indicates to the user that the program is waiting for input. In the above output statement the prompt message is between double quotes. The second statement extracts a string of characters from `cin` and puts it into `word`. Another statement:

```
cout << translation << "\n\n";
```

outputs `translation` to the screen. The `\n` symbol stands for the *newline* character, so `"\n\n"` ends the output line and leaves an additional blank line on the screen. As you can see, several `<<` operators can be chained together in one statement. The same is true for `>>` operators.

⌘ ⌘ ⌘

We can use the same `>>` operator for reading files. First we have to *open* an existing file with a given name for reading and associate it with an input stream. In the following statement, `apstring fileName` contains the file name and `inpFile` is the name that a programmer has given to the input stream associated with the file:

```
...
// Open dictionary file:

ifstream inpFile(fileName.c_str());

    // Declare an input file stream inpFile associated
    //   with a file whose name is in the apstring fileName.
...
```

Now we can use the `>>` operator to read data from the file. For example:

```
...
inpFile >> word >> translation;
...
```

(Likewise, we can *create* a new file with a given name and associate it with an output stream. We can then write data into the file using the `<<` operator.)

File I/O classes are defined in the header file `fstream.h`.

2.11. *Lab:* Compile and Run

Add some comments to the dictionary program. Create a project that combines the Dictionary program and the `apstring` class. Build and run the program. Make sure the data file DICT.DAT is placed in the current directory and is accessible to the program. Test whether the program reacts gracefully to error conditions, such as when the DICT.DAT file is not found. Create a small dictionary file for another language, name it DICT.DAT, and run the program again (without recompiling) to demonstrate that it works with different data files.

2.12. Summary

The text of a program is governed by rigid rules of syntax and style. The syntax is checked by the compiler, which does not allow a program with syntax errors to compile. The style is intended to make programs more readable and, even though it is not checked by the compiler, plays a very important role in producing acceptable code.

Comments complement the program code, document functions, and explain obscure places in the code. Comments can be also used to "comment out" (temporarily disable) statements in the program.

The text of the program contains ***reserved words***, which are used for a particular purpose in the language, as well as some names determined by the programmer. C++ is <u>case-sensitive</u>, so all words must be spelled with upper- and lowercase letters rendered correctly. All reserved words use lowercase letters.

A program consists of functions and must have a function called `main()`, which gets control first. Functions must be declared before they can be used. This is accomplished by placing ***function prototypes*** somewhere near the top of the program. The actual function code is called the ***body*** of the function. It is placed inside braces in the function ***definition***.

A programmer gives names to functions, variables, and constants, trying to choose names that make the program more readable. Names may contain letters, digits, and the underscore character. They cannot start with a digit.

C++ provides a vast collection of preprogrammed functions and classes, grouped in the standard library and in the class libraries. Prototypes for library functions and class definitions are contained in ***header files*** which are included into your program using the `#include` preprocessor directive.

Program code consists mostly of declarations and executable statements, which are normally terminated with a semicolon. The statements may be organized in nested blocks placed within braces. Inner blocks are usually indented in relation to the outer block.

C++ syntax is not very forgiving and may frustrate a novice — there is no such thing as "just a semicolon."

3

Variables and Constants

3.1. Discussion

In the early days of computing, programmers referred to memory locations by their exact numeric addresses in the computer memory. A programmer had to remember the addresses and how each location was used — a very tedious process. C++ and other high-level languages let programmers refer to memory locations using symbolic names called *variables*. The programmer gives his variables meaningful names that reflect their role in the program. The compiler takes care of all the details — allocation of memory space for the variables and representation of data in the computer memory.

The term "variable" is borrowed from algebra because, as in algebra, variables can assume different values and can be used in *expressions*. The analogy ends there, however. In a computer program, variables are actively manipulated by the program. A variable may be compared to a slate on which the program can, from time to time, write a new value and from which it can read the current value. For example, a statement

```
a = b + c;
```

does not represent an algebraic equality, but rather a set of instructions:

1. Get the current value of b;
2. Get the current value of c;
3. Add the two values;
4. Assign the result to a (write the result into a).

The same is true for

```
a = 4 - a;
```

It is not an equation, but a set of instructions for changing the value of a:

1. Take the current value of variable a;
2. Subtract it from 4;
3. Assign the result to a (write the new value into a).

In C++, a statement

```
someName = expression;
```

represents an ***assignment*** operation which ***evaluates*** (finds the value) of the expression on the right side of the = sign and assigns that value to (writes it into) the variable `someName`. The `'='` sign in C++ is pronounced "gets the value of." (If you want to <u>compare</u> two values, use another operator, `==`, to mean "is equal to.")

⌘   ⌘   ⌘

C++ recognizes different *data types* of variables depending on what kind of data they can contain. A variable of type `int`, for example, represents an integer, and a variable of type `double` represents a real number.

A data type is a logical notion used in programming languages — the computer memory itself is just a uniform sequence of bits and bytes, 0's and 1's. The data types help the compiler check the code for errors and allow more efficient computations.

The goal of this chapter is to learn the following concepts and elements of C++ syntax:

- The syntax and placement of variable declarations;
- Built-in data types;
- `typedef` (used to rename data types);
- Literal and symbolic constants;
- Initialization of variables in declarations;
- Some elements of output formatting;
- The *scope* of variables and symbolic constants.

3.2.   *Case Study:* Fastfood, a Point-of-Sale Program

To illustrate the use of variables and symbolic constants let us create a miniature POS (Point of Sale) system. POS is just a fancy industry term for a computerized cash register. We will implement a POS program for a fast food restaurant which, at least at the beginning, sells only two types of sandwiches — hamburgers and cheeseburgers.

A brief session with our program will look as follows:

```
Next item (0 to quit) ==> 1h
Next item (0 to quit) ==> 0
Total:          1.19
Sales tax:      0.06
Total due:      1.25
==> 2.00
Change:         0.75

Another customer (y/n)? y
Next item (0 to quit) ==> 2c
Next item (0 to quit) ==> 3h
Next item (0 to quit) ==> 0
Total:          6.35
Sales tax:      0.32
Total due:      6.67
==> 10
Change:         3.33

Another customer (y/n)? n
```

The bold font shows the user's input. 'h' stands for hamburger and 'c' for cheeseburger. The program calculates the total, adds the sales tax, and calculates change from the paid amount.

We can begin designing this program by first taking a very general view of the task, then gradually filling in the details. We split the program task into large subtasks. Then each subtask is split into smaller subtasks or steps, and so on. This approach is called ***top-down*** program design and ***step-wise refinement***. In our POS program, the task can be split into three steps:

1. Take the customer's order.
2. Add sales tax.
3. Collect the payment.

We may decide to implement the first and third steps as separate functions. Let's call them `TakeOrder` and `GetPayment`. The second step can be accomplished in just one line of code, which we can implement inside the `GetPayment` function. The `TakeOrder` and `GetPayment` functions are called from `main()`:

FASTFOOD.CPP

```
/* FASTFOOD.CPP

    This program implements a POS system for a fast food
    restaurant.

    Author: B. King
    Rev. 1.0    04/15/98
*/

#include <iostream.h>

// Function prototypes
double TakeOrder();
void GetPayment(double amt);

//****************************************************************
//***********               Main               *****************
//****************************************************************

int main()

{
    char nextCustomer;
    double amt;

    nextCustomer = 'y';
    while (nextCustomer == 'y') {
        amt = TakeOrder();
        if (amt > 0.)
            GetPayment(amt);
        cout << "Another customer (y/n)? ";
        cin >> nextCustomer;
    }
    return 0;
}

...
...
```

The calls to `TakeOrder()` and `GetPayment(...)` are placed inside a `while` loop that keeps repeating the statements in it until the user answers "n" to the "Another customer (y/n)?" question.

The `TakeOrder()` function accepts the customer's order and returns the total purchase amount. The `GetPayment(amt)` function adds the sales tax, receives the cash amount handed in by the customer and calculates change. The code for these functions will be discussed later.

3.3.   Declarations of Variables

The `main()` function above uses two variables: `nextCustomer` and `amt`. `nextCustomer` receives a 'y' or 'n' value from the user. A 'y' input indicates that the program should process the next customer; any other input breaks the `while` loop and terminates the program. The `amt` variable holds the dollar amount of the order.

All variables must be *declared* before they can be used.

In the POS program this is accomplished by the following declarations:

```
...
char nextCustomer;
double amt;
...
```

`char` and `double` are reserved words. They are examples of C++ ***built-in*** data types: variables of the `char` type may hold one character, and the `double` type is for double-precision real numbers.

The general format of a declaration is

```
sometype someName;
```

where *sometype* defines the type of the variable (a built-in data type for now, but it can also be a ***user-defined*** data type, as explained later), and `someName` is the name given by the programmer to his particular variable. Several variables of the same type may be declared together. For example:

```
double amt1, amt2, amt3;
```

A variable can be declared only once within its ***scope*** (scope refers to the space in the program where the variable is "visible" — see Section 3.10).

3.4. Data Types

C++ has the following eleven ***built-in*** types designated by reserved words:

```
char            unsigned char
int             unsigned int
short           unsigned short
long            unsigned long
float
double
long double
```

Because variables of different types occupy different amounts of memory space, we say that they have different *sizes*.

The exact implementation of types depends on the computer system, compiler, and operating environment. In the 16-bit architecture, for example, the `int` type may be implemented as a two-byte (16-bit) memory location (the same as a `short`). The most significant bit represents the sign of the number. In this case, its range is between -2^{15} and $2^{15}-1$. These are useful numbers to remember:

$$-2^{15} = -32768$$

$$2^{15}-1 = 32767$$

In the 32-bit architecture the `int` type is usually implemented as a four-byte (32-bit) memory location.

Table 3-1 summarizes the common implementation and use of built-in types. `char`, `int`, `short`, `long`, and the corresponding unsigned types are collectively called ***integral*** types.

In this book we will mostly use the `char`, `int`, and `double` data types.

You can find the sizes of different types for your compiler and environment by using the C++ `sizeof(x)` operator, where x may be the name of a data type or of a particular variable. The following program, for example, will print out a table of sizes for four common types:

TYPE	SIZE	USE
char	1 byte	One character, or a small integer in the range from -128 to 127.
unsigned char	1 byte	A small non-negative integer in the range from 0 to 255 or one byte of memory.
int	2 or 4 bytes	An integer in the range from -2^{15} to $2^{15}-1$ or from -2^{31} to $2^{31}-1$, respectively.
unsigned int	2 or 4 bytes	A non-negative integer in the range from 0 to $2^{16}-1$ or from 0 to $2^{32}-1$.
short	2 bytes	An integer in the range from -2^{15} to $2^{15}-1$.
unsigned short	2 bytes	A non-negative integer in the range from 0 to $2^{16}-1$.
long	4 or 8 bytes	An integer in the range from -2^{31} to $2^{31}-1$ or from -2^{63} to $2^{63}-1$.
unsigned long	4 or 8 bytes	A non-negative integer in the range from 0 to $2^{32}-1$ or from 0 to $2^{64}-1$.
float	4 bytes	A real number in floating point representation.
double	8 bytes	A double-precision real number in floating point representation.
long double	10, 12 or 16 bytes	An extended-precision real number in floating point representation.

Table 3-1. Built-in Data Types.

SIZE.CPP

```
// SIZE.CPP
//
// Prints out the size of int, long, float and double

#include <iostream.h>

int main()

{
    cout << endl;
    cout << "TYPE  SIZE " << endl;
    cout << "---------- " << endl;
    cout << "int    " << sizeof(int) << endl;
    cout << "long   " << sizeof(long) << endl;
    cout << "float  " << sizeof(float) << endl;
    cout << "double " << sizeof(double) << endl;

    return 0;
}
```

C++ compilers also provide a special header file, limits.h, which defines the ranges for integral types, and another header file, float.h, which provides useful constants for floating-point types.

It is a programmer's responsibility to make sure that the results of computations fit within the range of the selected type and that precision is adequate for the floating point computations.

3.5.   Renaming Data Types with typedef

C++ provides the typedef statement for naming new data types. For example, a statement in your program:

```
typedef unsigned char BYTE;
```

can introduce a new type name, BYTE, for the unsigned char type. Then, the declarations

```
        unsigned char b;
```
and
```
        BYTE b;
```

become identical and can be used interchangeably.

Sometimes it is desirable to use an alias (an abstract name) for a data type, because that lets you change the type for all variables that are used for a particular purpose using only one `typedef` statement. In our POS program, for example, we could use the alias MONEY for the `double` type and declare all variables that represent dollar amounts with the MONEY type:

```
...
typedef double MONEY;

...
int main()

{
    MONEY amt;
    ...
```

`typedef` statements are usually placed near the top of the program or in your own header file, which you can include by using `#include`.

3.6. Constants

Constants represent memory locations whose values do not change while the program is running. Your source code may include *literal constants* and *symbolic constants*. Examples of <u>literal constants</u> are decimal representations of integers and real numbers and characters in single quotes, for example:

```
'y', 'H'             — characters;
 7,  -3              — integers;
 1.19, .05, 12.     — float or double numbers.
```

Character constants also include a special set of non-printable characters that are sometimes called *escape* characters (the term derived from printer control commands). Escape characters are represented in C++ by an alias — a designated printable character — preceded by a backslash. The escape characters include:

```
\a      alert (bell)
\t      tab
\n      newline (line feed)
\r      carriage return
\f      form feed
\'      single quote
\"      double quote
\\      backslash
```

For example, an output statement

```
cout << "Change: " << '\a' << change << endl;
```

inserts a "bell" into the output. This will normally sound the speaker on a personal computer in addition to displaying the dollar amount of change on the screen.

Symbolic constants are <u>named by the programmer</u> and are declared in a manner similar to variables, except that the declarations are preceded by the reserved word `const` and some value must be assigned to the constant. For example:

```
const double hamburgerPrice = 1.19;
```

The general form of symbolic constants' declarations is

```
const sometype name1 = value1, name2 = value2,...;
```

where *sometype* is a data type (a built-in data type or a previously defined type) followed by a list of symbolic names with their values. A constant may be also initialized to some expression, but the expression must contain only constants, either literal constants or previously declared symbolic constants. For example:

```
const double hamburgerPrice = 1.19;
const double cheeseburgerPrice = hamburgerPrice + .20;
```

Or:

```
const double hamburgerPrice = 1.19,
             cheeseburgerPrice = hamburgerPrice + .20;
```

It may seem, at first, that symbolic constants are redundant and we can simply use their literal values throughout the program. For example, instead of writing

```
    ...
    const double taxRate = .05;
    ...
    taxAmt = amt * taxRate;
```

we could simply write

```
    ...
    taxAmt = amt * .05;      // Sales tax rate = 5%
```

> **The most important reason for using symbolic constants is easier program maintenance. If the program is modified in the future and the value of a constant has to be changed, only the constant declaration has to be changed by the programmer.**

A programmer who uses literal constants will have to search through the whole source code and replace the old value with the new one wherever it occurs. This is tedious and can easily cause errors.

Another advantage of symbolic constants is that they may make the code more readable and self-explanatory if their names are well chosen. The name can explain the role a constant plays in the program, making additional comments unnecessary.

It is also easier to change a symbolic constant into a variable if a program modification requires that. For example, in a simplified version of the Fastfood program, we can declare prices as constants. In a later upgrade, we can simply remove the `const` specifier and add a function for setting new prices.

Symbolic constants, like variables, are declared with a particular data type and are defined only within their scope. This introduces more order into the code and gives the compiler additional opportunities for error checking — one more reason for using symbolic constants.

On the other hand, there is no need to clutter the code with symbolic names assigned to universal constants such as 0 or 1 if these values inherently belong in the code.

3.7.   Initialization of Variables

In C++ a variable's declaration may also initialize it to some value. For example:

```
double totalAmt = 0.;
char sandwich = 'h';
```

In a more general form, a variable may be initialized to the value of an expression. The expression may include literal constants (e.g. numbers) and previously initialized symbolic constants and variables. For example:

```
double change = moneyIn - amtDue;
```

The variable `change` may be initialized this way only if `moneyIn` and `amtDue` have already received valid values.

3.8. *Case Study:* Fastfood Continued

We are now ready to complete our fast food restaurant POS system by adding in the prices of sandwiches and the `TakeOrder()` and `GetPayment(...)` functions. The completed program looks as follows:

FASTFOOD.CPP 💾

```
/* FASTFOOD.CPP

    This program implements a POS system for a fast food
    restaurant.

    Author: B. King
*/

#include <iostream.h>

double TakeOrder();
void GetPayment(double amt);

//*********************************************************************
//**********               Prices               ****************
//*********************************************************************

const double hamburgerPrice = 1.19,
             cheeseburgerPrice = hamburgerPrice + .20;


//*********************************************************************
//**********                Main                ****************
//*********************************************************************

int main()

{
    char nextCustomer = 'y';
    double amt;

    while (nextCustomer == 'y') {
        amt = TakeOrder();
        if (amt > 0.)
            GetPayment(amt);
```

Continued ➲

```
            cout << "Another customer (y/n) ? ";
            cin >> nextCustomer;
        }
        return 0;
    }

    //*****************************************************************
    //***********        TakeOrder, GetPayment        *************
    //*****************************************************************

    double TakeOrder()

    // Allows the operator to enter menu items.
    // Returns the total order amount.

    {
        double totalAmt = 0.;
        int howMany;
        char sandwich = '?';

        // Repeat while sandwich is not equal to blank
        while (sandwich != ' ') {

            // Prompt for the next item
            cout << "Next item (0 to quit) ==> ";

            // Input the number and type of sandwich
            cin >> howMany;
            if (howMany > 0)
                cin >> sandwich;
            else
                sandwich = ' ';

            // Add the price to the total amount
            if (sandwich == 'h')
                totalAmt = totalAmt + hamburgerPrice * howMany;
            else if (sandwich == 'c')
                totalAmt = totalAmt + cheeseburgerPrice * howMany;
        }

        return totalAmt;
    }

    //*****************************************************************
```

Continued

```
void GetPayment(double amt)

// Displays order total, sales tax, and total amount due;
//   calculates change.

{
    const double taxRate = .05;          // Sales tax rate = 5%
    double taxAmt, moneyIn;

    cout << "Total: " << amt << endl;
    taxAmt = amt * taxRate;
    cout << "Sales tax: " << taxAmt << endl;
    amt = amt + taxAmt;
    cout << "Total due: " << amt << endl;
    cout << "==> ";
    cin >> moneyIn;

    double change = moneyIn - amt;  // Declared and initialized here.
    cout << "Change: " << change << endl << endl;
}
```

The `TakeOrder()` function uses three variables. `double totalAmt` is initialized to 0.; as items are added to the order, their prices are added to `totalAmt`.

`int howMany` holds the requested number of sandwiches, and `char sandwich` indicates the kind of sandwich, `'h'` or `'c'`. The function prompts the user for the next item and adds it to the order. This step is repeated inside the `while` loop until the user enters 0 for the number of sandwiches. Then the program sets the value of `sandwich` to `' '` (blank space) to indicate that the order is completed and it is time to break out of the `while` loop.

The `GetPayment(...)` function takes the dollar amount of the order as its argument. It displays that amount, calculates and displays the sales tax, displays the total due, and prompts the user to enter the amount paid. It then calculates and displays the amount of change. This function uses a constant `taxRate` and two variables, `taxAmt` and `moneyIn`. The third variable, `change`, is declared near the end of the function code.

In C++ variables can be declared at any reasonable place in the code, but it is better, at least at the beginning, to declare all variables at the top of the function body.

We have declared `change` near the end only to demonstrate that this is allowed, as long as a variable has not been used anywhere above its declaration.

3.9.   Output Formatting

If you compile and run the above code, you will see that the `GetPayment(...)` function produces ugly output because the dollar amounts are displayed with different numbers of digits after the decimal point. C++ provides ways to control the format of numbers *inserted into the output stream* (that is, printed out with the `cout <<` operator). This is accomplished by using control elements inserted into the output, called I/O *manipulators*. Actually we have already used one manipulator, `endl`, to indicate the end of a line in the output. Here we introduce two more manipulators: `setw(d)` and `setprecision(d)`. These require a special header file, `iomanip.h`, that must be included into your program after `iostream.h`, as follows:

```
...
#include <iostream.h>
#include <iomanip.h>
...
```

`setw(d)` sets the width of the output field to `d` and can be used to align numbers in the output. The width setting remains in effect only for the next output item. `setprecision(d)` sets the number of digits after the decimal point for floating point numbers. This setting remains in effect until changed. We also need to set special *format flags*, `showpoint` and `fixed`, which tells `cout` always to show the decimal point and the trailing zeroes in floating point numbers (if, for example, we want to see 4.00 rather than 4):

```
cout.setf(ios::showpoint | ios::fixed);
```

Most compilers right-justify the output value in its output field by default. But some compilers may need a special instruction to right-justify the output:

```
cout.setf(ios::right, ios::adjustfield);
```

By using these tools (without going too deeply into their meaning or syntax at this time) we can achieve a prettier output:

```
...
#include <iostream.h>
#include <iomanip.h>

...

void GetPayment(double amt)

// Displays order total, sales tax, and total amount due;
//    calculates change.

{
    const double taxRate = .05;          // Sales tax rate = 5%
    double taxAmt, moneyIn;

    cout << setprecision(2);   // Show two digits after the decimal
                               //    point.  Remains in effect until
                               //    changed.
    cout.setf(ios::showpoint | ios::fixed);
                               // Set flags to always show the
                               //    decimal point and trailing zeroes.
    // Some compilers may also require (usually default):
    cout.setf(ios::right, ios::adjustfield);
                               // Set flags to right-justify
                               //    the output in its field.

    cout << "Total:     " << setw(8) << amt << endl;
    taxAmt = amt * taxRate;
    cout << "Sales tax: " << setw(8) << taxAmt << endl;
    amt = amt + taxAmt;
    cout << "Total due: " << setw(8) << amt << endl;
    cout << "==> ";
    cin >> moneyIn;

    double change = moneyIn - amt;
    cout << "Change:    " << setw(8) << change << endl << endl;
}
```

3.10. Scope of Variables and Constants

You have noticed that each function in the above program uses its own variables. Can a variable or a constant declared in one function be used in another function? Can a variable or a constant be declared in such a way that it is usable in several functions? These questions are related to the subject of *scope*.

In C++ a variable is defined only within a certain space in the program called the *scope of the variable*. The same is true for symbolic constants. The scope rules work exactly the same way for variables and symbolic constants.

Scope discipline helps the compiler to perform important error checking. If you try to use a variable or constant outside its scope, the compiler detects the error and reports an undeclared name. The compiler also reports an error if you declare the same name twice within the same scope and a warning if you try to use a variable before it has been assigned a value.

C++ programmers distinguish *local* variables declared within functions from *global* variables declared outside of any function. A beginner should declare all global variables near the top of the program and all local variables at the top of the function's code. The scope of a <u>global</u> variable extends from its declaration to the end of the program module (source file). The scope of a <u>local</u> variable declared at the top of a function extends from the declaration to the end of the function body (closing brace).

A <u>global</u> variable or constant is usable in any function below its declaration. The value of a global variable is maintained as long as the program is running. For example, it can be set in one function and used in another function. A global variable *goes out of scope* and its memory location is released only when the program finishes its execution.

A <u>local</u> variable exists only temporarily while the program is executing the function where that variable is declared. When a program passes control to a function, a special chunk of memory (a *frame* on the system *stack*) is allocated to hold that function's local variables. When the function is exited, that space is released and all local variables are destroyed.

(There is a way to override the temporary nature of local variables by using the C++ reserved word `static`. A *static* local variable still has local scope, but its value is preserved between successive calls to the function.)

As we mentioned earlier, local variables and constants in C++ do not have to be declared at the top of the function but can be declared anywhere in the function code. But the rules for declarations inside nested blocks may be confusing and such declarations may lead to elusive "bugs." Some examples are presented in the "Advanced Scope Rules" section below, but we recommend that you skip it on your first reading and simply place all declarations of local variables at the tops of functions.

⌘   ⌘   ⌘

It is good practice to use as few global variables and constants as possible and always to use different names for local and global variables.

C++ allows you to use the same name for a global and a local variable, with the local variable taking precedence over the global one in the function where it is declared. This may lead to errors that are hard to catch if you inadvertently declare a local variable with the same name. Consider, for example, the following code:

```
// BADCODE.CPP

...
const double hamburgerPrice = 1.19; // global constant
double amt;                         // global variable

void TakeOrder()

{
    ...
    amt = hamburgerPrice; // amt is not declared in TakeOrder(),
                          //   so this refers to the global variable
    ...
}

int main()

{
    double amt;  // local variable declared here by mistake.
                 //   It has the same name as a global variable.
                 //   The syntax is OK, but that was not the
                 //   intention!
    TakeOrder();
    cout << amt; // output is garbage, because the value of (local)
                 //   amt is undefined.
    ...
}
```

Use global variables and constants only when they indeed represent quantities you will refer to throughout the program, and give them <u>conspicuous</u> names. Excessive use of global variables is a sure sign of bad program design, because it is not obvious where and how they are used. Making changes to such a program may be difficult.

> **It is perfectly acceptable to use the same name for local variables in different functions. In fact this is a good practice if the variables represent similar quantities and are used in a similar way.**

But never try to economize on declarations of temporary local variables within functions and on passing arguments to functions by resorting to global variables.

3.11. Advanced Scope Rules

The scope of a local variable extends from its declaration to the end of the ***block*** in which the variable is declared. Blocks are usually delineated by braces, but implied blocks can also exist within `if-else` and `for/while` control structures that consist of one statement. Blocks may be nested, and a variable's scope includes the appropriate nested blocks.

Example 1:

```
void SyntaxError()

{
    int a = 1;               // ==> Beginning of scope for a

    while (a != 0) {
        int b = a;           // ==> Beginning of scope for b
        if (b != 0) {
            int c = b;           // ==> Beginning of scope for c
            cout << c;
        }                        // <== End of scope for c
        else
            c = a;
            // *** Syntax Error -- undeclared c ***
            // (used out of scope)
    }                            // <== End of scope for b
}                            // <== End of scope for a
```

Nested declarations can become confusing and cause errors, especially if the same name is used for variables declared in different blocks. The compiler reports an error if the same name is used twice in one block (at the same level), but it does allow the same name in different or embedded blocks and they are treated as totally different variables, with the innermost declaration having precedence, as shown in the example below:

Example 2:

```
#include <iostream.h>

void WrongCode()

{
    int a;
    int b = 0;

    cout << "Enter an integer: ";
    cin >> a;
    if (a > 0)
        int b = a;   // A new local variable b is declared here.
                     //    the value of the "outer" b has not changed
    else
        int b = -a; // Same here.

    cout << "Absolute value of " << a << " is " << b << endl;
    // The output for b is always 0.
}
```

To correct the problem we have to simply eliminate the extraneous declarations:

```
#include <iostream.h>

void WorkingCode()

{
    int a;
    int b = 0;

    cout << "Enter an integer: ";
    cin >> a;
    if (a > 0)
        b = a;            // b, declared outside, is assigned a value "a"
    else
        b = -a;

    cout << "Absolute value of " << a << " is " << b << endl;
}
```

The program will also work if we eliminate the outer declaration, but then we have to duplicate the output statement, which is undesirable:

```
#include <iostream.h>

void NotElegant()  // Working but not elegant code (with repetition)...

{
    int a;

    cout << "Enter an integer: ";
    cin >> a;
    if (a > 0) {
        int b = a;
        cout << "Absolute value of " << a << " is " << b << endl;
    }
    else {
        int b = -a;
        cout << "Absolute value of " << a << " is " << b << endl;
    }
}
```

3.12. *Lab:* Statistics for Fastfood

Modify the FASTFOOD.CPP program to collect and report "day's" statistics (where a "day" is one run of the program). Count up the total dollar amount of sales and the number of customers. Implement these quantities as <u>local</u> variables declared in main(...), initially set to 0. Is it easy to implement the total count of sold sandwiches as a local variable in main(...), too?

Write a separate function PrintDayTotals(...) that displays the totals, and call this function from the main program before exiting the program. Also try to calculate and display the average payment per customer.

3.13. enum Data Types

Sometimes, it is convenient to introduce a special data type for integer variables that can take only a few different values and to refer to these values by their symbolic names. This is accomplished with *enumerated* types, which a programmer can define using the reserved word enum. The syntax is illustrated in the following examples:

```
enum STATUS {FAILED, OK};
enum COLOR {BLUE = 1, GREEN, RED = 4};
```

In the above example, STATUS and COLOR become two new data types. As opposed to built-in data types, they are called *user-defined* types. The names in the enum list (inside the braces) become in effect new defined constants.

Whenever a value is omitted in the enum constant names list, it is set, by default, to the previous value plus one. The first value, if omitted, is set to 0.

FAILED and OK, for example, become defined constants of the type STATUS. Their actual values are 0 and 1, respectively. BLUE, GREEN and RED become defined constants of the type COLOR with the respective values 1, 2, and 4.

The programmer can put these definitions near the top of the program or in his own header file and then use them for variable and function declarations. For example:

```
...
enum STATUS {FAILED, OK};

// *** Function prototypes ***

STATUS InitializeModem();  // returns a value of the type STATUS;
                           //    the returned value can be only
                           //    FAILED or OK.
...
int main()

{
    STATUS ret = OK;       // Declares a variable called ret of
                           //    the type STATUS and initializes its
                           //    value to OK.
    ...
    ret = InitializeModem();
    if (ret == OK) {       // If ret is equal to OK...
        ...
    }
    ...
}
```

3.14. Summary

Variables and symbolic constants allow programmers to refer to memory locations by name. Variables and constants have to be declared before they can be used. The declaration of a variable includes the data type of the variable and an optional initial value. Several variables of the same type may be declared in the same declaration.

```
sometype name1, name2, ...;
sometype name1 = expr1, name2 = expr2, ...;
```

Symbolic constants must be declared with some initial value, which may be an expression combining literal constants (e.g. numbers) and previously defined constants:

```
const sometype name1 = expr1, name2 = expr2, ...;
```

C++ has char, int, short, and long built-in data types for representing integers of various sizes. char also represents single characters. Each of these integral types can be used with the unsigned keyword, which is a reserved word used to shift the range of represented numbers into the non-negative integer range. Real numbers of various size and precision are represented by the float, double, and long double built-in data types.

C++ provides the sizeof operator, which returns the memory size (in bytes) for storing a particular data type or a specific variable or constant. The limits.h and float.h header files contain useful constants that define ranges and precision for integral and floating point data types.

C++ also supports *enumerated* data types that are *user-defined*. An enumerated type is a special case of an integer type, but variables of that type may only take a small number of predefined values. The enum type definition gives symbolic names to these values.

4

Arithmetic Expressions

4.1. Discussion

Arithmetic expressions are written the same way as in algebra and may include literal and symbolic constants, variables, the arithmetic operators +, −, *, and /, and parentheses.

The order of operations is determined by parentheses and by the rank of operators: multiplication and division are performed first (left to right), followed by addition and subtraction. You can also use the minus symbol for negation.

4.2. Data Types in Expressions

C++ allows programmers to mix different data types in the same expression. Each operation in the expression is performed according to the types of its operands, and its result receives a certain type, even if it is only an intermediate result in the computation. The type of the result depends only on the types of the operands, not their values.

If the two operands have the same type, the result of the operation automatically gets the same type. This has serious consequences, especially for multiplication and division of integers.

In multiplication, the product may be much larger than each of the factors and may simply fall out of range. In the following code, for example:

```
#include <iostream.h>

int main()

{
    short a = 1000, b = 40;

    long x = a * b;
    cout << x << endl;
    ...
}
```

the output will be not 40000, as expected, but –25536! This is due to the C++ rules for handling types in expressions. Even though the final result, a `long`, is large enough to hold 40000, the intermediate result is a `short` because both operands, a and b, have the type `short`. A "short" number uses only two bytes and its value cannot exceed $2^{15} - 1 = 32767$. When a product gets out of the "short" range, the most significant bit is set and interpreted as a negative sign; the result here is –25536 (which is actually equal to $2^{16} - 40000$).

The same rule applies to division. The output of the following program is not 0.9, as expected, but 0.

```
#include <iostream.h>

int main()

{
    int a = 9, b = 10;

    double x = a / b;
    cout << x << endl;
    . . .
}
```

The reason is that when both operands are integers, their quotient is truncated to an integer first, which in this case is 0, even though the final result is declared as a floating point type, `double`.

If the two operands have different types, the operand of the "smaller" type is **promoted** (i.e. converted) to the "larger" type. All floating point types are considered larger than integral types, and the type which can hold values in a larger range is considered larger. For example, in the following code:

```
#include <iostream.h>

int main()

{
    double a = 9.;
    int b = 10;

    double x = a / b;
    cout << x << endl;
    . . .
}
```

b is promoted (converted) to a `double` prior to computing the ratio, because a is a `double`. The result will be displayed correctly as 0.9.

(The `char` data type in C++ plays a dual role: `char` variables can hold an ASCII code of a character or a small integer value. `char` operands in arithmetic expressions are first promoted to `int` and the result has the `int` data type.)

The result of the computation is automatically converted to the type of the variable to which it is assigned. You have to make sure that the type of the variable is adequate for holding the result of the computation.

4.3.   Type Conversions with the Cast Operator

C++ provides the so called "cast" operator for explicitly converting values from one type into another. The syntax is

> (*sometype*) *expression*

or

> *sometype* (*expression*)

where *sometype* is the name of the data type into which you are converting the value, and *expression* is either a constant or a variable or a parenthesized expression. The first form of cast is the older form, inherited from C. The second form is the newer form, introduced in C++.

The following code works correctly because the types of the operands are explicitly "cast as" appropriate types prior to computations:

```
#include <iostream.h>

int main()

{
    int a = 4000, b = 2000;

    cout << "a * b = " << double(a) * double(b) << endl;
    ...
}
```

Newer compilers support yet another form of the cast operator recently added to the C++ standard. This operator, called **static cast**, has the form:

> static_cast<*sometype*> (*expression*)

For example:

```
cout << "a * b = "
     << static_cast<double> (a) * static_cast<double> (b) << endl;
        // Static cast operator added to the C++ standard
```

We will always use either the newer form of cast or the static cast operator.

Your code will be safer and better documented if you indicate explicit type conversions using the cast operator, where necessary, rather than relying on implicit type conversions.

4.4.   Compound Assignment Operators

C++ has convenient shortcuts for combining arithmetic operations with assignment. The following table summarizes the *compound assignment* operators:

Compound assignment:	Is the same as:
a += b;	a = a + b;
a -= b;	a = a - b;
a *= b;	a = a * b;
a /= b;	a = a / b;

For example, the following statement:

```
...
amt = amt + taxAmt;
...
```

can be rewritten as:

```
...
amt += taxAmt;
...
```

The latter form may seem cryptic at the beginning, but, once you get used to it, it becomes attractive — not only because it is more concise, but also because it emphasizes the fact that the same variable is being modified.

Similarly, the following code:

```
...
    // Add the price to the total amount
    if (sandwich == 'h')
        totalAmt = totalAmt + hamburgerPrice * howMany;
    else if (sandwich == 'c')
        totalAmt = totalAmt + cheeseburgerPrice * howMany;
...
```

is better expressed as:

```
...
    if (sandwich == 'h')
        totalAmt += hamburgerPrice * howMany;
    else if (sandwich == 'c')
        totalAmt += cheeseburgerPrice * howMany;
...
```

Note that += has lower rank than the arithmetic operators, so the expression to the right of += is evaluated first, before the result is added to the left-hand side. For example:

```
a += b - c;        // Same as: a = a + (b - c)
```

4.5.   Increment and Decrement Operators

C++ has special ***increment/decrement*** operators (one of which gave the language its name). These operators are used as shorthand for incrementing or decrementing an integer variable:

Increment/Decrement:	Is the same as:
a++;	a = a+1;
a--;	a = a-1;
++a;	a = a+1;
--a;	a = a-1;

Increment and decrement operators may be used in expressions. That is where the difference between the a++ and ++a forms and between the a-- and --a forms becomes very important. When a++ is used, the value of the variable a is incremented <u>after</u> it has been used in the expression; for the ++a form, the value of the variable a is incremented <u>before</u> it has been used. The same is true for a-- and --a. This is summarized in the table below:

Increment/Decrement in an expression:	Is the same as:
a = b++;	{ a = b; b = b+1; }
a = b--;	{ a = b; b = b-1; }
a = ++b;	{ b = b+1; a = b; }
a = --b;	{ b = b-1; a = b; }

Consider, for example, the following program:

```
#include <iostream.h>

int main()

{
    int a = 10, b = 20, c;

    cout << "Initial values:\n";
    cout << "a = " << a    << " b = " << b << endl << endl;

    c = a++ * --b;
    // The above statement works the same as the following statements:
    // {
    //     b = b - 1;
    //     c = a * b;
    //     a = a + 1;
    // }

    cout << "c = " << c << endl << endl;
    cout << "Final values:\n";
    cout << "a = " << a << " b = " << b << endl << endl;

    return 0;
}
```

When compiled and executed, it generates the following output:

```
Initial values:
a = 10 b = 20

c = 190

Final values:
a = 11 b = 19
```

4.6.   The Modulo Division Operator

In addition to four arithmetic operations +, –, *, and /, C++ has the % operator for integers:

```
    a % b
```

which is read "a modulo b," and means the remainder when a is divided by b. For example, 31 % 7 is equal to 3 and 365 % 7 is 1. If a is negative, a % b is negative or zero (e.g. –31 % 7 is –3 and –28 % 7 is 0). The % operator has the same rank as * and /.

The compound assignment operator %= combines % with assignment. So

```
    a %= b;
```

is the same as:

```
    a = a % b;
```

4.7. *Lab:* Three Means

x is the **arithmetic mean** between two numbers, a and b, if $a - x = x - b$.

The arithmetic mean is equal to $\dfrac{a+b}{2}$.

x is the **geometric mean** between two positive numbers a and b, if $\dfrac{a}{x} = \dfrac{x}{b}$.

The geometric mean is equal to $\sqrt{ab}$.

x is the **harmonic mean** between a and b, if $\dfrac{1}{a} - \dfrac{1}{x} = \dfrac{1}{x} - \dfrac{1}{b}$.

The harmonic mean is equal to $\dfrac{2}{\dfrac{1}{a} + \dfrac{1}{b}}$.

Fill in the blanks in the following program that computes the three means:

MEANS.CPP

```
// MEANS.CPP
//
// This program calculates the arithmetic, geometric and harmonic
// means of two positive integers.
//
// Author: Meanie M.
//

#include <iostream.h>
#include <math.h>        // Includes the prototype of
                         //   the standard library function
                         //   double sqrt(double x) -- square root of x.

double ArithmeticMean (short a, short b)

{
    return double(a+b) / 2.;
}

double GeometricMean (short a, short b)

{
    ...
}
```

Continued

```
double HarmonicMean(short a, short b)

{
    ...
}

int main()

{
    short a, b;

    cout << "Enter two positive integers a and b ==> ";
    cin >> a >> b;
    cout << "Arithmetic mean of " << a << " and " << b
         << " = " << ArithmeticMean(a,b) << endl;

    cout << "Geometric mean of " << a << " and " << b
         << " = " << GeometricMean(a,b) << endl;

    cout << "Harmonic mean of " << a << " and " << b
         << " = " << HarmonicMean(a,b) << endl;

    return 0;
}
```

Compile and test the program with several input values ranging from 1 to 30000. For example:

```
1.  a = 1,      b = 2;
2.  a = 3,      b = 5;
3.  a = 20000,  b = 30000.
```

Explain the test results. Fix bugs in the functions, if any, but <u>do not</u> change the functions' arguments `short` data type. Re-test the program.

Note that for $a, b > 0$, the values of all three means should be between a and b, and

$$\frac{2}{\dfrac{1}{a}+\dfrac{1}{b}} \leq \sqrt{ab} \leq \frac{a+b}{2}$$

4.8.   Summary

Arithmetic expressions are written the same way as in algebra and may include literal and symbolic constants, variables, the arithmetic operators +, -, *, and /, and parentheses.

The result of an arithmetic operation has the same type as the operands. If the operands have different types, the operand of the "smaller" type is automatically converted (promoted) to the "larger" type. (For example, an `int` may be promoted to a `long` or a `double`, a `char` may be promoted to a `short` or an `int`.) C++ provides a cast operator that explicitly converts a variable or constant from one data type into another.

It is a programmer's responsibility to make sure that the values of variables and all the intermediate and final results in arithmetic expressions fit within the range of the chosen data types, and that these types satisfy the precision requirements for computations.

5

Arrays, apvector and apmatrix Classes

5.1. One-Dimensional Arrays

C++ programmers can declare several consecutive memory locations of the same data type under one name. Such memory blocks are called *arrays,* and the individual memory locations are called the *elements* of the array. The number of elements is called the *size* of the array.

Suppose we want to add soda to our fast food restaurant menu. Suppose it comes in three sizes: small, medium, and large. Instead of having a separate constant or variable to hold the price of each size of the drink, we can declare an array of three elements. For example:

```
double sodaPrice[3];  // array of three elements of the type double
```

Arrays can be initialized by placing a list of values, separated by commas, within braces. For example:

```
double sodaPrice[3] = {.59, .79, .99};
```

Individual elements of an array are accessed using *indices* (also called *subscripts*). An index is an integer value placed in square brackets after the array name to indicate the consecutive number of the element. In C++ the elements of an array are numbered starting from 0.

In the above example, the three soda prices can be referred to as `sodaPrice[0]`, `sodaPrice[1]`, and `sodaPrice[2]`, respectively.

The following statements declare an array of 100 integer elements:

```
const int MAXCOUNT = 100;
int a[MAXCOUNT];
```

The elements of this array can be referred to as `a[0]`, `a[1]`, ... , `a[99]`.

The power of arrays lies in the fact that a subscript can be a variable (or any expression). A program can refer, for example, to `a[i]`, where `i` is some integer variable. When the program is running, this is interpreted as the element of the array whose subscript is equal to the current value of `i`. For example, if the variable `i` at some point gets the value 3 and the program accesses `a[i]` at that point, a[i] will refer to a[3], which is the fourth element of the array (a[0] being the first element).

The index can be any expression. For example:

```
const int SIZE = 100;
int a[SIZE];
    ...
    int i = 3;
    ...
    a[2*i] = 0;
    a[2*i+1] = 1;
```

⌘   ⌘   ⌘

Let us return to our Fastfood example. We can add the following statements to our program to handle small, medium and large orders of soda:

```
...
const double sodaPrice[3] = {.59, .79, .99};

...

double TakeOrder()

{
    ...
    int sodaSize;

    ...
        cout << "Soda size (Small: 1; Medium: 2; Large: 3) ==> ";
        cin >> sodaSize;
        amt += sodaPrice[sodaSize-1];
        // [...-1] because the elements of the array are numbered
        //  0, 1 and 2, while the entered value is 1, 2 or 3.
    ...
}
```

5.2. The apvector Class

The C++ compiler does not keep track of the size of a declared array, nor does it verify that a subscript value is a valid number that points to an element of the array.

It is a programmer's responsibility to make sure that every subscript value falls into the valid range from 0 to size-1, where size is the size of the array.

For example, we may declare

```
int buffer[10];
```

and then write by mistake:

```
int i;
...
i = 10;
buffer[i] = 0;   // Error! Subscripts must be in the range
                 //   from 0 to 9. 10 is an illegal subscript
```

We can compile and run this program, but unpredictable things including a system crash could happen when we set `buffer[10]` to 0. This memory location is actually outside of our array; it may be used by another variable or constant, or it may store a function's return address!

Thus the use of C++ arrays requires extra caution. It would be desirable to have a mechanism that would check the subscript values while the program is running and warn the programmer about illegal subscripts. The `apvector` class, implemented by the AP C++ Development Committee, provides such a mechanism. This class is a subset of the `vector` class from the STL (Standard Template Library).

The AP Committee recommends that students <u>always</u> use the `apvector` class instead of built-in C++ arrays. All programming examples in this book follow this recommendation.

We refer to standard C++ arrays as "built-in" arrays because they are a standard feature of the C++ programming language. The `apvector` class is a helpful tool provided by the AP C++ Committee. In this book we may say "array" to refer informally to an `apvector` object.

In addition to checking subscripts, the `apvector` class offers three other advantages. First, it keeps track of the size of an array and provides a function `length()` that returns the size. With a built-in array, the programmer has to keep track of its size and explicitly pass it to functions that work with that array. Second, an `apvector` object can be resized. The size of a built-in array, once declared, must remain constant. Third, the actual storage for the `apvector` elements comes from a large pool of system memory called *free store* through a mechanism known as dynamic memory allocation (see Chapter 11). That is why apvector objects are sometimes called "dynamic arrays." Local built-in arrays are placed on the system stack, and a large array may overflow the stack.

5.3.   Declaring and Using apvector Variables

The apvector class is designed to work with vectors of different data types: integers, doubles, and other types. Such classes are called *templated* classes; they are explained in Part 2. The code for the apvector class is placed in a header file, apvector.h, which must be included at the top of your program:

```
#include "apvector.h"
```

At this point we need to know how to declare an apvector variable without going too deeply into the meaning of the required syntax (which is a bit tricky).

> **When you declare an apvector variable you have to specify the data type of its elements in angular brackets and the size of the vector in parentheses.**

For example:

```
apvector<int> v(10);   // Declare apvector v of 10 integers.
```

In the above declaration, apvector<int> serves as a new data type, v is the name of your variable, and 10 in parentheses is an "argument" that helps to "construct" your variable. This declaration follows the pattern:

```
sometype myVar(list of arguments);
```

When you declare a vector, you can set all its elements to the same "fill" value by placing that value in parentheses after the size of the array, separated by a comma. For example:

```
apvector<double> x(100, 99.9);
      // Declare apvector x of 100 doubles.
      // Set all its values equal to 99.9.
```

> **Unlike built-in arrays, the apvector class does not let you initialize the elements of a vector with a list of different values.**

Instead, you have to initialize the elements of a vector in separate assignment statements. For example:

```
apvector<double> sodaPrice(3);

sodaPrice[0] = .59;
sodaPrice[1] = .79;
sodaPrice[2] = .99;
```

It rarely makes sense to declare a `const` vector because then all its elements will be set to the same value. For example:

```
const apvector<int> v1(100, 1);
        // All 100 elements of vector v1 are forever set to 1.
```

⌘ ⌘ ⌘

You can access the individual elements of a vector by using subscripts in brackets — the same way as with built-in arrays:

```
x[0] = 0;
...
x[i] = x[j];
```

The subscript-checking code in the `apvector` class aborts your program and displays an error message when the program uses a subscript value that is out of bounds.

⌘ ⌘ ⌘

The `apvector` class has its own assignment operator, which copies the whole array. For instance, you can write:

```
apvector<int> a(100, 0), b;
        // a is a vector of 100 integers initially set to 0.
        // b is initially empty -- its size is 0.
...
b = a; // Copy vector a into b.  The size of b is properly
        //   adjusted to hold 100 elements.
```

Use the assignment of vectors with discretion, because it may involve moving a lot of bytes in memory and make your code very inefficient.

The `length()` function returns the size of the vector. The size is initially set when the vector is declared, but it may change as a result of calling the resize(...) function or after an assignment. length() is a ***member*** function of the apvector class; it is called using "dot" notation. For example:

```
apvector<double> buffer(1000);
int len;
...
len = buffer.length(); // len is set to 1000.
```

The resize(...) function lets you change the size of the vector. For example:

```
buffer.resize(2000); // Set the new size to 2000.
```

The resize(...) function may be used when the size of the array is not known in advance, but is entered by the user or read from a file. For example:

```
apvector<double> sample; // Declare an empty array
                         //   (initial size is 0).
int n;

cout << "Please enter the size of your sample: ";
cin >> n;
sample.resize(n);
```

If the new size is smaller than the original size, the vector's tail is chopped off and the tail elements are lost.

5.4.   Passing apvector Arguments to Functions

Functions that take apvector arguments are declared in basically the same way as functions with any other types of arguments. However, the argument name in the prototype and in the function header is usually preceded by the & (ampersand) symbol. For example:

```
void SomeFun(apvector<int> &x);
```

The ampersand tells the compiler that the function works with the original vector, not with its temporary copy. This is essential if your function <u>changes</u> the elements (or the size) of the vector. But even if your function does not change the vector, the ampersand is still very important because it prevents unnecessary copying of the vector. Without it your program may compile and run correctly but be awfully slow.

If your function <u>does not change</u> the vector, you can document (and enforce) that fact by adding the keyword `const` to the argument type. For example:

```
int AddElements(const apvector<int> &a);
```

Normally, your function will first need to retrieve the size of the array. This is accomplished by calling the `length()` member function. For example:

```
int AddElements(const apvector<int> &a)

// Returns the sum of the elements of the array a

{
    int len = a.length();
    ...
```

Code that accesses all the elements of an array requires a `for` or a `while` loop. These iterative statements are described in Chapter 7, but we can get a glimpse of how they work here:

```
int AddElements(const apvector<int> &a)

// Returns the sum of the elements of the array a

{
    int len = a.length();
    int i = 0, sum = 0;

    while (i < len) { // Repeat as long as i < len
        sum += a[i];
        i++;
    }
    return sum;
}
```

Or, with the `for` loop:

```
int AddElements(const apvector<int> &a)

// Returns the sum of the elements of the array a

{
    int len = a.length(), i, sum = 0;

    for (i = 0;   i < len;   i++)
        sum += a[i];

    return sum;
}
```

5.5.   Two-Dimensional Arrays

Two-dimensional arrays are used to represent rectangular tables or matrices of elements of the same data type. The following example shows how a 2-D array of "doubles" can be declared and initialized:

```
const int ROWS = 2;
const int COLS = 3;

double a[ROWS][COLS] = {
    {0.000, 0.111, 0.222},
    {1.000, 1.111, 1.222}
};
```

We access the elements of a 2-D array with a pair of indices, each placed in square brackets. We can think of the first index as a "row" and the second as a "column." Both indices start from 0.

In the above example,

```
a[0][0] = 0.0;    a[0][1] = 0.111;    a[0][2] = 0.222;
a[1][0] = 1.0;    a[1][1] = 1.111;    a[1][2] = 1.222;
```

A 2-D array is stored in a contiguous block of memory. Its total size is the product of the dimensions of the array; in our example it is ROWS*COLS = 6. The elements of the array are arranged "by row." More precisely, for each value of the <u>first</u> index, 0, 1, ... etc. the elements with the <u>second</u> index changing from 0 to its maximum value are stored sequentially in memory. Thus, in our example, the order of the elements in the computer memory is:

```
0.    0.111    0.222    1.    1.111    1.222
```

⌘ ⌘ ⌘

You can also declare three-dimensional and multi-dimensional arrays in a manner similar to two-dimensional arrays. Arrays in three or more dimensions are not used very often. In this book we do not go beyond two dimensions.

5.6.   The `apmatrix` Class

The `apmatrix` class, provided by the AP C++ Development Committee, implements two-dimensional arrays with "safe" subscripts.   As with the `apvector` class, a program that attempts to use an out-of-bounds subscript value is aborted with an error message.

A program that uses the `apmatrix` class needs to include the `apmatrix.h` header file:

```
#include "apmatrix.h"
```

`apmatrix` variables are declared similarly to `apvector` variables, but they are "constructed" with two arguments: the number of rows and the number of columns. For example:

```
apmatrix<double> table(5, 3);
  // Declare a matrix of doubles with 5 rows and 3 columns.
```

You can add the third argument, the "fill" value:

```
apmatrix<char> stars(2, 80, '*');
  // Declare a matrix of chars with 2 rows and 80 columns,
  //    and with all elements initially set to '*'.
```

Instead of the `length()` function in the `apvector` class, the `apmatrix` class provides two functions for accessing the dimensions of a matrix: `numrows()` and `numcols()`. These member functions of the `apmatrix` class are called using "dot" notation. For example:

```
int AddElements(const apmatrix<int> &m)

// Returns the sum of the elements in the matrix m

{
    int nRows = m.numrows(), nCols = m.numcols();
    int row, col, sum = 0;
    ...
```

The `resize(...)` function takes two arguments: the new dimensions.   For example:

```
apmatrix<double> m;   // Declare an empty matrix
int nRows, nCols;
...
cin >> nRows >> nCols;   // Read new dimensions
m.resize(nRows, nCols);  // Set new dimensions
```

5.7. *Lab:* Reverse an Array

The following program reverses the order of the elements in an array:

REVERSE.CPP

```
// REVERSE.CPP
//
// This program reverses the order of the elements in an array.
//
// Author: Leon Noel
//

#include <iostream.h>
#include "apvector.h"

void Reverse(apvector<int> &a);

int main()

{
    apvector<int> test(6);
    int i;

    // Set the test values in the array:
    test[0] = 1;    test[1] = 1;    test[2] = 2;
    test[3] = 3;    test[4] = 5;    test[5] = 8;

    // reverse the array:
    Reverse(test);

    // Display the array:
    for (i = 0;   i < 6;   i++)
        cout << test[i] << ' ';
    cout << endl;

    return 0;
}
```

Continued ☞

```
void Reverse(apvector<int> &a)

// Reverses the elements of the array

{
    int i, ...

    i = ...
    j = ...
    while(...) {
        ...
    }
}
```

Fill in the blanks and test the program. The output should be:

```
8  5  3  2  1  1
```

You can advance simultaneously from both ends of the array, swapping pairs of elements. Swapping two elements can be accomplished as follows:

```
int temp;
...
temp = a[i];
a[i] = a[j];
a[j] = temp;
```

(If your program appears not to do anything, you may be swapping things back into their original places.)

For "extra credit":

Modify the above program so that it flips the elements of a square two-dimensional array apmatrix<int> m(SIZE,SIZE) symmetrically about the main diagonal (the line that connects the upper left and lower right corners). In linear algebra this operation is called *transposing* a square matrix.

5.8.   Summary

C++ allows programmers to declare ***arrays*** — blocks of consecutive memory locations under one name. An array represents a collection of related values of the same data type. You can refer to the specific elements of an array by placing the element's subscript (index) in brackets after the array name. A subscript can be any integer variable or expression. In C++, the subscript of the first element of an array is 0 and the subscript of the last element is `len-1`, where `len` is the size of the array.

Programmers can also declare and use two-dimensional and multi-dimensional arrays. We can refer to an element in a 2-D array by placing two subscripts after the array name. Think of the first index as a "row" and the second as a "column." Both subscripts start from 0.

The `apvector` and `apmatrix` classes, provided by the AP C++ Development Committee, implement one- and two-dimensional arrays, respectively, with "safe" subscripts. Unlike built-in arrays, these classes check that the subscript values used by the program (while it is running) fall within the legal range, and abort the program with an error message if the program attempts to use an illegal subscript. The AP Committee recommends that students <u>always</u> use the `apvector` and `apmatrix` classes instead of built-in C++ arrays.

Programs that use the `apvector` or `apmatrix` classes must include the `apvector.h` and/or `apmatrix.h` header files at the top of the program.

The `apvector` and `apmatrix` classes are templated classes designed to work with different data types. When declaring an `apvector` or an `apmatrix` variable, specify the data type of its elements in angular brackets and the size of the vector or dimensions of the matrix in parentheses. For example:

```
apvector<int> v(10);      // Declare apvector v of 10 integers.
apmatrix<double> m(4,7);  // Declare apmatrix m of doubles
                          //   with 4 rows and 7 columns.
```

The size (length) of the vector is returned by the `length()` function. For example:

```
int len = v.length();
```

The dimensions of a matrix are returned by the `numrows()` and `numcols()` functions. For example:

```
int nRows, nCols;
. . .
nRows = m.numrows();
nCols = m.numcols();
```

Functions that take `apvector` or `apmatrix` arguments use the `&` (ampersand) character in their prototypes and header lines. The ampersand is placed in front of each `apvector` or `apmatrix` argument to indicate that the function works with the original object, not its temporary copy. The optional `const` keyword assures that the function does not change that argument.

6

Logical Expressions and `if-else` Statements

6.1. Discussion

The sequential flow of control from one statement to the next during program execution may be altered by the four types of control mechanisms:

1. Calling a function.
2. Iterative statements (loops).
3. Conditional (if-else) statements.
4. switch statements.

We have already seen that calling a function is a convenient way to interrupt the sequential flow of control and execute a code fragment defined elsewhere. We have also used a while loop, which instructs the program to repeat a fragment of code several times. while is an example of an *iterative* statement; these are fully explained later, in Section 7.2.

In this chapter we will study the if-else statement, which tells the program to choose and execute one or another fragment of code depending on the values of some variables or expressions. The if-else control structure allows **conditional branching**. Suppose, for instance, we want to find the absolute value of an integer. The function that returns an absolute value may look as follows:

```
int abs(int x)

{
    int ax;

    if (x >= 0)        // If x is greater or equal to 0
        ax = x;        //    do this;
    else               // else
        ax = -x;       //    do this.
    return ax;
}
```

Or, more concisely:

```
int abs(int x)

{
    if (x < 0)         // If x is less than 0
        x = -x;        //    negate x;
    return x;
}
```

There are special CPU instructions called ***conditional jumps*** that support conditional branching. The CPU always fetches the address of the next instruction from a special register, which, in some systems, is called the Instruction Pointer (IP). Normally, this register is incremented automatically after the execution of each instruction so that it points to the next instruction. This causes the program to execute consecutive instructions in order.

A conditional jump instruction tests a certain condition and tells the CPU to "jump" to the specified instruction depending on the result of the test. If the tested condition is satisfied, a new value is placed into the IP, which causes the program to skip to the specified instruction (Figure 6-1). For example, an instruction may test whether the result of the previous operation is greater than zero, and, if it is, tell the CPU to jump backward or forward to a specified address. If the condition is false, program execution continues with the next consecutive instruction.

```
        . . .
        cmp AH,7            ; Test for BW card
        je M11             ; Goto BW card init
        xor ax,ax          ; Fill for graphics modes
        jmp short M13      ; Goto clear buffer
M11:    mov CH,08h         ; Buffer size on BW card (2048)
        mov AX,' '+7*256   ; Fill char for alpha
M13:    rep stosw          ; Fill the regen buffer with
        . . .              ;    blanks
```

Figure 6-1.   80x86 Assembly language code with the je ("Jump if Equal to 0") instruction.

(There are also ***unconditional jump*** instructions that tell the CPU to jump to a specified address in the program by unconditionally placing a new value into the IP, for example, jmp short in Figure 6-1)

In high-level languages, conditions for jumps are written using relational operators such as "less than," "greater than," "equal to," and so on, and the logical operators "and, " "or," and "not." Expressions combining these operators are called ***logical*** or ***Boolean*** expressions in honor of British mathematician George Boole (1815-1864), who studied formal logic and introduced ***Boolean Algebra***, an algebraic system for describing operations on logical propositions. The value of a Boolean expression may be either true or false.

6.2.   `if-else` Statements

The general form of the **if-else** statement in C++ is:

```
if (condition)
    statement1;
else
    statement2;
```

where *condition* is a logical expression and *statement1* and *statement2* are either simple statements or **compound statements** (blocks surrounded by braces). The `else` clause is optional, so the `if` statement can be used by itself:

```
if (condition)
    statement1;
```

When an `if-else` statement is executed, the program evaluates the condition and then executes *statement1* if the condition is true and *statement2* if the condition is false. When `if` is coded without `else`, the program evaluates the condition and executes *statement1* if the condition is true. If the condition is false, the program skips *statement1*.

6.3.   "True" and "False" Values

C++ does not have special values for "true" and "false." Instead, "true" is represented by any non-zero integer value, and "false" is represented by the zero value. Thus a logical expression is simply a special case of an arithmetic expression: it is considered "false" if it evaluates to zero and "true" otherwise.

A proposal is being considered by the C++ Standards Committee to add the "Boolean" data type `bool` to the C++ built-in types. The proposal would make `true` and `false` — the only two values a Boolean variable can take — reserved words. The newer C++ compilers already support the `bool` data type. If their compiler does not support the `bool` type, C++ programmers do it themselves. They might add the following definitions to their code (or place them in a header file):

```
typedef int bool;        // defines bool as an alias for int
const bool false = 0;    // defines false as 0
const bool true = 1;     // defines true as 1
```

In this book we assume that the `bool` data type and the `false` and `true` constants are built in, but the programs on disk may contain the line

```
#include "bool.h"
```

BOOL.H contains the definition for the `bool` type and the `false` and `true` constants, in case your compiler does not have them. You may comment out this `#include` line (or the definitions inside BOOL.H) if your compiler has the built-in `bool` type.

After the `bool` type and the `true` and `false` constants have been defined, programmers can write declarations as follows:

```
. . .
bool aVar = false;
. . .
```

6.4.   Relational Operators

C++ recognizes six relational operators:

Operator	Meaning
>	Greater than
<	Less than
>=	Greater than or equal
<=	Less than or equal
==	Is equal
!=	Is not equal

In C++, the result of a relational operation has the `bool` (or `int`) type. It has a value equal to `true` (or `1`) if the comparison is true and `false` (or `0`) otherwise.

Note that in C++ the "is equal" condition is expressed by the "`==`" (double "`=`") operator, while a single "`=`" means assignment. Inadvertently writing = instead of == renders your conditional statement worse than meaningless, <u>without</u> generating a syntax error. However, some of the more "thoughtful" compilers do generate a warning against this pernicious bug.

Relational operators are mostly used for conditions in `if` statements and in iterative statements. Strictly speaking, they could be used in arithmetic expressions, too, because they have a value of 0 or 1 and will be promoted to the `int` type; however, such usage is unusual.

In C++, it is common to use integer variables or expressions as logical expressions. For example:

```
int count;
...
if (count)
    ...
```

The above is a C++ idiom, which means exactly the same thing as:

```
int count;
...
if (count != 0)   // if count not equal to 0
    ...
```

6.5.   Logical Operators

C++ has two binary logical operators, "and" and "or," and one unary logical operator, "not." They are represented by the following symbols:

Operator	Meaning
&&	and
||	or
!	not

The expression

```
condition1 && condition2
```

is true if and only if <u>both</u> condition1 <u>and</u> condition2 are true.

The expression

```
condition1 || condition2
```

is true if <u>either</u> condition1 <u>or</u> condition2 or both are true.

The expression

```
!condition1
```

is true if and only if `condition1` is false.

The following code:

```
bool match;
...
if (!match)
    ...
```

is identical to:

```
bool match;
...
if (match == false)
    ...
```

Like relational operators, the results of the logical operators `&&`, `||`, and `!` have the `int` (integer) data type: `1` represents true and `0` represents false.

The "and," "or," and "not" operations are related to each other in the following way:

```
not (p and q) = not(p) or  not(q)
not (p or  q) = not(p) and not(q)
```

These two formulas are called **De Morgan's laws**. De Morgan's laws are properties of formal logic, but they are useful in practical programming as well. In C++ notation, De Morgan's laws take the following form:

```
!(p && q) == (!p || !q)

!(p || q) == (!p && !q)
```

A programmer may choose one of the equivalent forms; the choice depends on which form is more readable. Usually it is better to distribute `!` ("not"). For example:

```
if (size <= 0 || a[0] == -1)
```

is much easier to read than:

```
if (!(size > 0 && a[0] != -1))
```

6.6.   Order of Operators

In general, all binary operators have lower precedence then unary operators, so unary operators, including ! ("not"), are applied first.   You have to use parentheses if ! applies to the entire expression. For example:

```
if (!x > 0)   //    You probably wanted:
              //    if (!(x > 0));
              //    You got:
              //    if ((!x) > 0);

   . . .
```

Relational operators (>, < , ==, etc.) have lower rank than all binary arithmetic operations (+, *, etc.), so they are applied after the arithmetic operators. For example, you can write simply:

```
if (a + b >= 2 * n)             // OK
   . . .
```

when you mean:

```
if ((a + b) >= (2 * n))         // Redundant inside parentheses
   . . .                        //    needlessly clutter
                                //    the code.
```

The binary logical operators && and || have lower rank than arithmetic and relational operators, so they are applied last. For example, you can write simply:

```
if (x + y > 0 && b != 0)        // OK
```

as opposed to:

```
if ((x + y > 0) && (b != 0))     // Redundant parentheses.
```

When && and || operators are combined in one logical expression, && has higher rank than || (i.e. && is performed before ||), but it is a good idea to always use parentheses to avoid confusion and make the code more readable. For example:

```
// Inside parentheses not required, but recommended for clarity:
if ((x > 2 && y > 5) || (x < -2 && y < -5))
    ...
```

The rules of precedence for the operators that we have encountered so far are summarized in the table below:

Highest	!	(unary)-	(cast)	++	--	sizeof
↑	*	/	%			
	+	-				
	<	<=	>	>=		
	==	!=				
↓	&&					
Lowest	||					

In the absence of parentheses, binary operators of the same rank are performed left to right, and unary operators right to left. If in doubt — use parentheses!

6.7.   Short-Circuit Evaluation

In the binary logical operations `&&` and `||`, the left operand is always evaluated first. There may be situations when its value predetermines the result of the operation. For example, if *condition1* is false, then *condition1* `&&` *condition2* is false, no matter what the value of *condition2*. Likewise, if *condition1* is true, then *condition1* `||` *condition2* is true.

If the value of the first (left) operand in a binary logical operation unambiguously determines the result of the operation, the second operand is <u>not</u> evaluated. This rule is called *short-circuit evaluation*.

If the expression combines several `&&` operations at the same level, such as

    condition1 && condition2 && condition3 ...

the evaluation of conditions proceeds from left to right. If a <u>false</u> condition is encountered, then the remaining conditions are <u>not evaluated</u>, because the value of the entire expression is false. Similarly, if the expression combines several `||` operations at the same level,

```
condition1 || condition2 || condition3 ...
```

the evaluation proceeds from left to right only until a <u>true</u> condition is encountered, because then the value of the entire expression is true.

The short-circuit evaluation rule not only saves the program execution time but is also convenient in some situations. For example, it is safe to write:

```
if (y != 0 && x/y > 3)
    ...
```

because x/y is not calculated when y is equal to 0. Similarly,

```
if (i >= 0 && i < SIZE && a[i] == 0)
    ...
```

makes sure that an element a[i] of the array is tested <u>only</u> when the index i is within the legal range between 0 and SIZE-1.

6.8. *Case Study:* Day of the Week Program

To illustrate the use of conditional statements and Boolean expressions, let us consider a program that deals with dates. The program will calculate the day of the week for a given date.

The dialog with the program, which we call Weekday, looks as follows:

```
Please enter a date (e.g. 11 23 2001) ==> 6 1 2000
6-1-2000, Thursday
```

It is easy to foresee which functions will be needed to carry out this task. We will need a function to check whether the entered date is valid. Then we will have to deal with leap years, which will require a function that determines whether a given year is a leap year. Of course, we also need a function that finds the day of the week for a given date. The easiest way to figure this out is to calculate the total number of days elapsed from some known fixed date, such as 01-01-1900, which was a Monday. We will need a function for that, too.

We will first implement these functions, then write the main program. This is called a ***bottom-up*** approach. The date functions we have identified are fairly general: they will help us to solve the problem at hand, but we can also use them later for other, similar tasks. By not focusing exclusively on a particular task but taking a slightly more general view of relevant functions, we can enhance the *reusability* of code, usually without extra cost for the project we are working on.

Let us begin with the `LeapYear(...)` function. This function takes an `int` argument (the year) and returns a Boolean value:

```
                                              WEEKDAY.CPP

bool LeapYear (int year)

// "year" must be between 1900 and 2999.
// Returns true if "year" is a leap year.

{
        //  true, if year is divisible by 4, and ...
        //     ... either not divisible by 100, or divisible by 400.

    return (year % 4 == 0 &&
               (year % 100 != 0 || year % 400 == 0));
}
```

This function returns the value of one logical expression, which has the type `bool`. Extra parentheses around

```
    (year % 100 != 0 || year % 400 == 0)
```

are important, because `&&` has precedence over `||`.

⌘ ⌘ ⌘

The other two functions require some tables: the number of days in each month and the number of days from the beginning of the year to the beginning of a month. We can implement them as global constant arrays:

```
                                              WEEKDAY.CPP

const int daysInMonth[12] =
    { 31, 28, 31, 30, 31, 30, 31, 31, 30, 31, 30, 31 };

// Days from the beginning of the year
//    to the beginning of the month:

const int daysToMonth[12] =
    { 0,   31,  59,  90, 120, 151, 181, 212, 243, 273, 304, 334 };
```

Continued ⇗

```
const char *dayName[7] = {
    "Sunday",
    "Monday",
    "Tuesday",
    "Wednesday",
    "Thursday",
    "Friday",
    "Saturday"
};

const int DAY0 = 1; // Day of week for 01-01-1900 is Monday = 1.
```

The above declarations use standard built-in arrays because it is convenient to initialize the constant values within the declarations. We could use the apvector class instead and write a special function that would set the values of the "constants" (but then we could not formally declare them as constants). It would look as follows:

```
apvector<int> daysInMonth(12);
...
void InitDateConstants()

{
    daysInMonth[0] = 31;
    ...
}
```

The keyword const cannot be used in the apvector version.

If we use built-in arrays, however, the keyword const in the declarations prevents the program from altering these arrays, so there is no danger of overwriting wrong memory locations by using a bad subscript. The worst thing that can happen if a subscript is out of range is an incorrect result. We do have to be careful to use correct subscripts: 0 through 11 for daysInMonth and daysToMonth, and 0 through 6 for dayName.

The asterisk in the declaration

```
const char *dayName[7] = {
```

indicates that dayName is an array of character strings (more precisely, pointers to character strings).

We have also supplied a universal constant DAY0 set to 1, which indicates that January 1, 1900 was a Monday.

⌘   ⌘   ⌘

The ValidDate(…) function simply verifies that the month, day, and year have valid values. This function returns a bool value — true if the date is valid, and false otherwise:

WEEKDAY.CPP

```
bool ValidDate (int month, int day, int year)

// Returns true if month-day-year is a valid date between
//    01-01-1900 and 12-31-2999.

{
    bool valid = false;  // First assume the date is invalid.
    int days;

    // If year and month have valid values:
    if (year >= 1900 && year <= 2999 &&
                            month >= 1 && month <= 12) {

        // Get the number of days in this month from the table:
        days = daysInMonth[month-1]; // (-1, because the indices
                                     //   of an array start from 0.)

        // If February of a leap year -- increment the number
        //   of days in this month:
        if (month == 2 && LeapYear(year))
            days++;

        // Check that the given day is within the range.
        //   If so, set valid to true:
        if (day >= 1 && day <= days)
            valid = true;
    }

    return valid;
}
```

The third function calculates the total number of days elapsed since 01-01-1900. Let us call it DaysSince1900(…). This number may be quite large, more than 400,000 for the year 2999, and it may overflow an int variable if the int data type is implemented as a 16-bit value. To be on the safe side, let's make this function return a long value:

WEEKDAY.CPP

```
long DaysSince1900 (int month, int day, int year)

// Returns the number of days elapsed since 01-01-1900
//  to month-day-year

{
    long days;

    // Calculate days to 01-01 of this year with correction for
    //   all the previous leap years:
    if (year == 1900)
        days = 0;
    else
        days = long(year - 1900) * 365
            + (year - 1901) / 4         // +1 for each 4th year
            - (year - 1901) / 100       // -1 for each 100th year
            + (year - 1601) / 400;      // +1 for each 400th year,
                                        //     starting at 2000

    // Add days for previous months with correction for
    //   the current leap year:
    days += daysToMonth[month-1];
    if (LeapYear(year) && month > 2) days++;

    // Add days since the beginning of the month:
    days += day - 1;

    return days;
}
```

Note the cast to `long` in the calculation of the number of days:

```
days = long(year - 1900) * 365
    . . .
```

Without it, an `int` value for the entire expression would be calculated first, because all the operands would have the `int` type and the result could be truncated before being assigned to the `long` variable `days`. Note also the use of integer division to compensate for the leap years since 1900:

```
    . . .
    + (year - 1901) / 4         // +1 for each 4th year
    - (year - 1901) / 100       // -1 for each 100th year
    + (year - 1601) / 400;      // +1 for each 400th year
```

The expression `+(year-1901)/4` adds a day to the calculation for every fourth year (starting in 1905) that has gone by. Likewise, `-(year-1901)/100` subtracts a day for every 100th year that has passed. Finally, starting at 2001, +(year-1601)/400 adds a day back for 2000 and every 400th year.

⌘ ⌘ ⌘

The DayOfWeek(...) function returns an integer between 0 (Sunday) and 6 (Saturday). This function takes a known date (01-01-1900), takes its day of the week (Monday = 1), adds the number of days elapsed since that date, divides the result by 7 and takes the remainder:

WEEKDAY.CPP

```
int DayOfWeek (int month, int day, int year)

// Returns the day of the week for a given date:
//    0 -- Sunday, 1 -- Monday, etc.

{
    return int((DAY0 + DaysSince1900(month, day, year)) % 7);
}
```

Note, that the expression has to be cast back into the int type, because DaysSince1900(...) returns a long value.

⌘ ⌘ ⌘

Finally, we can create the main program that implements the user interface and calls the functions described above:

WEEKDAY.CPP

```
// WEEKDAY.CPP
//
//    This program calculates the day on which the
//    user's birthday (or any other date) falls.
//
//    Author: Cal Lenders
//    Rev 1.0
//

#include <iostream.h>

//**************************************************************
//*************    Tables and functions     *******************
//**************************************************************

...
```

Continued ☞

```
//**********************************************************
//************                main                **************
//**********************************************************

int main()

{
    int month, day, year;
    int weekday;

    cout << "Please enter a date (e.g. 11 23 2001) ==> ";
    cin >> month >> day >> year;

    if (!ValidDate(month, day, year)) {
        cout << "*** Invalid date ***\n";
        return 1;
    }

    weekday = DayOfWeek(month, day, year);

    // Display the entered date and the name of the calculated
    //   day of week:
    cout << month << '-' << day << '-' << year << ", "
         << dayName[weekday] << endl;

    return 0;
}
```

Note the expression:

```
    if (!ValidDate(month, day, year)) {
        ...
```

which reads: "if <u>not</u> ValidDate..."

6.9.   *Lab:* Holidays

Write a program that calculates and displays the dates of Labor Day (first Monday in September), Memorial Day (last Monday in May), Thanksgiving (fourth Thursday in November), and Election Day (first Tuesday after the first Monday in November) for a given year. Re-use the functions and definitions from the Weekday program, but replace the main program with new code. The program should prompt the user for a desired year and calculate and display the holiday names and their respective dates.

6.10. if-else if and Nested if-else

Sometimes, a program needs to branch three or more ways. Consider the *sign(x)* function:

$$sign(x) \ = \ \begin{cases} -1, & \textit{if} \ \ x < 0; \\ 0, & \textit{if} \ \ x = 0; \\ 1, & \textit{if} \ \ x > 0. \end{cases}$$

sign(x) can be implemented in C++ as follows:

```cpp
int Sign (double x)     // Correct but clumsy code...
{
    int s;

    if (x < 0.)
        s = -1;
    else {
        if (x == 0.)
            s = 0;
        else
            s = 1;
    }
    return s;
}
```

This code is correct, but it is a bit cumbersome. The x < 0 case seems arbitrarily singled out and placed at a higher level than the x == 0 and x > 0 cases. Actually, the braces in the outer else can be removed, because the inner if-else is one complete statement. Without braces, the compiler always associates an else with the nearest if above it. The simplified code without braces looks as follows:

```cpp
int Sign (int x)    // Correct, but still clumsy...
{
    int s;

    if (x < 0.)
        s = -1;
    else
        if (x == 0.)
            s = 0;
        else
            s = 1;
    return s;
}
```

It is customary in such situations to arrange the statements differently: the second
`if` is placed next to the first `else` and one level of indentation is removed, as
follows:

```
int Sign (int x)    // The way it should be...

{
    int s;

    if (x < 0.)
        s = -1;
    else if (x == 0.)   // This arrangement of if-else is a matter
        s = 0;          //   of style.  The second if-else is
    else                //   actually nested within the first else.
        s = 1;
    return s;
}
```

This format emphasizes the three-way branching that conceptually occurs <u>at the
same level</u> in the program, even though technically the second `if-else` is ***nested***
in the first `else`.

A chain of `if-else if` statements may be as long as necessary:

```
if (condition1) {
    ...                 // 1st case
}
else if (condition2) {
    ...                 // 2d case
}
else if (condition3) {
    ...                 // 3d case
}
...
...
else {
    ...                 // Last case
}
```

This is a rather common structure in C++ programs and it is usually quite
readable. For example:

```
...
if (points >= 92)
    grade = 'A';
else if (points >= 84)
    grade = 'B';
else if (points >= 70)
    grade = 'C';
else if (points >= 55)
    grade = 'D';
else
    grade = 'F';
...
```

A different situation occurs when a program requires true hierarchical branching with nested if-else statements, as in a decision tree:

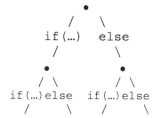

Consider, for example, the following code:

```
...
// Surcharge calculation:
if (age <= 25) {
    if (accidents)
        surcharge = 1.4;  // Premium surcharge 40%
    else
        surcharge = 1.2;  // Surcharge 20%
}
else {    // if age > 25
    if (accidents)
        surcharge = 1.1;  // Surcharge 10%
    else
        surcharge = .9;   // Discount 10%
}
...
```

Here the use of nested if-else is justified by the logic of the task. It is possible to rewrite the second part of it as if-else if, but then the logic becomes confusing:

```
    ...
    // Surcharge calculation (more confusing):
    if (age <= 25) {
        if (accidents)
            surcharge = 1.4;   // Premium surcharge = 40%
        else
            surcharge = 1.2;   // 20%
    }
    else if (accidents)
        surcharge = 1.1;   // Premium surcharge = 10%
    else
        surcharge = .9;    //  Discount 10%
    ...
```

When `if-else` statements are nested in your code to three or four levels, the code becomes intractable. This indicates that you probably need to restructure your code, perhaps using separate functions to handle individual cases.

Nested `if`s can often be substituted with the `&&` operation:

```
    if (condition1)
        if (condition2)
            statement;
```

is exactly the same (due to the short-circuit evaluation) as:

```
    if (condition1 && condition2)
        statement;
```

6.11. Common `if-else` Errors

1. Extra semicolon:

```
    if (condition);    // Compiled as:  if (condition) /* do nothing */;
        statement;     //                   statement;
```

2. Missing semicolon before `else`:

```
    if (condition)
        statement1     // Syntax error caught by the compiler
    else
        statement2;
```

3. Omitted braces:

```
if (condition)            // Compiled as: if (condition)
    statement1;           //                  statement1;
    statement2;           //              statement2;
```

4. "Dangling" else:

```
if (condition1)          // Compiled as: if (condition1) {
    if (condition2)      //                  if (condition2)
        statement1;      //                      statement1;
else                     //                  else
    statement2;          //                      statement2;
                         //              }
```

6.12. Summary

The general form of a conditional statement in C++ is:

```
if (condition)
    statement1;
else
    statement2;
```

where *statement1* and *statement2* can be either simple statements (terminating with a semicolon) or compound statements (a block of statements within braces). *condition* may be any arithmetic or logical expression.

There are no special values for "true" and "false" in C++: any non-zero integer value is interpreted as true, and a zero value is interpreted as false. Newer C++ compilers have built-in bool data type and true and false constants. If a particular compiler does not have the bool data type, programmers may add the definitions

```
typedef int bool;
const bool false = 0;
const bool true = 1;
```

to their program, or put them in a header file.

Usually, conditions are written with the relational operators

<	less than
<=	less than or equal
>	greater than
>=	greater than or equal
==	is equal
!=	is not equal

and the logical operators

&&	and
||	or
!	not

It is useful for programmers to know two properties from formal logic called ***De Morgan's laws:***

```
!(a && b) = !a || !b
!(a || b) = !a && !b
```

Use the

```
if...
else if...
else if...
...
else ...
```

structure for multiway branching and use nested `if-else` for hierarchical branching.

7

Iterative Statements: while, for, do-while

7.1. Discussion

Loops or *iterative statements* tell the program to repeat a fragment of code several times or as long as a certain condition holds. Without iterations, a programmer would have to write separately every instruction executed by the computer, and computers are capable of executing millions of instructions per second. Instead, programmers can implement solutions to problems using fewer instructions, some of which the computer repeats many times. A formal description of the procedural steps needed to solve a problem is called an *algorithm*. Designing, implementing, and understanding algorithms is a crucial programming skill, and iterations are a key element in non-trivial algorithms.

Iterations are often used in conjunction with arrays. We need to use iterations if we want to perform some process on all the elements of an array. For example, we might want to find the largest element of an array, or the sum of all the elements.

C++ provides three convenient iterative statements: `while`, `for`, and `do-while`. Strictly speaking, any iterative code can be implemented using only the `while` statement, but the other two add flexibility and make the code more concise and idiomatic.

7.2. `while` and `for` Loops

The general form of the `while` statement is:

```
while (condition) {
    statement1;
    statement2;
    ...
}
```

condition can be any arithmetic or logical expression; it is evaluated exactly the same way as in an `if` statement.

Informally the `while` statement is often called the *while loop*. The statements within braces are called the *body* of the loop. If the body consists of only one statement, the braces surrounding the body can be dropped:

```
while (condition)
    statement1;
```

It is important <u>not</u> to put a semicolon after while(condition). With a semicolon, the body of the loop would be interpreted as an empty statement, which would leave *statement1* completely out of the loop.

⌘   ⌘   ⌘

The following function returns the sum of all integers from 1 to *n*:

```
int AddUpTo (int n)

// Returns the sum of all integers from 1 to n, if n >= 1,
//   and 0 otherwise.

{
    int sum = 0;
    int i = 1;

    while (i <= n) {
        sum += i;
        i++;            // increment i
    }
    return sum;
}
```

We can discern three elements that must be present, in one form or another, with any while loop: initialization, a test of the condition, and incrementing.

1. Initialization

The variables tested in the *condition* must first be initialized to some values. In the above example, i is initially set to 1 in the declaration int i = 1.

2. Testing

The condition is tested <u>before</u> each pass through the loop. If it is false, the body is not executed, iterations end, and the program continues with the next statement after the loop. If the condition is false at the very beginning, the body of the while loop is <u>not executed at all</u>. In the AddUpTo (...) example, the condition is i <= n. If n is zero or negative, the condition will be false on the very first test (since i is initially set to 1). Then the body of the loop will be skipped and the function will return 0.

3. Incrementing

At least one of the variables tested in the condition must change within the body of the loop. Otherwise, the loop will be repeated over and over and never stop, and your program will **hang**. The change of a variable is often implemented with increment or decrement operators, but it can come from any assignment or input statement. At some point, however, the tested variables must get such values that the condition becomes false. Then the program jumps to the next statement after the body of the loop.

In the AddUpTo(...) function, the change is achieved by incrementing the variable i:

```
    ...
    i++;        // increment i
    ...
```

These three elements — initialization, testing, and incrementing (change) — must be present, explicitly or implicitly, with every while loop.

In the following more concise and efficient but less obvious implementation of the AddUpTo(...) function, the numbers are added in reverse order, from n to 1:

```
int AddUpTo (int n)

// Returns the sum of all integers from 1 to n, if n >= 1,
//   and 0 otherwise.

{
    int sum = 0;

    while (n > 0)
        sum += n--;

    return sum;
}
```

In this code, initialization is implicit in the value of the argument n passed to the function, and the change (actually <u>decrementing</u>) is buried inside a compound assignment statement.

⌘   ⌘   ⌘

The for loop is a shorthand for the while loop that combines initialization, condition, and increment in one statement. Its general form is:

```
for (initialization;   condition;   increment) {
    statement1;
    statement2;
    ...
}
```

where *initialization* is a statement that is <u>always</u> executed once before the first pass through the loop, *condition* is tested before each pass through the loop, and *increment* is a statement executed at the end of each pass through the loop.

A typical example of a for loop is:

```
for (i = 0;   i < n;   i++) {
    ...
}
```

The braces can be dropped if the body of the loop has only one statement.

The AddUpTo(n) function can be rewritten with a for loop as follows:

```
int AddUpTo (int n)

// Returns the sum of all integers from 1 to n, if n >= 1,
//   and 0 otherwise.

{
    int sum = 0;
    int i;

    for (i = 1;   i <= n;   i++)
        sum += i;

    return sum;
}
```

Initialization and increment statements may be composed of several statements separated by commas. For example:

```
int AddUpTo (int n)

// Returns the sum of all integers from 1 to n, if n >= 1,
//   and 0 otherwise.

{
    int i, sum;

    for (sum = 0, i = 1;   i <= n;   i++)
        sum += i;

    return sum;
}
```

Or, as written by a person determined not to waste any keystrokes:

```
int Add (int n)
{
    for (int s = 0; n > 0; s += n--);
    return s;
}
```

(In this inconsiderate code, the body of the for loop is empty — all the work is done in the "increment" statement.)

⌘   ⌘   ⌘

The following function calculates *n*! (*n factorial*), which is defined as the product of all numbers from 1 to *n*:

```
long Factorial (int n)

// Returns 1 * 2 * ... * n, if n >= 1 (and 1 otherwise).

{
    long f = 1;
    int k;

    for (k = 2;   k <= n;   k++)
        f *= k;

    return f;
}
```

7.3. *Lab:* Fibonacci Numbers

Write and test a program that calculates the *n*-th Fibonacci number.

The sequence of Fibonacci Numbers is defined as follows: the first number is 1, the second number is 1, and each consecutive number is the sum of the two preceding numbers. In other words,

$$F_1 = 1;$$
$$F_2 = 1;$$
$$F_n = F_{n-1} + F_{n-2} \quad \text{(for } n > 2\text{)}.$$

The first few numbers in the sequence are 1, 1, 2, 3, 5, 8, 13, ... The numbers are named after Leonardo Pisano (Fibonacci), who invented the sequence in 1202. The numbers have many interesting mathematical properties and even some computer applications.

Your main program should prompt the user for a positive integer *n*, call the Fibonacci(n) function, and display the result. Note that Fibonacci numbers grow rather quickly, so it is a good idea to keep them in variables of the long or even long double data type and to request small *n* when you test your program.

The Fibonacci(n) function can be based on one iterative loop. You can have it keep two previously calculated numbers f1 and f2, find the next number f3 = f1 + f2, and then, before the next pass through the loop, shift the values between variables as follows:

```
...
f1 = f2;
f2 = f3;
...
```

7.4. The do-while Loop

The do-while loop differs from the while loop in that the condition is tested <u>after</u> the body of the loop. This assures that the program goes through the iteration at least once. The general form of the do-while statement is:

```
do {
    ...
} while (condition);
```

The program repeats the body of the loop as long as *condition* remains true. It is better always to keep the braces, even if the body of the loop is just one statement, because the code without them is hard to read.

do-while loops are used less frequently than while and for loops. They are convenient when the variables tested in the condition are calculated or entered within the body of the loop rather than initialized and incremented. For example:

```
...
char answer;

do {
    ProcessTransaction();
    cout << "Another transaction (y/n)? ";
    cin >> answer;
} while (answer == 'y');
...
```

If for some reason you do not like do-while loops, you can easily avoid them by using a while loop and initializing the variables in such a way that the condition is true before the first pass through the loop. The above code, for example, can be rewritten as follows:

```
...
char answer = 'y';    // Initially answer is set equal to 'y'.

while (answer == 'y') {
    ProcessTransaction();
    cout << "Another transaction (y/n)? ";
    cin >> answer;
}
...
```

7.5. break and continue

The reserved words break and continue can be used only inside a body of a loop. (The break statement can be also used inside a switch; see Section 8.6.) break instructs the program to immediately break out of the loop and continue with the next statement after the body of the loop. continue tells the program to skip the rest of the statements on the current iteration and go to the next pass through the loop. Both of these statements must always appear inside a conditional (if or else) statement — otherwise some code in the body of the loop would be skipped every time, and the compiler would generate a warning: "Unreachable code in ..."

In the following example, the program calculates the sum of the reciprocal squares of the first N positive integers:

$$\frac{1}{1^2} + \frac{1}{2^2} + \frac{1}{3^2} + ... + \frac{1}{N^2}$$

This series converges to $\pi^2/6$ and can be used to approximate π. The loop ends when we have added 100 terms, or when the last added term is less than a given threshold `epsilon`, whichever happens first:

```cpp
#include <iostream.h>
#include <math.h>

int main()

{
    const double epsilon = .000001;
    double x, xSum = 0.;
    int k;

    for (k = 1;    k <= 100;    k++) {
        x = 1. / double(k);     // Calculate x = 1/k;
        x *= x;                 // Square x;
        xSum += x;              // Add it to the sum.

        // *** Break out of the loop if x is less than epsilon ***
        if (x < epsilon)
            break;
    }
    cout << "Pi is approximately equal to " << sqrt(6. * xSum) << endl;
    return 0;
}
```

The following function checks whether an integer n is a prime. We have to check all potential factors m but only as long as $m^2 \leq n$ (because if m is a factor, then so is n/m and one of the two must be less or equal to the square root of n). The function uses `break` to reduce the number of iterations:

```
bool IsPrime (int n)

// Returns true if n is a prime, false otherwise.

{
    int factors = 0;

    if (n <= 1)
        return false;

    for (int m = 2;    !factors;    m++) {
        if (m * m > n)
            break;
        if (n % m == 0)
            factors++;
    }
    return (factors == 0);
}
```

Another way to break out of the loop is to put a `return` statement inside the loop. For example:

```
...
for (int m = 2;    ;    m++) {
    if (m * m > n)
        break;
    if (n % m == 0)
        return false;       // Not a prime.
}
return true;
...
```

In the above code, the condition in the `for` loop is empty. An empty condition is considered always "true." The `break` or `return` is used to break out of the loop.

There is a C++ idiom

```
for(;;)
    ...
```

which means simply "repeat." The only way to get out of this loop is to use `break` or `return`.

⌘ ⌘ ⌘

The following code uses `continue` in calculating the sum and product of all primes less then or equal to *N*:

```
...
const int N = 100;

...
int sum = 0;
long product = 1;
int p;

for (p = 2;   p <= N;   p++) {
    if (!IsPrime(p))
        continue;
    sum += p;
    product *= p;
}
...
```

Note that although the increment statement is actually executed at the end of each iteration through a for loop, continue does not skip it.

Thus, in the above example, p++ is properly executed on every iteration.

This is not so with while loops, where the "increment" statement is a part of the body of the loop.

Be careful with continue in while loops: it may inadvertently skip the increment statement, causing the program to hang.

This would happen in the following version of the above example:

```
...
int p = 2;

while (p <= N) {           // This code hangs for N >= 4, because p
    if (!IsPrime(p))       //    never gets incremented after
        continue;          //    the first non-prime p = 4 is
                           //    encountered.
    sum += p;
    product *= p;
    p++;
}
...
```

7.6.   A Word About `goto`

C++ also has the `goto` statement, which implements an unconditional jump to a specified statement in the program, but its use is considered highly undesirable because it violates the principles of structured programming. The format is:

```
goto label;
```

where *label* is some name chosen by the programmer. The label, followed by a colon, is placed before the statement to which you want to jump. For example:

```
{
    ...
    if (cmd == 'y')
        goto quit;
    ...
quit:
    return;
}
```

`goto` does not have to be inside a loop.

The use of the `goto` statement is strongly discouraged.

7.7.   Iterations and Arrays

Iterations are indispensable for dealing with arrays for two reasons. First, if an array is large and we want to access every element (for example, to find the sum of all the elements), it is not practical to repeat the same statement over and over again in the source code:

```
sum = 0;
sum += a[0];
sum += a[1];
...
...
sum += a[999];
```

As we have seen, we can use a simple `for` loop instead and save 998 lines of code:

```
sum = 0;
for (i = 0;   i < 1000;   i++)
    sum += a[i];
```

Second, a programmer may not know in advance the exact size of an array. The program may declare an array with a <u>maximum possible</u> size, but the actual number of elements can become known only when the program is running. Or the program may use an `apvector` and resize it as necessary. The only way to deal with such a "variable-length" array is through iterations, usually a `for` loop. This is illustrated in the following example:

```cpp
// GRADES.CPP
//
// This program finds the average grade for a number
//   of students' grades, entered from the keyboard.

#include <iostream.h>
#include <iomanip.h>
#include "apvector.h"

double Average(const apvector<int> &a);

int main()

{
    int nStudents, i;
    apvector<int> grades;     // An empty array (the size is 0).
    double avgGrade;

    // Enter the number of students:
    cout << "Enter the number of students: ";
    cin >> nStudents;         // The actual number of students' grades
                              //   is entered here
    if (nStudents <= 0)
        return 1;
    grades.resize(nStudents);
                              // Set the size of the array to nStudents.

    // Enter students' grades and save them in the grades array:
    cout << "Enter students' grades:\n";
    for (i = 0;   i < nStudents;   i++)
        cin >> grades[i];

    // Compute and display the average grade:
    cout.setf(ios::showpoint | ios::fixed);
    cout << "Average grade is "
         << setprecision(1) << Average(grades) << endl;

    return 0;
}
```

Continued ☞

```
double Average (const apvector<int> &a)

// Returns the average of the elements of the array a.

{
    int i, n = a.length(), sum = 0;

    for (i = 0;   i < n;   i++)
        sum += a[i];

    return double(sum) / n;
}
```

Recall that an `apvector` argument is normally passed to a function "by reference," that is, its name is preceded by an ampersand character. If the function does not change the array, then the `const` keyword is used. For example:

```
double Average(const apvector<int> &a);
```

Passing arguments "by reference" is explained later, in Chapter 11.

(A note for the impatient. Normally, when an argument is passed to a function, its value is copied on the system stack. If the function changes that value, only the copy changes, not the original. There is also another method of passing an argument — "by reference." Then the <u>address</u> of the variable, not its value, is copied on the stack. When we pass an `apvector` to a function, we want to pass it by reference to avoid copying the whole array. Also, if a function changes some elements of the array, then we <u>must</u> pass it by reference so that the change occurs in the original array, not in a copy.)

7.8.   *Lab:* Students' Grades

The program below reads students' grades from a data file, GRADES.DAT, into an array. It then computes and displays the average, highest, and lowest grades. Study the `ReadNumbers (...)` function, which reads the numbers from a file into an array. Supply the missing functions `MaxElement (...)`, `MinElement (...)`, and `AddElements (...)`, whose prototypes have been provided.

(To find the largest element of an array you can declare a variable such as `aMax`, initialize it to the value of the first element, then scan through the remaining elements of the array and update `aMax` each time you encounter an element that is larger.)

```
                                              ┌─────────────────────┐
                                              │  GRADES.CPP    [💾]  │
                                              └─────────────────────┘
// GRADES.CPP
//
// This program reads students' grades from a file, GRADES.DAT,
//   and finds the average, the highest and the lowest grade.
//
// Author: Mark Avgerinos
// Date 05-21-1999
//

#include <iostream.h>
#include <fstream.h>  // Supports file I/O
#include <iomanip.h>
#include "apvector.h"

//************************************************************
//**************** Function Prototypes  ******************
//************************************************************

bool ReadNumbers (char fileName[], apvector<int> &a);
int AddElements (const apvector<int> &a);
int MaxElement (const apvector<int> &a);
int MinElement (const apvector<int> &a);

//************************************************************
//****************           Main          ******************
//************************************************************

int main()

{
    const int MAXSTUDENTS = 100;
    int nStudents;
    apvector<int> grades(MAXSTUDENTS);
    double avgGrade;

    if (!ReadNumbers("GRADES.DAT", grades)) {
        cout << "Cannot open GRADES.DAT.\n";
        return 1;
    }

    nStudents = grades.length();
    if (nStudents == 0) {
        cout << "GRADES.DAT file contains no numbers.\n";
        return 1;
    }

    cout << nStudents << " students\n";
```

Continued ➯

```
        avgGrade = double(AddElements(grades)) / nStudents;
        cout.setf(ios::showpoint | ios::fixed);
        cout << "The average grade is "
             << setprecision(1) << avgGrade << endl;
        cout << "The highest grade is "
             << MaxElement(grades) << endl;
        cout << "The lowest grade is "
             << MinElement(grades) << endl;

        return 0;
    }


//****************************************************************
//*****************          Functions          ******************
//****************************************************************

bool ReadNumbers (char fileName[], apvector<int> &a)

// Reads integers from a file "fileName" into the array a.
// Returns true if the file is opened sucessfully, false otherwise.

    {
        int n = 0, len = a.length();

        // Declare a variable "inpFile" of the data type "ifstream"
        //    -- input file stream -- and open the file with the
        //    requested name "fileName" for reading:

        ifstream inpFile(fileName);

        // Checks that the file exists:

        if (!inpFile)
           return false;

        // Extract numbers from the file input stream
        //    (i.e., read numbers from the file into the array)
        //    until the end of file is reached or the array is full:

        while (n < len && inpFile >> a[n])
           n++;

        // Resize the array to the actual number of grades read:
        a.resize(n);

        return true;
    }


//****************************************************************
```

Continued ☞

```
int AddElements (const apvector<int> &a)

// Returns a[0] + a[1] + ... + a[len-1]

{
    ...
    ...
}

//*************************************************************

int MaxElement (const apvector<int> &a)

// Returns the value of the largest element of the array a.

{
    ...
    ...
}

//*************************************************************

int MinElement (const apvector<int> &a)

// Returns the value of the smallest element of the array a.

{
    ...
    ...
}
```

Create your own test file, GRADES.DAT. It should contain up to 100 integers, which may be placed on separate lines or several per line; the program does not care. Compile and test the program, including special test cases when the file does not exist and when it is empty.

7.9.   Iterations and Two-Dimensional Arrays

If we want to process all the elements of a matrix (two-dimensional array), it is convenient to use nested for loops. For example:

```
apmatrix<int> grid(25, 80);
int nRows, nCols, row, col;
...
nRows = grid.numrows();
nCols = grid.numcols();
for (row = 0;   row < nRows;   row++) {
    for (col = 0;   col < nCols;   col++) {
        cout << grid[row][col] << "   ";
    }
    cout << endl;
}
```

Now that we are equipped with convenient `for` loops, the task of transposing a matrix (that is, flipping the elements of a square two-dimensional array symmetrically about the main diagonal as in the "extra credit" Lab assignment in Section 5.7) can be implemented with just a few lines of code:

```
void Transpose(apmatrix<double> &m)
{
    int size = m.numrows(); // or m.numcols();
    double temp;

    for (i = 1;   i < size;   i++) {
        for (j = 0;   j < i;   j++) {
            // Swap m[i][j] and m[j][i]
            temp = m[i][j];
            m[i][j] = m[j][i];
            m[j][i] = temp;
        }
    }
}
```

7.10. *Lab:* John Conway's "Game of Life"

The Game of Life is a simulation game introduced by British mathematician John Conway. It became popular in 1970, when Martin Gardner brought it to the attention of readers of *Scientific American*. The simulation takes place on a rectangular grid. Each cell of the grid may be "dead" (vacant) or "alive" (occupied by an "organism"). The initial configuration of alive cells goes through a series of generations. In each successive generation, some alive cells die and some new cells are born in vacant places depending on the total number of alive neighbors of the cell. The "births" and "deaths" follow the following rules:

1. A neighbor of a given cell has a common side or corner with that cell. Each cell inside the grid has 8 neighbors.

2. An alive cell with two or three alive neighbors remains alive in the next generation; an alive cell with less than two alive neighbors dies (of loneliness); a cell with four or more alive neighbors also dies (of overcrowding).

3. A vacant cell becomes alive in the next generation if it has exactly three alive neighbors.

4. All births and deaths take place at exactly the same time, so that the change from one generation to the next is instantaneous.

The following program implements a simplified one-dimensional version of The Game of Life. In this version, the organisms live in a one-dimensional array and a cell remains alive or is born if it has exactly one alive neighbor and dies if neither or both its neighbors are alive.

LIFE1D.CPP

```
// LIFE1D.CPP

// This program implements The Game of One-Dimensional Life.
//
// Author: Priscilla Wornum

#include <iostream.h>
#include <iomanip.h>
#include "apvector.h"

const int SIZE = 13;  // The size of the grid.  In the 1-D version
                      //    the "grid" is a one-dimensional array.

const char ALIVE = 'x';
const char DEAD = '.';

apvector<char> grid(SIZE);

void NextGeneration()

// Creates the next generation on the grid.

{
    apvector<char> newgrid(SIZE);
    int i, neighbors;
```

Continued

```
    // Count alive neighbors of each cell and
    //    calculate the new grid:

    for (i = 0;   i < SIZE;   i++) {
        neighbors = 0;
        if (i > 0 && grid[i-1] == ALIVE)
            neighbors++;
        if (i < SIZE-1 && grid[i+1] == ALIVE)
            neighbors++;
        if (neighbors == 1)
            newgrid[i] = ALIVE;
        else
            newgrid[i] = DEAD;
    }

    // Update the grid:

    grid = newgrid;
}

//****************************************************************

void DisplayGrid(int generation)

// Displays the current generation on the grid.

{
    int i;
    cout << setw(4) << generation << ": ";

    for (i = 0;   i < SIZE;   i++)
        cout << grid[i];
    cout << endl;
}

//****************************************************************

void LoadGrid()

// Reads the initial grid configuration.

{
    int i;

    cout << "Enter initial configuration ('x' or '.'): ";
    for (i = 0;   i < SIZE;   i++)
        cin >> grid[i];
    cin.ignore(80, '\n'); // Skip all remaining input to
                          //    the end of the line.
}
```

Continued ➯

```
//*************************************************************

int main()

{
    int generation = 0;

    LoadGrid();
    DisplayGrid(generation);          // Display initial configuration.

    char next;
    for(;;) {
        cout << "Next (y/n)? ";
        cin >> next;
        if (next != 'y')
            break;
        NextGeneration();
        generation++;
        DisplayGrid(generation);
    }
    return 0;
}
```

Adapt this program for the "real" (two-dimensional) Game of Life. Make `grid`
an `apmatrix` of 20 rows by 50 columns. For the sake of simplicity, declare `grid`
as a global variable rather than passing it to functions as an argument. (As a rule
we avoid using global variables, but here the whole program deals with this grid;
there is no need to be too dogmatic about the rules.) Declare the dimensions of
the array as symbolic constants.

Modify the `LoadGrid(...)` function to read the initial grid configuration from a
file with a given name. The input file is simply a picture:

```
.................................................
...x.............................................
....x............................................
..xxx............................................
.................................................
           (...etc.)
```

There are a number of interesting life-sustaining configurations.[*] A few famous
ones, nicknamed "Glider," "Cheshire Cat," and "Harvester," are provided on the
accompanying diskette (LIFE_GLI.DAT, LIFE_CAT.DAT, LIFE_HRV.DAT).

---

[*] For more information on The Game of Life see Martin Gardner's *Wheels, Life, and Other Mathematical Amusements*, 1983.

7.11. Summary

C++ offers three iterative statements:

```
while (condition) {
    ...
}

for (initialization;    condition;    increment) {
    ...
}

do {
    ...
} while (condition);
```

In a `while` loop, the variables tested in the *condition* must be initialized before the loop, and at least one of them has to change inside the body of the loop. The program tests *condition* before each pass through the loop. If *condition* is false at the very first test, the `while` loop is skipped, and the program jumps to the first statement after the body of the loop. Otherwise the program continues iterations for as long as *condition* holds true.

The `for` loop combines *initialization*, *condition*, and *increment* (change) in one statement. The *initialization* statement is executed once, before the loop. *condition* is tested before each pass through the loop, and if it is false, the loop is skipped and the program jumps to the next statement after the body of the loop. The *increment* statement is executed at the end of each pass through the loop.

The `do-while` loop is different from the `while` loop in that *condition* is tested after the body of the loop. Thus, the body of a `do-while` loop is always executed at least once.

A `break` statement inside the body of a loop tells the program to jump immediately out of the loop to the first statement after the body of the loop. A `continue` statement in the loop tells the program to skip the remaining statements in the body of the loop on the current iteration and jump to the top of the loop for the next iteration. `break` and `continue` may appear only inside some `if` or `else` statement, because otherwise some statements inside the body of the loop would be unreachable. One should be careful with `continue` in `while` loops, because it may inadvertently skip the statements that increment or change variables tested in the condition, causing the program to "hang."

The switch Statement

8.1. Discussion

There are situations when a program must take one of several actions depending
on the value of some variable or expression. Such situations often arise when the
program is processing commands, events, menu choices, or transactions of
different types. If the program has to handle just two or three possible actions,
you can easily use `if-else if` statements:

```
int x = expression;        // Evaluate the expression
                           //    and save its value in x

if (x == valueA) {         // Take action A
    statementA1;
    statementA2;
    ...
}
else if (x == valueB) {    // Take action B
    statementB1;
    statementB2;
    ...
}
else {                     // Take some default action
    ...
}
```

(*valueA* and *valueB* are constants or constant expressions.)

When the number of possible actions is large, the use of `if-else if...`
becomes cumbersome and inefficient. C++ provides a special mechanism, the
`switch` statement, for handling such situations. Its general form is:

```
switch (expression) {

    case valueA:        // Take action A
      statementA1;
      statementA2;
      ...
      break;

    case valueB:        // Take action B
      statementB1;
      ...
      break;

    ...
    ...

    case valueZ:        // Take action Z
      statementZ1;
      ...
      break;

    default:            // Take some default action
      ...
      break;
}
```

valueA, valueB, ... , *valueZ* are integer or character <u>constants</u>. When a switch is compiled, the compiler creates a table of these values and the associated addresses of the corresponding "cases" (code fragments). When the switch is executed, the program first evaluates *expression* to an integer. Then it finds it in the table and jumps to the corresponding "case." If the value is not in the table, the program jumps to "default." The break statement at the end of a "case" tells the program to jump out of the switch and continue with the first statement after the switch. switch, case, default, and break are C++ reserved words.

8.2. *Case Study:* The Calculator Program

The following program emulates a toy calculator with four operations: +, −, *, /.
A session with the program may look as follows:

```
Enter operand1 operation (+ - * /) operand2
For example:
Next: 1+2
  (or '0q' to quit)

Next: 1 + 2
= 3
Next: 4 / 0
*** Division by zero ***
Next: 4 : 2
= 2
Next: 0q
```

The program uses a `switch` statement to handle the four operations:

CALC.CPP

```cpp
// CALC.CPP
//
// This program emulates a calculator with +, -, *, and / operations.
//
// Author: T.I. Childs

#include <iostream.h>

int main()

{
    char op;            // operation sign
    double x, y;        // operands

    cout << "Enter operand1 operation (+ - * /) operand2\n"
         << "For example:\n"
         << "Next: 1+2\n"
         << "   (or '0q' to quit)\n\n";

    for (;;) {          // Repeat the "for" loop until break
        cout << "Next: ";
        cin >> x;
        cin >> op;
        if (op == 'q')
            break;                          // break from for(;;)
        cin >> y;
```

Continued

```
switch (op) {

  case '+':
    cout << "= " << x + y << endl;
    break;

  case '-':
    cout << "= " << x - y << endl;
    break;

  case '*':
    cout << "= " << x * y << endl;
    break;

  case '/':
  case ':':
    if (y == 0.) {
        cout << "*** Division by zero ***\n";
        break;                  // Break out from the switch.
    }

    cout << "= " << x / y << endl;
    break;

  default:
    cout << "*** Invalid operation ***\n";
    break;
  }
 }
 return 0;
}
```

8.3. *Case Study:* Menu

The switch statement is a convenient way to process commands entered by a user. A program can display a *menu* and ask the user to enter a number or a letter that signifies the desired choice. The input is processed by the switch, which may call the appropriate functions to perform selected actions. The switch is normally placed inside a loop that processes user commands until told to quit. In the following example, menu choices are designated by letters:

```
          One Of Each, Inc.
      Inventory Control System

          (S)how inventory item
          (A)dd item
          (R)emove item
          (L)ist inventory
          (Q)uit

Next command ==>  S
```

The above menu comes from the inventory control program presented below. The program is in its embryonic stage. Since we don't yet know how to deal with character strings and we have not yet studied data structures, we cannot conveniently represent the names, available quantities, or other characteristics of the inventory items. At this stage we will represent each inventory item by a "part number" (an integer) and will not keep track of available quantities. So all the program does, at this point, is add, remove, and display elements of an integer array.

MENU.CPP

```cpp
// MENU.CPP
//
// This program illustrates the use of simple one-character
//    commands.  The program displays a menu, accepts a command
//    and executes it.  The application is an embryonic
//    "Inventory Control System" which, at this stage of development,
//    only maintains a list of "inventory items" (integers).
//    Items are stored in an integer array. The "quantity" is
//    not supported -- it is set to 1 for all inventory items.
//
// Author: Bill Wares
//

#include <iostream.h>
#include <iomanip.h>
#include <ctype.h>                   // Declares toupper(ch)
#include "apvector.h"

const int QUANTITY = 1;              // Quantity for each item is set
                                     //    to 1 in this preliminary version.
```

Continued ➯

```
// Function prototypes:

int Find (const apvector<int> &inventory, int partNum);
void Show (const apvector<int> &inventory, int partNum);
void Add (apvector<int> &inventory, int partNum);
void Remove (apvector<int> &inventory, int partNum);
void List (const apvector<int> &inventory);

//************************************************************
//****************           main           ****************
//************************************************************

int main()

{
    apvector<int> inventory;    // Array of items (initially empty)
    char cmd;
    int partNum;

    cout << "\n            One Of Each, Inc.\n";
    cout << "        Inventory Control System\n";

    for(;;) {  // Repeat (until break)

        // Show the menu and prompt:

        cout << "\n";  // Output a blank line

        cout << "\t (S)how inventory item\n";        // '\t' is tab
        cout << "\t (A)dd item\n";
        cout << "\t (R)emove item\n";
        cout << "\t (L)ist inventory\n";
        cout << "\t (Q)uit\n";
        cout << endl;
        cout << "Next command ==> ";

        // Accept command:

        cin >> cmd;                // Read one char.
        cin.ignore(80, '\n');      // Skip remaining input (up to 80
                                   //   chars) to the end of the line.
        cmd = toupper(cmd);        // Convert letter to upper case
                                   //   to allow lower case input
                                   //   for commands (for convenience).

        // Quit if 'Q'

        if (cmd == 'Q')
            break;                     // Quit processing commands

        cout << "\n\n*****************************************\n";
```

Continued ⇨

```
// Process command:

switch (cmd) {

   case 'S':                  // Show inventory item information

      cout << "Part number: ";
      cin >> partNum;
      Show(inventory, partNum);
      break;

   case ...
   ...
   ...

   }

   cout << "*****************************************\n";
   }
   return 0;
}
...
```

Note the use of the `cin.ignore(80, '\n')` and `toupper(cmd)` calls:

```
...
cin >> cmd;                  // Read one char.
cin.ignore(80, '\n');        // Skip remaining input (up to 80
                             //    chars)to the end of the line.
cmd = toupper(cmd);          // Convert letters to upper case
                             //    to allow lower case input
                             //    for commands (for convenience).
...
```

`cin.ignore(80, '\n')` tells the input stream to skip all input characters (up to 80) until the user hits the <ENTER> key. This allows the users to enter full words for commands (even though only the first letter is used). `toupper(ch)` returns the corresponding uppercase character for an alphabetic character `ch`. It does not modify any other characters. This standard library function is declared in the header file `ctype.h`, along with `tolower(ch)` and other useful functions that convert and identify different subsets of characters.

8.4. *Lab:* "One of Each" Inventory System

Complete the switch statement in the Menu program introduced in the previous section. Study the Add(...) and Remove(...) functions below and supply code for the Show(...) and List(...) functions. Then compile and test the program.

MENU.CPP

```
//*****************************************************************
//***************          Functions          ********************
//*****************************************************************

int Find (const apvector<int> &inventory, int partNum)

// Finds the part number, partNum, in the inventory array.
// Returns its index if found, -1 otherwise.

{
    int i, nItems = inventory.length();

    for (i = 0;   i < nItems;   i++)
        if (inventory[i] == partNum)
            return i;
    return -1;
}


//*****************************************************************

void Show (const apvector<int> &inventory, int partNum)

// Displays inventory information for the given part number.

{
    ...
    ...
}


//*****************************************************************
```

Continued

```
void Add (apvector<int> &inventory, int partNum)

// Adds the new inventory item with the specified part number,
//   partNum, to the inventory list.
//   Checks whether partNum is already in the list.

{
    int nItems;

    if (Find(inventory, partNum) >= 0)
        cout << "already registered in the inventory list.\n";
    else {
        nItems = inventory.length();
        inventory.resize(nItems+1);
        inventory[nItems] = partNum;
        cout << "added to the inventory list.\n";
    }
}

//****************************************************************

void Remove (apvector<int> &inventory, int partNum)

// Removes the item partNum from the inventory list, if it
//   is there.  Displays an appropriate message if partNum is not
//   in the list.

{
    int i, j, nItems;

    i = Find(inventory, partNum);
    if (i < 0)
        cout << "not found.\n";
    else {
        nItems = inventory.length();
        for (j = i+1;   j < nItems;   j++)  // Shift items
            inventory[j-1] = inventory[j];  //  to fill the gap.
        inventory.resize(nItems - 1);
        cout << "removed from the inventory list.\n";
    }
}

//****************************************************************

void List (const apvector<int> &inventory)

// Displays the inventory list.

{
    ...
    ...
}
```

Note that arrays are not very convenient if you must remove elements from the middle, because a gap appears. You can fill it by shifting the next element and all the subsequent elements to the left by one.

For "extra credit":

Keep the elements of your inventory array *sorted* (ordered) in ascending order by the part number. Instead of adding a new element at the end of the array, you have to find the right place where to insert the new element. You have to create an empty slot for the new element by shifting all subsequent elements to the right (starting from the last element in the array and working your way back to the marked spot — Figure 8-1). The new element is then inserted into the created vacant slot.

(The search operation is more efficient with sorted arrays. When the array is in random order, you have to scan through the whole array to find an element with the given value or to ascertain that no such element is in the array. This is how the Find(...) function works. This method is called *sequential search.* If you use sequential search on a sorted array, you can terminate the search as soon as you find an element that is equal to or larger than the target value. More importantly, on a sorted array you can use the *binary search* method which, for large arrays, is much more efficient than sequential search. The binary search method is explained in Section 9.3.)

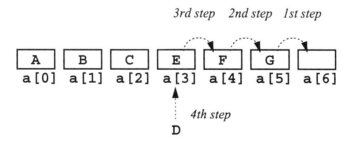

Figure 8-1.   Inserting a new value into the middle of an array.

8.5.   Details of the `switch` Statement

Note the following properties of the `switch` statement:

1. The expression evaluated in a `switch` must have an integral type (integer or `char`). It is often simply one variable, like `op` in the calculator example.

2. All "cases" must be labeled by constants. A "case" cannot be labeled by a variable or an expression that contains variables.

3. The same action may be activated by more than one constant label. For example:

```
case '/':          // both '/' and ':' signify division
case ':':
  ...
```

4. There may be a `break` in the <u>middle</u> of a "case," but then it must be inside an `if` or `else`, otherwise some code in that "case" would be unreachable. Such a `break` tells the program to jump out of the switch immediately. For example:

```
case '/':
  ...
  if (y == 0.) {
      cout << "*** Division by zero ***\n";
      break;    // Jump out of the switch
  }
  ...
  break;         // Jump out of the switch
```

5. The `default` clause is optional. If not specified, the default action is "do nothing."

6. It is a common mistake to omit `break` at the end of a "case."

> **The `switch` syntax does not require that each "case" end with a `break`. Without a `break`, though, the program <u>falls through</u> and continues with the next "case." This C++ feature may lead to annoying bugs, and programmers usually take special care to put a `break` at the end of each "case."**

Unusual situations, where a programmer intentionally allows the program to "fall through" from one "case" to the next, call for a special comment in the code.

8.6.   Breaks in Nested Loops and Switches

Loops and switch statements use the same break keyword. A break must always appear inside a loop or switch.

In situations where there is a switch within a loop or a loop within a switch, or a loop within a loop, or a switch within a switch... break affects only the innermost loop or switch that contains it.

In the calculator program, for example, we used a break within a switch which is within a for loop. That break breaks out of the switch, but not out of the for loop. Likewise, in the following code:

```
for (x = 0.;    x <= 1.;    x +=.01)
    for (y = 0.;    y <= 1.;    y +=.01)
        if (x*x + y*y >= r*r) break;

cout << "x = " << x << " y = " << y;
```

break would tell the program to jump out of the <u>inner</u> loop, but not out of the outer loop. So if the programmer intended to quit all iterations over y <u>and</u> x when the if (*condition*) became true, he has a "bug." The correct code would be:

```
bool quit = false;
for (x = 0.;   x <= 1. && !quit;   x +=.01)
    for (y = 0.;    y <= 1.;    y +=.01)
        if (x*x + y*y >= .64) {
            quit = true;
            break;
        }
cout << "x = " << x << " y = " << y;
```

If a break is within a loop which is within a "case," the break works only for the loop, and another break is needed for the "case." For example:

```
switch(cmd) {
  ...

  case 1000:  // Find a prime between 1000 and 2000
    for (p = 1000; p <= 2000;   p++)
        if (IsPrime(p))
            break;            // Break out of the "for" loop.
    break;                    // Break out of the switch.

  ...
}
```

8.7. Summary

The general form of a `switch` statement is

```
switch (expression) {

    case valueA:        // Take action A
       statementA1;
       statementA2;
       ...
       break;

    case valueB:        // Take action B
       statementB1;
       ...
       break;

    ...
    ...
    default:            // Take the default action
       ...
       break;
}
```

where *valueA*, *valueB*, etc., are some integer or character constants. The switch evaluates *expression* and jumps to the "case" labeled by the corresponding constant value, or to the default "case" if no match has been found. A `switch` can be used to replace a long `if-else if` sequence and is convenient for processing menu commands, events, or transactions that require different actions.

The `break` statement is used to break out of a loop or a switch. A `break` must be inside a loop or switch. In the case of nested loops or switches, a break tells the program to break out of the <u>innermost</u> loop or switch that contains it but does not affect the control flow in the outer switches or loops.

9

Algorithms

9.1. Discussion

There is a subtle but crucial gap between solving a problem and simply expressing the solution in a particular language or notation. Knowing all the rules of English grammar and spelling won't help you give directions from point A to point B unless you know how to get there. Until now, we have mostly focused on the style and syntax of C++. As a result, we have acquired substantial expressive power; now we can use many features of the C++ language to solve problems.

A method of performing a task or solving a problem can be described at different levels of abstraction. In computer applications, an analyst can describe a method in more or less abstract terms to a computer programmer. It helps if the analyst knows the capabilities of computers and the general principles of computer programming, but he does not have to know any specific programming language. The programmer can then describe the method in C++ or Pascal or LISP, allowing any computer that has a compiler for that language to translate the program from a still abstract high-level programming language to a precise list of instructions for a specific CPU.

Unless the problem it's solving is completely trivial, a program is based on one or several *algorithms*. A formal definition of an algorithm is elusive, which is a sure sign that the notion is fundamentally important. Basically, an *algorithm* is a more or less abstract and formal step-by-step recipe that tells how to perform a certain task or solve a certain problem on a computer. The paradox of this definition, however, is that algorithms existed long before computers. One of the most famous, Euclid's Algorithm for finding the greatest common factor of two integers, dates back to about 300 B.C. You may also recall the algorithm for long division of numbers, often used in the pre-calculator era. The question of whether computers have evolved the way they are to support the implementation of algorithms or whether algorithms (as they are understood now) gained prominence due to the advent of computers belongs to the chicken-and-egg category.

An algorithm may describe a method for accomplishing a task without relying on any particular programming language or any particular computer model. In fact, an algorithm can be used without any computer by a person equipped with a pencil and paper.

Various tools and notations have been developed for describing and teaching algorithms. Flowcharts, for example, use graphical representation. The flowchart in Figure 9-1 represents an algorithm for finding the sum of all the elements of an array. Rectangles represent processing steps; rhombuses, conditional branching points. Another representation is called ***pseudocode***. It uses operations similar to those defined in programming languages, but without paying much attention to syntax or data types; this produces a shorthand that all programmers, regardless of the language they use, can read and understand. For example:

```
Input: a[0], ... a[N-1]
    1. i ← 0    // arrow means "set to" - same as = in C++
    2. sum ← 0
    3. Repeat steps 4-5 while i < N
    4. sum ← sum + a[i]
    5. i ← i+1
Output: sum
```

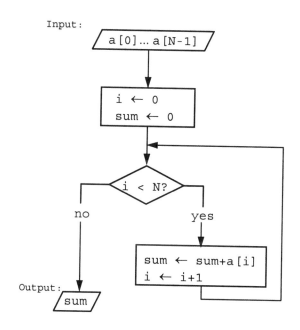

Figure 9-1. Flowchart for finding the sum of elements of an array.

In the rest of this chapter we will consider three classical examples of algorithms: ***selection sort***, an algorithm for arranging the elements of an array in ascending (or descending) order; ***binary search***, an algorithm for quickly finding the element with a given value in a sorted array; and ***Euclid's Algorithm*** for finding the greatest common factor of two integers. We will first explain each algorithm informally and then implement it as a C++ function.

9.2.   Selection Sort

Given an array of numbers, the task is to rearrange the elements of the array in ascending order.

We are looking for a general algorithm that works for an array of any size and for any values of its elements. There are many algorithms for accomplishing this task (called *sorting* algorithms), but the most straightforward one is probably *selection sort*. It involves the following steps:

```
Selection sort:
    1. Initialize a variable n to the size of the array.
    2. Find the largest among the first n elements.
    3. Make it swap places with the n-th element.
    4. Decrement n by 1.
    5. Repeat steps 2-4 while n ≥ 2.
```

At the first iteration we find the largest element of the array and swap it with the last element. The largest element is now in the correct place, from which it will never move again. We decrement n, pretending that the last element of the array does not exist anymore, and repeat the procedure until we have worked our way through the array. The iterations stop when there is only one element left, because it has already been compared with every other element and is guaranteed to be the smallest.

The Sort (...) function below implements this algorithm for an array of the type double:

ALGORTHM.CPP

```
void Sort(apvector<double> &a)

// Sort a[0], ..., a[size-1] in ascending order.

{
    int i, iMax, n;
    double aTemp;
    int size = a.length();

    for (n = size;   n >= 2;   n--) {

        // Find the index "iMax" of the largest element
        //    among a[0], ..., a[n-1]:

        iMax = 0;
        for (i = 1;   i < n;   i++)
            if (a[i] > a[iMax])
                iMax = i;

        // Swap a[iMax] with a[n-1]:

        aTemp = a[iMax];     // Save a[iMax] in a temporary location.
        a[iMax] = a[n-1];    // Copy a[n-1] to a[iMax].
        a[n-1] = aTemp;      // Copy saved value to a[n-1].

        // Decrement n (accomplished by n-- in the "for" loop).
    }
}
```

A similar procedure will sort the array in descending order; instead of finding the largest element, we can simply find the smallest element of the array.

Sorting is a common operation in computer applications and a favorite subject for studying and comparing algorithms. Several other sorting algorithms are presented later, in Part 2.

9.3. Binary Search

Suppose we have an array of a certain size and we want to find the location of a given "target" value in that array (or to ascertain that it is not there). This task is called *searching*. If the elements of the array are in random order, we have no choice but to check the value of each element until we find the target element (or finish scanning through the whole array). This may be time-consuming if the array is large. For an array of 1,000,000 elements we will examine an average of

500,000 elements before finding the target (assuming that the target value is always somewhere in the array).

It turns out that if our array is sorted, there is a much faster searching algorithm, the **binary search**. Let's say our array is sorted in ascending order and we are looking for the target value *x*. Take the middle element of the array and compare it with *x*. If they are equal, the target element is found. If *x* is smaller, the target element must be in the left half of the array, and if *x* is larger, the target must be in the right half of the array. In any event, each time we repeat the same procedure, we narrow the range of our search by half. This sequence stops when we find the target or get down to just one element, which happens very quickly.

Using the binary search method, an array of 3 elements requires at most 2 comparisons. An array of seven elements requires at most 3 comparisons. An array of 15 elements requires at most 4 comparisons, and so on. In general, an array of $2^n - 1$ (or less) elements requires at most *n* comparisons. So an array of 1,000,000 elements will require at most 20 comparisons ($2^{20} - 1 = 1,048,575$) which is much better than 500,000. (That is why this method is called "divide and conquer.")

The binary search algorithm for an integer array, sorted in ascending order, is implemented in the following function `Search(…)`:

ALGORTHM.CPP

```
int Search(const apvector<int> &a, int target)

// Performs binary search on the array
//    a[0] < a[1] < ... < a[size-1].
//    Looks for an element a[k] equal to "target".
// Returns k if the target is found; -1 otherwise.

{
    int left = 0, right = a.length() - 1, middle;
    int k = -1;

    while (left <= right) {

        // Take the index of the middle element between
        //    "left" and "right":

        middle = (left + right) / 2;

        // Compare  this element to the "target" value
        //    and adjust the search range accordingly:
```

Continued ⇗

```
    if (target > a[middle])
        left = middle + 1;
    else if (target < a[middle])
        right = middle - 1;
    else {      // target must be equal to a[middle]
        k = middle;
        break;
    }
  }

  return k;
}
```

One way to understand and check code is to *trace* it manually on some representative examples. Let us take, for example:

```
Given:
    size = 6;
    a[size] = {8,13,21,34,55,89}
      (a[0] =  8; a[1] = 13; a[2] = 21; a[3] = 34;
       a[4] = 55; a[5] = 89);
    target = 34.

Initially:
    left =  0; right = size-1 = 5.

First iteration:
    middle = (0+5)/2 = 2;
    a[middle] = a[2] = 21;
    target > a[middle] (34 > 21)
      ==> Set left = middle + 1 = 3; (right remains 5).

Second iteration:
    middle = (3+5)/2 = 4;
    a[middle] = a[4] = 55;
    target < a[middle] (34 < 55)
      ==> Set right = middle - 1 = 3; (left remains 3).

Third iteration:
    middle = (3+3)/2 = 3;
    a[middle] = a[3] = 34;
    target == a[middle] (34 = 34)
      ==> Set k = middle = 3; break.

Return: 3.
```

A more comprehensive check should also include tracing special situations (e.g., when the target element is the first or the last element, or is not in the array) and "degenerate" cases when `size` is equal to 1 or 0.

We also have to make sure that the function terminates — otherwise, the program may hang. This is better accomplished by logical or mathematical reasoning than by tracing specific examples, because it is hard to foresee all the possible paths of an algorithm. We know that our `Search(...)` function terminates because on each iteration the difference `right-left` decreases by at least 1. So eventually we either break out of the loop via `break` (when the target is found), or reach a point where `right-left` becomes negative, `right` becomes smaller than `left`, and the condition in the `while` loop becomes false.

9.4.   Euclid's Algorithm for Finding GCF

Given two positive integers, *m* and *n*, their greatest common factor GCF*(m,n)* is defined as the largest integer *d* such that both *m* and *n* are evenly divisible by *d*. For example,

GCF(1001, 4235) = 77

One way to find the greatest common factor of two integers is to obtain the prime factorization for each number and then take the product of all shared primes. For example,

1001 = 7 · 11 · 13;

4235 = 5 · 7 · 11 · 11;

GCF(1001, 4235) = 7 · 11 = 77

This method works well for small numbers, but its implementation on a computer would be rather cumbersome and inefficient. Euclid's *Elements* contains the description of an elegant "computer" algorithm for finding the GCF. (Perhaps Euclid should be credited with defining, in principle, the architecture and capabilities of the modern computer.)

Euclid's Algorithm is based on the following simple observations:

1. If m is evenly divisible by n then GCF$(m, n) = n$;
2. If m is divided by n and r is the remainder $(r \neq 0)$, then

$$GCF(m, n) = GCF(n, r)$$

This is true because

$$m = qn + r$$

If a divisor d divides evenly into both m and n , it also divides evenly into r. Conversely, if d divides into both n and r, it also divides into m. Thus, the set of all common factors of m and n is the same as the set of all common factors of n and r, and GCF$(m, n) =$ GCF(n, r).

In Euclid's algorithm we repeatedly substitute smaller numbers n and r for the previous pair m and n, as long as r is not equal to zero. When $r = 0$, we return the answer n.

Figure 9-2 shows a flowchart for this algorithm.

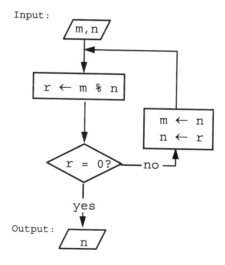

Figure 9-2. Flowchart for Euclid's Algorithm.

It is implemented in the following C++ code:

ALGORTHM.CPP

```
int GCF(int m, int n)

// Returns the greatest common factor of two positive integers
//    m and n.

{
    int r;

    for(;;) {  // Repeat (until break)
        r = m % n;              // r = "m modulo n" i.e. the remainder
                                //    when m is divided by n.
        if (r == 0)             // i.e. if n evenly divides m
            break;
        m = n;                  // Substitute values: m becomes n and
        n = r;                  //    n becomes r.  GCF(m,n) = GCF(n,r).
    }
    return n;
}
```

Let us trace the above code for *m* = 1001, *n* = 4235:

```
Given:
    m = 1001; n = 4235;

First iteration:
    r = 1001 % 4235 = 1001;
    m = 4235;
    n = 1001;
```

In this example *m* happens to be less than *n,* so the first iteration does nothing but swap them. This can be avoided if we stipulate that *m* must be greater or equal to *n*. It often happens, however, that a good algorithm works under more general conditions than anticipated. So the above function works for *m* < *n* as well.

```
Second iteration:
    r = 4235 % 1001 = 231;
    m = 1001;
    n = 231;

Third iteration:
    r = 1001 % 231 = 77;
    m = 231;
    n = 77;
```

```
Fourth iteration:
    r = 231 % 77 = 0;
    break;

Return n = 77;
```

The GCF(...) function always terminates, because on each iteration we first calculate r < n, then set the new value of n equal to r. So the value of n decreases on each iteration, and at some point the break condition, r == 0, must become true.

9.5. *Lab:* Practice in Algorithms

In these exercises we are looking for economical solutions that do not use temporary arrays.

1. Write the following function and a main program to test it:

```
void CumulativeSum(const apvector<double> &a, apvector<double> &s)

// Calculates and places in the array "s" cumulative sums:
//    s[0] = a[0]
//    s[1] = a[0] + a[1]
//    ...
//    s[size-1] = a[0] + a[1] + ... + a[size-1]
```

Don't forget to resize the vector s to the appropriate size first.

2. The array pages contains page numbers for a reading assignment. The page numbers are in ascending order, but they may be written in an abbreviated form: the leading digits in a page number may be dropped if they are the same as in the previous number. For example, 413, 15, 21, 1001, 3 actually means 413, 415, 421, 1001, 1003. Write and test a function

```
void ExpandNumbers (apvector<int> &pages)
```

that converts abbreviated numbers into the correctly expanded numbers and places them into the same array.

3. Write and test a function that generates Pascal's triangle:

```
void PascalTriangle(apvector<int> &tr, int n)
// Generates the n-th row of Pascal's triangle in tr
```

The triangle, named after the French mathematician Blaise Pascal (1623-1662), looks like this:

```
row 0:            1
row 1:           1 1
row 2:          1 2 1
row 3:         1 3 3 1
row 4:        1 4 6 4 1
  . . .         . . . . . . . . . .
```

All the numbers on the sides of the triangle are 1, and each number inside the triangle is the sum of the two numbers above it. The elements in the *n*-th row are the coefficients in the expansion of $(x+y)^n$. For example:

$$(x + y)^4 = x^4 + 4x^3 y + 6x^2 y^2 + 4xy^3 + y^4$$

(As it happens, the coefficient in the *k*-th position in the *n*-th row is also equal to the number of possible different ways to choose *k* objects out of *n*. For example, there are 6 different ways to choose 2 objects out of 4.)

An output statement strategically placed within `PascalTriangle(...)` will print out the whole triangle up to the *n*-th row. Simplified output may look as follows:

```
1
1   1
1   2   1
1   3   3   1
1   4   6   4   1
```

With a little extra work, you can insert the necessary number of spaces at the beginning of each line so that the output triangle is symmetrical:

```
            1
          1   1
        1   2   1
      1   3   3   1
    1   4   6   4   1
```

9.6. Summary

It is not easy to formalize the concept of an algorithm. To do this properly, we would need a very abstract mathematical model of a "computing machine." A set of instructions enabling such a machine to accomplish a certain task would represent an algorithm for that task.

Informally, an algorithm is a step-by-step "recipe" for carrying out a task. An algorithm must be general enough to work for a reasonably general formulation of the task. Algorithms use abstract versions of the operations and control structures (such as assignment, iterations, conditional branching, etc.) that can be expressed more specifically in various programming languages. Thus an algorithm is an abstract blueprint for a computer program and must be readily convertible into a working program.

The correctness of an algorithm can be ascertained informally by trying it out on a representative set of examples or proven more formally through logical or mathematical reasoning. Logical errors in algorithms will creep into programs as "bugs." Besides careful logical examination of the algorithm and its implementation as a program, one way of getting rid of bugs is to trace the code with some examples, either manually or with the help of a debugger.

10

Monte Carlo Methods

10.1. Discussion

Monte Carlo methods are computer models that involve some chance or probabilistic behavior. (Monte Carlo is a famous gambling resort in Monaco.) In this chapter, we will consider applications of a Monte Carlo method for estimating areas, volumes, or integrals that are hard to calculate by analytical methods.

Suppose we have a figure in the x-y plane and we want to estimate its area. Suppose the figure lies within some known rectangle and for each point with coordinates (x, y) we can tell whether the point belongs to the figure or not. The area of interest may be the area under the graph of some function $y = f(x)$ and bounded by the x-axis and two vertical lines: $x = a$ and $x = b$ (Figure 10-1). Such an area is called the **definite integral** of the function $f(x)$ on the interval $[a,b]$. Assuming that $f(a) \geq f(x) \geq 0$ for any x between a and b, this area lies within the rectangle

$$\{a \leq x \leq b; \ 0 \leq y \leq f(a)\}$$

A point (x, y) from the rectangle lies inside or on the border of the figure when (x, y) is on or under the curve, that is, when $y \leq f(x)$.

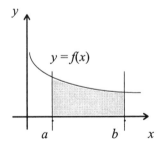

Figure 10-1.   The area under the curve is called *definite integral* of a function.

The idea of the Monte Carlo method is to throw many random points uniformly distributed over the rectangle that contains our area of interest. Some points will land inside the figure, and other points will land outside. The fraction of all points that land inside should be approximately equal to the ratio of the area of the figure to the area of the rectangle.

The C++ standard library includes a function `rand()` that returns a "random" number. `rand()` is an unusual function. Normally, a function called with the same arguments or with no arguments returns the same value. But the whole point of `rand()` is that it returns a different, "random" value on every call. This is accomplished by saving some internal state of the random number generator and updating it after each call. The numbers returned by `rand()` could not possibly be true random numbers, because they are calculated according to some procedure and because their sequence repeats after a number of calls to `rand()`. Nevertheless, these numbers have a rather uniform distribution over their range, and the length of the period before repetition is quite long (e.g. 2^{32}). Numbers produced by a random number generator procedure are called ***pseudorandom*** numbers.

By default, successive calls to `rand()` always generate the same sequence. Another library function, `srand(unsigned seed)`, "seeds" the random number generator, so that the starting point of the random sequence changes. If necessary, the seed can be derived from the system clock or some other random event.

`rand()` is declared in the header file `stdlib.h`. It returns an integer between 0 and `RAND_MAX`. `RAND_MAX` is a constant also defined in `stdlib.h` (usually $2^{15}-1$).

A number returned by `rand()` can be scaled to any desired range $[a,b]$. For example:

```
const double a = -10., b = 10.;
double x;
...
x = a + double(rand()) * ((b-a) / RAND_MAX);
```

The number of points used in the Monte Carlo method depends on the desired accuracy and the properties of the random number generator. Even with a very large number of points, the accuracy of the estimate is still limited by the granularity of the grid of possible random coordinates. If random integers between 0 and `RAND_MAX` are scaled to the interval $[a,b]$, all scaled values fall on a discrete grid with the step equal to `(b-a)/RAND_MAX` (Figure 10-2).

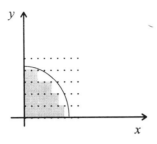

Figure 10-2.   Accuracy of the Monte Carlo method is limited by the
granularity of the grid of random points.

Random points are generated and tested within a loop:

```
for (n = nPoints;   n > 0;   n--) {  // A loop that goes down to
                                     //   0 is slightly more
                                     //   efficient.

    x = a + double(rand()) * ((b-a) / RAND_MAX);
    y = ...
    ... // if (y <= f(x)) increment count
    ...
}
```

10.2. *Case Study:* Estimating the Perimeter of an Ellipse

The program below uses Monte Carlo to estimate the perimeter of an ellipse. This number may be useful, for example, for finding the length of the elliptical orbit of a planet or a satellite. The Earth's equator is not quite round, but slightly elliptical, too. In a special case, when the ellipse is a circle, the perimeter (circumference) is, of course, simply $2\pi R$. In the general case the perimeter can be expressed as $4ER$, where $2R$ is the major axis of the ellipse and E is the so-called elliptic integral. E is equal to the area under the curve

$$f(x) = \sqrt{1 - \tfrac{1}{2}\sin^2 x}$$

from $x=0$ to $x=\pi/2$ (Figure 10-3). The coefficient $\frac{1}{2}$ corresponds to the particular elongation of the ellipse that we have chosen.*

Note that we have started with the problem of finding the <u>length</u> of a curve (ellipse) but restated it in terms of finding an integral, which is the <u>area</u> under a (different) curve.

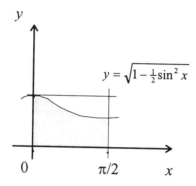

Figure 10-3.   Perimeter of an ellipse is determined by the area under the curve.

The `sin(x)` function, which calculates the sine of an angle measured in radians, is provided in the C++ standard library.

---

* The elliptic integral E is defined as:

$$E = \int_0^{\frac{\pi}{2}} \sqrt{1 - k^2 \sin^2 x}\ dx$$

The parameter k determines the elongation of the ellipse and is usually defined in terms of the modular angle: k = sin α.

In our test program, we have chosen $\alpha = 45°$, so $k = \frac{\sqrt{2}}{2}$ and $k^2 = \frac{1}{2}$.

MONCARLO.CPP

```
// MONCARLO.CPP
//
//   This program calculates the perimeter of an ellipse.
//   One quarter of the perimeter of an ellipse with the
//   larger radius 1 is equal to the so-called
//   "elliptic integral" E -- the area under the curve
//   y = sqrt(1 - (k*sin(x))^2) on the interval 0 <= x <= pi/2.
//   The parameter k describes the shape of the ellipse and is
//   usually expressed in terms of the so-called "modular angle":
//   k = sin(alpha), where alpha is the angle between the minor
//   axis and the line that connects its end to a focus of
//   the ellipse.  For a circle, alpha = 0 and k = 0.
//   The integral is calculated by using the Monte Carlo method.
//
//   Author: B. Random
//   Date: 2/29/1999
//

#include <iostream.h>
#include <iomanip.h>
#include <stdlib.h>    // Declares rand() and RAND_MAX
#include <math.h>      // Declares sin(x)

const double PI = 3.14159265358979323846;

// Modular angle (in degrees and radians):
const double alpha = 45;
const double alpha_radians = alpha * PI / 180.;

// k defines elongation of the ellipse:
const double k = sin(alpha_radians);

//*************************************************************

double MonteCarlo (long nPoints)

//   This function calculates the elliptic integral E.
//   It generates "nPoints" (pseudo)random points in the
//   rectangle { 0 <= x <= pi/2;  0 <= y <= 1 }, finds
//   the fraction of all points that fall under the curve,
//   and calculates the corresponding fraction of the area of
//   the rectangle.

{
    double x, y, f;
    long n, count = 0;
```

Continued ✍

```
    for (n = nPoints;    n > 0;    n--) {

        // Generate a random point:
        //    0 <= x <= pi/2
        //    0 <= y <= 1

        x = double(rand()) * (.5 * PI / RAND_MAX);
        y = double(rand()) / RAND_MAX;

        // Calculate 1 - (k * sin(x))^2

        f = k * sin(x);
        f *= f;                    // Square f
        f = 1 - f;

        // Increment the counter if the point (x,y) is on or under
        //    the curve:

        if (y*y <= f) count++;
          // (more efficient than: if (y <= sqrt(f)) ...)
    }

    //   count                             E
    //  -------  =  ---------------------------------------
    //  nPoints       area of rect {0 <= x <= pi/2; 0 <= y <= 1}

    return (double(count) / double(nPoints)) * (.5 * PI);
}

//*************************************************************

int main()

{
    long n;
    double ellipsePerim;

    cout << "Enter the number of random points in Monte Carlo ==> ";
    cin >> n;
    ellipsePerim = 4. * MonteCarlo(n);

    cout << "The perimeter of the ellipse with a modular angle of "
         << alpha << " degrees\n"
         << " and a major axis of 2 units is approximately = "
         << setprecision(3) << ellipsePerim << endl;

    return 0;
}
```

The output of the program is 5.407 for 100,000 points — quite close to the 5.4024 value from the table of elliptic integrals.

10.3. *Lab:* Estimating π Using the Monte Carlo Method

The purpose of the lab is to find out whether you can get a good approximation of π by using a Monte Carlo method. The easiest way to get π with Monte Carlo is from the formula for the area of a circle. As we know, the area of a circle of radius R is πR^2. The area of a quarter of a circle with a radius of 1 and the center at (0,0) should be equal to π/4. We can estimate that area by generating random points (x,y) uniformly distributed over the square $\{\, 0 \le x \le 1;\ 0 \le y \le 1 \}$. A point (x,y) is inside the circle when $x^2 + y^2 \le 1$.

Modify the program shown in the previous section to get an estimate of π, and experiment with different numbers of random points used. Compare the results with the actual value of π.

11

Pointers, References, Dynamic Memory Allocation

11.1. Discussion

In a C++ assignment statement

```
a = b;
```

the variables a and b play different roles. Think of a as a place and b as a thing: b tells which value the program should use, and a tells where to put it. Anything that can be on the left side of the assignment operator is called *lvalue* (from "left value") and anything on the right side *rvalue* (from "right value").

Any valid expression can be used as an rvalue. For example, we can write

```
a = b + 1;
```

Not so for lvalues. If we write

```
a - 1 = b;
```

the C++ compiler generates an error message, "lvalue required in ..." a-1 is not an lvalue.

Note that the word "address" has been carefully avoided in our discussion, as if it were inappropriate to mention it in good society — the menial job of dealing with the actual addresses of variables has been left to the C++ compiler. This has made our lives much easier, but it has also prevented us from doing many useful things. Now the time has come to bring addresses explicitly into our programs.

C++ offers not one, but two parallel mechanisms for dealing with addresses: *pointers* and *references*. Pointers are an older mechanism that C++ inherited from C along with many traditional C idioms and methods of handling arrays and linked structures. Some standard C++ library functions, left over from C, use pointers as arguments and/or return values. References are a newer method that originated in C++.   C++ class libraries, especially I/O stream operators and functions, use references. Thus, we have no choice but to learn and use both.

Both pointers and references are variables (or constants) that hold memory addresses as their values. The two mechanisms use two different notations, and each mechanism has its own traditional uses.

The rest of this chapter explains the use of pointers and references for the following purposes:

- Passing arguments to functions **by reference** (i.e., passing the argument's address, as opposed to its value, to a function).

- **Dynamic memory allocation** (i.e., temporarily grabbing a chunk of free memory for use in your program).

- Using pointers or references as return values from functions.

In Part 2 we will see how pointers are used to create linked structures such as linked lists. But the first step is to learn how to declare pointers and references and assign values to them.

11.2. Pointers and References: Declarations and Assignments

For any built-in or user-defined data type, SOMETYPE, C++ provides two automatically defined data types. One is designated SOMETYPE* and called "a pointer to SOMETYPE" (or "SOMETYPE pointer"); the other is designated SOMETYPE& and called "a reference to SOMETYPE" (or "SOMETYPE reference"). For example, a variable of the data type double* is a <u>pointer</u> to a double; a variable of the type double& is a <u>reference</u> to a double.

Variables or constants of both double* and double& types hold the <u>addresses</u> in computer memory of variables (or of symbolic constants) of the type double.

In general, variables (or constants) of both the SOMETYPE* and SOMETYPE& types hold <u>addresses</u> of variables (or of symbolic constants) of the type SOMETYPE. The difference between SOMETYPE* and SOMETYPE& is in notation: in how the pointers and references are declared, initialized, and used in programs.

C++ provides the operator "address of," which is denoted by the & symbol. It can be applied to a variable, a symbolic constant, or to an element of an array, and returns its address in the form of a <u>pointer</u> of the corresponding type. For example, if we have

```
double x;
```

then the expression &x means "address of x" and has the type double* (a pointer to a double"). We can declare a variable, say px, of the type double* and initialize it to the address of x:

```
double x;
double* px = &x;   // Variable px is a pointer to a double;
                   //   Its initial value is the address of x.
```

As we have already mentioned, pointers and references offer similar capabilities but use different syntactic notation. We can declare a variable, say rx, of the type double& (*reference* to a double) and initialize it to the address of x:

```
double& rx = x;    // Variable rx is a reference to a double;
                   //   Its initial value is the address of x.
```

Note that when initializing the pointer px, you must explicitly apply the & ("address of") to x. When you are initializing the reference rx, the & is implicit: the compiler knows it has to take the <u>address</u> of x (as opposed to its value) because it is initializing a <u>reference</u> variable.

⌘   ⌘   ⌘

Pointers and references are peculiar variables. Their values are memory addresses which are represented by some positive integers and are usually expressed "in hex" (hexadecimal notation). You can take a look at one if you want to. For example:

```
#include <iostream.h>

int main()

{
    double PI = 3.14;
    double* ptrPI = &PI;   // Declares a variable ptrPI and
                           //   initializes it to the address of the
                           //   previously declared variable PI.

    cout << "Value of PI = " << PI << endl;
        << "Address of PI = " << ptrPI << endl;

    return 0;
}
```

The output may be something like

```
Value of PI = 3.14
Address of PI = 0x194a0ffc
```

We never use the exact numeric values of pointers or references in programs because these values are determined at run time and may be different each time we execute our program depending on where the program is loaded in memory.

The things that we <u>can</u> do with pointers and references are the following:

1. We can assign addresses of variables or constants to pointers and initialize references.
2. We can get hold of or modify the value stored at a given address, (i.e., the value "pointed to" by a pointer or "referred to" by a reference).
3. We can copy the values of pointers to other pointers.
4. We can pass pointers and references to functions.
5. We can increment or decrement addresses, or, in general, calculate a new address by adding an offset (a positive or a negative integer) to a given address.

The latter capability, called "pointer arithmetic," is convenient for handling built-in arrays. There is a close relationship between built-in arrays and pointers, but the `apvector` class hides this relationship from programmers and obviates the pointer arithmetic. The relationship between built-in arrays and pointers is discussed in Appendix B.

⌘ ⌘ ⌘

You might wonder why we need pointers and references of different types. An address is an address, whether it points to an `int`, a `char` or a `double`. And in a typical computer, all addresses are represented in the same way.

Different pointer and reference types are needed only at the logical level to maintain the integrity of C++ data type checking, conversions, and input/output operations, and to support pointer arithmetic.

If necessary, one pointer type can be converted into another pointer type using the cast operator. For example:

```
...
int* pn;        // pn is pointer to int
char* pc;       // pc is pointer to char
...
pc = static_cast<char *> (pn);
```

The cast is purely logical — nothing actually happens to the address represented by a pointer. C++ provides a "generic" pointer type, `void*`, which can be cast into any specific pointer type when necessary.

⌘ ⌘ ⌘

Let us consider the following declarations:

```
. . .
char  c = '$';    // c is a char initialized to '$'.
char* p = &c;     // p is a char* (pointer to char) initialized
                  //   to the address of c.
char& r = c;      // r is a char& (reference to char) initialized
                  //   to the address of c.
. . .
```

The initialization of a pointer is <u>optional</u> — you can assign its value later — but a <u>reference must be initialized</u> to some address when it is declared, and that address cannot be changed.

In the above examples, we have been using `double*` or `char&` for the corresponding type names. In C++ syntax, however, the `*` or `&` symbol does not have to be attached to the type name. We can let it hang freely in the middle or attach it to the declared variable (or constant) name instead:

```
Identical declarations:

char*  p;
char * p;
char  *p;

char&  r;
char & r;
char  &r;
```

Moreover, we can have several variables of types `SOMETYPE`, `SOMETYPE*` and `SOMETYPE&` interspersed in the same declaration list. For example:

```
char c, *p = &c, &r = c;  // Declares: 1. char c;
                          //           2. char* p, initialized to
                          //              the address of c;
                          //           3. char& r, initialized to
                          //              the address of c.
```

This kind of a declaration list is rather common. Note the multipurpose use of the `&` symbol as both the "address of" operator (e.g. `. . .= &c`) and the reference type indicator (as in `&r=. . .`) in declarations.

Because such lists can separate a variable from its antecedent data type, it is better to attach the * or & symbol to the <u>name of the declared variable</u> rather than to the data type name. From now on, we will adhere to this practice and use

```
SOMETYPE *c;
```

instead of

```
SOMETYPE* c;
```

⌘ ⌘ ⌘

Ultimately, the *raison d'être* for pointers and references is the values to which they point or refer.

> **If p is a pointer, *p represents the rvalue or lvalue to which p points.**

Consider carefully the following example, which illustrates what pointers are all about:

```
...
char aVar = 'A',
     bVar = 'B';
char *p = &aVar;        // p is declared as a char* variable.
                        //   p is initially set equal to the
                        //   address of aVar (*p temporarily
                        //   becomes an alias to aVar).
cout << *p << endl;     // Output: A
p = &bVar;              // Set p to address of bVar.
cout << *p << endl;     // Output: B

p = &aVar;              // Set p to address of aVar again.
*p = 'Z';               // (Indirectly) set aVar to 'Z'.
p = &bVar;              // Set p to address of bVar.
*p = 'Y';               // (Indirectly) set bVar to 'Y'.
cout << aVar
     << bVar << endl;   // Output: ZY
...
```

Note that both p and *p can be used both as rvalues and lvalues — they are found both on the right and left sides of assignment statements. Also note the multipurpose use of the * symbol: as a pointer type indicator in declarations and as the **_dereference_** operator, which transforms a pointer into the value (lvalue or rvalue) to which it points.

With references the notation can be confusing at first, because reference variables are used in an unusual way. For any "normal" variable x, the name x in the program represents either its own lvalue (location) if x is in the left side of an assignment, or its own rvalue (value) if x is in the right side of an assignment. Thus, the statement

```
x = x + 1;
```

actually means: "Take the value of x, add 1, and save the result in the location reserved for x." However:

If r is a reference variable, the name r represents not its own location or value but, <u>indirectly</u>, the location or value at the <u>address contained in r</u>.

Thus, the statement

```
r = r + 1;
```

means: "r contains some address. Take the value <u>at that address</u>; add 1; save the result in the location <u>at that address</u>." r's own value (which is that "some address") does not change.

If r is a reference variable, &r represents r's own value; that is, the address to which r refers.

In some older compilers &r could be used as either an lvalue or an rvalue, but now its use is restricted to rvalue, so &r = . . . is not allowed.

11.3. Passing Arguments to Functions by Reference

Reference variables in programs are used primarily for passing arguments to functions *by reference*.

In one of the previous sections we described the Sort (...) function, which included code to swap the values of two elements in an array. It may be reasonable to implement this code as a separate function, Swap (...) . Let us try to implement and test the Swap (...) function:

```
#include <iostream.h>

void Swap (double x, double y)

// Trying to swap x and y... but it does NOT work!

{
    double temp;

    temp = x;
    x = y;
    y = temp;
}

int main()

{
    double x = 1.111, y = 2.222;

    cout << "x = " << x << " y = " << y << endl;
    Swap(x,y);
    cout << "x = " << x << " y = " << y << endl;
    return 0;
}
```

When we compile and run the program, the output is:

```
x = 1.111 y = 2.222
x = 1.111 y = 2.222
```

Nothing happened — the numbers have not been swapped. To explain why, we need to understand the way C++ code calls functions. When a function is called, the arguments are made available to the function by copying them to a place where the function can reach them. This place may be a *frame* on the *system stack* — an area in memory pointed to by a special *Stack Pointer* (SP) CPU register. The function code has access to the SP and therefore knows where to find the arguments. Some compilers have the option of placing the arguments into general purpose CPU registers. In any event, the values of arguments are copied into a new location.

Inside a function, its arguments act as new variables whose values have been initialized to values passed to the function by the calling code. The arguments play the same role as local (temporary) variables, and they disappear after the function is exited.

In the "Swap" example, x and y in main() and x and y in the Swap(...) function represent different memory locations, despite the fact that we chose to give them the same names. So only the temporary copies of x and y swap places. The originals remain intact.

Our mistake was that we passed the <u>values</u> of x and y to Swap(...). This is called **passing arguments by value**. To correct the situation, we need to give Swap(...) access to the <u>addresses</u> of x and y — a method known as **passing arguments by reference**. Naturally, C++ provides two ways of doing this, through either pointers or references.

The older method, using pointers, is inherited from C. In this method we declare the arguments of the Swap(...) function as having the double* (pointer to a double) type and explicitly pass the addresses of x and y to the function when we call it:

```
#include <iostream.h>

void Swap (double *px, double *py)

// Swaps *px and *py
//
//   *** Older style, uses pointers ***
//

{
    double temp;

    temp = *px;
    *px = *py;
    *py = temp;
}

int main()

{
    double x = 1.111, y = 2.222;

    Swap(&x, &y);              // pass addresses of x and y to Swap(...)
    ...
}
```

The newer, C++ method uses references. In this method, the arguments to Swap(...) are declared to be of the double& (reference to a double) type. When we call Swap(x,y), the compiler automatically passes the addresses of x and y to the function instead of their values, because <u>that is what the function expects</u>:

```
#include <iostream.h>

void Swap (double &x, double &y)

// Swaps x and y, passed by reference.
// x and y become aliases of some variables in the calling
//    function.

{
    double temp;

    temp = x;
    x = y;
    y = temp;
}

int main()

{
    double x = 1.111, y = 2.222;

    Swap(x,y);              // Passes references to x and y to Swap(...)
                            //    (because Swap expects arguments of the
                            //    reference type).
    ...
}
```

Note that <u>the only thing</u> we have changed from our original misguided attempt is one line in the `Swap (...)` definition, where we have added two `&`'s. This simplicity is what makes references convenient.

In the future, we will <u>always use references</u> rather than pointers when we need to pass the address of a variable to a function.

Arguments passed as references must be lvalues. If we write something like:

```
    ...
    Swap(x, y+1)
    ...
```

the compiler will generate an error message because `y+1` is not an lvalue.

Passing arguments by reference may be done for two reasons. We need to pass an argument by reference if we want to modify or calculate its value inside the function. We may also want to pass an argument by reference if the argument takes a lot of space.

Copying a value of a built-in data type to the stack is not a problem, but when we deal with user-defined data types such as vectors, matrices, or **structures** (Chapter 13), we realize that copying a large object is inefficient. It is better to pass such an argument by reference (that is, to copy to the stack only its address) even if we do not want to modify it.

If we pass an argument to a function by reference but want to protect that argument from being changed inside the function, we can use the const keyword: this in effect casts the function argument as a constant and therefore forbids the function code to change it:

```
void MyFunction(const SOMETYPE &x)    // x is passed by reference
                                      //   only for efficiency;
                                      //   Its value remains unchanged.

{
    ...
}
```

11.4. *Lab:* Quadratic Formula

Define and test a function that finds the solutions of a quadratic equation

$$ax^2 + bx + c = 0$$

Make it a Boolean function that returns true if real solutions exist and false otherwise. Pass the coefficients a, b, and c by value. Place the calculated solutions into two variables passed to the function by reference.

Recall that the formulas for the solutions of a quadratic equation are:

$$x_1 = \frac{-b + \sqrt{b^2 - 4ac}}{2a} \qquad x_2 = \frac{-b - \sqrt{b^2 - 4ac}}{2a}$$

You will need to use the sqrt(double z) standard library function for calculating the square root. It is declared in math.h.

11.5. The Null Pointer

A pointer of any type can be set to 0. This is often used in programs to indicate that the pointer does not currently point to anything meaningful.

Some programmers use the symbolic constant NULL, defined as 0, specifically for inactive pointers. NULL is a relic from C, and it can be found in one or several header files. It is defined as:

```
#define NULL 0
```

or, for "large memory models," as:

```
#define NULL 0L      // Long integer equal to 0
```

It may be also defined as:

```
const void *NULL = 0; // Pointer of the type "void *" set to 0.
```

In many C++ compilers, the NULL definition is included in iostream.h.

C++ programmers often write simply 0 in their programs but refer to it as "null" when they talk about it.

A pointer of any type can be also compared to "null." For example:

```
    if (p != 0)   // if p is not null ...
        ...
```

or, simply:

```
    if (p)      // non-zero value means true, null means false.
        ...
```

11.6. Dynamic Memory Allocation: `new` and `delete`

When we declare a variable, a symbolic constant, or an array, the compiler automatically allocates memory for it. If a constant, a variable, or an array is declared outside of any function (or, if the declaration is preceded with the keyword `static`), the memory is allocated in the special, permanent "static" memory segment of the program. If a variable or an array is *local* (declared inside a function), then the memory is allocated temporarily on the system stack and released when the function is exited.

C++ provides a mechanism for allocating a contiguous block of memory explicitly at any time in the program. Each program has a special pool of free memory, called the *free store*. A program may request some space from the free store to hold a value or an array of the specified (built-in or user-defined) data type. This is accomplished by using the `new` operator. The `new` operator returns a pointer of the appropriate data type, which points to the reserved space.

In the following code, `SOMETYPE` stands for some built-in or user-defined type:

```
int n;
SOMETYPE *s, *t;
...
n = 100;
...
s = new SOMETYPE;          // Allocates one location of SOMETYPE.
...
t = new SOMETYPE[n];       // Allocates an array of n
                           //   locations of SOMETYPE.
```

The first `new` reserves one location of the type `SOMETYPE` and returns a pointer to it, which is then assigned to s. The second `new` reserves an array of n=100 elements of the type `SOMETYPE` and returns a pointer to its first element, which is assigned to t. The size of the requested array is essentially an argument given to the `new` operator. It is specified inside the <u>square</u> brackets and can be any expression that evaluates to a positive integer.

The `new` operator may fail if the program runs out of memory. In that case, it returns a null pointer. It is a good idea to check the pointer returned by `new` and take some corrective action or display an error message if it returns a null. For example:

```
void MyFunction()
{
    char *p;

    ...
    p = new char[10000];
    if (!p) {
        cout << "Memory allocation error in MyFunction.\n";
        return;
    }
    ...
}
```

⌘   ⌘   ⌘

Memory allocated with new remains at the program's disposal until it is explicitly returned to the free store by the delete operator. delete has the following syntax:

```
delete s;              // Deallocate one memory location pointed
                       //    to by s.
...
delete [] t;           // Deallocate an array pointed to by t.
```

new and delete work as a pair. new reserves a contiguous block of memory in the free store and returns a pointer to it. The memory remains at the program's disposal until it is freed by the delete operator. delete returns the memory pointed to by a pointer to the free store. This mechanism is called *dynamic memory allocation*.

The words "new" and "delete" do not imply, of course, that a new block in the computer memory is created and then deleted. These words should be construed to mean that a new entity (a pointer of a particular data type and a memory location to which it points) is created and later deleted from the realm of your program.

new and delete do not have to be called within the same function, but the program must somehow maintain the pointer returned by new, and it must use delete to free the memory before exiting.

The dynamic memory allocation mechanism maintains its own internal list of sizes and addresses of all allocated memory blocks. That is how delete knows how many bytes it has to return to the free store. delete can only delete a pointer allocated with new, but "deleting" a null pointer is permitted and has no effect.

⌘   ⌘   ⌘

Dynamic memory allocation plays an important role in the implementation of the `apvector` and `apmatrix` classes. When we declare a vector of a certain size, the code dynamically allocates a memory buffer of that size and places the pointer to that buffer into the vector descriptor. When the `apvector` variable goes out of scope, the code calls the `delete` operator to release its memory buffer.

Since in this book we use `apvector` and `apmatrix` classes instead of built-in arrays, it is never necessary to allocate an array. The `apvector` class does it for us. Therefore, we only need to use

```
    s = new SOMETYPE;          // Allocates one location of SOMETYPE.
```
and
```
    delete s;
```

There is no need for

```
    t = new SOMETYPE[n];       // Allocates an array of n
```
and
```
    delete [] t;
```

⌘   ⌘   ⌘

It would make little sense to dynamically allocate a simple `int` or `double` variable because it can be declared (allocated automatically on the stack), and it may take less space and may be easier to handle than a pointer to a dynamically allocated location. Dynamic memory allocation is useful primarily for the following purposes:

1. Allocating a temporary (local) array that is too large for the system stack.

2. Allocating an array whose size is not known in advance but rather calculated or entered at some point in the program.

3. Implementing classes, such as `apvector` and `apmatrix`.

4. Allocating structures, especially nodes of linked data structures: lists, trees, etc.

It is this last use that is most important to us here. Unfortunately, we are not quite ready to explain it fully until we know what structures, nodes, and linked lists are. At this point, we have to be content with the following informal explanation.

In C++, you can define a new data type that combines several data elements, often of different data types. The new type may be defined using the keyword `struct`:

```
struct SOMETYPE {  // Defines a new data type SOMETYPE as a structure
   ...
};
```

One or more elements in the structure may be pointers to other structures. In particular, one element of a structure may be a pointer to another structure of the same type. Let us consider, for example:

```
struct NODE {
   int info;
   NODE *next;   // "next" is a pointer to NODE
};
```

You can dynamically allocate a series of NODE structures using the new operator. You can set the value next in the first node equal to the pointer to the second node. In general, you can set the next pointer in each "node" to the following "node" (except the last node, in which next is set to null). In this way you create a *linked list* of nodes in which each node contains, as one of its data elements, the pointer to the "next" node. Data structures of this kind are very flexible. You can insert, remove, and rearrange the elements of a linked list by manipulating a pointer or two rather than moving many bytes in memory.   Structures are discussed in detail in Chapter 13, and linked lists in Part 2.

11.7. Returning Pointers or References from Functions

In C++, functions can return pointers or references as well as other data types. A function that returns a pointer is declared as:

```
SOMETYPE *MyFunction(...)
```

and a function that returns a reference is declared as:

```
SOMETYPE &MyFunction(...)
```

where SOMETYPE stands for a built-in or user-defined data type.

In what situations do we need such functions? To what may the returned pointer or reference point or refer? There are three possibilities:

1. The returned pointer may point to a variable (or an array) dynamically allocated within the function.

2. The pointer may be derived from the function arguments and point to an array or some element of the array passed to the function as an argument.

3. The pointer may point to some global constant, variable, array, or array element declared outside the function.

The returned pointer can be also null, indicating that it does not point to anything. Some of the above possibilities also apply to references.

A pointer or reference returned from a function should <u>never</u> be set to the address of a local variable or local array in that function, because when the function is exited, all local variables are destroyed. The pointer or reference will be left dangling — pointing to some vacant area on the system stack. The value at that location is undetermined, and writing anything to that location may crash the system. So such a pointer would be both useless and dangerous outside the function.

In this book we will be concerned primarily with the following two situations.

A function returns the pointer to a variable that was dynamically allocated inside the function:

```
SOMETYPE *MyFunction(...)
{
    SOMETYPE *p;
    ...
    p = new SOMETYPE;
    ...
    return p;
}
```

A function returns a reference originally passed to the function as an argument:

```
SOMETYPE &MyFunction(SOMETYPE &arg, ...)
{
    ...
    return arg;
}
```

In particular, C++ stream I/O functions and operators often return a <u>reference</u> to the same stream. For example, the `put` member function that writes a character to a file returns the data type `ostream&` (reference to an output stream) and returns the reference to the stream for which it is called: `outFile.put(ch)` returns `outFile`. The same is true of other stream member functions and the insertion and extraction operators. That is why we can chain together several insertion operators:

```
cout << a << b << ...
```

Or, rather strange (and not advised):

```
cout.put('H').put('i').put('!') << endl; // Prints "Hi!\n"
...
(cin >> ch).ignore(80, '\n');  // read one char, ignore the rest
```

11.8.   Summary

For any data type `SOMETYPE`, there are two other data types that are automatically defined in C++: `SOMETYPE*` (a pointer to `SOMETYPE`) and `SOMETYPE&` (a reference to `SOMETYPE`). Both can hold the address of a variable, a symbolic constant, or an array element of the data type `SOMETYPE`.

Pointers and references must be initialized to some address before they can be used. A pointer can be also set to "null" (zero) to indicate that it does not point to anything meaningful.

References are used primarily for passing arguments to functions "by reference," i.e., passing the argument's address instead of its value to a function. If a function's argument is declared to be of reference type, the compiler automatically knows to pass its <u>address</u>, as opposed to its <u>value</u>, to the function. For example:

```
// The Swap(...) function takes arguments
//   of double& (reference to double) type.

void Swap (double &x, double &y);
```

The function is called as usual:

```
Swap(a, b);
```

but x and y inside the function become aliases for a and b in the calling code.

A C++ program can at any time request a contiguous block of memory sufficient to hold a value or an array of values of a specified data type, `SOMETYPE`. The memory is allocated from a pool of free memory, called the free store, using the `new` operator. For example:

```
SOMETYPE *p;
p = new SOMETYPE;  // Allocate a variable of the specified type.
```

The allocated memory remains at the program's disposal until it is explicitly freed and returned to the free store using the `delete` operator:

```
delete p;
```

The mechanism provided by the `new` and `delete` operators is called dynamic memory allocation. It is useful for allocating temporary arrays, allocating arrays whose size is not known in advance, and creating new "nodes" in linked data structures such as linked lists, trees, and so on. Pointers are indispensable for creating and updating such structures.

12

Strings

12.1. Discussion

Processing text constitutes a large part of computer applications. Text is handled in reading and parsing text files (such as the source code of computer programs), word processing, data entry, communications, and so on. Segments of text are stored in character arrays, which C++ programmers refer to as *character strings*. An array may be larger than the actual text string it is holding at the moment, so the program needs to know where the string ends.

C++ has no built-in mechanism for maintaining the length of a string. Instead, C and C++ programmers place a special marker, a *null character*, at the end of each string. The null <u>character</u> (not to be confused with the null <u>pointer</u>) is simply a character constant with the value 0.

It is better to use the "escape" character constant '\0' rather than simply 0 to denote the null character in your code. This emphasizes that the null character has the data type char and that your code is dealing with characters rather than integers.

C++ syntax allows programmers to use literal character strings (text in double quotes):

```
char hello[14] = "Hello, World!";
```

A null character is automatically appended at the end of a literal string. (Note that the string is declared as an array of fourteen characters to leave space for the null character after the phrase's thirteen characters.) Other than that, a null character is neither required nor automatically assumed to be present anywhere in C++ syntax — it is simply a convention used by C/C++ software developers, standard library functions that deal with strings, and input/output classes. Character arrays that hold text and follow the null termination convention are referred to as *null-terminated strings*.

The null character can be tested for in Boolean expressions. As usual, any non-zero value represents "true" and the null character (zero) means "false." If s is a pointer to a string, then *s (the character currently pointed to by s) can be checked for zero value as the terminating condition in a loop as s advances along the string. This was widely used in C idioms. Sometimes, though, compact and idiomatic formulation can cross the line into obscurity:

```
// Copy string s1 to s2:
while (*s2++ = *s1++);          // Get it?
```

C compilers have many functions in the standard library for handling null-terminated strings. These functions are available in all C++ compilers as well. But most C++ programmers prefer to use a special string class, because it is easier to use and helps to avoid bugs. A string class is provided in class libraries that come with compilers and in various libraries of classes created by organizations or individual programmers. The implementation of a string class may still be based on null-terminated strings, but the details are hidden from the programmer who is using the class: she only needs to know the ***class interface*** — that is, the convention for using the class operators and functions.

In this book we will use the `apstring` class provided by the AP C++ Development Committee. The Committee recommends that students always use the `apstring` class for representing and handling strings.

In this chapter we will study the following topics related to strings:

- String constants
- Standard library functions for null-terminated strings
- Stream I/O functions and operators for strings
- How to use the `apstring` class (Section 12.5 and Labs 12.6 and 12.7).

12.2. Literal Strings

A *literal string* is a string of characters in double quotes. The string may include "escape" characters such as `'\t'` (tab), `'\"'` (double quote), `'\n'` (newline), etc. A null character, `'\0'`, is automatically appended at the end of a literal string.

The number of bytes required to store a literal string is one more than the length of the string — one byte is added for the null character. For instance, the string `"Wow"` takes 4 bytes. `""` (two double quotes with nothing in between) represents an empty string, which consists of only the null character and takes one byte.

Literal strings are used in two different ways: (1) for initializing character arrays and (2) as initial values of pointers or as `char*` values (rvalues) in expressions.

It is important to distinguish these two situations because the strings are stored in different places in computer memory depending on the situation. When a string is used to initialize a character array, it is placed into that array. When a string is used to initialize a pointer, it is stored in the special segment of the program's memory which holds program constants.

Let us consider array initialization first:

```
char msg[20] = "Hello";
```

When a character array is initialized to a literal character string, the string and its terminating null character are simply placed into the array.

The compiler checks that the size of the array is large enough to hold the string and its terminating null (although some compilers simply drop the null if there is no room for it). If the string is too long, the compiler reports an error. The above declaration is simply shorthand for:

```
char msg[20] = {'H', 'e', 'l', 'l', 'o', '\0'};
// msg[0] = 'H', ..., msg[5] = '\0',
// msg[6] ... msg[19] remain not initialized.
```

A programmer can leave it to the compiler to calculate the length of the array by omitting its size in the declaration. For example,

```
char msg[] = "Hello";
```

is the same as:

```
char msg[6] = "Hello";
```

⌘ ⌘ ⌘

Now let us see how literal strings are used as pointers. In the following declaration, the char* variable name is initialized to "Sunshine":

```
char *name = "Sunshine";
```

The string "Sunshine" (with its terminating null) is stored in the program's memory together with other constants, and the pointer name is set to the address of the string's first character.

When a literal string is used in an expression or as a function argument, it is treated as a pointer (of the `char*` data type) pointing to the first character of the string.

In the following code, for example, the `char*` variable `errMsg` is set to point to different literal strings depending on the circumstances:

```
char *errMsg = 0;   // Pointer errMsg is initialized to
                    //   the null pointer.
...
if (...)
    errMsg = "File does not exist.";
...
if (...)
    errMsg = "Memory allocation error.";
...
if (errMsg)         // if errMsg is not a null pointer...
    cout << errMsg << endl;
```

Note that in the above code `errMsg` is a <u>pointer</u>, not an <u>array</u>. When the program is running, the text strings are not copied anywhere; only the address in `errMsg` changes its value.

C++ programmers can also declare arrays of pointers and initialize them to addresses of literal strings. For example:

```
char *nameOfDay[7] = {   // Array of 7 pointers to char.
    "Sunday",
    "Monday",
    "Tuesday",
    "Wednesday",
    "Thursday",
    "Friday",
    "Saturday"
};
```

The above declaration allocates an array of seven pointers to `char`. The null-terminated strings, "Sunday" etc., are placed somewhere in the segment of the program's memory that holds constants, and the pointers in the array are set to the respective addresses of those strings.

⌘ ⌘ ⌘

A confusion between the two situations — when an array is initialized with a literal string, and when a pointer is set to point to a literal string — leads to bugs that are hard to find. This is another good reason for using a string class.

> A typical string class allows a programmer to initialize a string class
> object (variable) with a literal string and to assign a value to a string
> class variable from a literal string.

For example:

```
#include "apstring.h"      // Include the definition of the apstring
                           //   class into your program.
...
    apstring str1 = "Hello";
                           // Declare a variable str1 of the type
                           //   apstring and assign it the value "Hello"

    apstring str2;
    str2 = "Sunshine";     // Assign the value "Sunshine" to str2.
    ...
```

In both the declaration and assignment above, the characters from the literal string
are actually copied into the internal character buffer associated with each
apstring object.

12.3. Standard Library Functions for Strings

The standard C++ library provides many functions for handling null-terminated
strings and converting text to numbers.   The following list presents several
commonly used string functions.   If you want to learn about all the functions
available, refer to the compiler documentation or on-line help.

The string functions are declared in the string.h header file.

```
unsigned strlen(const char *s);
    // Returns the length of the string s (the character count
    //   excluding the null character).

char *strcpy(char *dest, const char *src);
    // Copies the string src into dest.
    // Returns a pointer equal to dest.

char *strcat(char *dest, const char *src);
    // Appends the string src to the string at dest.
    // Returns a pointer equal to dest.
```

```
char *strchr(const char *s, int c);
   // Returns a pointer to the first occurrence of
   //   the char c in the string s, or a null pointer if not found.
   //   c is declared as int, but normally a char is used.
   //   For example:
   //       dot = strchr(fileName, '.');
   // (The terminating null is considered a part of the string, so
   //       strchr(s, '\0') returns a pointer to the
   //       terminating null.  This can be useful.)

int strcmp(const char *s1, const char *s2);
   // Returns 0 if s1 and s2 are identical strings.
   //   Otherwise returns c1 - c2 where c1 and c2 are the
   //   first pair of different characters in the corresponding
   //   positions in s1 and s2.  The return value is negative
   //   if s1 is alphabetically earlier than s2.

char *strstr(const char *s, const char *ss);
   // Returns a pointer to the first occurrence of the
   //   substring ss in s, or null if not found.

char *strlwr(char *s);
   // Converts all letters in the string s into the lower case.
   //   Other characters remain unchanged.
   // Returns s.

char *strupr(char *s);
   // Converts all letters in the string s into the upper case.
   //   Other characters remain unchanged.
   // Returns s.
```

The standard library also contains conversion functions for reading a number from a string. These functions are declared in `stdlib.h`. (In some compilers, `atof(...)` may be declared in `math.h`.)

```
int atoi(const char *s);
   // Converts an ASCII string (optional sign, then digits)
   //   into an integer.
   // Example:  atoi("-1001") returns -1001.

long atol(const char *s);
   // Converts an ASCII string (optional sign, then digits)
   //   into a long integer.

double atof(const char *s);
   // Converts an ASCII string (optional sign, digits,
   //   optional decimal point) into a double.
```

The following code extracts hours, minutes, and seconds from a "time" string of the form "`hh:mm:ss`":

```
...
char time[] = "01:12:55";
...
if (strlen(time) != 8) {
    cout << "Invalid time string.\n";
    return;
}
char *s = time;
hour = atoi(s);          // atoi scans the string as long as it
                         //   finds digits. It will stop at ':'.
s = strchr(s,':') + 1;   // Set s to point to the first char
                         //   after ':'.
mins = atoi(s);
s = strchr(s,':') + 1;   // Set s to point to the first char
                         //   after the next ':'.
secs = atoi(s);
...
```

12.4. Input and Output for Strings

Normally, when you output a pointer by passing it to the stream insertion operator `<<`, the output is some memory address in hexadecimal notation. A pointer to a character (`char*` type) is an exception. The output stream implementation assumes that a `char*` pointer points to a null-terminated string and outputs that string rather than the pointer. That is why, in the following example, all three output statements print "Hello, World!":

```
char a[20] = "Hello, World!";
char *p = "Hello, World!";

cout << "Hello, World!" << endl;
cout << a << endl;
cout << p << endl;
```

Note that the insertion operator `<<` does not automatically append a newline character at the end of a null-terminated string. You have to supply the newline character separately by inserting `endl` or `'\n'` after the string:

```
// Three equivalent ways to output a line of text:
cout << "A rose by any other name would smell as sweet,\n";
cout << "A rose by any other name would smell as sweet," << endl;
cout << "A rose by any other name would smell as sweet," << '\n';
```

⌘   ⌘   ⌘

The extraction operator `>>` assumes that a `char*` argument points to a character array and reads a string of characters into that array. There are, however, two problems. First, the array must be large enough to hold the string. If a mischievous user enters a very long string, it will overrun the declared array and overwrite some memory in your program. Second, the extraction operator reads only one "word". It skips all white space (spaces, tabs, newline characters) preceding the string, reads a contiguous string without any white space characters in it, and stops reading when it encounters the first white space character or the end of file. When you execute the following code, for example,

```
int main()

{
    char firstName[30], lastName[30];

    cout << "Enter your name: ";
    cin >> firstName >> lastName;
    ...
```

and you type:

```
<TAB>Albert Einstein<SPACE><ENTER>
```

the program will correctly skip the tab, place "Albert" into `firstName` (with a terminating null) and "Einstein" into `lastName` (also with a null). The remaining space, newline, and any other input will remain in the input stream. But what if you entered "John J. Jingleheimer Schmidt, Jr."? Your program would be better off reading the whole string before parsing (analyzing) it to extract the necessary information.

The input stream class provides the `getline(...)` member function for reading a whole string of text, including all white space characters. This function takes three arguments: a pointer to a character array, a maximum number of characters to read, and the "delimiter" character:

```
cin.getline(char str[], int maxcount, char delim);
```

The function extracts characters from the input stream (e.g., `cin` for the keyboard) and places them into the `str` array until one of three things happens: (1) it reads a character equal to `delim`; (2) it reads `maxcount-1` characters (leaving one vacant space for the terminating null character); (3) it reaches the end of file. If the function encounters the delimiter character, the function extracts it from the input stream but <u>does not store it</u> in the array. `getline(...)` <u>always adds a terminating null</u> to the string.

In the following code:

```
char line[81];

cin.getline(line, 81, '\n');
```

getline(...) reads a line of text of up to 80 characters, stops at the newline character (placed into the input stream when you hit the <ENTER> key), consumes the newline character, and appends a null to the array.

The delim argument is optional: if not specified, it defaults to '\n'. So:

```
cin.getline(line, 81);
```

is the same as:

```
cin.getline(line, 81, '\n');
```

If your line (up to and including '\n') is equal to or longer than maxcount, getline(...) leaves the tail of the line in the input stream. Like the other stream I/O functions, getline(...) works not just for cin but for any file input stream. When the input stream is at the end of file, getline(...) puts the stream into an error state, which can be tested as a condition. For example:

```
if (!file.getline(...))    // Read the line.  If failed ...
    ...
while (file.getline(...)) // Call getline while it reads
                          //   successfully.
    ...
```

The following program reads and prints all lines in a text file, splitting the lines that are longer than LINELENGTH characters:

GETLINE.CPP

```
//  Prints a file, splitting the lines that are longer than
//     LINELENGTH.

#include <iostream.h>
#include <fstream.h>

const int LINELENGTH = 32;   // 32 characters per line

int main()

{
```

Continued

```
    char fileName[40];
    char line[LINELENGTH+1];     // +1 for the terminating null

    cout << "File name: ";
    cin >> fileName;             // Read one word into fileName.

    ifstream f1(fileName);       // Open file for reading
    if (!f1) {
        cout << "Cannot open " << fileName << ".\n";
        return 1;
    }

    // Read lines while available (until the end of file).
    while (f1.getline(line, LINELENGTH+1)) {
        cout << line << endl;
    }

    cout << "*** END OF FILE ***\n";
    return 0;
}
```

When compiled and run on the following file:

LIMERICK.TXT

```
There once lived a poet named Sage
Whose lines never fit on a page
```

the program will print:

```
File name: limerick.txt
There once lived a poet named Sa
ge
Whose lines never fit on a page
*** END OF FILE ***
```

⌘   ⌘   ⌘

Unfortunately, the `getline(...)` function does not tell the program whether it ever got to the `'\n'` character or not. So there is no easy way to tell whether or not the line was too long. There is another function, `get(...)`, which works exactly the same way as `getline(...)` but leaves the delimiter in the input stream.

The only difference between `get(...)` and `getline(...)` is that `get(...)` always leaves the delimiter in the input stream.

You can get rid of the `'\n'` left by `get (...)` together with the unwanted tail of the line by using the `ignore (...)` function:

```
cin.ignore(int maxcount, char delim);
```

`cin.ignore (...)` skips as many as `maxcount` characters up to and including the delimiter character. You can tell it to skip a large number of characters up to the delimiter `'\n'`:

```
cin.get(line, 81);        // Read up to 80 characters,
cin.ignore(1000, '\n');   // Skip "all" (as many as 1000) chars
                          //   to the end of the line, including '\n'.
```

The following is a modified version of the program for printing a file. In this version, the long lines are truncated instead of being split:

```
//  Prints a file, truncating the lines to the first
//     LINELENGTH characters.

#include <iostream.h>
#include <fstream.h>

const int LINELENGTH = 32;

int main()

{
    ...
    // Uses get(...) instead of getline(...) to always leave '\n'
    //    in the input stream.

    while (f1.get(line, LINELENGTH+1)) {
        cout << line << endl;
        f1.ignore(1000, '\n');  // Skips to and consumes '\n'.
    }
    ...
}
```

This version will print:

```
File name: limerick.txt
There once lived a poet named Sa
Whose lines never fit on a page
*** END OF FILE ***
```

12.5. The `apstring` Class

This section describes the `apstring` class provided by the AP C++ Development Committee. This class defines a new user-defined data type, `apstring`, and allows us to handle character strings more or less the same way as we handle built-in data types such as `int` or `double`.

The definition of the class and declarations of its functions and operators must be included into the program; as usual, they are placed in a header file, `apstring.h`. The actual code for the class functions and operators is placed in the source file, `apstring.cpp`.

`apstring.cpp` can be compiled separately; it can be integrated with the rest of your program using the project management component of your compiler. Your compiler documentation or on-line "help" will tell you exactly how to do it.

The `apstring` class provides three ways to declare a string:

```
#include "apstring.h"
...

apstring str1;              // Declare an empty string;
apstring str2 = "Hello";    // Initialize to a literal string
apstring str3 = str2;       // Initialize to a previously defined string
```

C++ allows programmers to redefine the meaning of standard operators (a feature called ***operator overloading***). The `apstring` class redefines the assignment operator as making a copy of a string and the + and += operators as concatenation of two strings or appending a character to a string. This lets us write things like:

```
apstring h = "Hello", s;

h += ", ";
s = h + "Sunshine" + '!';
// Now the value of s is "Hello, Sunshine!"
```

The relational operators are redefined to compare strings. For example:

```
apstring name1, name2;
...
if (name1 == name2)
    ...

if (name1 != name2)
    ...
```

The `<`, `<=`, `>`, and `>=` operators compare strings using the ASCII order of characters. In particular, all uppercase letters are "smaller" than all lowercase letters.

⌘   ⌘   ⌘

The `apstring` class is implemented in such a way that you can still access individual characters in a string using subscripts, the same way you do with built-in character arrays. As with the `apvector` and `apmatrix` classes, the `apstring` class verifies at run time that the subscripts used in the program are within the legal range. The subscripted string element can be used both on the left and on the right side of the assignment operator. For example:

```
apstring str = "bat";
char ch;


...
if (str[0] == 'b') {
    ch = str[0];
    str[0] = str[2];
    str[2] = ch;
}
```

The `length` member function returns the current length of the string (excluding the null terminator):

```
apstring str = "bat";
int len = str.length();
cout << len;            // Output: 3
```

The following function returns `true` if all the characters in a string are digits. It uses the `isdigit` function defined in the standard header file `ctype.h`:

```
#include <ctype.h>  // Defines isdigit(...)
#include "apstring.h"

bool AllDigits(const apstring &str)

{
    int i, len = str.length();

    for (i = 0;   i < len;   i++)
        if (!isdigit(str[i]))
            return false;

    return true;
}
```

Note that the `apstring` argument is passed to the function <u>by reference</u>. As with `apvector` and `apmatrix` variables, this eliminates unnecessary copying of the string. The keyword `const` indicates that the function does not change the string.

⌘   ⌘   ⌘

The `apstring` class also provides the `find(...)` function that helps you find a given character or a substring in the string, and the `substr(...)` function that builds a new string equal to a substring in the given string.

The first form of `find(...)` is

```
int find(char ch);
```

It returns the position of the first occurrence of the character `ch` in the string. If the `ch` character is not found, the function returns a special constant value, `npos` (currently set to -1 in `apstring.cpp`). For example:

```
apstring fileName;
int i = fileName.find('.');  // if fileName is "TEST.DAT"
                             //    i is set to 4.
if (i == npos)      // if '.' is not found, use the default extension
    fileName += ".TXT";
```

The second form of `find(...)` takes an `apstring` as an argument and returns the position of its first occurrence as a substring. For example:

```
apstring msg = "Hello, Sunshine!";
apstring target = "Sun";

int i = msg.find(target); // i is set to 7.
```

This form of `find(...)` returns the position of the first character in the matching substring or `npos` when the substring is not found.

The `apstring` class "knows" how to convert a literal string in double quotes into an `apstring` object. This makes it possible to pass a literal string to a function that expects an `apstring` argument, for instance to the `find(...)` function (as well as to your own functions). So you can write:

```
int i = msg.find("Sun");
```

Another member function,

```
apstring substr(int pos, int len);
```

builds and returns the substring that starts at position `pos` and has the length `len`.
For example:

```
apstring fileName = "TEST.DAT", ext;
ext = fileName.substr(5, 3); // ext gets the value "DAT".
```

⌘   ⌘   ⌘

The `c_str()` member function returns the pointer to the actual null-terminated
string associated with the `apstring` object. This function is needed to convert an
`apstring` object into a `const char*` for use with classes and functions that do
not understand apstrings. For example:

```
apstring fileName;
...
ifstream file(fileName.c_str());
    // The ifstream class does not understand
    //   the argument of the apstring type, so you can't write simply
    //   ifstream file(fileName);
    // The ifstream class expects a char* argument, and c_str()
    //   performs the conversion.
```

⌘   ⌘   ⌘

In the `apstring` class, the `<<` operator displays the string, and the `>>` operator
reads one word. For example:

```
#include <iostream.h>
#include "apstring.h"
...
    apstring prompt = "Please enter the file name: ", fileName;
    cout << prompt;
    cin >> fileName;
    ...
```

These operators are implemented with the help of similar operators for null-
terminated strings.

The `apstring` class also provides a version of the `getline` function, which
reads a whole line of text from `cin` or from a file. This is not a member function,
but a "free-standing" function that takes two arguments, the name of the input
stream and an `apstring` variable. The function returns a reference to the same
stream:

```
istream &getline(istream &inputFile, apstring &str);
```

For example, to read one line of text from `cin` you can use:

```
apstring line;
getline(cin, line);
```

Here is a version of the Limerick program from the previous section, rewritten with the `apstring` class:

```
// This program uses the apstring class to print a file

#include <iostream.h>
#include <fstream.h>
#include "apstring.h"

int main()

{
    apstring fileName, line;

    cout << "File name: ";
    cin >> fileName;                    // Read one word into fileName.

    ifstream f1(fileName.c_str());  // Open file for reading.
       // c_str() is the apstring class's member function that returns
       //    the pointer to the actual null-terminated string
       //    associated with the apstring object.

    if (!f1) {
        cout << "Cannot open " << fileName << ".\n";
        return 1;
    }

    // Read lines while available (until the end of file).
    while (getline(f1, line))
        cout << line << endl;

    cout << "*** END OF FILE ***\n";
    return 0;
}
```

This version handles the lengths of text lines automatically. It will print:

```
File name: limerick.txt
There once lived a poet named Sage
Whose lines never fit on a page
*** END OF FILE ***
```

12.6. *Lab:* Palindromes

Write and test a Boolean function

```
bool Palindrome(const apstring &text);
```

This function will take a string `text` as an argument and return `true` if `text` is a palindrome (the same when read forward or backwards, as in "Madam, I'm Adam"). In testing for a palindrome, ignore all spaces, punctuation marks, apostrophes, and other non-alphanumeric characters, and consider lower- and uppercase letters the same. Don't let your function change the original string.

As a first step, you can implement and test `Palindrome(...)` for only one word made of only lowercase letters; then you can add code to skip non-alphanumeric characters and to compare characters case-blind.

The `ctype.h` header file declares useful functions and macros for determining the type of the character (`isalpha(c)`, `isdigit(c)`, and so on) and for converting characters to the upper or lower case. In particular, you might want to use `isalnum(char c)`, which returns `true` if `c` is a letter or a digit, and `toupper(char c)`, which returns the corresponding upper case for 'a' - 'z' and the unchanged character for all other characters.

Use the `getline(...)` function, described in the previous section, to get a test phrase from the user.

12.7. *Lab:* GREP

"GREP" is an old utility program from UNIX that scans a file or several files for a given word and prints out all lines in which that word occurs. (According to The New Hacker's Dictionary, the name "GREP" comes from the "qed/ed" editor commands g/re/p — globally search for the regular expression and print the lines.)

Write a simplified version of GREP that looks for a word in one file. A "word" is defined as a contiguous string of alphanumeric characters. For every line that contains the word, print out the line number and the line, like this:

```
Line    29: You are my sunshine
```

In a command-line-oriented operating system such as MS DOS or UNIX, programs often receive some initial data from the command line. The parameters passed to the program from the command line are called ***command line arguments***. A utility like GREP would normally be invoked with command line arguments. GREP takes two: the word and the file name. For example:

```
C> grep sunshine song.txt
```

C/C++ supports a form of the function `main(...)` that accepts command line arguments. This form of `main(...)` is:

```
int main(int argc, char *argv[])
```

`argc` and `argv` are <u>traditional names</u> for the arguments. `argc` indicates how many words there are on the command line (including the program name). `argv` is an array of pointers to the command line words: `argv[0]` points to the program name, `argv[1]` points to the first argument, etc. `argv[i]` should be treated as literal constant strings. If you need to change one of the command line words, you must copy it first into a temporary character array or into an `apstring` variable. Otherwise, `argv[i]` can be used simply as a pointer to a constant character string.

Integrated Development Environments usually provide an option for setting command line arguments. For example, in Turbo C++ 4.5, you can enter the command line arguments in the Options/Environment/Debugger dialog box. You program may check whether the arguments are supplied and display a help message if they are missing or prompt the user for the required input.

The search for a matching word can be accomplished by using the `apstring`'s member function `find(...)`. This function will find the target word even if it occurs as part of another word in the line. If you want to find only matches between complete words, write your own function.

The following code provides a few initial steps for setting up the GREP program and an example of how a program gets hold of its command line arguments:

GREP.CPP

```
// GREP.CPP
//
// This program reads a file and prints out all lines
//    where a given word occurs.
//
// Usage:
//    C> grep word fileName
//
// Author: Yu Nix
// Date: 01/12/70

#include <fstream.h>
#include <iomanip.h>
#include <ctype.h>
#include "apstring.h"

int main(int argc, char *argv[])

{
    apstring word, fileName;
    apstring line;
    int lineNum = 0;

    // Get the arguments from the command line:

    if (argc >= 3) {           // At least 3 words
                               //    on the command line.
        word = argv[1];        // argv[1] is the word to search for.
        fileName = argv[2];    // argv[2] points to the file name
    }
    else {
        cout << "Enter the word to search for: ";
        cin >> word;
        cout << "Enter the file name: ";
        cin >> fileName;
    }

    // Create input stream for the file:

    ifstream file(fileName.c_str());     // Open file for reading
    ...
}
```

For "extra credit":

Supply and use your own function

```
FindCaseBlind(const apstring &line, const apstring &word);
```

that matches only complete words and performs case-blind comparison of letters.

12.8. Formatted Output to a Character Array

The standard library does not offer direct functions for converting numbers into character strings, but there is a powerful general-purpose mechanism that allows programmers to write formatted "output" — text and numbers — into a string. You can associate a character array with an output stream. All the "output" to that stream, produced by the insertion operator <<, I/O manipulators, and all other stream I/O functions, will be directed into your character array (rather than to the screen or to a file). This feature works with null-terminated strings. Without going too deeply into the details of the syntax, let us see how it is done:

```
#include <iostream.h>
#include <strstream.h> // Defines stream I/O classes for charater arrays
#include <iomanip.h>   // Only if manipulators setw(...),
                       //   setprecision(...), etc. are used.

...
const int SIZE = 100; // Maximum length of the
                      //   output string, e.g. 100.
   ...
   char buffer[SIZE];           // Declares the character array.

   ostrstream os(buffer, SIZE);
                          // Declares a string-type output
                          //   stream, "os", and associates
                          //   it with "buffer".

   // All output to os now goes into buffer.
   // For example ...

   double pi = 3.14159;
   os << "PI =";
   os << setw(5) << setprecision(2) << pi << ends;

   //  ... places "PI = 3.14" into buffer (ends is a manipulator
   //     that appends the null character, instead of endl).

   ...
   // If the previous string in buffer is no longer necessary,
   //   and you want to reuse buffer:

   os.seekp(0);                // "Rewind" os
                               //   (Re-positions internal stream
                               //     pointer to the beginning
                               //     of buffer).
   os << ...                   // Now the output will go to buffer,
                               //   starting at the beginning again.
```

A similar method can be used for "input" from a string, but instead of ostrstream, we use istrstream:

```
...
istrstream is(buffer);    // Creates an input stream "is" and
                          //   associates it with "buffer", where
                          //   "buffer" is a null-terminated string.
is >> ...

is.seekg(0);              // Re-positions internal stream
                          //   pointer to the beginning of buffer.
```

For example, the task of extracting hours, minutes and seconds from a time string "hh:mm:ss" can be accomplished as follows:

```
#include <strstream.h>
    ...
int hour, mins, secs;
char time[9] = "02:13:54";

istrstream timestr(time);

timestr >> hour;
timestr.ignore(1, ':');              // Skip ':'
timestr >> mins;
timestr.ignore(1, ':');
timestr >> secs;
    ...
strcpy(time, "12:02:01");   // Copy new data into "time" array
timestr.seekg(ios::beg);    // "Rewind" the timestr stream
timestr >> hour;
    ...
```

Note the use of two different functions for repositioning streams: seekp(...) for output streams and seekg(...) for input streams. "p" probably stands for "put", "g" for "get".

12.9. Summary

C++ programmers can use literal constant strings, which consist of some text placed between double quotes. Literal strings may include escape characters ('\n', '\t', '\\', etc.) The C++ compiler automatically appends a null character to a literal character string. Literal strings can be used to initialize character arrays and apstring class variables.

The stream I/O insertion and extraction operators `<<` and `>>` treat `char*` pointers differently from other pointers. Their implementation assumes that the pointer points to a character array. The `<<` operator expects a null-terminated string and prints the string. The `>>` operator skips all white space, reads one word into the array, and appends a terminating null. To read a whole string, programmers use the `getline(...)` function:

```
myFile.getline(char str[], int maxcount, char delim = '\n');
```

The `apstring` class offers a more convenient and safer way for handling strings. It verifies that all subscripts fall within the legal range. The `apstring` class redefines the `=` operator for copying strings, the `+` and `+=` operators for concatenating strings, and the relational operators for comparing strings alphabetically. It also provides member functions that find a character or a substring in a string, and extract a substring from a string.

The `apstring` class uses the `<<` and `>>` operators for displaying the string and reading one word. The `getline(...)` function, provided with the `apstring` class (not to be confused with `cin.getline(...)` or `myFile.getline(...)`), can be used to read a whole line of text from `cin` or from a file. For example:

```
    ...
    apstring str;
    getline(myFile, str);
    ...
```

13

Structures

13.1. User-Defined Types

Up until now we have taken an oversimplified view of software design. We focused only on its procedural side — describing a programming task through a hierarchy of subtasks and implementing them as functions — and completely ignored the other, equally important second side: structuring the <u>data</u> involved in the task. We can design and implement many computer applications more efficiently if we take as a starting point not the procedures but the data: not what we have to do, but what kind of data we have to deal with, and how to represent it. For example, when we design a computerized inventory control system, we may begin by asking questions such as: What is an inventory item? Which data elements and data types are needed to describe it? How should we organize the inventory data? What other data elements (e.g., purchase orders, dates, backorder items, etc.) have to be represented, and how? And so on.

C++ offers a simple and convenient mechanism for imposing structure on the data involved in a programming task. A programmer may combine elements that have different data types (including built-in types, user-defined types, arrays, pointers, and so on) into one structure, defining this as a new ***user-defined*** data type. This is accomplished by using the keyword `struct` and listing the elements of the structure inside braces, separated by semicolons. The elements of the structure are called structure ***members***; the programmer gives each member a name that lets the program access it.

The following structure, for example, can represent an inventory item in an inventory control system:

```
struct INVENTORYITEM {
    int partNum;
    apstring description;
    int quantity;
    double price;
};
```

The power of structures lies in the fact that once defined, the structure name becomes a new data type in the program; it can be used pretty much the same way as the built-in data types.

In particular, we can declare variables, arrays, pointers, and references of that type. In the above example, for instance, INVENTORYITEM becomes a new data type. This lets us write declarations such as:

```
INVENTORYITEM newItem;
INVENTORYITEM *ptrItem;
INVENTORYITEM inventory[10000];
apvector<INVENTORYITEM> inventory(10000);
```

We can also use the new operator to dynamically allocate one element or an array of the new data type. For example:

```
INVENTORYITEM *ptrItem = new INVENTORYITEM;
INVENTORYITEM *inventory = new INVENTORYITEM[5000];
```

The general form of a structure definition is:

```
struct newtypename {
    sometype1 name1;
    sometype2 name2;
    ...
    sometypek namek;
};
```

Note that a structure definition (as opposed to a function definition) requires a semicolon after the closing brace.

We prefer to use all caps for the new data types' names — this is just a question of taste.

Once a data type is defined, the programmer can use it in definitions of new types.

Suppose, for instance, that we have defined the DATE structure:

```
struct DATE {
    int month;
    int day;
    int year;
};
```

Now if we want to add the date of the last shipment to INVENTORYITEM, we can simply add one member:

```
struct INVENTORYITEM {
    int partNum;
    apstring description;
    int quantity;
    double price;
    DATE lastShipped;           // Date of the last shipment.
};
```

The members of a structure occupy a contiguous block of memory and its total size is the sum of the sizes of all members. The programmer can determine the total size of a structure by using the `sizeof` operator.

User-defined types' definitions may be placed into a separate header file. This is convenient if a programmer re-uses the same data types in different projects. The file is included into the program using the `#include` directive, as usual, but the name of the header file is placed in <u>double quotes</u> rather than angular brackets to indicate that the compiler should look for it in the current project directory rather than the compiler include directory. The syntax looks as follows:

```
// MYFILE.H

struct DATE {
    ...
};
...

// MYPROG.CPP

#include "myfile.h"

...
```

13.2. Initialization and Assignments

A symbolic constant or a variable of a user-defined `struct` type may be initialized in its declaration by listing the values of its elements inside braces, separated by commas. For example:

```
struct DATE {
    int month;
    int day;
    int year;
};

    ...

const DATE firstDay = {01, 01, 1900};
const DATE lastDay = {12, 31, 2000};
DATE currentDay = {6, 1, 1998};
```

Unfortunately, this simple method does not apply when the structure has `apvector`, `apmatrix`, or `apstring` members. We will learn how to initialize such structures later, using constructors with initializer lists.

> **C++ aims to make user-defined types work the same way as built-in types. In particular, it allows us to initialize a variable to some previously initialized variable or constant and to use the assignment operator with the usual syntax.**

For example:

```
ID_INFO someGuy = johnQPublic;
ID_INFO otherGuy;
...
otherGuy = someGuy;
```

> **The = operator in the initialization and assignment means member-by-member assignment: each member of the structure on the right side is copied into the corresponding member of the structure on the left side.**

However, a programmer must keep in mind that an innocuous assignment statement may conceal a lot of byte-copying if the structures are large.

Also be careful if a structure contains pointers. Since the assignment is done member by member, the corresponding pointer on the left side of the assignment will become simply a replica of the pointer on the right side, and it will point to <u>the same</u> location. As we will see later, this can cause problems.

13.3. Accessing Structure Members

The members of a structure can be accessed in two ways: either through the variable itself, or through a pointer to the variable. To access a member through the variable, we append its name to the variable's name, separating the two by a dot (" . ").

For example:

```
struct DATE {
    int month;
    int day;
    int year;
};


    . . .
    DATE lastShipped, today;
    . . .
    today.year = 1998;
    . . .
    lastShipped.month = today.month;
    . . .
```

The following program prints a date:

```
#include <iostream.h>
#include <iomanip.h>

struct DATE {
    int month;
    int day;
    int year;
};

int main()

{
    DATE date;

    date.month = 1;
    date.day = 1;
    date.year = 2001;
```

Continued ☞

```
        cout.setf(ios::right, ios::adjustfield);
        cout << setfill('0')                    // Show leading zeroes
            << setw(2) << date.month << '-'
            << setw(2) << date.day   << '-'
            << setw(4) << date.year
            << setfill(' ')                      // Reset the leading char
            << endl;                             //   back to space.

        return 0;
    }
```

The output will be:

```
01-01-2001
```

⌘   ⌘   ⌘

**To access a member through a pointer, we append its name to the
pointer's name, separating the two by an arrow "->"
(two characters: - followed by >).**

For example:

```
    DATE *p;
    ...
    p = &today;            // or, say: p = new DATE;
    p->year = 2001;
    ...
    int day = p->day;
```

⌘   ⌘   ⌘

You can also access structure members through a reference using "dot" notation.
For example:

```
    DATE today, &r = today;
    ...
    r.year = 2001;    // Actually sets today.year to 2001.
```

⌘   ⌘   ⌘

There are more complex situations when a structure member is an array or another
structure, or when we have an array of structures. The syntax for handling these
situations is rather logical. As an example, let us consider the following
definitions and declarations:

```
struct VERTEX {
    int x;
    int y;
};

struct POLYGON {
    int nSides;
    apvector<VERTEX> vertices;
};
    ...
    POLYGON polygon;
    POLYGON *p = &polygon;
    apvector<POLYGON> drawing; // A "drawing" is made of many polygons.
```

The following examples show how we can refer to various elements of structures of arrays and arrays of structures:

```
int n = polygon.nSides;          // Number of sides in polygon.

VERTEX v = polygon.vertices[i];  // The i-th vertex in polygon.

VERTEX *pv = &polygon.vertices[i]; // Pointer to the i-th vertex
                                   //    in  polygon.

int x = polygon.vertices[i].x;   // x-coordinate of the i-th
                                 //    vertex in polygon.

int n = p->nSides;               // Number of sides in polygon,
                                 //    pointed to by p.

int x = p->vertices[i].x;        // x-coordinate of the i-th vertex
                                 //    in polygon, pointed to by p.

int n = drawing[n].nSides;       // Number of sides in the n-th
                                 //    polygon in drawing.

int x = drawing[n].vertices[i].x; // x-coordinate of the i-th
                                  //    vertex in the n-th polygon
                                  //    in drawing.
```

The order of operations is less obvious when a member of a structure is a pointer to another structure or a pointer to an array. For example:

```
struct COUNTRY {
    POLYGON *border;              // A pointer to a polygon "border"
    apvector<POLYGON> states;    // An array of polygons
                                  //    (states).
};
    ...
    COUNTRY usa;
    ...
    usa.border = new POLYGON;
    usa.states.resize(50);
    ...

    int n = usa.border->nSides;          // Number of sides in the polygon
                                          //    pointed to by border in usa.

    int y = usa.border->vertices[i].y;  // y coordinate of the i-th vertex
                                          //    in the polygon pointed to
                                          //    by border.

    VERTEX v =
          usa.states[n].vertices[i];    // The i-th vertex of the
                                          //    n-th state in the array
                                          //    pointed to by states.
```

> ...This is the cow with the crumpled horn,
> That tossed the dog,
> That worried the cat,
> That killed the rat,
> That ate the malt
> That lay in the house that Jack built...

When these expressions become too long, a programmer can split them into manageable pieces. For instance:

```
POLYGON *state = &usa.states[n]; // A pointer to the n-th state
int sides = state->nSides;
int x = state->vertices[i].x;
int y = state->vertices[i].y;
```

as opposed to:

```
int sides = usa.states[n].nSides;
int x = usa.states[n].vertices[i].x;
int y = usa.states[n].vertices[i].y;
```

If your nested data structures become too complex, though, you should probably re-examine your design.

13.4. Passing and Returning Structures to and from Functions

Passing a structure to a function <u>by value</u> involves copying the whole structure to the system stack. It is usually more efficient to pass the structure <u>by reference</u>, because then only its address is put on the stack. If we do not want to modify the structure inside the function, it is safer to add the keyword const to the function argument. The following function prints the DATE structure, which is passed to it by reference:

```
void PrintDate(const DATE &date)

// Prints the date as mm-dd-yyyy

{
    cout << setfill('0')                  // Show leading zeroes
         << setw(2) << date.month << '-'
         << setw(2) << date.day   << '-'
         << setw(4) << date.year
         << setfill(' ');                 // Reset the leading char
                                          //   back to space.
}
```

If the structure will be modified inside the function, you need to pass it by reference (you could also pass it by pointer, but we prefer the former method). The following function, for example, scales the coordinates of a point:

```
struct POINT {
    int x;
    int y;
};

...
const double SCALE_FACTOR = .1;
...

void ScalePoint (POINT &point)

//  Scales the point coordinates by SCALE_FACTOR.

{
    point.x *= SCALE_FACTOR;
    point.y *= SCALE_FACTOR;
}
```

⌘ ⌘ ⌘

A less intuitive notion is that a function can <u>return</u> a structure. The function must be declared to have the type of the structure, and the `return` statement must return a value of the type of the structure. The example below shows how the `ScaledPoint(…)` function is defined and used. It takes a `POINT` type argument (passed by reference for efficiency) and returns the scaled point:

```
...

POINT ScaledPoint (const POINT &point)

//  Returns a point with coordinates scaled by SCALE_FACTOR.

{
    POINT scaled;

    scaled.x = point.x * SCALE_FACTOR;
    scaled.y = point.y * SCALE_FACTOR;
    return scaled;
}

int main()

{
    POINT point1, point2;

    point1.x = 100;
    point1.y = 200;
    point2 = ScaledPoint(point1);
    ...
}
```

It seems desirable to deal with user-defined data types the same way that we deal with built-in types. Hence the idea of returning structures from functions. For small structures that are calculated inside functions, this leads to elegant code. But it is not very practical for large structures, especially if we want to change just a couple of values in the structure. Consider how much waste is involved in the following code:

```
struct BIGSTRUCT {
    int count;
    apvector<double> x;   // May hold many elements
};

BIGSTRUCT Reset(BIGSTRUCT b)

{
    BIGSTRUCT temp = b;      // Copies structure b to temp.
    temp.count = 0;
    return temp;             // Copies temp to the result.
}
```

```
int main()

{
    BIGSTRUCT b1;

    b1 = Reset(b1);         // Copies b1 to the argument, and then
                            //    the result back into b1.
    ...
}
```

The same result can be accomplished without any copying:

```
...
void Reset(BIGSTRUCT &b)

{
    b.count = 0;
}

int main()

{
    BIGSTRUCT b1;

    Reset(b1);
    ...
}
```

⌘   ⌘   ⌘

The above example should not be confused with functions that return <u>a pointer</u> to a structure. When a pointer is returned, no copying is necessary. For example:

```
BIGSTRUCT *NewBigStruct()

// Allocates a new BIGSTRUCT and sets b.count to 0.
// Returns a pointer to the new structure.

{
    BIGSTRUCT *p = new BIGSTRUCT;    // Allocate BIGSTRUCT
    if (!p) {
        cout << "*** Memory allocation error in NewBigStruct ***\n";
        return 0;           // Return null pointer.
    }
    p->count = 0;
    return p;                           // Return a pointer to newly
                                        //    allocated BIGSTRUCT.
}
```

13.5. Input/Output for User-Defined Types

The ideal of treating user-defined data types exactly the same way as built-in types finds an obstacle in stream I/O insertion and extraction operators. These operators have been programmed to handle all built-in types properly, but how can they know about user-defined types? It turns out that there is a solution to this problem based on the C++ feature known as *function and operator overloading*.

"Overloading" means using the same name for two or more different functions or the same symbol for two or more different operators. The difference between these functions (or operators) is in the number or data types of their arguments.

Let us take the stream insertion operator << as an example. This operator actually takes two operands: the output stream and the output value. There are many different forms of the insertion operator for handling output values of different data types: char, int, etc. From the compiler's perspective, different forms of the << operator are <u>different operators</u> even though they use the same symbol. The compiler automatically invokes the appropriate form of the operator based on the data type of the operand. There is nothing unusual in this. We don't pay any attention, for instance, to the fact that we can use the same + operator to add both integers and floating point numbers.

In C++ we can also use the same name for two functions that take arguments of different data types. For the compiler, these are two entirely different functions. For instance,

```
void PrintOut(int x);
```

and

```
void PrintOut(double x);
```

can be defined in the same program without any conflict. The compiler selects which one to call <u>based on the type of the argument</u>: for an int value it calls PrintOut(int), and for a double value it calls PrintOut(double). This is called *function overloading*.

⌘　⌘　⌘

In C++ the difference between operators and functions is minimal: an operator is a function, except that it is invoked in the program using different syntax. The operator represented by a *X* symbol is defined as a function with the name "operator*X*".

For instance, if we want to, we can write:

```
cout.operator<< (x);    // Call member function operator<< with
                        //   the argument x.
```

rather than the usual:

```
cout << x;
```

Our goal is to define a new overloaded form of the `<<` operator that handles the DATE data type. We would like to write:

```
DATE date = {12, 31, 2000};

cout << date;
```

and receive the output:

```
12-31-2000
```

To overload the `<<` operator we need to define a new function `operator<<(...)`. In our case, this function will take two arguments: a reference to the output stream and a reference to a DATE structure. To follow the convention, the function has to return a reference to the same stream. The data type `ostream` is defined in `iostream.h`.

Emulate the following example to overload the `<<` operator for a user-defined data type.

OVERLOAD.CPP

```
#include <iostream.h>
#include <iomanip.h>

struct DATE {
    int month;
    int day;
    int year;
};

ostream &operator<< (ostream &os, const DATE &date)

// Usage:
//    os << date;
// Prints the date as mm-dd-yyyy.
// (Requires <iostream.h> and <iomanip.h>.)

{
    os.setf(ios::right, ios:: adjustfield);
    os << setfill('0')                    // Show leading zeroes
        << setw(2) << date.month << '-'
        << setw(2) << date.day   << '-'
        << setw(4) << date.year
        << setfill(' ');                  // Reset the leading char
                                          //    back to space.

    return os;
}
```

The above code is almost identical to the `PrintDate(...)` function from the previous section. But to overload the `<<` operator we have to name the new function `operator<<`.

13.6. *Lab:* Updating Your Inventory

Review the "One of Each" Inventory System from Section 8.4. In that program, inventory items were defined simply as integers. Enhance the program by defining a new data type that would represent an inventory item as a <u>structure</u> including part number, part description, and quantity.

Declare the inventory array not as `apvector<int>`, but as an `apvector` of the newly defined data type. Modify the processing of the menu commands accordingly. Prompt the user, where necessary, for part description and quantity.

Modify the `Find(...)`, `Show(...)`, `Add(...)`, `Remove(...)`, and `List(...)` functions appropriately. You will also need to change the function arguments:

1. The Add(...) function should now take three arguments: the part number, description, and quantity. Alternatively, it can take one argument — the inventory item structure (const, passed by reference). The part description should be verified and the specified quantity should be added to the available quantity if the item is already in the array.

2. The Remove(...) function should take an additional argument quantity. The specified quantity should be subtracted from the available quantity. If the requested quantity exceeds available inventory, display a message to backorder the difference.

    For "extra credit":

3. Implement and use an overloaded << operator to display structures of the inventory item data type.

13.7. *Programming Project:* Enhancements to the Dictionary Program

Remember the Dictionary program in Chapter 2? Read it again and make the following modifications:

1. Accept the dictionary file name from the command line. If not specified, use the default file name DICT.DAT.

2. Add the part of speech indicator (e.g. adjective, noun, verb, etc.) to the dictionary data file lines and add a member to hold the part of speech indicator in the ENTRY structure. Have the program display the part of speech indicator together with the translation.

3. Manually arrange the entries in the dictionary file in alphabetical order. Modify the FoundWord(...) function to use <u>binary search</u> on the dictionary array.

4. If a word is not found in the dictionary, ask the user whether he wants to add the word. Implement a function that inserts a word into the dictionary in the correct alphabetical place.

Develop a comprehensive QA (quality assurance) plan and test the program.

For "extra credit":

5. Define and use overloaded stream insertion and extraction operators for the ENTRY structure.

6. Allow multiple entries for the same word in the dictionary data file and show all translations for the word.

7. Allow the user to enter sentences and make the program "translate" the sentence (i.e., all the words in the sentence).

8. If words have been added to the dictionary, ask the user whether he wants to save the modified dictionary. Implement a function to save the dictionary in a file (in the same format).

Part Two

Classes and
Data Structures

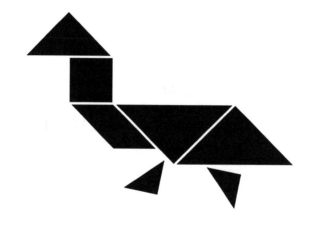

14

Modularity

14.1. Discussion

If you don't know much about cars and you take a look under the hood of an automobile, you will see a number of interconnected modules and parts designed to fit neatly into a restricted space. You may also observe that all the car's wheels are the same and that different car models may have identical or interchangeable parts.

Computer programs are a different kind of artifact, one whose structure is not readily available for inspection by the user. If he could peek "under the hood" of software systems, the user might find all sorts of things ranging from elegant designs to monstrous tangles.

One obvious way to reduce chaos and introduce some order into any complex project is to divide it into reasonably independent pieces. A large, well-structured software system typically comprises a number of *modules* that can be created and tested independently of each other. Each module implements a set of related data structures and functions.   Modern programming languages and software development environments, including C++, provide support for this modular approach.

Software modules can be compiled separately and then linked into one executable program.

The benefits of modular software design, besides cleaner structure and more efficient implementation, include easier software maintenance and reusability. In a bird's-eye view of the project, each module exists to carry out a certain task. Once the interfaces between the modules are defined, each module can be implemented and even modified independently of the other modules.   This property is called *locality*. A tested module can be used in other projects that present the same task. This property is called *reusability*. Since software's main costs are development and maintenance, not physical production, tested reusable code is essentially free.

Modularity is, of course, widely used in the physical world. Once the connections and the size of a dishwasher are standardized, a kitchen designer can proceed with the overall design with an "abstract" dishwasher in mind. The specific model will be installed later and can be replaced easily in case of a malfunction or upgrade.

In this chapter we discuss the more traditional approach to modularity in which each module implements a set of related functions. This will prepare us for later chapters where we will consider a more advanced concept of modularity associated with C++ classes.

14.2.   Example: Dates Revisited

As an example, let us consider a software application that processes banking transactions. In all likelihood this application will have to deal with dates. Even before knowing all the details, we can predict that this application will need functions that validate and compare dates and convert them into different formats. These functions can fit neatly into a separate module, which would deal only with a structure defined for representing dates.

Let us start by defining the DATE structure:

```
struct DATE {
    int month;
    int day;
    int year;
};
```

We can then think of functions useful for the tasks at hand. For example:

```
    ...
bool ValidDate(const DATE &date);
int DaysBetween(const DATE &date1, const DATE &date2);
bool Earlier(const DATE &date1, const DATE &date2);
void AddDays(const DATE &date1, DATE &date2, int days);
ostream &operator<< (ostream &os, const DATE &date);
    ...
```

Other functions may be added later, as the application takes shape. Some reasonable functions may be included for completeness even if they are not immediately useful for this application, because the extra effort is minimal and they may be useful for testing or for a future application. The same or another member of the development team can implement the actual code.

14.3.   Program Modules and Header Files

In C++ the source code for each module is implemented in a separate file. The file that handles dates, for example, may be called DATES.CPP. How would other modules "know" about the definitions and functions in DATES.CPP? One approach would be to include the file's text into the main program by putting

```
#include "dates.cpp"
```

somewhere in the main program. This would be equivalent to copying the source code from DATES.CPP into the main program — the modules would be combined at the source code level. Any change to DATES.CPP would require recompilation of all modules that use the date functions, and the object code for them would be repeated in every module that uses them. This approach would make it difficult to maintain the integrity of large software systems and would waste both space and compilation time.

A better approach, which is supported in C++ and other modular languages, is to compile the modules separately and then combine them into one executable program.   The modules don't need to know the details of each other's implementation, but they do need to share some definitions and declarations. In C++ this is accomplished by means of header files. We have already used standard library modules and system header files provided with the compiler. There is nothing that would prevent a programmer from creating his own header files.

Programmers create their own header files to let modules share definitions and declarations.

C++ recognizes two forms of the #include directive. One form uses angular brackets and is used with system header files provided with the compiler. For example:

```
#include <iostream.h>
```

The other form uses double quotes instead of angular brackets. This form is reserved for header files that you have written or that your organization has supplied. For example:

```
#include "apstring.h"
#include "dates.h"
```

The difference between the two forms is in the order in which the file directories are searched for header files. The double quote form indicates that the search should start with the current user directory, that is, the same directory where all the programmer's source code is located; the angular bracket form indicates that the search should start with the compiler system directories and not look into the current directory at all.

In our example, we can put the definition of the DATE structure and the function prototypes for the date functions into a separate header file. Following the convention, we name this file DATES.H — the same name as the respective source module but with the extension ".H."

DATES.H

```
// DATES.H
//
// Header file for the DATES module
//
//    Author: Cal Lenders
//    Rev 1.0
//

#include <iostream.h>

struct DATE {
    int month;
    int day;
    int year;
};

// Function Prototypes:

bool ValidDate(const DATE &date);
int DaysBetween(const DATE &date1, const DATE &date2);
bool Earlier(const DATE &date1, const DATE &date2);
void AddDays(const DATE &date1, DATE &date2, int days);
ostream &operator<< (ostream &os, const DATE &date);
```

The code in DATES.CPP may look as follows:

```
                                        ┌─────────────────────────┐
                                        │ DATES.CPP         [💾]   │
                                        └─────────────────────────┘
// DATES.CPP
//
// DATES module
//
//    Author: Cal Lenders
//    Rev 1.0
//

#include "dates.h"

const int daysInMonth[12] =
    { 31, 28, 31, 30, 31, 30, 31, 31, 30, 31, 30, 31 };

// Days from the beginning of the year
//    to the beginning of the month:

const int daysToMonth[12] =
    { 0,   31,  59,  90, 120, 151, 181, 212, 243, 273, 304, 334 };

const char *monthName[12] = {
    "January", "February", "March",
    ...
};

//****************************************************************

bool LeapYear (int year)

// year must be between 1900 and 2999.
// Returns true if "year" is a leap year.

{
    ...
}

//****************************************************************

bool ValidDate(const DATE &date)

// Returns true if date contains a valid date between
// Jan 1, 1990 and Dec 31, 2100.

{
    ...
}

//****************************************************************
```

Continued ✍

```
static int DaysSince1900(const DATE &date)

// date contains a valid date
//    (between Jan 1, 1990 and Dec 31, 2100).
// Returns number of days passed since Jan 1, 1990.

{
    ...
}

//*************************************************************

int DaysBetween(const DATE &date1, const DATE &date2)

// date1 and date2 must contain valid dates.
// Returns number of days passed from date1 to date2.

{
    return DaysSince1900(date2) - DaysSince1900(date1);
}

//*************************************************************

bool Earlier(const DATE &date1, const DATE &date2)

// date1 and date2 must contain valid dates.
// Returns true if date1 is earlier than date2, false otherwise.

{
    return DaysBetween(date1, date2) > 0;
}

//*************************************************************

void AddDays(const DATE &date1, DATE &date2, int days)

// date1 contains a valid date and days is >= 0.
// Fills date2 with a new date obtained by
//    adding days to date1.

{
    ...
}

//*************************************************************
```

Continued

```
ostream &operator<< (ostream &os, const DATE &date)

// Usage:
//   cout << date;
// Prints the date, as in "January 1, 1990".

{
    os << monthName[date.month - 1] << ' '
       << date.day << ", "
       << date.year;

    return os;
}
```

The header file is included into each module that needs to use the functions and structures defined in it, but the functions' actual code is not duplicated. Each module can be compiled separately.

A separate test program may be created for testing all the date functions:

TESTDATE.CPP

```
// TESTDATE.CPP
//
// This program is used to test the dates functions defined in
//   DATES.CPP.

#include <iostream.h>
#include "dates.h"

int main()

{
    DATE date1, date2;
    int days;

    cout << "Enter three numbers: month, day, year\n"
         << "    (e.g. 7 4 1999) ==> ";
    cin >> date1.month >> date1.day >> date1.year;
    if (ValidDate(date1))
        cout << date1 << endl;
    else {
        cout << "*** Invalid date ***\n"
             << " (Valid dates are between Jan 1, 1990 and\n"
             << "        Dec 31, 2100).\n";
        return 1;
    }
```

Continued

```
    cout << "Enter number of days to increment this date ==> ";
    cin >> days;

    AddDays(date1, date2, days);
    cout << "The new date is " << date2 << endl;

    if (DaysBetween(date1, date2) == days)
        cout << "Test ok.\n";
    else
        cout << "Error in AddDays or DaysBetween.\n";

    return 0;
}
```

A special program, the linker, is used to put the modules together. We will discuss the linker in Section 14.5.

14.4. Module Hierarchies

Large projects may involve hierarchies of modules. One approach to good software architecture is to arrange functions in layers based on their "level of functionality" and the "level" of data structures that they deal with. For example, functions that deal with different types of transactions in a banking application may form a separate layer positioned above the layer that deals with dates. Each layer can be implemented as a separate module or several modules.

In an ideal architecture, each layer uses only functions and data structures from the layer immediately below it. Changes in the implementation of a module normally do not disturb other modules. In a "layered" design, even changes to the interface of a module do not propagate through the whole system but affect only the layer above it.

This kind of layered design creates a dilemma related to the use of header files. A higher layer may have its own header file which requires definitions from lower layers. For example, the module processing transactions, TRANS.CPP, may use its own header file, TRANS.H. Declarations and definitions in TRANS.H may require the DATE structure from DATES.H, so the programmer may decide to include DATES.H at the top of TRANS.H:

```
// TRANS.H

...
#include "dates.h"
...
```

It may be difficult, though, to keep track of which header files are included within other header files. Suppose another header file (say, ACCOUNTS.H) also includes DATES.H. Now suppose both TRANS.H and ACCOUNTS.H are included into the same module. Then DATES.H will be included <u>twice</u> and the compiler will generate error messages that structures and constants in DATES.H are already defined.

To get around this problem, programmers often use conditional compilation preprocessor directives to eliminate duplicate inclusions of the same code. At the beginning of the header file, a programmer defines a constant that identifies that file. The constant's name should be unusual to avoid clashes with other names; for example, it may start and end with a few underscore characters. The text of the header file is placed between the `#ifndef`-`#endif` preprocessor directives and is included only if the constant is <u>not defined</u> above; that is, only if that header file has not yet been included in this module. For example:

```
// DATES.H

#ifndef _DATES_H_    // Include statements below only if the
                     //   name _DATES_H_ is not defined.

#define _DATES_H_    // Now the name _DATES_H_ becomes defined

#include <iostream.h>

struct DATE {
    int month;
    int day;
    int year;
};

. . .
. . .


#endif     // End of conditional compilation for #ifndef _DATES_H_
```

The same trick is used in system header files. Note that we have included `iostream.h` into DATES.H because we needed the definition of the `ostream` type. But although we have included <u>both</u> `iostream.h` and DATES.H into TESTDATE.CPP, the conditional compilation in `iostream.h` prevents duplicate definitions.

14.5. Linking

The process of combining different object modules into one executable module is called *linking*. Linking, in a nutshell, involves the following steps. When the compiler finds a function definition (not the prototype, but the actual code), it places the function's name and its address (relative to the beginning of the module) into a special table of *global* (a.k.a. *public*) symbols. This function can be used from other modules. When a compiler finds the first call to a function that is not defined in the given module, it places the function's name in a special table of *external* symbols and reserves some logical external address for it, leaving that address temporarily undefined. This indicates that the function's code should be found in some other module. Each object module has a table of "globals" and a table of "externals."

(Actually, as we discussed in Section 13.5 of Part 1, C++ supports function *overloading*: functions with the same name but different sets or data types of arguments are considered by the compiler to be entirely different functions. Thus, a complete function *signature*, including its name and the types of all its arguments, is stored in the tables of globals and externals.)

A special program, the *linker*, examines the set of object modules that you have specified in the linking command. It combines all the code contained in them and tries to *resolve* all external references by finding their names and addresses among the globals of other modules. The logical addresses of externals are then replaced with their actual addresses in the combined code, and the linker creates an executable file.

The linker is provided to you together with other development tools.

In case of problems, the linker reports errors. One common error is "Unresolved external: YourFunction." This happens when none of the specified modules contains YourFunction's code. Another possible error is "Multiple definitions of YourFunction," which occurs when two or more modules define functions with the same signature. Note that many modules may contain the <u>declaration</u> of the function (i.e., the function prototype) but only one module may contain the actual code (the function's <u>definition</u>).

⌘   ⌘   ⌘

In large projects it is convenient to combine the object modules into one or more *object module libraries* using a utility program called the *librarian*. A librarian also helps to maintain a library and allows you to add, replace, and delete modules and list their globals and externals.

The linker is capable of searching specified libraries. It examines each library and picks only those modules that contain remaining unresolved externals.

C++ compilers all come with standard object module libraries containing standard functions. Libraries with various useful functions are also available from third-party vendors. The vendors can provide the documentation, the header files, and the object code while keeping their source code confidential — another advantage of integration at the object module level!

In modern development environments, the process of linking is transparent to the user. The project maintenance facility usually allows programmers to specify which modules should be included into the current project; pressing a key or clicking on a menu item automatically compiles all the necessary modules and links them into an executable file.

14.6. Global and Static Variables

Several modules may not only use the same functions but also share global constants or variables.

A constant or variable declared outside of any function is not only global in its own module, but is automatically considered global between modules; its name and data type are included in the table of globals and passed to the linker.

Other modules may gain access to that variable or constant by declaring it with the `extern` keyword:

```
// Defining module:

int age_of_universe;
apstring hello = "Hello, World";
const double pi = 3.141592654;

// Another module:

extern int age_of_universe;
extern apstring hello;
extern const double pi;
```

A global variable or constant cannot be declared without the `extern` modifier in more than one module because the linker will generate error messages about multiple definitions of a global symbol. On the other hand, `extern` declarations do not conflict with the actual declaration:

```
extern apstring hello;              // Redundant, but OK.
apstring hello = "Hello, World";
```

So `extern` declarations may be placed in the header file, which is a good way to insure consistency of external declarations between modules.

The `extern` modifier can be also used with function prototypes, but it is redundant, since a function is assumed by default to be external unless it is defined in the same module.

Global variables are "considered harmful" even in one module and should be avoided at all costs between modules because they violate <u>locality</u> **and make the project structure intractable. If used, they should be carefully documented.**

⌘   ⌘   ⌘

It is possible to declare a global variable or a function within one module but hide it from the other modules. This is done by using the keyword `static` in the declaration. For example:

```
static bool LeapYear(int year);

static const int daysInMonth[12] =
    {31,28,31,30,31,30,31,31,30,31,30,31};

static const int daysToMonth[12] =
    {0,31,59,90,120,151,181,212,243,273,304,334};

static const char *monthName[12] = {
    "January", "February", "March",
    "April", "May", "June",
    "July", "August", "September",
    "October", "November", "December"
};


static bool LeapYear(int year)

{
    ...
}
```

Static variables and functions are not placed into the table of globals and are not reported to the linker.

Static declarations belong in the source file; it wouldn't make much sense to place them in a header file. It is good practice always to use `static` for variables, constants and functions restricted to one module; this documents that they are used only in this module and allows other modules to use the same name without conflict.

14.7.   Inline Functions

C++ allows programmers to declare fragments of code as *inline functions*. An inline function pretends to be a normal function, but instead of implementing it as a real function, the compiler just inserts a copy of the inline function's code whenever it encounters a call to the function. Inline functions avoid the overhead associated with calling a function but make the executable code bigger. They should be used only for very short functions.

Inline functions may neither be static nor external. If an inline function is to be accessible to many modules, it should be defined in a header file. For example:

```
// DATES.H

...
int DaysBetween(const DATE &date1, const DATE &date2);

inline bool Earlier(const DATE &date1, const DATE &date2)
{
    return DaysBetween(date1, date2) > 0;
}
...
```

Inline functions may use prototypes but usually don't need them because their short code can be defined together with the declaration.

14.8. Summary

Modularity is essential for sound software design. Modular programs are easier to develop and test, especially for a team of programmers. They are also easier to understand and maintain because certain changes can be implemented locally and do not require extensive modifications or retesting of the entire application.

Modules should be designed, implemented, and documented with an eye to their possible future use in other projects. It is desirable to create reusable modules, isolating more general functions from more application-specific functions.

Each module is usually implemented in two separate files, a header file and a source file. The header file may contain constants, function prototypes, inline functions, definitions of data structures, and declarations of external variables. The source code contains function definitions (code) and static variables and functions. The header file is #include-ed into the source code and into other modules.

The modules are compiled separately and linked together into one executable program by a linker program. Object modules may be combined into object module libraries by using a librarian utility program. The linker can search specified libraries for modules that supply remaining unresolved external references and include them into the executable file.

15

Classes

15.1.   Discussion

The evolution of programming languages is driven in part by the development of general ideas about the nature of programming and its methodology. Classes in C++ represent an attempt to foster a programming style in which code is more modular, maintainable, and reusable. They are also an important step towards ***Object-Oriented Programming*** (OOP).

(In OOP a program is designed as a set of actively interacting objects of different types. The types of objects are often arranged in taxonomic hierarchies in which one type of object is viewed as a special case, "a kind of" object of a more general type. An object combines certain attributes and data with procedures (often called ***methods***) for processing specific conditions, calls, or messages that the object receives from other objects. A full explanation of OOP methodology is beyond the scope of this book.)

This effort has had only partial success. Just using classes does not guarantee well-structured or easily maintainable code; like any powerful tool, classes actually give software designers and developers the added responsibility of using them properly. In addition to structural flexibility, classes also offer unprecedented syntactic freedom, particularly in redefining the meaning of standard operators. This freedom can easily be abused by a novice, leading to intractable code. In this chapter we will cover the essential features and properties of classes, leaving more exotic features for later chapters.

In previous chapters we have seen that we can implement a functional module by defining some data structures and some functions that operate on those structures. Classes take this concept one step further by allowing programmers to define data elements and functions that operate on them as one entity, a ***class***, and by imposing certain restrictions on the use of its elements.

In the following example, the definition of a class DATE combines data elements and function prototypes:

```
class DATE {

  private:

    int month;
    int day;
    int year;

  public:

    bool Valid();
    int DaysTo(const DATE &date2);
    ...
};
```

Both data elements and functions are called *members* of the class.

Like structures, classes are treated as user-defined data types.

The syntax for classes is similar to the syntax for structures. Variables and pointers of the class type may be declared in the same way as built-in and structure types. For example:

```
int main()

{
    DATE date, *dateptr;
    ...
    dateptr = new DATE;
    *dateptr = date;
    ...
}
```

15.2.   Public and Private Members, Encapsulation

You may notice the `private` and `public` keywords in the class definition. When we use structures, all data elements of the structure are accessible to any function, as long as the instance of the structure is in the function's scope. If we define:

```
struct DATE {
    int month;
    int day;
    int year;
};
```

then we can write:

```
int main()

{
    DATE date;
    ...
    date.year = 1999;
    ...
}
```

Not so with classes.

> **In classes, all members are divided into two categories:** *private* **and** *public*. **The public members, both data elements and functions, can be used anywhere in the program (as long the class instance is in scope). They define the interface between the class and the rest of the program. The private members are hidden within the class and are accessible only to member functions. They determine the internal structure and workings of the class.**

(There is no connection between *public* members of a class and *public* (global) functions or variables in a module.)

The `public` and `private` keywords in the class definition designate members of a particular type. The groups of private and public members can be interspersed freely in the class definition, but it is customary to group together all private members and all public members. The first group is <u>private</u> by default unless overridden with the `public` keyword. However, it is better to explicitly label the first section as private or public for clarity.

Strictly speaking, a C++ `class` definition has exactly the same syntax as a `struct` definition. The only difference between a `struct` and a `class` is that in a `struct` the first group of members is by default <u>public</u>, and in a `class`, private. However, programmers usually do not use private members or member functions with `struct` — this is because C, where `structs` come from, has no classes and no public or private members.

The main idea of classes is to combine data elements and functions in one entity and to hide data elements within the class by making them accessible only to member functions. This concept is called *encapsulation*. For example, the innocent-looking code:

```
class DATE {

  public:
    ...

  private:

    int month;
    int day;
    int year;
};

int main()

{
    DATE date;
    date.month = 12;
    ...
}
```

would generate the compiler error:

```
Error ...: 'DATE::month' is not accessible in function main()
```

Some theorists believe that data structures are more susceptible to change over the lifetime of a program than function declarations. Encapsulation assures that any change to (private) data elements remains <u>local</u>: it does not affect the rest of the program outside the class member functions. Locality makes program maintenance easier. If, for example, we decided at some point to represent month in DATE as a char instead of an int, we would have to change only the member functions. The code outside the class would remain intact.

The default rule notwithstanding, it is common in programs and computer books to list the public class members first, followed by the private members. The rationale is that the <u>user</u> of a class is interested only in the class interface, not its implementation. In this book, however, we are often interested in the implementation of a class. It is easier to understand what the member functions do after taking a look at the data on which they operate, so sometimes we list the private members first.

A class designer typically has to provide special public functions, often referred to as *accessors*, for accessing private data members. The functions that set or change the values of private members are often called *modifiers*. For example:

```
class DATE {

  public:
    ...
    // Accessors:
    int GetMonth() {return month;}
    ...
    // Modifiers:
    void SetMonth (int a_month);
    ...

  private:

    int month;
    int day;
    int year;

};
```

Accessors and modifiers may seem redundant, but they offer some advantages. One advantage is that modifiers can check the arguments to ensure that class data members always have valid values:

```
void DATE::SetMonth(int a_month)

{
    if (a_month >= 1 && a_month <= 12)
        month = a_month;
}
```

The advantage of accessors is that the internal representation of a data member may change without changing the code outside the class:

```
class DATE {

  public:
    ...
    int GetMonth() {return int(month);}
    ...

  private:

    char month;
    int day;
    int year;
};
```

⌘ ⌘ ⌘

A class may have accessors and other member functions that do not change any data members of the class. It is a good practice to declare such functions "constant" by adding the keyword `const` at the end of the function's prototype and the function's header line. For example:

```
// apstring.h

class apstring {

  public:
    ...
    int length() const;
    ...
};

// apstring.cpp

...
int apstring::length() const

// Returns the length of the string

{
    ...
}
```

The keyword `const` documents and enforces the fact that the function does not change the data members of the class. If a `const` function attempts to change a class member or call a non-`const` function, the compiler reports an error.

⌘ ⌘ ⌘

Unfortunately, attempts at total encapsulation sometimes fall short of expectations. Deadlines and other pressures from the real world often force programmers to bypass full encapsulation and use some public data members. Others may implement encapsulation in letter but not in spirit, providing redundant access functions but not performing data validation, or leaving the class interface too dependent on the particular internal data representation. Designing a class that strikes a balance between private and public members becomes an elusive art. The ideal of total encapsulation in C++ also fails because the private class members are included along with public members in class definitions, which are placed in header files. They are not usable outside the class, but any change to the private members of a class requires recompilation of all modules that use the class.

15.3.   Implementation of a Class

A class is usually implemented as two separate files: a header file and a source
file. The header file serves the same purpose as header files in the procedural
modules discussed earlier (see Section 14.3): it contains the definition of the class
and is included into modules that use the class. It is also included into the class's
source file.   The source file contains the bodies of the member functions.
Sometimes a few related classes may be implemented in one module, sharing one
header file and one source file. The header file may also contain other structures,
constants and types useful for the class:

```
// STUDENT.H

enum GENDER {MALE, FEMALE};

struct DATE {
    int month;
    int day;
    int year;
};

class STUDENT {

  private:

    int age;
    GENDER gender;
    DATE dob;
    bool ValidDate(const DATE &date);
    . . .

  public:

    int id;
    . . .
    GENDER GetGender() {return gender;}
    void SetGender(GENDER a_gender);
    void SetGender(char c_gender);  // Second (overloaded) version.
    DATE GetDOB() {return dob;}
    void SetDOB(const DATE &date);
    . . .
};
```

**Short member functions may be defined inside the class definition.
These are automatically treated as inline functions.**

The bodies of other member functions are placed in the source file, which usually
has the same name as the header file with the extension ".CPP":

```
// STUDENT.CPP

...
bool STUDENT::ValidDate(const DATE &date)

{
    return (date.year >= 1950 && date.year <= 2100);
}

...

void STUDENT::SetDOB(const DATE &date)

{
    if (ValidDate(date)) dob = date;
}

...

void STUDENT::SetGender (GENDER a_gender)

{
    gender = a_gender;
}

void STUDENT::SetGender (char c_gender)

{
    if (c_gender == 'M')
        gender = MALE;
    else if (c_gender =='F')
        gender = FEMALE;
}
```

Note some important features in the above code.

1. Function names are preceded by STUDENT::. Functions in different classes and outside of any classes may have the same names. In fact, allowing the same function names in different objects is a useful feature of the object-oriented approach, because it is desirable to give the same names to semantically close behaviors regardless of the specific type of an object. The definition of the function ValidDateOfBirth(...), for example, may be different in the STUDENT class and in the PRESIDENT class. C++ compilers do not automatically assume that all functions in a given source file belong to the same class. To distinguish definitions of functions that belong to a particular class, their names are prefixed with the class name and the *scope resolution symbol* ::.

2. Private and public functions are defined the same way in the source file. The division into public and private members is specified only in the class definition.

3. All member functions can refer to any private or public data members or functions just by using their names. The scope resolution prefix automatically puts all class members in scope.

4. Member functions can be overloaded, just like ordinary functions (for example, see SetGender(...) above). Overloading adds flexibility to class use.

⌘ ⌘ ⌘

The class data members' names often clash with the obvious choices for arguments' names in member functions. In the above example, we would be tempted to use:

```
void STUDENT::SetGender(GENDER gender)

{
    ...         // gender = gender ???
}
```

But we cannot, because the name gender is already used for a class member. This may eventually become a nuisance. Some programmers use a standard prefix in all names of class members, such as:

```
class STUDENT {
    ...
    int mAge;
    GENDER mGender;
    ...
}
```

Others use a prefix for arguments:

```
void STUDENT::SetGender(GENDER a_gender)

{
    ...
    gender = a_gender;
}
```

```
void STUDENT::SetAge(int an_age)

{
    ...
    age = an_age;
}
```

Yet others deal with it on a case-by-case basis. You also have to be very careful not to declare local variables whose names clash with class member names.

15.4.   Syntax for Accessing Class Members

We have seen that all class members are in scope and can be accessed simply by their names inside member functions. Outside the class, we need to associate a class member with a variable or a pointer of the class type that represents a particular instance of the class.

The syntax for accessing a class's public <u>data</u> members outside the class is the same as for accessing `struct` members. For example:

```
// STUDENT.H

class STUDENT {

  public:

    int id;
    ...
};

// TEST.CPP

#include "student.h"

...

int main()

{
    STUDENT student, *studentPtr;
    ...
    student.id = 269;
    studentPtr = new STUDENT;
    studentPtr->id = student.id;
    ...
}
```

The syntax for invoking member <u>functions</u>, however, is new. It imitates the syntax for accessing a data member of a structure or a class by placing the class instance name first, followed by a dot or an arrow (for a pointer), followed by the member function's name and arguments. For example:

```
// TEST.CPP

int main()

{
    STUDENT student, *studentPtr;
    int age;
    ...
    studentPtr = new STUDENT;
    age = student.GetAge();
    studentPtr->SetAge(age);
    ...
}
```

15.5.   Constructors and Destructors

C++ aims to make user-defined types as easy to use as built-in types. In particular, user-defined types may be declared, and their values initialized, the same way as built-in types. Some classes, however, may require a special initialization procedure before they can be used: they may need members initialized, arrays allocated for internal storage, etc. When they are no longer useful, class instances may require some final cleaning up before they disappear: they may need memory released, etc. C++ makes the initialization and clean-up automatic, transparent to the programmer. This is accomplished by two special public class member functions called the *constructor* and *destructor*.

The constructor has the same name as the class. The destructor has the name of the class preceded by ~. For example:

```
// apstring.h

class apstring {

  public:

    apstring(const char str[]); // Constructor from a literal string
    ...
    ~apstring();                 // Destructor

  private:

    int mLength;       // The actual length of the string
    int mCapacity;     // The size of the available string buffer
    char *mCstring;    // Pointer to the string buffer
};
```

```
// apstring.cpp

apstring::apstring(const char str[])

// Constructor: builds an apstring from a null-terminated string,
//   such as "abcd".

{
    mLength = strlen(str);        // Get the length of the string
    mCapacity = mLength + 1;      // +1 to hold the terminating null
    mCstring = new char[mCapacity]; // Allocate the string buffer
    strcpy(mCstring, str);        // Copy str into the buffer
}
```

In the above example the constructor is used to initialize the mLength and mCapacity members of apstring, to allocate the string buffer, and to copy the string characters into it.

Neither the constructor nor the destructor has a return type, not even void. In addition, destructors do not take any arguments. Both constructors and destructors can be inline functions.

You do not have to define a constructor or destructor. If you don't, C++ generates a default constructor with no arguments (see Section 21.4).

⌘　⌘　⌘

It may be a good exercise to create a simple class and write a constructor and a destructor that print out messages. This will make clear at what point a test program calls them.

⌘   ⌘   ⌘

Like ordinary functions, constructors can be overloaded. For example:

```
// apstring.h

class apstring {

  public:

    apstring();                    // Constructor: makes an empty string
    apstring(const char str[]); // Constructor from a literal string
    ...
```

The source code has to define all forms of overloaded constructors. For example:

```
// apstring.cpp

apstring::apstring()

// Constructor: Builds an empty string.

{
    mLength = 0;
    mCapacity = 1;
    mCstring = new char[1]; // Allocate the string buffer for one char
    mCstring[0] = '\0';        // The string buffer has only a null char
}

apstring::apstring(const char str[])

// Constructor: builds an apstring from a null-terminated string,
//   such as "abcd".

{
    mLength = strlen(str);       // Get the length of the string
    mCapacity = mLength + 1;     // +1 to hold the terminating null
    mCstring = new char[mCapacity]; // Allocate the string buffer
    strcpy(mCstring, str);       // Copy str into the buffer
}
```

Destructors cannot be overloaded.

Constructors and destructors are called <u>automatically</u>. The constructor is called when a variable of the class type is declared, or when one is created with the `new` operator. The destructor is called when the variable goes out of scope or is deleted with the `delete` operator.

For global variables, the constructor is called before `main()` and the destructor is called after `main()`, before the program returns to the operating system. If you create a new object with the `new` operator, you are responsible for deleting it with `delete`.

When a class constructor takes arguments, an instance of that class (i.e., a variable or a constant of the class data type) has to be declared with the corresponding argument values placed in parentheses after the variables' name. For example:

```
DATE date(12, 31, 1999);
ifstream inpFile("TEST.DAT");
apstring fileName("TEST.DAT");
```

The same applies to creating instances of a class with the `new` operator. For example:

```
DATE *pDate = new DATE(12, 31, 1999);
```

⌘   ⌘   ⌘

If a constructor takes one argument, then you can use the conventional form of initialization of a constant or a variable as well. For example:

```
apstring fileName = "TEST.DAT";
```

The two forms—

```
apstring fileName("TEST.DAT");
```
and
```
apstring fileName = "TEST.DAT";
```

—are interchangeable; both call the constructor

```
apstring::apstring(const char str[]);
```

It is largely a matter of taste which form of declarations you use. Some programmers always use the parenthesized form because it is more general: it works for constructors with one argument as well as constructors with two or more arguments. It is also used in *initializer lists*, as explained in Section 21.2. Actually, the parenthesized form is also acceptable with built-in data types, and some C++ purists use only that form. For example:

```
int count(0); // The same as: int count = 0;
```

But this takes some getting used to.

Our preference is to use the assignment form for built-in types and for single-argument constructors whenever, conceptually, the constructor <u>copies or converts</u> the argument into the class instance. The argument data type must be the same or closely related to the class. So we write:

```
apstring fileName = "SAMPLE.TXT";
```

but

```
ifstream inpFile("SAMPLE.TXT");
```

In both cases the class object is constructed with one argument, a literal string. But in the first case the literal string is converted and copied into the variable of type `apstring`, while in the second case the constructor simply opens the file with the given name.

⌘ ⌘ ⌘

C++ allows you to declare functions with default values for some of their arguments. The arguments with default values must be grouped at the end of the argument list. The default values for the arguments are supplied in the function prototype. For example:

```
void LoadDictionary(apvector<ENTRY> &dict,
        const apstring &fileName = "DICT.DAT", int maxwords = 1000);
```

A call to a function with default values for its arguments may omit these arguments in the call. For example, you can call the above `LoadDictionary(...)` function with three, two, or just one argument:

```
LoadDictionary(dict);
    // The same as: LoadDictionary(dict, "DICT.DAT", 1000);

LoadDictionary(dict, "FRENCH.DAT");
    // The same as: LoadDictionary(dict, "FRENCH.DAT", 1000);

LoadDictionary(dict, "SPANISH.DAT", 20000);
    // Values for all arguments are supplied explicitly.
```

This feature can be used with class constructors. For example, we could declare a constructor for the DATE class with the default argument:

```
date::date(int month, int day, int year = 2000);
```

Then both declarations

```
DATE date1(12, 31, 1999);
DATE date2(1, 1);   //  Same as:  DATE date2(1, 1, 2000);
```

become valid.

15.6. *Lab:* Add a Constructor to the apstring Class

Examine the declarations and the code for constructors for the apstring class. Add a constructor that would allow you to declare an apstring of a given length, filled with a given character. Use a for loop to set all the characters in the string buffer to the "fill" character; don't forget to add the terminating null ('\0') character at the end.

Use the new constructor to print a line that contains 13 stars.

For "extra credit":

Supply a default value for the char argument so that if the fill character is not specified in the declaration, the string is filled with spaces.

Write a program that prints a "triangle" with seven rows of stars:

```
      *
     ***
    *****
   *******
  *********
 ***********
*************
```

Use your new constructor to declare two strings of the required lengths, one filled with spaces and the other filled with stars. Place these declarations inside the loop that prints the rows of the triangle. Besides these declarations, all you need is one output statement, so your code will be very concise.

The above solution illustrates how constructors do the work behind the scenes. But it also illustrates the common tradeoff in C++ between code clarity and performance. In a more conservative approach, you can declare one large enough string outside the loop. Initially this string is filled with spaces. Then, within the loop, you can flip a couple of characters from spaces to stars and print the string.

Implement this solution, too. Your code will be just a bit longer and perhaps not as elegant, but it will run faster. Explain why.

15.7.   *Lab:* Vending Machine Class

Write a class SODA that simulates a soda vending machine. The class should keep track of the total money deposited into a machine and the inventory for several brands. For the sake of simplicity, initialize the inventories to the same number for all drink brands. Place the initialization code in the class constructor. Have the constructor display instructions for use of the machine. The destructor should print a message about the total money collected in the machine.

The public members, in addition to the constructor and the destructor, should be three functions:

```
void AddMoney(int cents);
void ReturnMoney();
void DispenseDrink(int brand);
```

DispenseDrink(...) should check whether the chosen brand is available and enough money deposited, print appropriate messages, and report the customer's change.

The other functions should print appropriate messages; for example, AddMoney (...) may display the total amount deposited by the customer.

Make the drink price a private member of the class (you may want to provide a function to set it to a desired value). Since we have not yet covered how to declare and use static members in a class, declare the brand names in a separate static array outside the class:

```
static const int BRANDS = 5;
static const char *brandName[BRANDS] = {
    "PepC++",
    . . .
};
```

Write a small test program that will use your class. It will display a menu of three items ("Add Money," "Select Drink," "Return Money") and call! the appropriate class member function.

15.8.   Summary

Classes in C++ implement user-defined types with great flexibility. They combine functions and data elements in one entity and implement "members-only" access to their private members. All data elements may be hidden from non-member functions and made accessible only through public member functions — a concept known as encapsulation.

Each class has two special functions, a constructor and a destructor, which are called automatically when a variable of a class type is created and destroyed.

Classes, if used properly, enforce modularity and facilitate code maintenance and reusability. However, they also may present many pitfalls for the uninitiated.

16

Templates

16.1.   Discussion

C++ is a strongly typed language: every variable or function argument must be declared with a particular built-in or user-defined type. This helps programmers avoid some errors and helps compilers produce more efficient code. In many cases, however, the desired functionality is identical for different data types and can be expressed with exactly the same code simply by substituting one type for another. For example, a function that swaps two integers:

```
void Swap (int &a, int &b)

{
    int temp = a;  a = b;  b = temp;
}
```

will become a function that works for doubles if we simply substitute `double` for `int` everywhere in the code. If we define our own type:

```
struct POINT {
    int x;
    int y;
};
```

and substitute `POINT` for `int` everywhere in the `Swap(...)` function, the new function will swap two "`POINTS`":

```
void Swap (POINT &a, POINT &b)

{
    POINT temp = a;  a = b;  b = temp;
}
```

Thanks to the function overloading feature of C++, all these functions can coexist without any conflict: the compiler knows which one to call based on the types of the specified arguments. It may be quite tedious for the programmer, though, to copy the same code over and over. More importantly, any change would have to be duplicated in all forms of the function. It may also be difficult to foresee all the necessary forms of a function, so that the new forms may have to be added later. These drawbacks undermine the ideal of easily maintainable and reusable code.

Recognizing these difficulties, the designers of C++ have added to the later versions of the language a feature called *parameterized types*, or *templates*. This feature automates the process of writing multiple forms of the same function with arguments of different types. Instead of a concrete data type — `int`, `double`, `POINT` — you write your code with an arbitrary parameter name, which the compiler replaces with different concrete data types when it learns how the function is used. In other words, the data type itself becomes a parameter for the function's template.

Templates can be also used with classes. The `apvector` and `apmatrix` classes are examples of templated classes that work with elements of different data types.

16.2. Syntax for Templates

A templated function's prototype and definition are preceded with the expression:

```
template <class typeparameter>
```

`template` and `class` are reserved words, and *typeparameter* is any name of your choice which will be used as replacement for concrete type specifiers. The keyword `class` here has little relation to C++ classes, but it is required, and forgetting it causes a syntax error.

The templated function `Swap (...)` looks like this:

```
template <class SOMETYPE>
void Swap (SOMETYPE &a, SOMETYPE &b)

{
    SOMETYPE temp = a; a = b; b = temp;
}
```

A templated function can be called with any built-in type or any user-defined type implemented with `typedef`, `enum`, `struct`, or `class`.

More elaborate functions may use two or more parameterized types. The syntax is:

```
template <class typeparameter1, class typeparameter2, ...>
```

16.3.   Classes with Parameterized Types

A templated class can use parameterized types anywhere in its definition where a built-in or user-defined type would be appropriate.   The statement

```
template <...>
```

precedes the definition of the class.

As an example, let us consider the `apvector` class.   As we know, this class implements dynamic arrays with the data type of the array elements as a parameter in the class definition.   The authors of the class chose the name `itemType` for that parameter:

```
// apvector.h

template <class itemType>
class apvector {

  public:

    // Constructors/destructor:
      apvector();                      // Default constructor
      apvector(int size);              // Initial size of vector is size

      apvector(int size, const itemType &fillValue );
                                       // Fills the array with fillValue
      apvector(const apvector &v);     // Copy constructor
      ~apvector();                     // Destructor

    // Overloaded assignment operator:
      const apvector &operator= (const apvector &v);

    // length and resize functions:
      int  length() const;
      void resize(int newSize);

    // Overloaded subscripting operator []:
      itemType &operator[] (int index);

  private:

      int  mSize;                      // Number of elements in the array
      itemType *mBuffer;               // Pointer to the buffer that
                                       //   holds elements of the vector
};
...
```

In a templated class each member function or operator is a templated function. For example:

```
// apvector.h
...

template <class itemType>
int apvector<itemType>::length() const

{
    return mSize;
}
```

The first line declares that length() is a templated member function (even though it does not use any itemType arguments). apvector<itemType> in the second line is the full name of the class that precedes the scope resolution operator. The above syntax is cumbersome and redundant, but we have no other choice if we want to code templated classes.

In a templated class the bodies of all member functions are placed in the header file. They cannot be placed in a separate .cpp file because the compiler can generate their code only after it sees how the class is used. This is explained in more detail in the next section.

For templated classes the data type parameter is instantiated when we declare variables or constants of the class type. This is accomplished by placing the actual data type (any built-in or previously defined data type) in angular brackets after the class name. For example:

```
// MYPROG.CPP

...
#include "apvector.h"

struct ENTRY {
...
};

...
int main()

{
    apvector<double> sample(100);
    apvector<int> counts(1000, 0);
    apvector<apstring> text;
    apvector<ENTRY> dict(MAXWORDS);
    ...
```

The code that uses the above declarations essentially treats `apvector<int>`, `apvector<double>`, `apvector<apstring>` and `apvector<ENTRY>` as four new data types.

16.4.   How to Use Templates

The compiler generates code for a templated function only when it sees that it is used and figures out how. If the templated function is used with different data types, the compiler will generate several overloaded functions, one for each form used.

The same applies to templated classes.

The code of the member functions in a templated class is placed in the class's header file because this code must be included into each source module that uses the class.

Templates save space in source code and simplify code maintenance at the <u>source</u> level. But they undermine modularity at the <u>object</u> (compiled) code level. Any change in the body of a member function requires recompilation of each program or module that uses the class.

Templates do not save space in the executable program, because each form of a function or a class used in the program has its own code. In fact, it is very easy to end up with several very similar pieces of code in the same compiled module and several identical pieces of code in different modules.

Templates are convenient for small general-purpose functions, especially inline functions such as `swap`, `abs`, `max`, `min`, and so on. They are also useful for generalized implementations of common algorithms. For example, templated implementations of binary search, sort, or merge may apply to any objects for which the operators `==`, `<=`, etc. are defined. Data structures such as list, stack, queue can be implemented as templated classes usable with elements of any data type.

Like all tricky C++ features, though, templates have some pitfalls. Some programmers may get carried away with the idea of the universal applicability and eternal life of their programs and clutter their code with templates that make it unreadable. In the end, each template (and perhaps even the whole program...) may be used only once.

⌘   ⌘   ⌘

A more technical difficulty is making sure that a templated function or class works properly with all the specific types for which it is intended. The requirements for these types have to be documented.

Suppose we wrote a templated function Sum(...) that returns the sum of the elements of a vector:

```
template <class SOMETYPE>
SOMETYPE Sum(const apvector<SOMETYPE> &v)

{
    SOMETYPE total = 0;
    int i, n = v.length();

    for (i = 0;   i < n;   i++)
        total += v[i];

    return total;
}
```

This function will work properly when used with apvector<int> or apvector<double>.   But what happens if we decide to try it for apvector<apstring>?   After all, the apstring class has the += operator, which appends a string to the left-hand side. So we could expect that the Sum(...) function returns all the elements of v concatenated together in one string. That would make sense, but unfortunately it doesn't work! The problem arises from the innocuous declaration

```
    SOMETYPE total = 0;
```

This is the same as

```
    SOMETYPE total(0);
```

and it assumes that SOMETYPE has a constructor with one integer argument. But the apstring class does not have such a constructor; the linker will report an error that the function apstring::apstring(int) is undefined. We could add the following constructor to the apstring class:

```
// Constructors:
...
apstring(int len) // builds a string of length len,
                  //   filled with spaces
```

Then, if SOMETYPE is apstring,

```
SOMETYPE total = 0;
```

would declare an empty string, and Sum (...) would work properly.

16.5.   *Lab:* Adding Functions to the apvector Class

1. Add the member functions max(), min(), and sum() to the apvector class. These functions should return the largest element, the smallest element, and the sum of all elements, respectively. The new functions should work for all numeric types of vector elements. Test the new class on vectors of ints and doubles.

2. Recall the modified version of the apstring class that you created in Lab 15.6. That version has the additional constructor:

   ```
   apstring(int len, char fill = ' ');
   ```

   Test your max(), min(), and sum() functions on apvector<apstring> with the modified apvector and apstring classes.

16.6.   Summary

Templates are a convenient tool for getting around the strong type checking in C++. Many small functions, as well as general-purpose algorithms and data structures, can be implemented as templates. Templates are also a useful tool for demonstrating these data structures and algorithms in a type-independent manner.

The templates reduce the source code's size and improve its maintainability and reusability by eliminating repetitive overloaded definitions. However, the templates do not reduce the size of the executable code. On the contrary, they are deceptive in making it very easy to produce multiple pieces of very similar compiled code in the same module or identical code fragments in different compiled modules.

The syntax for templates is cumbersome and hard to remember without some "cookbook" examples. Overuse of templates may render your code unreadable and may offset all the benefits of easier maintenance by making it impossible to understand your program in the first place.

When you write code with templates, you should understand and document what kinds of objects the template is intended for and make sure these objects can interpret all the operators applied to them in the template's code.

17

Linked Lists

17.1.   Data Structures and Abstract Data Types

This chapter opens our discussion of a series of data structures that constitute a standard set of tools in software design and development. These include lists, stacks, queues, trees, and other structures.

A data structure combines a method for data organization with methods of accessing and manipulating the data.

For example, an array becomes a data structure for storing a set of elements when we provide functions to insert and remove an element. Similar functionality can be achieved with a ***linked list*** structure, which we will explain shortly. At a very abstract level, we can think of a general "list" object: a list contains a number of elements; we can insert elements into the list and remove elements from the list.

An abstract description of a data structure, with the emphasis on its properties, functionality, and use rather than a specific implementation, is referred to as an ***Abstract Data Type*** (***ADT***). An ADT defines an ***interface*** (set of access methods) to an abstract data organization without specifying the details of implementation.

A "List" ADT, for example, may be specified as follows:

```
"List" ADT:

Data organization:

    Contains a number of data elements arranged in
    a linear sequence.

Functions:

    Create an empty List;
    Insert an element into List;
    Remove an element from List;
    Traverse List (process or print out all elements
      in sequence, visiting each element once);
    Destroy List.
```

The "List" ADT can be further specialized. We can require, for example, that an element always be inserted at the "tail" of the list and removed from the "head" of the list. Such an ADT can be called a "Queue"; it describes the "first-in-first-out" (FIFO) data access method. Or we can require that the elements in the list be arranged in ascending alphanumeric order and stipulate that the insert function put the new element into the right place in the order. This can be called the "Ordered List" ADT.

The data structures and ADTs that we are going to study are not specific to C++ — they can be implemented in any programming language.

We have already seen (Part 1, Section 8.3 and Lab 8.4) that the "List" ADT can be implemented as an <u>array</u>. In the following sections we will show how to implement the "List" ADT as a *linked list* and discuss the advantages and disadvantages of each implementation.

The preferred C++ implementation of an ADT is a class.

But in this chapter we will implement linked lists in the old-fashioned way: as structures and functions that work with them. This will allow us to avoid some minor technical difficulties that we are not quite ready to handle.

17.2.   Linked List Data Structure

The elements of an array are stored in consecutive locations in computer memory. We can calculate the address of each element from its sequential number in the list. By contrast, the elements of a linked list may be scattered in various locations in memory, but each element contains <u>a pointer</u> to the next element in the list. The last element's pointer is set to null.

Metaphorically, we can compare an array to a book: we can read its pages sequentially or we can open it to any page. A linked list is like a magazine article: at the end of the first installment it says "continued on page 27." We read the second installment on page 27, and at the end it says "continued on page 36", and so on, until we finally reach the ♦ symbol that marks the end of the article.

We will refer to the elements of a linked list as "nodes." A node contains some information useful for a specific application and a pointer to the next node.

Let us say the information is represented by a data type SOMETYPE, which can be a built-in type, a string, or a structure. Let us call the pointer to the next node "next". We can combine these elements in a structure NODE:

```
struct NODE {
    SOMETYPE data;
    NODE *next;
};
```

Note two things about this definition. First, "next" is a name chosen by the programmer: it is not required by C++ syntax. We could have called it "link" or "nextptr" or "polliwog." The name of the structure, "NODE", is also chosen by the programmer.

Second, the definition is self-referential: it refers to the NODE* data type inside the NODE data type definition! C++ allows this as long as the member is a <u>pointer</u> to NODE. The definition would not make much sense if one of the members of NODE were a NODE. A pointer, on the other hand, takes a fixed amount of space; the compiler can calculate the size of the NODE structure without paying much attention to what type of pointer next is. The compiler uses the fact that next has the data type NODE* (as opposed to any other pointer type) only for type checking later in the code.

As an example, let us consider a list of departing flights on an airport display. The flight information may be represented in a FLIGHT structure:

```
struct FLIGHT {
    int  number;           // Flight number
    apstring destination;  // Destination city
    ...
};
```

Suppose a program has to maintain a list of flights departing in the next few hours, and we have decided to implement it as a linked list. A node of the list can be represented as:

```
struct NODE {
    FLIGHT flight;
    NODE *next;
};
```

⌘   ⌘   ⌘

When a program creates a linked list, it usually starts with an empty list. A new node is dynamically allocated from the free store using the new operator, and the desired information is copied into it. A newly created node is linked to the list by rearranging the pointers. Thus, a linked list does not have to have a predetermined size. Its maximum size is potentially limited only by the size of the free store, which may depend on the total computer memory. Since each node of the list is allocated with the new operator, the nodes have to be destroyed with the delete operator <u>one by one</u> when the list is no longer needed.

When we discuss the code involved in handling linked lists, it is sometimes convenient to use diagrams that represent the nodes and links (pointers). In Figure 17-1, the boxes represent nodes and the arrows represent the values of pointers. The pointer in the last node is null.

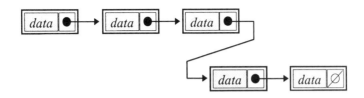

Figure 17-1. A linked list diagram.

17.3. Linked List Traversal

Let us give the name "head" to the variable that holds a pointer to the first node of the list:

```
NODE *head;
```

head is set to null when the list is empty:

```
NODE *head = 0;   // Declare an empty list.
```

After we build up our list, head points to the first node. Note that in this implementation head is <u>not a node</u>, just a pointer to the first node of the list. head->next points to the second node, and so on, with the pointer to each next successive node contained in the previous one's next element. If nodePtr is a variable of the NODE* data type and nodePtr points to a node in our list, then the value of nodePtr->next is the pointer to the next node (or nodePtr->next is null, if there is no next node). We can construct a for loop that goes through all the elements of the list in sequence as follows:

```
NODE *nodePtr;
for (nodePtr = head;   nodePtr;   nodePtr = nodePtr->next) {
    ...  // Process the list element pointed to by "nodePtr".
}
```

In this loop we first set nodePtr equal to head so that it points to the first element of the list. If the list is empty (i.e., head == 0), nothing else happens. Otherwise, we process the element pointed to by nodePtr. At the end of each iteration the value of nodePtr is updated so that it points to the next element of the list. The iterations proceed until nodePtr becomes null, indicating that we have processed the last element of the list.

A procedure that accesses and processes all elements of a data structure in sequence is called **traversal**. The above for loop is a simple and convenient way to traverse a linked list.

Due to the nature of linked lists, information stored in nodes is always accessed through a pointer to a node.

For example, if a list is defined as:

```
struct FLIGHT {
    int   number;          // Flight number
    apstring destination;  // Destination city
    ...
};

struct NODE {
    FLIGHT flight;
    NODE *next;
};
```

and nodePtr points to a node in the list, then the information in the node can be accessed as:

```
nodePtr->flight;
```

The individual elements of the FLIGHT structure can be accessed as:

```
nodePtr->flight.number;
nodePtr->flight.destination;
...
```

A function for traversing and displaying a list of departing flights may look as follows:

```
void DisplayList(NODE *head)

{
    NODE *node;

    for (node = head;   node;   node = node->next) {
        cout << node->flight.number <<   "   "
             << node->flight.destination << "   "
             ...
             << endl;
    }
}
```

(Since we always deal with pointers when we handle linked lists, we consider it too cumbersome to name a local variable `nodePtr`; we prefer simply `node`, as in the above example.)

When we are working with an array, we can access its elements sequentially <u>or</u> we can go directly to a particular element. For instance, if array `a` has 12 elements (`a[0]`,..., `a[11]`), and we want to access, say, the seventh element, we can go directly to `a[6]`. This property is called *random access*. A linked list is an inherently *sequential-access* structure: to get to a certain element we always have to start from the first node of the list and traverse the list until we get to the node we are looking for.

⌘   ⌘   ⌘

As we have seen, the `NODE  *head` variable plays a dual role: by pointing to the first node of the linked list, it also points to the whole list (Figure 17-2). We could introduce a special data type which would represent a linked list as a whole:

```
struct LIST {
    NODE *head;
};
```

But at the moment this seems redundant. When we need to pass a linked list to a function, we can simply pass the `head` pointer as we have done in the `DisplayList(...)` function above.

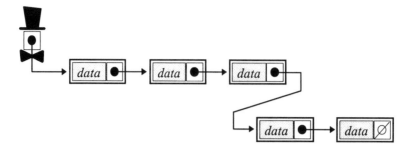

Figure 17-2. A linked list is defined by the head pointer.

17.4.   The Insert Function

Let us consider a list that contains character strings such as names of cities:

```
struct NODE {
    apstring city;
    NODE *next;
};
```

Suppose we want to add information to a linked list. We can define an Insert(...) function that inserts an element at the "head" (beginning) of the list. The function takes two arguments: a list (really a pointer to the first node of a list) and the information for the new node — in our case, a name of a city. We can make the function return a STATUS value, OK or FAILED:

```
enum STATUS {FAILED, OK};

STATUS Insert(NODE* &head, const apstring &city);
```

The Insert(...) function adds the node at the head of the list, and the added node becomes the new head. Therefore, the head of the list <u>changes</u> and has to be passed to the Insert(...) function <u>by reference</u>. This is expressed in the following syntax:

```
    ...   NODE* &head   ...
```
or
```
    ...   NODE *&head   ...
```

— "a reference to a pointer to a NODE..."

The first two steps are to allocate a new node and to copy the information into it. The final step is to "link" the node to the list:

```
                                                        LIST.CPP    💾
...
#include "apstring.h"
...


//************************************************************

STATUS Insert (NODE* &head, const apstring &city)

// Inserts "city" at the head of the linked list.
// Returns OK if successful, FAILED if could not
//    allocate a new node.

{
    NODE *newnode;

    // 1. Allocate a new node:

    newnode = new NODE;
    if (!newnode)
        return FAILED;        // Out of memory.

    // 2. Copy the information into the new node:

    newnode->city = city;

    // 3. Link the new node to the list:

    newnode->next = head;     // Append the old list to newnode.
    head = newnode;           // Change the head to newnode.

    return OK;
}
```

The "linking" action is illustrated in Figure 17-3.

When we implement linked list functions, we have to pay special attention to singular situations, such as when the list is empty or when we insert or remove a node at the head or tail of the list. Luckily, in this case we did not have to do anything special — the code works for an empty list as well. If head is null, newnode->next is appropriately set to null.

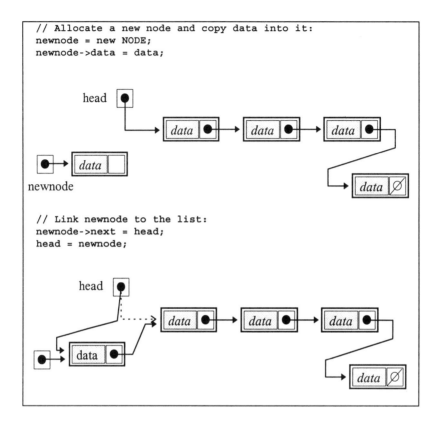

Figure 17-3. Inserting a new node at the head of a linked list.

⌘ ⌘ ⌘

Now let us implement the `InsertInOrder(...)` function. This function assumes that the list is arranged in alphabetical order and inserts a new element so that the order is preserved. The first two steps are the same — allocate a node and copy the information into it. But the linking step is slightly more complicated because we have to find the right place in the list to insert the new node. We have to keep track of two nodes so that we can insert the new node between them. Let's call them `node` and `prev` (for "previous"):

LIST.CPP

```
STATUS InsertInOrder (NODE* &head, const apstring &city)

// Inserts "city" in alphabetical order into the linked list.
//    Assumes that the list is arranged in alphabetical order.
//    Duplicate names are allowed.
// Returns OK if successful, FAILED if could not
//    allocate a new node.

{
    NODE *newnode;

    // 1. Allocate a new node:

    newnode = new NODE;
    if (!newnode)
        return FAILED;

    // 2. Copy the information into newnode:

    newnode->city = city;

    // 3. Link newnode to the list:

    //    3.1. Find the right place to insert newnode --
    //            between "prev" and "node":

    NODE *node = head, *prev = 0;

    while (node && node->city <= city) {
        prev = node;                 // ... advance node and prev
        node = node->next;
    }

    //    3.2. Link newnode between "prev" and "node":

    newnode->next = node;        // Append "node" to newnode.
    if (prev)
        prev->next = newnode;    // Insert after "prev".
    else
        head = newnode;          // No prev -- make newnode the
                                 //   new head.

    return OK;
}
```

The searching and "linking" steps are illustrated in Figure 17-4. Note that the function still works when the element has to be inserted at the end of the list: then node is null and newnode->next is set to null. If the element has to be inserted before head, then prev remains set to null and we appropriately change head to newnode. Verify that the above code works for an empty list as well.

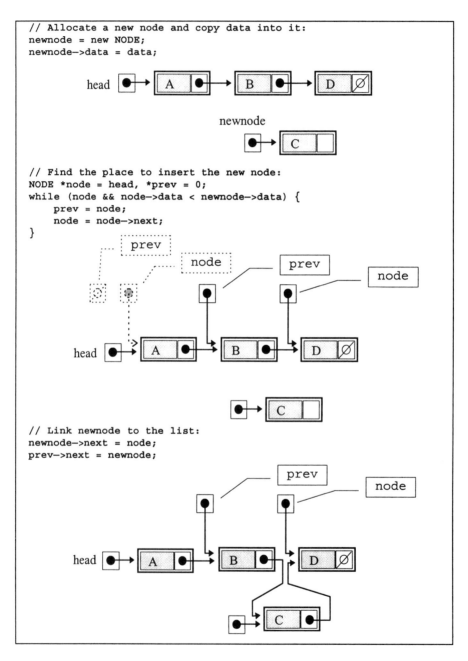

Figure 17-4. Inserting a new node into an ordered linked list.

Note that since there are situations where head changes, we have to pass
it <u>by reference</u> to the function.

17.5.   *Lab:* Creating, Traversing and Destroying a Linked List

Create a file containing a few names of cities in random order. Place each name
on a separate line. Write a program that reads the names from the file and puts
them into a linked list.

It is better to write a separate function that opens and reads the file and builds the
list. For example:

```
STATUS LoadList (NODE* &head, const apstring &fileName);
```

Implement and test three different versions of the LoadList (...) function:

1. LoadList1(...) calls the Insert (...) function within a loop.
2. LoadList2(...) calls the InsertInOrder(...) function within a loop.
3. LoadList3(...) builds the list directly. It keeps track of the tail of the list and
    appends elements at the tail.

In the third version, link each newly created node newnode to the tail as follows:

```
NODE *head = 0, *tail = 0, *newnode;

...
while (...) {  // For each line in the file...
    ...
    // Allocate newnode and copy info into it:
    ...

    newnode->next = 0;

    if (!head)             // If the list is empty...
        head = newnode;
    else
        tail->next = newnode;

    tail = newnode;        // Update tail
}
```

Provide the `DisplayList(...)` function to display your list after it has been created. What can you tell about the order of names in the list for each of the above three `LoadList(...)` functions?

Write a function that destroys a list:

```
void DestroyList(NODE *head);
```

The `DestroyList(...)` function must delete the nodes of the list <u>one by one</u>. You have to be careful not to delete a node before you have saved the pointer to the next node. The following code, for example, is <u>wrong</u>:

```
while (...) {
    // *** Wrong code! ***
    delete head;          // Delete node pointed to by "head".
    head = head->next;    // head->next is undefined, once memory
                          //   pointed to by "head" is released.
}
```

Instead, use a temporary variable to save the `next` pointer.

Call the `DestroyList(...)` function at the end of your program.

Some compilers provide a function that returns the total size of free memory. For example, the Borland C++ compiler for MS DOS has the function `coreleft()`, defined in `alloc.h`:

```
#include <alloc.h>
    ...
    cout << coreleft() << endl; // Display the size of free memory.
```

You can use the above statement to show the size of free memory at the beginning of the program, after creating a linked list, and at the end of the program after the list is destroyed. If the first and the third numbers are the same, your program is behaving itself.

17.6.   The Remove Function

Now let us consider how we can implement a `Remove(...)` function that removes the node with a given value from the list and deallocates its memory:

```
STATUS Remove (NODE* &head, const apstring &city);
```

If the list has several nodes that match the specified value, the version of the function presented here will remove only the first one it finds.

The code works as follows: we go along the list and keep pointers to the previous and the current nodes until we find a match. We then "unlink" the node and connect the previous node directly to the next node. Finally we delete the unlinked node:

LIST.CPP

```
STATUS Remove (NODE* &head, const apstring &city)

// Removes "city" from the list.
// Returns OK if successful, FAILED if not found.

{
    NODE *node, *prev;

    // 1. Find and unlink the node:

    //    1.1. Find the node to remove.  Keep track of
    //          the previous node:

    prev = 0;
    node = head;

    while (node && node->city != city) {
        prev = node;
        node = node->next;
    }

    if (!node)
        return FAILED;     // The target value not found in the list.

    //    1.2. Unlink the node:

    if (prev)
        prev->next = node->next;
    else
        head = node->next;

    // 2. Deallocate the node and release its memory:

    delete node;

    return OK;
}
```

Note that `head` is passed by reference because it may change. The "unlinking" action is illustrated in Figure 17-5.

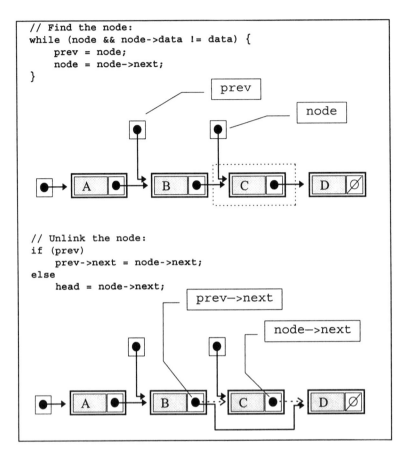

Figure 17-5. Removing a node from a linked list.

17.7. *Lab:* Maintaining a List

Write a menu-driven interactive program that maintains a linked list of names in alphabetical order. The program first loads the list from a file. It provides menu commands to display the list, insert or remove a name, and save the list in a file. The program destroys the list at the end.

You can adapt the menu-handling code from the "Inventory" program (Part 1, Section 8.3). You already have most of the linked list declarations and functions that you will need:

LIST.CPP

```
struct NODE {
    apstring city;
    NODE *next;
};

enum STATUS {FAILED, OK};

// Function prototypes:

STATUS LoadList (NODE* &head, const apstring &fileName);
void DisplayList (NODE *head);
STATUS Insert (NODE* &head, const apstring &city);
STATUS InsertInOrder (NODE* &head, const apstring &city);
STATUS Remove (NODE* &head, const apstring &city);
void DestroyList (NODE *head);
```

Test your program, paying special attention to singular situations such as first and last nodes and empty lists.

For "extra credit":

1. Add the function:

```
STATUS SaveList (NODE *head, const apstring &fileName);
```

2. Note that `InsertInOrder(...)` lets you insert a name which is already on the list. This creates duplicates on the list. Modify the `Remove(...)` function so that it removes (in one pass through the list) all the nodes that contain a matching name.

17.8.   Linked Lists vs. Arrays

In Section 17.1, we talked about the "List" ADT, which represents a collection of elements and functions that insert, remove, and find an element. As we have seen, the "List" ADT can be implemented as either an <u>array</u> or a <u>linked list</u>. Each of these implementations of the "List" ADT has its advantages and limitations, particularly for more specialized ADTs based on the "List" ADT.

The array implementation provides direct access to the *n*-th element of the array. This property, called **random access**, is important in many algorithms. For example, we saw that binary search, a very efficient algorithm for finding a value in a list, applies to a sorted array (an array whose values are arranged in ascending or descending order). Binary search requires access to the element directly in the middle between two elements, which is easy with arrays but inefficient with linked lists. Later, in Chapter 26, we will see how the random access property of arrays is used in calculating distributions of values, in *look-up tables*, and in *hash tables*. An array also provides *sequential access* to its elements — we can traverse an array both from beginning to end and backwards.

Arrays have two drawbacks, however. First, it is not easy to insert or remove an element at the beginning or in the middle of an array — a lot of bytes may need to be moved if the array is large. Second, we do not always know in advance the exact number of elements an array needs to store. We have to declare an array that will hold the maximum possible number of elements, and resize it later.

Linked lists get around both of these problems. First, an element can be easily inserted or removed from a linked list simply by rearranging the pointers. This is a crucial property if we have a frequently updated list containing large structures or records. Second, the nodes of a linked list are dynamically allocated only when new elements are added, so no memory is wasted for vacant nodes. (On the other hand, a linked list takes some extra memory to store pointers to nodes.)

17.9.   Linked Lists with a Tail and Doubly Linked Lists

In some applications we may need to insert elements at the <u>end</u> of the list. In a *queue* data structure, for example, we insert elements at the "tail" of the list and remove elements from the head of the list. In an ordinary linked list, we have to traverse the whole list to find its tail. We can make insertion at the end of the list much more efficient by maintaining an additional pointer to the last node of the list.

A linked list with an additional pointer to its tail is defined by two pointers: head and tail. For an empty list, both pointers are set to null. The Insert(…) and Remove(…) functions must update both head and tail pointers when necessary. For example:

```
STATUS Insert (NODE* &head, NODE* &tail, const apstring &city)

// Inserts city at the "tail" of the list.

{
    ...
    // Link newnode to the tail of the list:
    if (tail)
        tail->next = newnode;
    else                        // ...if list was empty...
        head = newnode;

    tail = newnode;             // Update tail.

    return OK;
}

STATUS Remove (NODE* &head, NODE* &tail, const apstring &city)

// Removes city from the list.

{
    ...
    // Unlink node from list:
    if (prev)                   // As before...
        prev->next = node->next;
    else
        head = node->next;
    if (node == tail)           // Update tail, if removing
        tail = prev;            //   the last node.

    delete node;

    return OK;
}
```

It is better to combine `head` and `tail` in one structure. For example:

```
struct LIST {
    NODE *head;
    NODE *tail;
};
...
LIST list = {0,0};  // Empty list
```

```
...
STATUS Insert (LIST &list, const apstring &city)

// Inserts city at the "tail" of "list".

{
    ...
    // Link newnode to the tail of the list:
    if (list.tail)
        list.tail->next = newnode;
    ...
}
```

⌘ ⌘ ⌘

Another variation on the linked list is the ***doubly linked list***. In a doubly linked list, each node contains a pointer to the previous node as well as a pointer to the next node. The list is defined by two pointers, head and tail (Figure 17-6).

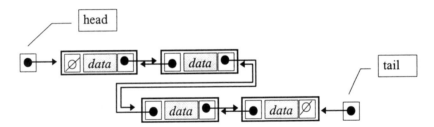

Figure 17-6. A doubly linked list.

A doubly linked list of city names can be defined as follows:

```
struct NODE {
    apstring city;
    NODE *prev;
    NODE *next;
};

struct LIST {
    NODE *head;
    NODE *tail;
};
```

list.head->prev and list.tail->next are always null.

We can traverse a doubly linked list both forward and backward. For example:

```
// Traverse doubly linked list in reverse order:
for (node = list.tail;   node;   node = node->prev) {
    ...
}
```

When you insert or remove a node from a doubly linked list, there is no need to keep track of a pointer to the previous node because this pointer is available from the current node:

```
prev = node->prev;
```

17.10. *Lab:* Doubly Linked List

Rewrite your "Maintaining a List" program from Section 17.7 using a doubly linked list.

Sometimes, when you program doubly linked lists, your code may set all the forward pointers correctly but leave the reverse pointers dangling or set incorrectly. A bug of this type may not immediately manifest itself in the program. Add a new function:

```
void DisplayListReverse(const LIST &list)
```

which will traverse the list backward, and add a corresponding command to the menu. This function will help you test the integrity of the reverse pointers in the list.

For "extra credit":

Write a function that matches a string of characters against a "pattern." A pattern is a string that may contain "wildcard" characters (e.g., '?'). A wildcard character matches any character in the corresponding position. For example, "New York," "New Haven," and "Newark" all match the pattern "New???????????".

Now write a function:

```
void MoveToTop(LIST &list, const apstring &pattern);
```

that will move all the nodes that match a given pattern to the top (beginning) of the list. The function should perform the operation in one traversal of the list and should keep the moved nodes in the same order (so that if "New Haven" was above "New York" and both were moved to the top of the list, "New Haven" would remain above.) Add a corresponding menu command and devise a comprehensive test for your function, including situations when there is no match or only one match, when the matching names include the first or the last node of the list, and so on.

17.11. Summary

A data structure is a method of data organization that includes methods of accessing and manipulating the data. An abstract description of a data structure with the emphasis on its properties, functionality, and use rather than on a specific implementation is called an Abstract Data Type (ADT). An ADT defines an interface (set of access methods) to an abstract data organization without specifying the details of its implementation.

A "List" ADT, for example, may be specified as a collection of elements and functions to create an empty list, insert and remove elements, and destroy the list. The "List" ADT may serve as a basis for more specialized ADTs such as the "Ordered List" ADT, the "Queue" ADT, and so on.

The "List" ADT can be implemented as an array or as a linked list. The array implementation has the random access property (i.e., it provides direct access to the n-th element of the array), which is important in many algorithms (e.g., binary search). But insertion and removal of elements at the beginning or in the middle of an array may be inefficient.

In a linked list, each node contains some information and a pointer to the next node. We access the list through a pointer to its first node. The last node's pointer is set to null. A new node can be inserted or removed easily by rearranging the pointers. The nodes of a linked list are dynamically allocated only when new elements are added, so no memory is wasted for vacant nodes. A linked list does not provide random access to its elements.

A procedure which accesses and processes all the elements of a data structure in sequence is called a traversal. The following `for` loop is a convenient expression for traversing a linked list:

```
NODE *node;
...
for (node = head;   node;   node = node->next) {
    ... // Process the list element pointed to by "node"
}
```

When a linked list is created in a program, we usually start with an empty list designated by a null pointer:

```
NODE *head = 0;
```

A variation of a linked list structure — the linked list with an additional pointer to the last node (tail) of the list — is convenient for implementing lists where elements are added at the tail of the list, as in the "Queue" ADT. In another variation, the doubly linked list, each node contains two pointers — one to the next node and one to the previous node. We can traverse a doubly linked list in both directions, forward and backward.

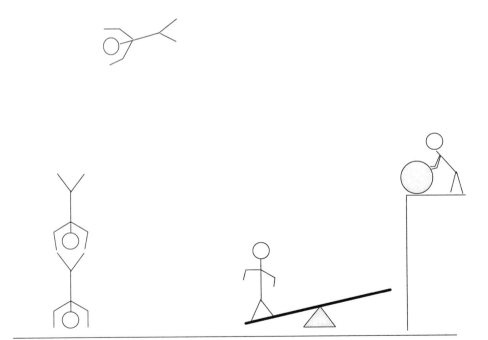

18

Stacks

18.1. Discussion

The *stack* is a data structure used for storing and retrieving data elements. The stack provides temporary storage in such a way that the element stored last will be retrieved first. This method is sometimes called LIFO — Last-In-First-Out (as opposed to the FIFO, or First-In-First-Out, method of a *queue*). In terms of abstract data types, the "Stack" ADT may be viewed as a specialization of the "List" ADT that implements the LIFO access method.

A stack usually holds elements of the same size, such as integers, doubles, or some records. The elements are said to be *on* the stack. The stack is controlled by two operations which are referred to as *push* and *pop*. Push adds an element to the top of the stack and pop removes the element from the top of the stack. These two operations implement the LIFO method.

A stack can be set up in different ways. One possible implementation uses an array and an integer index, called the *stack pointer*, which marks the current top of the stack. The stack usually grows toward the end of the array; the stack pointer is incremented when a new element is pushed onto the stack and decremented when an element is popped from the stack. In some implementations the stack pointer points to the top element of the stack, but many C++ programmers find it more convenient to point to the <u>next available vacant slot</u> on the stack. Figure 18-1 illustrates the latter implementation.

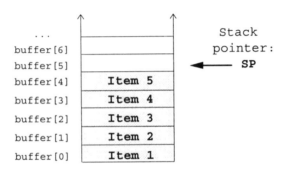

Figure 18-1. Stack Pointer points to the next vacant slot on the stack.

Another possible stack implementation uses a singly-linked list with elements added and removed at the head of the list. This implementation is more appropriate when the data elements are large records and the maximum size of the stack cannot be determined in advance. In this implementation, storage for the elements pushed onto the stack is dynamically allocated using the `new` operator and released with the `delete` operator after an element is popped from the stack and its copy returned to the calling function.

> **The stack mechanism is useful for temporary storage, especially for dealing with nested structures or processes: expressions within expressions, functions calling other functions, directories within directories, etc. The stack mechanism helps your program to untangle the nested structure and trace all its substructures in the correct order.**

The C++ compiler itself provides an example of effective stack use when it processes `#include` statements. The compiler must read all lines of code in the correct order, so when it encounters an `#include` line, it has to save the current location in the current file and branch off to process the included file. But the included file itself may have another `#include`, and we need to save that location, too, and branch off again. If we save it in the same place, the first location will be overwritten. That's where a stack becomes indispensable. Each time we encounter another `#include`, we push the current file location on the stack and branch off to process the included file. When we are done with the file, we pop the saved location from the stack and resume processing. The process allows us to handle `#include` statements nested to any depth, limited only by the stack's size. The procedure terminates when we have finished reading the current file and the stack is empty. The empty stack indicates that we are back at the top level of the initial file.

18.2. Array Implementation of Stack

In this section we will implement a stack using the array method. Let us write a simplified class that implements a stack of integers; a more general templated class that works with all data types, `apstack`, is discussed in the next section.

We begin by defining the class in the header file STACK.H:

STACK.H

```
// STACK.H
//
// Stack of integers implemented as an array.
//

#ifndef _STACK_H_
#define _STACK_H_

class STACK {

  private:

    int mSize;
    int mSp;
    int *mBuffer;

  public:

    STACK(int size = 100); // Constructor; default size is 100 elements
    ~STACK();
    void push(int item);
    void pop(int &item);
    bool isEmpty();
};

#endif    // _STACK_H_
```

The `mSize` element contains the maximum stack size, and `mSp` is the stack pointer. Note that `mBuffer` is not an array but just a pointer to an integer array. The actual array of the specified size is allocated in the constructor and released in the destructor. This is similar to the implementation of the `apvector` class.

The stack class member functions are coded in STACK.CPP:

STACK.CPP

```
// STACK.CPP
//
// Stack of integers implemented as an array.
//

#include "stack.h"
```

Continued

```
STACK::STACK(int size)

// Constructor: creates a stack of the specified size.
// (If fails, the size is set to 0.)

{
    mBuffer = new int[size];
    if (!mBuffer)
        mSize = 0;
    else
        mSize = size;
    mSp = 0;
}

//*************************************************************

void STACK::push(int item)

{
    if (mSp < mSize) {
        mBuffer[mSp] = item;   // Or, simply:
        mSp++;                 //    mBuffer[mSp++] = item;
    }
}

//*************************************************************

void STACK::pop(int &item)

{
    if (mSp > 0) {
        mSp--;                 // Or, simply:
        item = mBuffer[mSp];   //    item = mBuffer[--mSp];
    }
}

//*************************************************************

bool STACK::isEmpty()

{
    return mSp == 0;
}

//*************************************************************

STACK::~STACK()

// Destructor: frees buffer.

{
    delete [] mBuffer;
}
```

Normally the code for a general-purpose stack class would report errors such as trying to pop an item from an empty stack or push an item on a full stack. For instance, instead of `void push(…)` and `pop(…)` we could make them return a Boolean value that would indicate success or failure. We have decided not to do this because `push` and `pop` functions are `void` in the `apstack` class discussed in the following section.

18.3. The `apstack` Class

The `apstack` class is a templated class provided by the AP C++ Development Committee. It is patterned after the stack class from the STL (Standard Template Library).

The class implements the stack as an array in a manner very similar to the example from the previous section. But the `apstack` class can handle stack elements of any data type, not just integers. A stack of doubles, for example, can be declared as:

```
apstack<double> stack;
```

The `apstack` class automatically handles the size of the stack. There is no way to specify the desired size in the declaration. The constructor first allocates a small buffer for the stack elements; later the `push(…)` function may allocate a bigger buffer if the stack runs out of space. The most commonly used member functions are:

```
void push(const itemType &item);
void pop(itemType &item);
bool isEmpty();
```

The class has other member functions:

```
const itemType &top() const;
    // Returns the top element without removing it from the stack

void pop();
    // Overloaded version of pop(…) that removes the top element
    //    from the stack and discards it

int length() const;
    // Returns the number of elements on stack.

void makeEmpty();
    // Empties the stack
```

18.4. *Case Study and Lab:* **Music**

Tunes and songs often have repeating fragments. In a computer representation of a musical score it would be convenient to incorporate commands to replay specified fragments. In this section we will write a program that "plays" a tune with "repeat" commands. The repeating fragments may be nested to any depth, so that a fragment that is being replayed may contain another "repeat" command. Naturally, our program will use a stack to properly untangle the hierarchy of repeating fragments.

Since different hardware platforms may have different capabilities and software support for making sound, playing the actual music is left to those readers who want to learn how that is done on their particular system. Here, instead of representing a musical score and playing music, we will simply display the lyrics of songs. Consider a text file which, in addition to lines of text, may have "repeat" commands. A repeat command is a line in the file that has the following format:

```
#repeat fromLine toLine
```

where *fromLine* and *toLine* are two integers that represent the line numbers for the beginning and the ending line of the fragment to be repeated. For instance, the Beatles' *Hello, Goodbye* may be written as follows:

	SONG.TXT	

You say yes	//	1
I say no	//	2
You say stop	//	3
And I say go go go	//	4
	//	5
CHORUS:	//	6
Oh no	//	7
You say Goodbye	//	8
And I say hello	//	9
Hello hello	//	10
I don't know why	//	11
You say Goodbye	//	12
I say hello	//	13
#repeat 10 13	//	14
Why	//	15
#repeat 12 14	//	16
	//	17

Continued ☞

```
I say high              // 18
You say low             // 19
You say why             // 20
And I say I don't know  // 21
#repeat 5 16            // 22
```

We start numbering lines from 1 (not 0) and assume that all the line numbers in the script are correct and that there are no circular references that would put the program into an infinite loop. The program, with a few gaps, can be found in MUSIC.CPP. The program reads the lines of text from the specified file into an array of strings. It first calls the ShowTextSimple (...) function that displays the text as is, without processing #repeat commands. After that, it calls the ShowText (...) function that displays the text with all #repeat commands correctly processed.

MUSIC.CPP

```
// MUSIC.CPP
//
// This program displays the lyrics of a song written in a file
// with embedded #repeat commands.
//
// Author: J. Lennon and P. McCartney
//

#include <iostream.h>
#include <fstream.h>
#include <strstrea.h>
#include "apstring.h"
#include "apvector.h"
#include "apstack.h"

void ShowTextSimple (const apvector<apstring> &text,
                                     int fromLine, int toLine);
void Parse (const apstring &line, int &fromLine, int &toLine);
void ShowText (const apvector<apstring> &text, int fromLine, int toLine);

//*************************************************************

int main()

{
    const int MAXLINES = 1000;
    apvector<apstring> text(MAXLINES);
    apstring fileName;
    int nLines = 0;
```

Continued ✍

```
    // Prompt the user for a file name and open the file.
    // If no extension given, append the default extension ".txt":
    cout << "Text file name: ";
    cin >> fileName;
    if (fileName.find('.') == npos)
        fileName += ".txt";

    ifstream textFile(fileName.c_str());
    if (!textFile) {
        cout << "Cannot open " << fileName << ".\n";
        return 1;
    }

    // Read the lines from the file into an array of strings:
    while (nLines < MAXLINES && getline(textFile, text[nLines]))
        nLines++;

    // Show the text "as is":
    ShowTextSimple(text, 1, nLines);

    cout << "\n***********************************\n\n";

    // Show the text with correctly processed #repeat commands:
    ShowText(text, 1, nLines);

    return 0;
}

//****************************************************************

void ShowTextSimple (const apvector<apstring> &text,
                                        int fromLine, int toLine)

// Displays lines of text from fromLine to toLine.
// Lines are numbered starting from 1.

{
    while (fromLine <= toLine) {
        cout << text[fromLine-1] << endl;
        fromLine++;
    }
}

//****************************************************************
```

Continued ☞

```
void ShowText (const apvector<apstring> &text, int fromLine, int toLine)

// Displays lines of text from fromLine to toLine.
// Handles #repeat directives embedded in the text:
// #repeat fromNum toNum
//   (the first character in the line must be #; fromNum and toNum
//    are integers).
// Lines are numbered starting from 1.

{
    apstack<int> stack;
    apstring line;

    while (fromLine <= toLine || !stack.isEmpty()) {
        if (fromLine <= toLine) {
            line = text[fromLine-1];
            if (line.length() == 0 || line[0] != '#') {
                // Regular line
                cout << line << endl;
                fromLine++;
            }
            else {
                // #repeat line
                ...
                ...
                Parse(line, fromLine, toLine);
            }
        }
        else { // if (!stack.isEmpty())
            ...
            ...
        }
    }
}

//*****************************************************************

void Parse (const apstring &line, int &fromLine, int &toLine)

// Parses a repeat directive
// #repeat fromNum toNum
// extracts fromNnum and toNum and places them into fromLine, toLine.

{
    apstring discard;
    istrstream is( static_cast<char *>(line.c_str()) );
            // Creates an input stream associated with the string.
            // istrstream constructor takes one argument of the char* type.
            // c_str() converts apstring into const char*
            // static_cast converts const char* into char*

        is >> discard >> fromLine >> toLine;
}
```

The ShowText(...) function must handle two situations: a regular line and a #repeat line. In the first case it simply displays the line. In the second case, it saves the current values of the fromLine and toLine variables on stack, gets new values from the #repeat line, and continues processing. When done, the function pops the saved values from the stack and continues. When the current fragment is finished and the stack is empty, the function is done.

The Parse(...) function helps to extract the line numbers from a #repeat line. It uses the feature of I/O streams that allows you to associate an input stream with a null-terminated character string (see Chapter 12). This lets the program read individual items from the string the same way it reads from cin.

⌘   ⌘   ⌘

As a lab exercise, fill in the blanks in the ShowText(...) function. Don't forget that a stack is a LIFO structure, so the saved values must be popped in reverse order. Test your program using your own test files or the provided file SONG.TXT.

For "extra credit":

Find out how to play musical notes on your computer. Design a format for storing a tune in a file and modify the program to play a tune from a specified file.

18.5.   The Hardware Stack

What happens when a function is called? When function Caller calls function Task, how does Task know where to return control after it has finished? Obviously Caller has to pass along some return address so that Task can send the CPU to that address when it is through. Let us consider several possible locations where that return address can be stored.

The first guess is that it could go to some specially reserved memory location. This could work if Task did not call any other functions. If, however, Task called another function, SubTask, then its return address would go into the same memory location and overwrite the first return address. In a more elaborate scheme, the return address could go into some special memory area attached to the function code, for instance just before the beginning of the function code. This would solve the problem of functions calling other functions, because every function has its own storage for the return address. This is, in fact, how some early models of computers worked. A problem arises, however, if Task is allowed to call itself, or when there are circular calls: Task calls SubTask,

SubTask calls AnotherSubtask, AnotherSubtask calls Task. Task gets confused about whether to return control to AnotherSubtask or to Caller.

(The notion of a function calling itself may at first seem absurd. But, as we will explain later, such *recursive* calls are extremely useful for dealing with nested structures or branching processes, where substructures or branches are similar to the whole. Recursive functions can greatly simplify algorithms.)

Practically the only solution remaining is a stack. When Caller calls Task, it first pushes the return address on the stack. When Task has finished, it pops the return address from the stack and passes control back to it. Task can use the stack for its own purposes and for calling other functions: the only requirement is that it restore the stack pointer to its initial value before returning.

This way, functions can call each other without any conflict. In particular, a function can call itself or functions can call each other in a circular manner. In addition to the return address, though, we have to be careful with the arguments and local variables. If a function in the middle of its course calls itself, what becomes of its local variables? Again, the stack offers the solution. The function arguments and local variables can all reside on the stack. The stack pointer is adjusted to reserve some space for them when the function is called, and the stack pointer is restored when the function has finished its processing. That way we can use only one copy of the function code but multiple copies of the function return address, arguments, and local variables for every currently active copy of the function. The area of the stack that holds all the information for a particular function call is called a *frame*. Figure 18-2 illustrates the frames created on the stack after several function calls.

In modern computers the stack method is supported in hardware. The hardware stack does not require any special memory. It is implemented simply as a stack pointer *register* which can point to a desired memory location and can be modified either directly or by the push and pop CPU instructions. The CPU call instruction automatically pushes the address of the next instruction on the stack before passing control to a subroutine. The CPU ret (return) instruction automatically pops the return address from the stack and passes control back to that address.

When function Caller calls function Task, Caller first pushes the arguments that it wants to pass to Task on the stack, then passes control to Task. Task allocates some space on the stack for its own local variables. When Task has finished its job, it wipes out its local variables from the stack. Either the caller or the called function, depending on the convention, performs the final clean-up by removing the arguments from the stack.

When arguments are passed by value, the value of the argument is pushed on stack. That is why it's not a good idea to pass large structures by value. When an argument is passed by reference, only its address is pushed on stack.

⌘　⌘　⌘

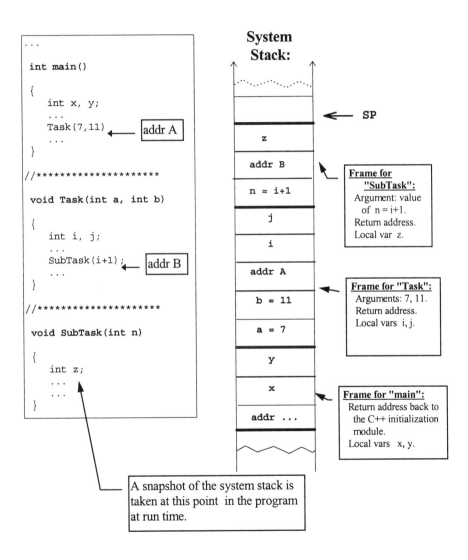

Figure 18-2. Frames on the system stack after a few function calls.

The hardware stack is also used for saving the system state when it is interrupted by an external event. Pressing any key on the keyboard, for example, generates a *hardware interrupt,* a situation that needs the CPU's immediate attention. When this happens, the address of the current CPU instruction is pushed on stack and control is passed to the special interrupt handling routine. This routine pushes all CPU registers on stack to save the current state. Then it receives and processes the pressed key and places its code into the keyboard buffer for later use by the running application. After that the keyboard routine pops all the registers from the stack (in reverse order) and returns control to the interrupted program. The stack helps to handle nested interrupts (when one interrupt comes in the middle of processing another interrupt) properly. (People often use a similar method when their tasks or conversations are interrupted.)

18.6. Summary

The stack is a data structure used for storing and retrieving data elements. A stack usually holds elements of the same size, such as integers, doubles, or some records. The elements are said to be "on the stack." The stack is controlled by two operations referred to as push and pop. Push adds an element to the top of the stack and pop removes the element from the top of the stack. These two operations implement the LIFO (Last-In-First-Out) data access method.

One possible implementation of a stack uses an array and an integer index, called the stack pointer, which marks the current top of the stack. The stack usually grows toward the end of the array; the stack pointer is incremented when a new element is pushed onto the stack and decremented when an element is popped from the stack.

The stack mechanism is useful for temporary storage, especially for dealing with nested structures or processes: it allows your program to untangle the nested structure and trace all its substructures in the correct order.

The templated `apstack` class implements a stack for elements of any data type. The most commonly used member functions are `push(...)`, `pop(...)` and `isEmpty()`:

```
apstack<int> stack;
int item;

stack.push(item);
stack.pop(item);
while (!stack.isEmpty())...
```

19

Recursion

19.1. Discussion

According to one of Euclid's axioms, "The whole is greater than the part." This may be true for the lengths of segments and the volumes of solids in geometry, but in the intangible world of computer software the whole is sometimes the same as the part, at least in terms of its structural description and use. Which is "greater," for example, a directory or a subdirectory in a tree-structured computer file system? A particular directory is "greater" than its subdirectories, because overall it contains more files (counting the files in all its subdirectories), than any subdirectory. But a directory is "the same" as its subdirectories, because any subdirectory is a directory. It holds its own files and its own subdirectories, and its structure and use are the same.

In another example, a C++ source file may have other C++ source files included in it by means of #include statements. The overall number of lines in the file and all included files together is larger than in any included file. But the structure of any included file is the same, because it is itself a source file, and it may have its own #include statements.

The above instances are examples of *recursive* structures whose substructures have the same form as the whole. Such structures are best handled by *recursive procedures*, which operate the same way on a substructure as on the whole structure. In computer software, recursive procedures and processes can be conveniently implemented by means of *recursive functions* whose code includes calls to themselves. We saw in Section 18.5 that in a modern computer system the same mechanism implements a function call whether the function calls itself or another function. All function arguments, the return address, and the local variables are kept in a separate frame on the system stack, so that several functions, including several copies of the same function, can be waiting for the control to be returned to them without any conflict. Multiple copies of the same function all share the same code (set of CPU instructions) but operate on different data.

It is no coincidence, then, that recursive structures and processes are especially common in the computer world. It is easier to implement and use a structure or a process when its substructures and subprocesses have the same form. The same function, for example, can deal with a directory and subdirectories, a file and included files.

Recursion is not specific to C++: it works the same way with any language that allows functions to call themselves.

19.2.   Examples of Recursive Functions

Let us consider two sketches of recursive functions based on the above discussion. (We will ignore minor implementation details.)

In the first example, the function `TotalDirectorySize(...)` calculates the sum of the sizes of all files in a directory and all its subdirectories (Figure 19-1). The directory can be represented in memory as some structure `DIR`, for instance a linked list of items with their attributes. Each item can be either a file or a subdirectory.

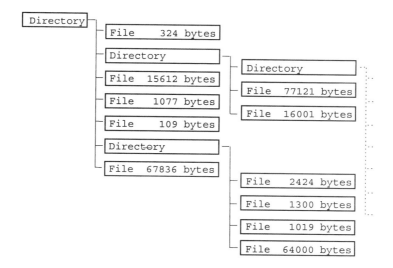

Figure 19-1. A tree-structured directory of files.

```
long TotalDirectorySize(const apstring &directoryName)

{
    long  sum = 0;

    <... Open and load directory (directoryName)>;

    for (... <all items in the directory>) {
        if (... <current item is a file>)
            sum += ... < size of this file>;
        else if (... <current item is a subdirectory>) {
            //  *** Recursive call to TotalDirectorySize ***
            sum += TotalDirectorySize(... <subdirectory name>);
        }
    }

    <... Close directory and remove from memory>

    return sum;
}
```

The `TotalDirectorySize(...)` function keeps calling itself until it reaches the bottom level in the directory hierarchy, where a subdirectory does not have any more subdirectories. Since the directories are nested only to some finite depth, the processing will eventually return to the top level and the function will successfully finish its work.

In the second example, the function `FindString(...)` finds and prints out all lines that contain the specified string in a source file and in all `#include`-ed files:

```
#include <iostream.h>
#include <fstream.h>
#include "apstring.h"

extern bool IncludeLine(const apstring &line);
extern void ExtractName(const apstring &line, apstring &name);

void FindString (const apstring &fileName, const apstring &target)

{
    apstring line;
    apstring inclFileName;

    // Open file:

    ifstream inpFile(fileName);
    if (!inpFile)
        return;
```

Continued ☞

```
// For all lines in the file:

while (getline(inpFile, line)) {
    if (!IncludeLine(line)) {        // Not an "#include" line
        if (line.find(target) != npos)
            cout << fileName << ":\n" << line << endl;
    }
    else {                           // "#include" line
        // Extract include file name from line into inclFileName
        ExtractName(line, inclFileName);

        // *** Recursive call to FindString ***
        FindString(inclFileName, target);
    }
}
}
```

This is how `FindString(...)` can be called from the main program:

```
int main()

{
    apstring fileName, str;

    cout << "Filename ==> ";
    cin >> filename;
    cout << "Target string ==> ";
    cin >> str;
    FindString(fileName, str);

    return 0;
}
```

The above examples demonstrate how compact the recursive implementation of a function can be. As discussed in Chapter 18, both `TotalDirectorySize(...)` and `FindString(...)` could be implemented with your own stack instead of recursion. You would have to push the current position in the hierarchy on stack, process all the lower levels, then pop the saved position from the stack and continue. The code would be longer and harder to understand. Recursive calls actually do a similar thing, but they automate the process for you by using the system stack.

⌘ ⌘ ⌘

In the following example we rewrite the `ShowText(...)` function from Section 18.4 with recursion instead of a stack. The `ShowText(...)` function now simply cycles through all the lines: when it finds a regular line it displays it; when it finds a #repeat command, it calls itself recursively:

```
// MUSIC.CPP
...
void ShowText (const apvector<apstring> &text, int fromLine, int toLine)

// Displays lines of text from fromLine to toLine.
// Handles #repeat directives embedded in the text:
// #repeat fromNum toNum
//    (the first character in the line must be #; fromNum and toNum
//     are integers).
// Lines are numbered starting from 1.

{
    apstring line;
    int fromNum, toNum;

    while (fromLine <= toLine) {
        line = text[fromLine-1];
        if (line.length() == 0 || line[0] != '#') {
            // Regular line
            cout << line << endl;
        }
        else {
            // #repeat line
            Parse(line, fromNum, toNum);
            ShowText(text, fromNum, toNum);
        }
        fromLine++;
    }
}
```

With recursion, this function is almost as simple as `ShowTextSimple(...)`!

19.3.   Base Case and Recursive Case

In all of the above examples, recursion helped us deal with some nested structures. In the last program, for example, we processed nested fragments of text. For each line of text there were two possibilities: it could be a regular line (a *base case*) or it could be a repeat command (a *recursive case*). In the base case there is no need to call the function recursively. Since structures can be nested only to some finite depth, the process eventually reaches the lowest level where only base case processing remains. Then no more recursive calls are made.

In some recursive functions, the base case is separated from the recursive case in a more explicit way. Let us consider an example of a recursive function where the process is branching and recursive in nature although there are no nested structures. Suppose we are building a computer word game that tries to make a valid word out of a given set of letters. The program will require a function that generates all permutations of the letters and matches them against a dictionary of words. The set of letters will be represented as a string of length n. Our strategy for generating all permutations is to place each element in turn in the last place in the array, then generate all permutations of the first $(n-1)$ elements. In other words, the Permutations (...) function will be recursive. The function takes two arguments: the string and the number n of characters in the leading fragment that have to be permutated. The base case is when n is equal to 1 — there is nothing to do except to report the permutation.

The function below is quite short and readable; still, it is hard to grasp why it works! We will return to it in Section 19.5, which explains the best way of understanding and debugging recursive functions.

```
inline void Swap (char &a, char &b){char temp = a; a = b; b = temp;}

void Permutations (apstring &str, int n)

{
    if (n <= 1);      // Base case:
                      // The permutation is completed -- report it
            cout << str << endl;          // (e.g., print it out)

    else {            // Recursive case:
        for (int i = 0;    i < n;    i++) {
            Swap (str[i], str[n-1]);
            Permutations(str, n-1);
            Swap (str[n-1], str[i]);
        }
    }
}
```

19.4.   When Not to Use Recursion

Any recursive function can be also implemented through iterations, using a stack if necessary. This poses a question: When is recursion appropriate, and when is it better avoided?

There are some technical considerations that may restrict the use of recursive functions:

1. If a function declares large local arrays, each frame on the system stack will be large, and the stack may overflow after a few recursive calls. A programmer may rather implement her own stack and save only the relevant variables there, leaving out any shared arrays.

2. When a function manipulates static or global variables or arrays, the recursive call may change their values in an unpredictable way unless the manipulation is done on purpose and thoroughly understood.

3. If performance is important, a function implemented without recursion may work faster.

But the most important rule is that recursion should be used only when it significantly simplifies the code without excessive performance loss. Recursion is especially useful for dealing with nested structures or branching processes. One typical example is algorithms for traversing tree structures, which are described in Chapter 22. On the other hand, when you are dealing with linear structures and processes, normally you can use simple iterations. The following test will help you to decide when to use recursion and when iterations. If the function calls itself more than once or if the recursive call is within a loop, it is justified to use recursion. If the function calls itself only once, you can probably do the same thing just as easily with iterations.

As an example, let us consider the `Factorial(n)` function, which calculates the product of all numbers from 1 to n. This function has a simple recursive form:

```
long Factorial (int n)

{
    if (n <= 1) // Base case:
        return 1;
    else         // Recursive case:
        return n * Factorial(n-1);
}
```

Our test shows that Factorial's code has only one recursive call. We are dealing with a linear process. It should be as easy to do the same thing with iterations, thus avoiding the overhead of recursive function calls:

```
long Factorial (int n)

{
    long factorial = n;

    while (n > 1) {
        n--;
        factorial *= n;
    }
    return factorial;
}
```

Both versions are acceptable, because the performance loss in the recursive version is small for small n, and the factorial of large n is far too large, anyway.

A more pernicious example is offered by the famous Fibonacci Numbers. These are defined as a sequence where the first two numbers are equal to one, with each consecutive number equal to the sum of the two preceding numbers:

$$1, 1, 2, 3, 5, 8, 13, ...$$

Mathematically this is a recursive definition:

$$F_1 = 1; \quad F_2 = 1;$$
$$F_n = F_{n-1} + F_{n-2} \quad (\text{for } n > 2).$$

It can be easily converted into a recursive function:

```
long Fibonacci(int n)

{
    if (n <= 2)      // Base case:
        return 1;
    else             // Recursive case:
        return Fibonacci(n-1) + Fibonacci(n-2);
}
```

It may seem, at first, that this function meets our test of having more than one recursive call to `Fibonacci`. But in fact, there is no branching here: `Fibonacci` simply recalls two previous members in the same linear sequence. Don't be misled by the innocent look of this code. The first term, `Fibonacci(n-1)`, will recursively call `Fibonacci(n-2)` and `Fibonacci(n-3)`. The second term, `Fibonacci(n-2)`, will call (again) `Fibonacci(n-3)` and `Fibonacci(n-4)`. The `Fibonacci(...)` calls will start multiplying like rabbits. To calculate the n-th member of the Fibonacci sequence, F_n, `Fibonacci(...)` will actually make more than F_n recursive calls, which, as we will see in the following section, may be quite a large number.

On the other hand, the same function implemented iteratively will need only *n* iterations:

```
long Fibonacci(int n)

{
    long f1 = 1, f2 = 1, next;

    while (n > 2) {
        next = f1 + f2;
        f1 = f2;
        f2 = next;
        n--;
    }
    return f2;
}
```

For our final example of when recursion is not appropriate, let us consider the selection sort algorithm for sorting an array of *n* elements in ascending order. The idea is to find the largest element and swap it with the last element, then apply the same method to the array of the first *n*–1 elements. This can be done recursively:

```
void SelectionSort(apvector<int> &v, int n)

{
    int i, iMax, vTemp;

    if (n == 1)      // Base case: array of length 1 -- nothing to do
        return;

    else {

        // Find the index of the largest element:
        for (iMax = 0, i = 1;   i < n;   i++)
            if (v[iMax] < v[i]) iMax = i;

        // Swap it with the last element:
        vTemp = v[n-1]; v[n-1] = v[iMax]; v[iMax] = vTemp;

        // Call SelectionSort for the first n-1 elements:
        SelectionSort(v, n-1);
    }
}
```

This is a case of so-called ***tail recursion***, where the recursive call is the last statement in the function: only the return from the function is executed after that call. Therefore, by the time of the recursive call, the local variables (except the arguments passed to the call) are no longer needed. Instead of recursion we can just update the argument(s) and send control back to the beginning of the function:

```
void SelectionSort(apvector<int> &v, int n)

{
  start:
    if (n == 1)        // Base case: nothing to do
         return;
    else {
         ...
         ...
         // Do SelectionSort for the first n-1 elements:
         n = n - 1;
         goto start;
    }
}
```

Or, if we get rid of `goto` and replace it with a `while` loop, we come to the same iterative code as we saw in Part 1 (Section 9.2):

```
void SelectionSort(apvector<int> &v, int n)

{
    int i, iMax, vTemp;

    while (n > 1) {

        // Find the index of the largest element:
        for (iMax = 0, i = 1;   i < n;   i++)
            if (v[iMax] < v[i]) iMax = i;

        // Swap it with the last element:
        vTemp = v[n-1]; v[n-1] = v[iMax]; v[iMax] = vTemp;

        n--;
    }
}
```

To quote the inventor of Pascal, Niklaus Wirth,

> In fact, the explanation of the concept of recursive algorithm by such inappropriate examples has been a chief cause of creating widespread apprehension and antipathy toward the use of recursion in programming, and of equating recursion with inefficiency.[*]

---

[*] Niklaus Wirth, Algorithms + Data Structures = Programs, Prentice Hall, 1976.

19.5.   Understanding and Debugging Recursive Functions

A common way of understanding and debugging non-recursive functions is to trace, either mentally or with a debugger, the sequence of statements and function calls in the code. Programmers may also insert some debugging print statements that will report to them the function's progress and the intermediate values of variables.

These conventional methods are very hard to apply to recursive functions, because it is difficult to keep track of your current location in the hierarchy of recursive calls. Getting to the bottom of the recursive process requires a detailed examination of the system stack — a tedious and useless process. Instead of such futile attempts, recursive functions can be more easily understood and analyzed with the help of a method known as ***mathematical induction***.

In a nutshell, mathematical induction works as follows. Suppose we have a series of statements

$$P_0, P_1, P_2, \dots, P_n, \dots$$

Suppose that:

1.   We can show that P_0 is true (the base case);
2.   We can prove that, for <u>any</u> $n \geq 1$, if P_{n-1} is true (***induction hypothesis***), then P_n is also true.

Then, if both conditions are met, we can conclude that all statements in the series are true.

This is so because P_0 implies P_1, P_1 implies P_2, and so on. However, we do not have to go through the entire logical sequence for every step. Instead, we can take a shortcut and just say that all the statements are true by mathematical induction.

⌘   ⌘   ⌘

As an exercise in mathematical induction, let us estimate the running time for the recursive Fibonacci function discussed in the previous section:

```
long Fibonacci(int n)

{
    if (n <= 2)      // Base case:
        return 1;
    else             // Recursive case:
        return Fibonacci(n-1) + Fibonacci(n-2);
}
```

We will prove that `Fibonacci(n)` requires not less than $(3/2)^{n-2}$ calls to the function. This is true for $n = 1$ and $n = 2$ (base cases), which both require just one call:

$$n{=}1{:}\ \ 1 > (3/2)^{1-2} = (3/2)^{-1} = 2/3;$$
$$n{=}2{:}\ \ 1 = (3/2)^{2-2} = (3/2)^{0}$$

For any $n > 2$, in addition to the initial call, the function calls `Fibonacci(n-1)` and `Fibonacci(n-2)`. <u>From the induction hypothesis</u> the number of calls for `Fibonacci(n-1)` is not less than $(3/2)^{n-3}$ and the number of calls for `Fibonacci(n-2)` is not less than $(3/2)^{n-4}$. So the total number of calls for `Fibonacci(n)` is not less than:

$$1 + (3/2)^{n-3} + (3/2)^{n-4}\ >\ (3/2)^{n-3} + (3/2)^{n-4} = (3/2)^{n-4}\,(3/2 + 1) =$$

$$(3/2)^{n-4} \cdot (5/2)\ >\ (3/2)^{n-4} \cdot (3/2)^{2} = (3/2)^{n-2}, \text{q.e.d.}$$

Assuming that a reasonably fast computer can execute a million calls per second (and that we somehow manage to represent very large Fibonacci numbers in memory), `Fibonacci(100)` would run for over $(3/2)^{98}$ / 10^6 seconds, or more than 5700 years! (The iterative implementation, by contrast, would run for 100 microseconds.)

You may notice a close conceptual link between recursion and mathematical induction. The key feature of mathematical induction is that we do not have to trace the sequence of statements to the bottom. We just have to first prove the base case and then, for an arbitrary n, show that <u>if</u> the induction hypothesis is true at all previous levels, <u>then</u> it is also true at the n-th level.

⌘ ⌘ ⌘

Let us see how mathematical induction applies to the analysis of recursive functions. As an example, let's take the `Permutations(...)` function from Section 19.3, which generates all permutations of a string of characters:

```
inline void Swap (char &a, char &b) {char temp = a; a = b; b = temp;}

void Permutations (apstring &str, int n)

{
    if (n <= 1)      // Base case:
                     // The permutation is completed -- report it
        cout << str << endl;          // (e.g. print it out)

    else {           // Recursive case:
        for (int i = 0;    i < n;    i++) {
            Swap (str[i], str[n-1]);
            Permutations(str, n-1);
            Swap (str[n-1], str[i]);
        }
    }
}
```

We will prove two facts about this code using mathematical induction:

1. `Permutations (...)` returns the string to its original order when it is finished.
2. `Permutations (str,n)` generates all permutations of the first n elements.

In the base case, $n = 1$, the function just reports the string and does nothing else — so both statements are true. Let us <u>assume</u> that both statements are true for any level below n (induction hypothesis). <u>Based on that assumption</u> let us prove that both statements are also true at the level n.

In the recursive case, the function swaps `str[i]` and `str[n-1]`, then calls `Permutations(str,n-1)`, then swaps back `str[n-1]` and `str[i]`. <u>By the induction hypothesis,</u> `Permutations(str,n-1)` preserves the order of characters in `str`. The two swaps cancel each other. So the order of characters is not changed in `Permutations(str,n)`. This proves Statement 1.

In the `for` loop we place every element of the string, in turn, at the end of the string. (This is true because the index `i` runs through all values from `0` to `n-1` and, as we showed above, the order of elements does not change after each iteration through the loop.) With each element placed at the end of the string we call `Permutations(str, n-1)`, which, <u>by the induction hypothesis,</u> generates all permutations of the first $n-1$ elements. Therefore, we combine each element placed at the end of the string with all permutations of the first $n-1$ elements, which generates all permutations of n elements. This proves Statement 2.

The above example demonstrates how mathematical induction helps us understand and, with almost mathematical rigor, prove the correctness of recursive functions.

By comparison, conventional code tracing and debugging and attempts at unfolding recursive calls to the very bottom are seldom feasible or useful.

19.6. *Lab:* The Towers of Hanoi

According to an ancient legend of the Far East, some monks in a monastery are trying to solve the puzzle of "The Towers of Hanoi." There are three pegs, with several disks on the first peg. The disks are arranged in order of decreasing diameter from the largest disk on the bottom to the smallest on top. The rules require that the disks be moved from peg to peg, one at a time, and that a larger disk never be placed on top of a smaller one. The objective is to move the whole tower from the first peg to the second peg.

1. Write a program that will solve the puzzle and print out all required moves for a specified number of disks.

2. Examine the number of moves required for 1, 2, 3, etc. disks, find the pattern, and come up with a formula for the minimum number of moves required for *n* disks. Prove the formula using the method of mathematical induction. Estimate how long it will take the monks to move a tower of 64 disks, assuming that they move two disks per second and make only correct moves.

19.7. *Lab:* Area Fill

An image is represented as a two-dimensional array of characters. Elements of the array, called pixels, (picture elements) have values '.' (white) and 'x' (black). An image may have a number of arbitrarily shaped blobs, contours, isolated pixels, etc. With each white pixel in an image we can associate a certain white area called the connectivity component of that pixel. This is defined as the set of all white pixels that can be connected to the given pixel with a continuous chain of white pixels.

Metaphorically we can think of all black pixels and contours as "walls" between white "containers". If we pour in black paint at a given point, then the container filled with black paint is the connectivity component of that point — a concept familiar to all users of "paint" programs. The AreaFill(...) function takes a specified white pixel in an image and fills the connectivity component of that pixel with black. The figure below illustrates this concept:

Before:

```
. . . . .xx. . . . . . . .
. . . .x. .xx. . . . . .
. . . .x. . . .xxxx. .
. . .x. . . . . . . .xxx
. .x. . .*. . . . . . . .
. . .x. . . . . . . .xx.
. . .x. .xxx. . .x.x
. . .x. .x. .x.x. . .
. .xxxx. . .x. . . .
. . . . . . . . . . . . . .
```

After:

```
. . . . .xx. . . . . . . .
. . . .xxxxx. . . . . .
. . . .xxxxxxxxx. .
. . .xxxxxxxxxxxx
. .xxxxxxxxxxxxxx
. . .xxxxxxxxxxxx
. . .xxxxxxxxxx.x
. . .xxxx. .xxx. . .
. . .xxxx. . .x. . . .
. . . . . . . . . . . . . .
```

```
* -- starting pixel
```

Write a class IMAGE that represents an image. Normally this class would be **derived** from the apmatrix<char> class: it would **inherit** all the elements and functions of apmatrix and we would be able to add new functions to it. But since we do not yet know how to use inheritance in C++ (see Chapter 28), we can just make the pixel matrix one member of the IMAGE class:

```
class IMAGE {
    ...
  private:

    apmatrix<char> mPixels;
    ...
```

Your IMAGE class does not need a constructor or destructor: the default code will do. Add three member functions:

```
  public:

    void Load(istream &file);
    void Display();
    void AreaFill (int row, int col);
```

The Load (...) function loads the image from a file. Assume that the first line in the file holds the dimensions of the image—the number of rows and the number of columns (two integers). The subsequent lines contain the appropriate number of dots and x's. Don't forget to resize your matrix after reading the image dimensions from the file but before filling it with data.

The Display() function displays the dimensions of the file and all the pixels.

The AreaFill (...) function fills the area starting from the pixel at the specified location. It is a recursive function: after filling a pixel, it proceeds with its four neighbors. Make sure you remain within the image boundaries and do not refill pixels that are already black.

The main program prompts the user for the image file name, loads and displays the image. Then it asks for the location of the starting pixel, calls `AreaFill(...)`, and displays the result.

Note that if the area to be filled is large, the `AreaFill(...)` function may go quite deeply into recursive calls and may overflow the system stack. Then your program may crash without warning. If this happens, you can increase the size of the stack by adjusting the appropriate setting in your compiler configuration.

> ### *For "extra credit":*

Implement the `AreaFill(...)` function using a more economical method of traversing horizontal lines. Fill the horizontal segment that contains the pixel. At the same time scan the adjacent lines above and below, find all segments that touch the newly filled pixels, and push on stack one pixel on each of these segments. Continue processing for all the saved pixels. This method doesn't use recursion, but rather relies on your own stack. Compare the execution times for this method and the four-neighbor recursive method (run the `AreaFill(...)` function multiple times; exclude the time for reading the file from disk to get a more accurate estimate).

19.8. Summary

Recursion is a programming technique based on functions calling themselves.

Recursive function calls are supported by the system stack, which keeps the function arguments, return address, and local variables in a separate frame for each call. Recursion is useful for dealing with <u>nested structures</u> or <u>branching processes</u> where it helps to create short, readable, and elegant code that would otherwise be impossible.

Recursion should generally be avoided in situations that deal with <u>linear</u> structures or processes, which can be as easily and more efficiently implemented with iterations.

The best way to understand and analyze recursive functions is by thinking about them along the lines of mathematical induction: attempts at unfolding and tracing recursive code "to the bottom" usually fail.

20

Queues

20.1. Discussion

The *queue* is a data structure used for temporary storage from which the data elements are retrieved in the same order as they were stored. This method is called FIFO — First-In-First-Out (as opposed to LIFO — Last-In-First-Out, the method of a stack). A queue can hold fixed-size elements, structures, or pointers to structures or strings. The queue is controlled by two functions: `enqueue` and `dequeue`. `enqueue` inserts an element at the *rear* of the queue and `dequeue` removes an element from the *front* of the queue. These two operations implement the FIFO method.

The queue structure is usually used for processing events that have to be processed in the order of their arrival, but not necessarily right away. The events are *buffered* in a queue while awaiting processing. Consider, for example, an application that implements an e-mail system. Each subscriber will have a mailbox, which can be implemented as a queue of messages. A newly arrived message is inserted at the rear of the queue, and the "Read Next" user command removes a message from the front of the queue.

(The term "queue" may sometimes refer to a more general implementation where in addition to removing elements at the front of the queue, the program can access them from the middle, reorder them, or prioritize them. In the above example, for instance, it is reasonable to display the whole list of messages and allow the user to chose which message she wants to read next.)

A queue can be implemented in different forms. One possible implementation uses a singly-linked list enhanced by an additional pointer to the tail of the list. Elements are added at the tail of the list and removed at the head of the list. In this implementation, storage for the elements is dynamically allocated using the `new` operator when an element is inserted and released with the `delete` operator when an element is removed from the queue.

Another implementation uses a *ring buffer*, which is simply an array used in a circular manner. If we used an array in a regular linear manner, we would have to shift the whole array forward whenever we removed the first element. In a ring buffer we simply adjust the pointer that defines the "logical" first element. The state of the queue is maintained with the help of two indices, `front` and `rear`.

`front` points to the first element in the queue, which will be returned by the next call to the `dequeue (...)` function; `dequeue (...)` also increments the `front` index. `rear` points to the empty slot following the last stored element. The `enqueue (...)` function stores the next element in the slot pointed to by `rear` and increments the `rear` index. Both `front` and `rear` wrap around the end of the array to the beginning (Figure 20-1). This mechanism helps to maintain a queue without shifting the whole array.

Queues are widely used at the system level for buffering commands or data between processes or devices. A personal computer has a keyboard queue implemented as a ring buffer. When a key is pressed, its code does not go directly to the active program but is placed in the keyboard buffer until the program requests it. Printer output may be buffered: the characters are held in the output buffer until the device is ready to receive them. An operating system may have a queue of print jobs waiting to be sent to a printer while other programs are running.

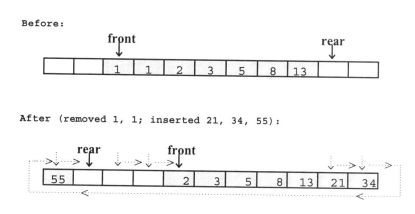

Figure 20-1. Ring-buffer implementation of a queue.

20.2. Ring Buffer and Linked List Queue Implementations

In this section we demonstrate two simplified classes that implement a queue of strings as a linked list and a queue of characters as a ring buffer. A more general templated class that works with elements of any data type, `apqueue`, is discussed in the next section.

The LLQUEUE class implements a queue as a linked list:

```
                                                    LLQUEUE.H    [disk]
// LLQUEUE.H
//
// Queue implemented as a linked list.

#ifndef _LLQUEUE_H_
#define _LLQUEUE_H_

#include "apstring.h"

struct QNODE {
    apstring info;
    QNODE *next;
};

class LLQUEUE {

  public:

    LLQUEUE();
    ~LLQUEUE();
    void enqueue (const apstring &item);
    void dequeue (apstring &item);
    bool isEmpty();

  private:

    QNODE *mFront;
    QNODE *mRear;
};

#endif     // _LLQUEUE_H_
```

The LLQUEUE constructor sets both front and rear pointers to null. The destructor deletes all elements remaining in the queue.

```
// LLQUEUE.CPP                                              LLQUEUE.CPP   💾
//
// Queue implemented as a linked list.

#include "llqueue.h"

LLQUEUE::LLQUEUE()

// Constructor

{
    mFront = 0;
    mRear = 0;
}

//****************************************************************

LLQUEUE::~LLQUEUE ()

// Destructor: deletes all elements remaining in the queue.

{
    QNODE *next;

    while (mFront) {
        next = mFront->next;
        delete mFront;
        mFront = next;
    }
    mRear = 0;
}

//****************************************************************

void LLQUEUE::enqueue (const apstring &item)

// Inserts item at the rear of the queue.

{
    // Allocate a new node and copy info into it:
    QNODE *newnode = new QNODE;
    if (newnode) {
        newnode->info = item;
        newnode->next = 0;
```

Continued ☞

```
        // Append the new node at the rear of the queue:
        if (mRear == 0)
            mFront = newnode;
        else
            mRear->next = newnode;
        mRear = newnode;
    }
}

//*********************************************************

void LLQUEUE::dequeue (apstring &item)

// Retrieves and removes the first element from the queue.

{
    // Retrieve the first element from the queue:
    if (mFront != 0) {
        item = mFront->info;

        // Remove the node from the front of the queue
        QNODE *next = mFront->next;
        delete mFront;
        mFront = next;
        if (mFront == 0) // If removed the last element...
            mRear = 0;
    }
}

//*********************************************************

bool LLQUEUE::isEmpty()

// Returns true if the queue is empty, false otherwise

{
    return mFront == 0;
}
```

Normally the code for a general-purpose queue class would report errors such as trying to get an item from an empty queue or memory allocation failure. For instance, instead of void enqueue (...) and dequeue (...) we could make them return a Boolean value that would indicate success or failure. We have decided to implement the enqueue (...) and dequeue (...) functions as void for the sake of compatibility with the apqueue class discussed in the following section.

⌘   ⌘   ⌘

The second class, RBQUEUE, implements a ring buffer for characters:

RBQUEUE.H

```
// RBQUEUE.H
//
// Queue implemented as a ring buffer.

#ifndef _RBQUEUE_H_
#define _RBQUEUE_H_

class RBQUEUE {

  public:

    RBQUEUE(int size = 1024);
    ~RBQUEUE();
    void enqueue (char c);
    void dequeue (char &c);
    bool isEmpty();

  private:

    char *mBuffer;
    int mSize;
    int mFront;
    int mRear;

    // Private helper function that calculates the next
    //   index with wrap-around.
    int NextIndex(int index);
};

#endif    // _RBQUEUE_H_
```

```
// RBQUEUE.CPP
//
// Queue implemented as a ring buffer.

#include "rbqueue.h"

RBQUEUE::RBQUEUE(int size)

// Constructor.

{
    mBuffer = new char[size];
    if (mBuffer)
        mSize = size;
    else
        mSize = 0;

    mFront = 0;
    mRear = 0;
}

//**************************************************************

RBQUEUE::~RBQUEUE()

// Destructor.

{
    delete [] mBuffer;
}

//**************************************************************

void RBQUEUE::enqueue (char c)

// Appends c at the end of the buffer.

{
    int i = NextIndex(mRear);
    if (i == mFront)                  // The queue is full
        return;
    mBuffer[mRear] = c;
    mRear = i;
}

//**************************************************************
```

Continued ➩

```
void RBQUEUE::dequeue (char &c)

// Retrieves and removes the element from the front of the buffer.

{
    if (mFront == mRear)        // The queue is empty
        return;
    c = mBuffer[mFront];
    mFront = NextIndex(mFront);
}

//*****************************************************************

bool RBQUEUE::isEmpty()

// Returns true if the queue is empty, false otherwise.

{
    return mFront == mRear;
}

//*****************************************************************

int RBQUEUE::NextIndex(int index)

// Calculates and returns the value of the next index
//    with wrap-around.

{
    index++;
    if (index == mSize)
        index = 0;

    return index;
}
```

The ring buffer implementation is slightly more efficient than the linked list because it avoids the overhead of dynamic memory allocation.

20.3.   The apqueue Class

The apqueue class is a templated class provided by the AP C++ Development Committee. The class implements the queue as a ring buffer in a manner very similar to the RBQUEUE class example from the previous section. But the apqueue class can handle queue elements of any data type. A queue of strings, for example, can be declared as:

```
apqueue<apstring> q;
```

The `apqueue` class automatically increases the size of the queue when necessary. There is no way to specify the desired size in the declaration. The constructor first allocates a small buffer for the queue elements; later the `enqueue (...)` function may allocate a bigger buffer if the queue runs out of space. The most commonly used member functions are:

```
void enqueue(const itemType &item);
void dequeue(itemType &item);
bool isEmpty();
```

The class has other member functions:

```
const itemType &front() const;
    // Returns the front element without removing it from the queue.

void dequeue();
    // Overloaded version of dequeue(...) that removes the
    //    front element from the queue and discards it.

int length() const;
    // Returns the number of elements in the queue.

void makeEmpty();
    // Empties the queue.
```

20.4. *Case Study:* Application of Queues

In this section we discuss the "Pizza Plus Co. Home Deliveries" program, which assigns delivery orders to available drivers. The program uses two queues: one for the pending pizza delivery orders, another for the available drivers. This is a typical situation where queues are used: the external events are not synchronized and must be processed on a first-come-first-serve basis, but only as resources become available.

The program uses the `apqueue` class for the queue of orders and for the queue of drivers.

```
// PIZZA.CPP
//
// Pizza Plus Co. Home Deliveries
// Author: Roman Crust
// Rev 1.1


#include <iostream.h>
#include <ctype.h>
#include "apstring.h"
#include "apqueue.h"

struct ORDER {
    apstring items;
    apstring address;
};

int main()

{
    char key = ' ';
    ORDER order;
    apstring driverName;
    apqueue<ORDER> pendingOrders;
    apqueue<apstring> availDrivers;

    cout << "\n*** Pizza Plus Co. Home Deliveries ***\n\n";

    while (key != 'Q') {

        // Show menu, get next command:

        cout << "     (N)ew order\n";
        cout << "     (D)river available\n";
        cout << "     (Q)uit\n";
        cout << "\n";
        cout << "Next command ==> ";
        cin >> key;
        cin.ignore(256, '\n');
        key = toupper(key);

        // Execute command:

        switch (key) {

          case 'N':    // Enter new order

            cout << "  Address ==> ";
            getline(cin, order.address);
```

Continued

```
                    cout << "   Ordered Items ==> ";
                    getline(cin, order.items);
                    cout << "\n";

                    pendingOrders.enqueue(order);
                    cout << "<OK>\n";
                    break;

                case 'D':    // Enter the name of available driver

                    cout << "   Driver Name ==> ";
                    getline(cin, driverName);
                    cout << "\n";

                    availDrivers.enqueue(driverName);
                    cout << "<OK>\n";
                    break;

                case 'Q':
                    break;

                default:
                    cout << "*** Invalid command ***\n";
                    break;
            }

            // Dispatch available drivers to deliver pending orders

            while (!availDrivers.isEmpty() && !pendingOrders.isEmpty()) {
                pendingOrders.dequeue(order);
                availDrivers.dequeue(driverName);
                cout << "\n\n*** Attention: " << driverName << "\n"
                     << "*\n"
                     << "*        " << order.items << "\n"
                     << "*   to:\n"
                     << "*        " << order.address << "\n"
                     << "******************\n\n";
            }
        }
    return 0;
}
```

The main program is basically one `while` loop that processes events. This is typical for an *event-driven* application. Such applications wait for the next event and process it when it arrives.

In an event-driven application the program maintains a queue of events. The first event simply reports that the program has started. Other events can be a keyboard key pressed, a mouse moved, or a message received from another program. On each iteration through the `while` loop, the program checks whether any events are available and processes the next available event. Sometimes processing an event may create new events that are queued to the same or other applications. For example, having received a click of a mouse button, the program may send messages to itself that certain menu selections were made, or to other programs that certain windows have to be repainted on the screen.

The "Pizza Deliveries" example deals only with external, "real-world" events. It displays a little menu for adding a new order or "checking in" an available driver (who presumably has just shown up for work or returned from the previous trip). The command is processed and either the new order is inserted into the `pendingOrders` queue or the driver's name is inserted into the `availDrivers` queue. After that, the program examines both queues, and if both are not empty, it matches the next driver to the next order and "prints" the order ticket.

In this example, it is not possible for both queues to have more than one element, so we could use

```
if (!availDrivers.isEmpty() && !pendingOrders.isEmpty()) ...
```

instead of

```
while (!availDrivers.isEmpty() && !pendingOrders.isEmpty()) ...
```

In a slightly modified version (e.g., one expanded to handle situations where the kitchen is behind) both queues could have several elements. Then a `while` loop would move both queues forward as far as possible.

20.5. *Lab:* e-Mail

Complete the program below, a mock e-mail system. The program maintains an array of subscribers identified by their names. Each subscriber has a mailbox, represented by a queue.

The e-mail program should include the functions `FindUser(...)`, `NewUser(...)`, and `Login(...)`. `FindUser(...)` returns the index of the user in the subscriber array with the matching name. `NewUser(...)` adds a new name to the subscriber array. `Login(...)` tries to find a subscriber with a given name, and if not found, automatically adds it to the array of subscribers. It returns the index of the logged-in subscriber.

The `ProcessCommand(...)` function, called from within a loop, shows a menu ("Read message", "Send message", "Quit") and implements the command entered. The "Read message" command displays the next message from the mailbox or the

"No new mail" message. The "Send message" command prompts the user for the recipient's name, subject, and (one-line) text, and posts the message to the recipient's mailbox. If a message is addressed to an unknown subscriber, his or her name is automatically added to the array of subscribers if space is available.

The sketch of the program can be found in EMAIL.CPP:

EMAIL.CPP

```
// EMAIL.CPP
//
//    This program sets up a toy e-mail system.
//
//    The program maintains a list of subscribers in an array.
//    Initially the list is empty.  The program adds new
//    subscribers automatically when a new name "logs in" and
//    when a message is addressed to a new name.
//    The list may have at most 10 subscribers.
//
//    Author: Eudora Scanty

#include <iostream.h>
#include <ctype.h>
#include <string.h>
#include "apstring.h"
#include "apqueue.h"

struct MESSAGE {
    apstring from;
    apstring to;
    apstring subject;
    apstring text;
};

struct SUBSCRIBER {
    apstring name;
    apqueue<MESSAGE> mailbox;
};

// Array of subscribers
//    (these constants and variables are declared as global because
//    they are central to this program and most of the functions
//    need them):

static const int MAXUSERS = 10;   // Maximum number of subscribers
static apvector<SUBSCRIBER> subscriber(MAXUSERS);
static int nUsers = 0;     // Current number of users

//*************************************************************
```

Continued

```
static int FindUser(const apstring &name)

// Returns the index of the user whose name matches
//    "name", or -1 if not found.

{
    ...
    ...
}

//****************************************************************

static int NewUser(const apstring &name)

// Adds a new user to the array of subscribers.
// Returns the index of the new subscriber or
//    -1 if failed.

{
    int n;

    if (nUsers >= MAXUSERS) {
        cout << "Cannot add " << name << " (out of space).\n";
        return -1;
    }
    ...
    ...
}

//****************************************************************

static int Login(const apstring &name)

// Finds the name in the subscriber array or
//    adds a new user with the given name if not found.
// Returns the index of logged-in user,
//    or -1 if failed.

{
    int n;

    n = FindUser(name);
    if (n < 0)
        n = NewUser(name);

    return n;
}

//****************************************************************
```

Continued ☞

```
static void ProcessCommands(int n)

{
    char key = ' ';
    apstring name;
    MESSAGE msg;
    int nDest;    // index of the destination subscriber.

    while (key != 'Q') {

        // Show menu, get next command:

        cout << "      (R)ead next message\n";
        cout << "      (S)end message\n";
        cout << "      (Q)uit\n";
        cout << "\n";
        cout << "Next command ==> ";
        cin >> key;
        cin.ignore(256, '\n');
        key = toupper(key);

        // Execute command:

        switch (key) {

          case 'R':     // Read next message

            ...
            ...

            break;

          case 'S':     // Send message

            ...
            ...

            break;

          case 'Q':        // Quit
            break;

          default:
            cout << "*** Invalid command ***\n";
            break;
        }
    }
}

//***************************************************************
```

Continued ☞

```
int main()

{
    apstring name;
    int n;

    for (;;) {
        cout << "Username (or 'Q' to quit): ";
        getline(cin, name);
        if (name == "Q" || name == "q")
            break;
        n = Login(name);
        if (n >= 0) {
            cout << "\nWelcome " << subscriber[n].name << "\n\n";
            ProcessCommands(n);
        }
    }

    return 0;
}
```

Fill in the blanks in the program. Develop a comprehensive QA (quality assurance) plan that will test your program under various conditions, paying special attention to singular conditions (e.g., the list of subscribers is empty or full, the mailbox is empty, the subscriber is not found, etc.).

20.6. Summary

The Queue is a data structure for storing and retrieving elements in a First-In-First-Out (FIFO) manner.

A queue can be implemented as a ring buffer, which is simply an array used in a circular way. The `front` index marks the beginning of the queue, where the next element will be removed; the `rear` index marks the end of the queue (the first available slot), where the next element will be inserted. Both pointers wrap around the end of the array.

Another queue implementation may use a singly-linked list with an additional pointer to the tail of the list, where the new elements will be inserted.

Queues are usually used for processing events that have to be handled in the order of their arrival but may have to wait for available resources or an appropriate time. Queues are widely used for system tasks such as scheduling jobs, passing data between processes, and input/output buffering for peripheral devices.

The templated `apqueue` class implements a queue for elements of any data type. The most commonly used member functions are `enqueue(...)`, `dequeue(...)` and `isEmpty()`:

```
apqueue<apstring> q;
apstring name;

q.enqueue(name);
q.dequeue(name);
while (!q.isEmpty())...
```

21

Classes: More Advanced Features

21.1. Discussion

By now we have covered most of the syntax and many features of C++, and you may be wondering: Why do we need more? We should bear in mind that a programming language is an artificial creation of its designers. Moreover, unlike a building or a bridge, a programming language does not have to take into account the laws of gravity or the strength of the materials—its "top floor" may weigh a hundred times more than the foundation. So it doesn't always make sense to ask why things are the way they are. Clearly C++ is a very rich language to which new features have been added over time. C++ sets out to tighten the rules and at the same time increase flexibility—two contradictory goals. So it often fights its own design flaws by adding new features and syntax.

In this chapter we explain several new features of C++ classes:

- Constructors with initializer lists;
- Two ways to overload an operator: as a member and as a non-member;
- *friend* functions and classes;
- Iterators;
- Static class members.

Initializer lists are needed because there is no other way to call constructors for those members of a class that are instances of another class. The `friend` keyword lifts restrictions on accessing private members of a class. Iterators help to cycle through all the elements of an array or linked list that is a private member of a class. Static members allow several instances of a class to share and control the same memory location.

Section 21.4 shows the standard recipe for coding the "canonical features" of a class: a default constructor, a copy constructor, and the overloaded assignment operator. In Section 21.9, we touch on a few design considerations related to the use of classes.

21.2. Initializer Lists

Suppose a class has a member of another class type:

```
class FIRSTCLASS {

   ...
   private:

      SECONDCLASS mPassenger;
      ...
};
```

Suppose that as part of the FIRSTCLASS constructor we need to initialize mPassenger with certain values. This is a problem: there is no place to call the appropriate constructor for mPassenger. If mPassenger were declared by itself, we could simply write:

```
SECONDCLASS mPassenger(x, y, z);
```

This declaration implicitly calls the appropriate constructor for mPassenger. But what can we do when mPassenger is a class member? If we try to initialize members of mPassenger directly, we will discover that private members of mPassenger are not accessible through FIRSTCLASS's constructor. *Initializer lists* come to the rescue. The syntax is:

```
// Constructor:

FIRSTCLASS::FIRSTCLASS(...) : mPassenger(x, y, z)

{
   ... // other code
}
```

In the above code, mPassenger(x,y,z) is not in the body of the constructor. It is more like a reminder that in the process of building an object of the FIRSTCLASS type, the program has to build its member mPassenger using the appropriate SECONDCLASS constructor, which knows how to interpret the arguments x, y, z.

x, y, z may be literal constants or global constants or variables defined above the constructor. They may also be arguments of the FIRSTCLASS constructor that are passed to members of the initializer list. For example:

```
// stack.h
// =======

class STACK {

  ...
  private:

    int mSize;
    int mSp;
    apvector<int> mBuffer;    // Holds stack elements. Size?
                             //   (cannot be initialized here).

};


// stack.cpp
// =========

// Constructor: builds a stack of the specified size.

STACK::STACK(int size)
          : mBuffer(size)   // size argument is passed to mBuffer

{
    mSize = size;
    mSp = 0;
}
```

In a more general case a class may have several members that are instances of other classes. Then we can list all their constructors, separated by a comma, after the colon:

```
FIRSTCLASS::FIRSTCLASS(...) : mItem1(...), ... , mItemk(...)

{
    ... // other code
}
```

Note that there is no need to list members without arguments in the initializer list because the default constructors for these members will be used automatically.

Some programmers prefer to initialize all class members, including members of built-in data types, in the initializer list. Often the constructor code then has nothing left to do. For example:

```
// stack.cpp

STACK::STACK(int size)
          : mSize(size),    // mSize = size;
            mSp(0),         // mSp = 0;
            mBuffer(size)
{}                          // Nothing to do!
```

⌘ ⌘ ⌘

Initializer lists are especially important when we use structures or classes whose members are vectors, matrices, or strings (represented by the `apvector`, `apmatrix`, or `apstring` types). Initializer lists are the only place where we can initialize such members to define the size of a vector, the dimensions of a matrix, or the contents of a string. Consider, for example, the following structure:

```
struct GAME {
    apstring mName;              // Game name
    apmatrix<char> mBoard;       // Game board
};
```

How do we tell the `mBoard` member what the dimensions of the matrix are? And how do we initialize the `mName` string with a particular name? If we used built-in arrays, we could write:

```
struct GAME {
    char mName[30];            // Game name
    char mBoard[3][3];         // Game board 3 by 3
};

GAME game = {"Tic-Tac-Toe"};   // Syntax with braces to initialize
                               //    struct members in declarations
```

But if we try something similar with `apstring` and `apmatrix`, the compiler will report syntax errors:

```
struct GAME {
    apstring mName;
    apmatrix<char> mBoard(3,3);    // Syntax error 1.
};

GAME tictactoe = {"Tic-Tac-Toe"};  // Syntax error 2.
```

The first error message will tell you that you cannot specify arguments in member declarations. The second error message will tell you that initialization with braces is not allowed for the structure GAME (because it contains members with types such as `apstring` or `apvector`).

But unless we specify the matrix dimensions our GAME structure is useless: the matrix dimensions are set to zero by default. What to do? Our first impulse might be to initialize each instance of GAME "manually," resizing the mBoard matrix as needed using the resize(...) function. We may think of writing a separate initialization function, or several functions, for doing this. For example:

```
void SetForTicTacToe(GAME &game)
// Initializes a GAME structure for Tic-Tac-Toe.
{
    game.mName = "Tic-Tac-Toe";
    game.mBoard.resize(3,3);
}

void SetForGo(GAME &game, int size)
// Initializes a GAME structure for Go.
{
    game.mName = "GO";
    game.mBoard.resize(size, size);
}
```

This approach is dangerous: we would have to remember to initialize every GAME object before we used it. Also, it would be impossible to declare const GAME objects. But more importantly, this approach would fail completely if GAME were not a struct but a class with encapsulated data members: then members of GAME would not be accessible to our initialization functions or any other code outside the GAME class.

A much better solution is to use initializer lists. We can provide a constructor for GAME that will pass the appropriate arguments to the apstring and apmatrix constructors:

```
struct GAME {
    apstring mName;             // Game name
    apmatrix<char> mBoard;      // Game board

    GAME();                     // Constructor: initializes GAME
                                //    for Tic-Tac-Toe.
};

// Constructor for struct GAME:

GAME::GAME()
      : mName("Tic-Tac-Toe"), mBoard(3,3)    // Initializer list
{
    ... // Any additional code if necessary
}
```

The initializer list, together with any short and simple code for the constructor, may also be placed inside the `struct` or `class` definition. For example:

```
struct GAME {

    apstring mName;             // Game name
    apmatrix<char> mBoard;      // Game board

    GAME()                      // Constructor for Tic-Tac-Toe
      : mName("Tic-Tac-Toe"), mBoard(3,3)
    {}
};
```

Now if your program declares the variable

```
    GAME game;
```

the object `game` will be created with the name "Tic-Tac-Toe" and a Tic-Tac-Toe board.

You can provide several constructors with different sets of arguments for your structure or class. Some of these arguments may be passed to the constructors of members that are strings, vectors, or matrices. For example:

```
class GAME {

  public:

    GAME()                      // Constructor for Tic-Tac-Toe
                                //    (default --no arguments)
      : mName("Tic-Tac-Toe"), mBoard(3,3)
    {}

    GAME(int size)              // Constructor for GO
                                //    (one argument--size)
      : mName("GO"), mBoard(size, size)
    {}

    GAME(const apstring &name, int size)
                                // Constructor for other games
      : mName(name), mBoard(size, size, ' ')
    {}

  private:

    apstring mName;             // Game name
    apmatrix<char> mBoard;      // Game board
};
```

Now if your program declares a GAME object with no arguments, the default constructor will be used and the object created will be a Tic-Tac-Toe board:

```
GAME game;    // Declare a game object for Tic-Tac-Toe.
```

If one integer argument is provided, the appropriate constructor will initialize mName to "GO" and create a square board of the specified size:

```
GAME game(19);  // Declare a game object for GO with
                //   the name "GO" and a 19 by 19 board
```

Given two arguments, a string and an int, the last constructor will be used. It will set the name to the specified string and build a square matrix mBoard of the specified size. It will also fill mBoard with spaces, because we specified the ' ' (the space char) fill value for the mBoard constructor in the initializer list. For example:

```
GAME game1("Reversi", 8);
                // Declare a game object for Reversi with
                //   the name "Reversi" and an 8 by 8 board,
                //   initially filled with spaces.
GAME game2("Hasami Shogi", 9);
```

21.3. Operator Overloading

Operator overloading is the C++ feature for changing the meaning of standard operators such as +, *, >=, and so on. We have already seen in Part 1 (Section 13.5) how << and >> are overloaded to represent I/O stream insertion and extraction operators for structures.

Class designers often overload operators because they want to support elegant syntax for using their classes. But the assignment operator is often overloaded out of necessity.

The assignment operator for copying class objects may be overloaded when the default, member-by-member assignment does not do the job properly. Arithmetic operators may be overloaded when a class represents some algebraic object (e.g., a fraction, a complex number, or a "big integer").

The apstring class overloads the + operator to signify concatenation of strings.

Recall that in C++ the difference between operators and functions is minimal. An operator X <u>is</u> a function with the name `operatorX(...)` (where X is a standard operator symbol +, *, etc.). C++ allows you to overload both unary and binary operators, but for the sake of simplicity let us limit our discussion to binary operators. A binary operator is a function that needs two arguments: a left-hand side and a right-hand side. The arguments do not necessarily have to be of the same data type.

There are two ways to overload an operator for a class: as a member of the class and as a free-standing operator (not a member of any class).

When an operator is overloaded as a member, a prototype for the operator is placed inside the class definition, together with other public member functions. The left-hand argument is implicit: it is the instance of the class that owns the operator.

```
class SOMECLASS {

  public:
    . . .
      resultType operatorX(argType b);
        . . .
};
```

Theoretically, a member operator can be used with the regular syntax for calling member functions:

```
    SOMECLASS a;
    argType b;
    resultType c;

    c = a.operatorX(b);
```

But the whole point of overloaded operators is that they allow you to use the operator syntax:

```
    c = a X b;    // The same as c = a.operatorX(b);
```

When an operator is overloaded as a free-standing operator, its prototype is placed <u>outside</u> the class definition and both arguments are explicit. Either argument can have the data type of our class.

```
class SOMECLASS {
    ...
};

resultType operatorX (argType1 a, argType2 b);
```

where *argType1*, *argType2*, or both is SOMECLASS. Again, theoretically it can be used as a regular function:

```
argType1 a;
argType2 b;
resultType c;

c = operatorX(a, b);
```

But of course it will be used as an operator:

```
c = a X b;
```

Each of the two methods—member and non-member overloading—has its own limitations.

> **When you use an operator overloaded as a class member, the first (left-hand-side) operand must always be of that class data type.**

Suppose, for instance, that in the apstring class you want to have three versions of the overloaded + operator: one for concatenating two strings, and two others for appending a character at the end and at the beginning of a string:

```
apstring str1, str2, result;
char ch;

result = str1 + str2;
result = str1 + ch;
result = ch + str2;
```

The first two forms of + may be overloaded as member operators of the apstring class, but the third must be a free-standing operator.

In the assignment operator

```
a = b;
```

the left-hand-side argument is, as a rule, of the class type. So the = operator is normally overloaded as a class member operator. The same is true for += and other compound assignment operators. But in the I/O stream extraction and insertion operators the left-hand-side argument has the type `istream` or `ostream`, respectively:

```
cin >> classVar;
cout << classVar;
```

So these operators have to be overloaded as free-standing operators.

The problem with free-standing operators is that they may not have access to the private members of the class. The class designer has to find a way around this. He may be able to use the class's constructors, public accessor member functions or operators, or he may provide additional "undocumented" accessors or public member functions that do the bulk of the work. For example:

```
// bigint.h
class BigInt {

  public:
    ...
    // facilitate operators ==, <, << without friends
    ...
    void Print (ostream &os) const;
    ...
};


...
ostream &operator<< (ostream &os, const BigInt &x);

// bigint.cpp
...
ostream &operator<< (ostream &os, const BigInt &x)

{
    x.Print(os);
    return os;
}
```

Alternatively he may declare the free-standing operator a *friend* to his class (see Section 21.6), thus explicitly giving it access to all private members of his class. The latter is the standard approach, but the AP C++ Development Committee does not require the knowledge of "friends" and avoids using "friends" in its materials.

The code for the overloaded operators is usually placed into the class implementation file, together with the code for member functions and non-member functions related to the class:

```
resultType SOMECLASS::operatorX (argType b)

// SOMECLASS member operator

{
    ...
}

resultType operatorX (argType1 a, argType2 b)

// Free-standing operator.  Usually, argType1, argType2, or both are
//    of the SOMECLASS type.

{
    ...
}
```

⌘ ⌘ ⌘

Let us consider three examples of overloaded operators from the apstring class. The first is the assignment operator, which is a member of the class. This operator is declared together with other public member functions in the class definition in apstring.h:

```
class apstring {

    public:
        ...
        const apstring &operator= (const apstring &str);
        ...
};
```

The syntax in this declaration has several elements. First of all, it declares a member function operator=:

```
const apstring & operator= (const apstring &str);
```

The return data type of this function is a constant reference to apstring:

```
const apstring & operator= (const apstring &str);
```

This allows assignments to be chained together:

```
str1 = str2 = str3;  // The same as:  str1 = (str2 = str3);
```

The keyword const indicates that the returned value cannot be modified. The return type is a reference but const prevents it from being used as an lvalue, such as:

```
    (str1 = str2) = str3;    // Not allowed!
```

The `operator=` function takes one argument of the `const apstring &` type:

```
    const apstring &operator= ( const apstring & str );
```

This means that `str` is passed by reference and that it may not be modified inside the operator code. The code for this operator can be found in `apstring.cpp`. It is discussed in the next section.

⌘   ⌘   ⌘

The second example is the overloaded `<<` operator. This is a free-standing operator. Its prototype is supplied in `apstring.h`, but it is placed <u>outside</u> the class definition:

```
class apstring {
     ...
};
...
ostream &operator<< (ostream &os, const apstring &s);
```

Like assignment this is a binary operator. And since it is a free-standing operator, it takes two arguments. The first argument is a reference to an output stream, the second is a constant reference to an `apstring`. The operator returns `os`, the reference to the same stream, so that `<<` operators can be chained together.

The code for this operator has been placed in `apstring.cpp`. It relies on the `c_str()` accessor member function which returns the pointer to the string buffer, a regular null-terminated string. The `<<` operator is already defined for null-terminated strings, so it can be used in the implementation of `<<` for the `apstring` class:

```
    ostream &operator<< (ostream &os, const apstring &s)
    {
        os << s.c_str();    // Or simply: return os << s.c_str();
        return os;
    }
```

⌘   ⌘   ⌘

The third example is the `+` operator, overloaded as a free-standing operator. Actually the `apstring` class offers three overloaded forms of `+`:

```
apstring operator+ (const apstring &str1, const apstring &str2);
apstring operator+ (const apstring &str, char ch);
apstring operator+ (char ch, const apstring &str);
```

Again, these prototypes are outside the class definition. All three forms return a new `apstring` object. All of them are implemented as non-member operators for the sake of the third form, where the first argument is not an `apstring` but a `char`. (The free-standing operator also lets us use a literal string as the first argument.)

Normally such operators would be declared `friend` to the `apstring` class:

```
class apstring {

  friend apstring operator+ (const apstring &str1, const apstring &str2);

  ...
};
```

But we can avoid using friends:

```
apstring operator+ (const apstring &str1, const apstring &str2)

// Concatenates str1 and str2 and returns the new string

{
    apstring result = str1;    // Construct result equal to str1.
    result += str2;            // append str2 using the += operator.
    return result;
}
```

In the above code `+=` is another overloaded operator, one overloaded as a member of the `apstring` class. `+=`, therefore, has access to the private members of `apstring` and, as you can see, does most of the work. This code is very short, but it is less efficient than a direct implementation of `+` (without `+=`) because the strings will be copied unnecessarily a couple of times.

21.4.   Canonical Features of a Class

In C++, classes represent user-defined types. It is desirable that these types behave, as much as possible, like built-in types. As a minimum, a well-constructed class should provide the "canonical" features needed to allow convenient object declarations and assignments:

```
// TEST.CPP

#include <iostream.h>

int main()

{
    SOMECLASS x;
    SOMECLASS y = x;
    ...
    y = x;
    ...
}
```

In this section we provide a recipe for implementing these features. The following techniques are used:

```
int main()

{
    SOMECLASS x;       // <== Default constructor
    SOMECLASS y = x;   // <== Copy constructor
    ...
    y = x;             // <== Overloaded assignment operator
    ...
}
```

The default constructor, copy constructor, assignment operator and destructor are considered canonical features of any well-defined class.

The default constructor does not take any arguments. The copy constructor takes one argument: a reference to an object of the same class. The overloaded assignment operator copies a class object. The destructor performs any required clean-up.

These features are especially important when dealing with templated classes, such as `apvector` and `apmatrix`, because these classes assume that the default constructor, copy constructor, and assignment work properly for their elements. For instance, if we use

```
apvector<SOMECLASS> v;
```

SOMECLASS must have a working assignment operator.

Copy constructors are also used in functions that return a class object. If a function returns a value of the SOMECLASS type, SOMECLASS must have a copy constructor.

⌘   ⌘   ⌘

What happens if you do not define the default constructor, copy constructor, or assignment operator? If you do not code some of the canonical features, the C++ compiler will supply their "automatic" versions (we use the word "automatic" here in order not to confuse different meanings of the word "default"). You have to consider carefully whether these automatic versions will do the job: quite often they do.

If you do not define any constructors, the automatic default constructor will be used. It calls the default constructors for each class member that has a user-defined (some other class) data type, and leaves all members of built-in data types uninitialized.

An automatic default constructor will be generated only if a class does not have any constructors at all.

Consider, for example, the following class with two data members:

```
class FLIGHT {
  ...

    int flightNumber;
    apstring destination;
};
```

The automatic default constructor will make destination an empty string because the apstring class has the default constructor that makes an empty string. flightNumber, however, will contain garbage.

The automatic copy constructor uses member-by-member assignment for built-in types and calls copy constructors for all user-defined (class) type members. Likewise, the automatic assignment operator will use member-by-member assignment.

This may work fine as long as all the class members have proper assignment operators and the class does not have any members that are pointers to arrays.

The automatic destructor simply executes destructors for all members of user-defined class types.

⌘   ⌘   ⌘

The canonical features are declared in the class definition as follows:

```cpp
class SOMECLASS {

  public:
    ...
    SOMECLASS();                      // Default constructor
    SOMECLASS(const SOMECLASS &x);   // Copy constructor
    const SOMECLASS &operator= (const SOMECLASS &x);
                                      // Assignment operator
    ~SOMECLASS()                      // Destructor
    ...
};
```

Let's see how these features can be coded in the `apstring` class:

```cpp
// apstring.h

class apstring {

  public:
    ...
    apstring();                       // Default constructor
    apstring(const apstring &str);    // Copy constructor
    const apstring &operator= (const apstring &str);
                                      // Assignment operator
    ...
  private:
    int mLength;        // Current length
    int mCapacity;      // Buffer capacity
    char *mCstring;     // Pointer to the char buffer
};

// apstring.cpp

#include "apstring.h"
...

apstring::apstring()

// Default constructor: builds an empty string.

            : mLength(0), mCapacity(1)
{
    mCstring = new char[1];
    mCstring[0] = '\0';   // Holds only the terminating null char.
}
```

Continued ☞

```
apstring::apstring(const apstring &str)

// Copy constructor

{
    mLength = str.length();
    mCapacity = mLength + 1;
    mCstring = new char[mCapacity];
    strcpy(mCstring, str.mCstring);   // Copy the char buffer
}
```

Note that the automatic member-by-member copy constructor wouldn't do the job for the `apstring` class because the `mCstring` pointer in the copy would simply be assigned to the value of `mCstring` in the original, making the `mCstring` pointers in the original and in the copy point to the same buffer. This situation would be fatal: if one string released or reassigned the buffer, the second would continue to point to it, not knowing about the change. That is why we need to code the copy constructor ourselves: to allocate a new buffer in the copy and copy the contents of the original buffer into it.

The same is true for the assignment operator. In addition, the code for the assignment operator must reallocate the buffer if the current buffer does not have enough capacity to hold the right-hand-side string:

```
const apstring &apstring::operator= (const apstring &str)

// Assignment operator

{
    int len;

    if (this != &str) {                    // Do not assign to itself!
        len = str.length();
        if (mCapacity < len + 1) {         // If not enough room--
            delete [] mCstring;            //    deallocate the buffer
            mCapacity = len + 1;           //    and allocate a new one
            mCstring = new char[mCapacity];
        }
        mLength = len;                     // Set the new length
        strcpy(mCstring, str.mCstring);    // Copy the string
    }
    return *this;             // Return the reference to itself!
}
```

The above code is pretty straightforward with the exception of two new idioms:

```
if (this != &str) // Compare this to the address of str
```

and

```
return *this;
```

These idioms are pretty standard in the code for an overloaded assignment operator. The first is used to make sure that an object is not assigned to itself. The second is used to return the reference to the class object (which is needed in order to chain several = operators together). Both idioms use the `this` pointer. `this` is a C++ reserved word which means "the pointer to the current object." In our case `this` has the type `apstring*`. Whenever we refer to class members, we could use the `this->` prefix. For example:

```
this->mLength = len;
```

is exactly the same as:

```
mLength = len;
```

`*this` (with a star) converts the type from `apstring*` to the `apstring&` required by the operator return type.

21.5.   Constructors as Casts

Besides the default constructor and the copy constructor, a well-designed class may provide constructors from other data types that are semantically closely related to the class. You can think of "closely related" types as those that can be cast into your class object.

For example, a "big integer" class object may represent very big integer numbers (as long arrays of digits). It is reasonable, though, to expect that a regular integer (type `int`) can be converted into a `BigInt`. To accomplish this, `BigInt`'s designer provides a constructor from `int`:

```
class BigInt {

  public:
    ...
    BigInt (int n);  // Constructor from int
    ...
};
```

The `apstring` class provides a constructor from a literal string:

```
class apstring {

  public:
    ...
    apstring(const char *s);   // A string in double quotes has the
                               //   const char* data type.
    ...
};
```

Constructors from related types take one argument. They play three important roles in programs: initialization of class objects, explicit casts, and implicit casts of function arguments and operands.

The first use of constructors from related types is initialization. For example:

```
    BigInt factorial = 1;
    apstring name = "Sunshine";
```

The above declarations actually imply casts:

```
    BigInt factorial = BigInt(1);
    apstring name = apstring("Sunshine");
```

The compiler makes sure that the appropriate constructor (`BigInt(int)` and `apstring(const char *)` in our examples) exists, and adds a call to it to your code.

The second use of constructors is for explicit casts. For example:

```
    BigInt x;
    int n;

    cin >> n;
    x = BigInt(n);   // Cast; calls the BigInt(int) constructor.
```

The third use is for implicit casts. Suppose your `BigInt` class has an overloaded + operator:

```
  BigInt operator+ (const BigInt &a, const BigInt &b);
```

This operator expects two `BigInt` arguments. Still, in the client program you can write:

```
BigInt x = 1, sum;
int n;
...
sum = x + n; // Same as: sum = x + BigInt(n); -- implicit cast
```

You can also write:

```
sum = n + x;
```

But if you write:

```
BigInt sum;
int m = 1, n = 1;
...
sum = m + n;  // Caution: the result may overflow!
```

then the regular + for integers will be executed first, and only the result will be converted into `BigInt` by calling the `BigInt(int)` constructor. So automatic promotion works pretty much the same way as for built-in types.

> **If a function or an operator is called with arguments of certain types, and that form of function or operator is not defined, the compiler tries to find casts that convert arguments into the required types. The compiler uses promotion rules for built-in types and constructors for user-defined class types. The compiler checks if the required conversion can be accomplished without ambiguity. But if in doubt, use explicit casts!**

21.6.   Friend Classes and Functions

The keyword `friend` is used to give a non-member function or operator access to all members (including the private members) of a class. `friend` declarations may appear anywhere within a class definition. For example:

```
class IMAGE {

  friend ostream &operator<< (ostream &file, const IMAGE &im);
  friend istream &operator>> (istream &file, IMAGE &im);
  friend void PrintImage (const IMAGE &im);

  private:
    ...
};
```

These declarations give operator<<, operator>>, and the PrintImage(...) function access to all private members of the class IMAGE.

Friend declarations do not make friend functions or operators members of the class, do not affect their code in any way, and do not replace function prototypes. They simply inform the compiler that these particular free-standing functions or operators are allowed to use private members of that class.

If necessary, a whole class may be declared a friend of your class. That gives all its member functions access to all the members of your class.

A friendship is not necessarily symmetrical. As a class designer, you determine your class's friends; users of your class cannot declare their classes friends to your class and gain access to its private members.

Friend classes and functions should be used judiciously because they weaken encapsulation.

21.7. Iterators

Encapsulation creates a particular problem in a simple situation where a class has an array or a list and a non-member function needs to access its elements one by one. For example, we may have a general-purpose linked-list class LIST with Insert(...) and Remove(...) functions, etc. This class does not know how its elements will be used. Another class or function may need at some point to traverse the list and, say, count the elements that match a given pattern. But the elements of the list are private members. One solution would be to make all the members of LIST public — a sin against encapsulation. Another approach is to declare each class and non-member function that seeks access to the list a friend, but that would ruin the generality of the LIST class because it is hard to foresee all functions that may need to traverse a list in the future.

Yet another solution could be to include the iteration functionality within the LIST class. We can add a data member that keeps track of the current position in the list and a member function that returns the data in the current node and advances to the next node. For example:

```
struct NODE {
    apstring data;
    NODE *next;
};

class LIST {

  private:

    NODE *head, *tail;
    NODE *current;

  public:

    ...
    void StartIterations() {
        current = head;
    }
    bool NextData(apstring &str) {
        if (!current)
            return false;
        str = current->data;
        current = current->next;
        return true;
    }
};
```

This is feasible, but it limits the iteration functionality to only <u>one iteration loop at a time</u>. The programmer must keep track of who is currently iterating through the list and make sure that no one else tries to do the same in the middle. Tasks which require nested `for` or `while` loops, such as finding duplicates in a list, would not be supported.

As usual, C++ successfully solves the problem (that it created for itself). The solution uses a complementary *friend* class, called an *iterator*, which implements just the iterations through the list. You can create several instances of the iterator and therefore run any number of iterators concurrently without any conflict.

The original class and the iterator class work together as a team. A constructor is provided for the iterator class which initializes it with the object of the original class. Another constructor — a copy constructor — initializes it with another iterator for nested iterations.

The following sketch of a linked list class provides an example:

```
// LIST.H

#include "apstring.h"

struct NODE {
    apstring data;
    NODE *next;
};

// *** Linked List class ***

class LIST {

  private:

    NODE *head, *tail;

  public:

    LIST();
    void Insert (const apstring &str);
    ~LIST();

    friend class LISTITER;

};

// *** Companion iterator class ***

class LISTITER {

  private:

    NODE *current;

  public:

    LISTITER(const LIST &list);        // Constructor from a LIST object
    LISTITER(const LISTITER &listiter); // Copy constructor

    bool NextData(apstring &str);
            // Places data from the current node into str and
            //    advances the current pointer.
            // Returns true if successful, false if at the end
            //    of the list.
};
```

ITERATOR.CPP

```
// LIST.CPP

#include "list.h"

// *** LIST implementation: ***

LIST::LIST()

// Default constructor: makes an empty list.

        : head(0), tail(0) // head and tail are set to null.
{}

void LIST::Insert (const apstring &str)

// Inserts str into the list.

{
    NODE *newNode;

    newNode = new NODE;
    newNode->data = str;
    newNode->next = 0;
    if (tail)
        tail->next = newNode;
    else
        head = newNode;
    tail = newNode;
}

LIST::~LIST()

// Destructor: deletes all nodes.

{
    NODE *temp;

    while (head) {
        temp = head->next;
        delete head;
        head = temp;
    }
}
```

Continued ⇗

```
// *** LISTITER implementation ***

LISTITER::LISTITER(const LIST &list)

// Constructor from LIST

{
    current = list.head; // Set current to the head of the list
}

LISTITER::LISTITER(const LISTITER &otheriter)

// Copy constructor

{
    current = otheriter.current;
    // This is redundant: we could use the automatic member-by-member
    //   copy constructor.  Here we intentionally want the pointer
    //   current in the original iterator and in the copy to point
    //   to the same memory location--a node in the list.
}

bool LISTITER::NextData(apstring &str)

// Places data from the current node into str and
//   advances the current pointer.
// Returns true if successful, false if at the end of the list.

{
    if (!current)
        return false;

    str = current->data;
    current = current->next;

    return true;
}
```

The following test program shows how a single iterator is used in the Print (...) function and two nested iterators are used in the PrintDuplicates (...) function:

ITERATOR.CPP

```
// TEST.CPP

#include <iostream.h>
#include "list.h"

void Print(LIST &list)

// Prints all elements in the list using one iterator.

{
    LISTITER listiter(list);
    apstring str;

    while (listiter.NextData(str))
        cout << str << ' ';
    cout << endl;
}

//*************************************************************

void PrintDuplicates(LIST &list)

// Prints all those elements in the list that have duplicates
//    by using two nested iterators.

{
    cout << "Duplicates:\n";

    LISTITER listiter1(list);
    apstring str1, str2;

    while (listiter1.NextData(str1)) {
        LISTITER listiter2 = listiter1;
        while (listiter2.NextData(str2)) {
            if (str1 == str2) {
                cout << '[' << str1 << ']' << endl;
                break;    // Break from the inner while loop.
            }
        }
    }
}

//*************************************************************
```

Continued 🖝

```
int main()

{
    LIST list;

    list.Insert("a");   // Automatic cast from const char* to
                        //   apstring.  Calls the apstring(const char*)
                        //   constructor.
    list.Insert("rose");
    list.Insert("is");
    list.Insert("a");
    list.Insert("rose");
    Print(list);
    cout << endl;

    PrintDuplicates(list);
    return 0;
}
```

The program generates the following output:

```
a rose is a rose

Duplicates:
[a]
[rose]
```

21.8.   Static Class Members

C++ lets you declare some data members of a class as *static*. Static members share the same memory for all instances of the class (i.e., for all declared variables of the class type). We can say that static members belong to the class as a whole, not to its specific instances.

> **In addition to data members, member functions can be declared static, too. Unlike regular member functions, these functions can be called without attributing them to a specific class instance. For that reason, static functions can access and manipulate only static data members.**

You can declare a member static by using the keyword `static` in its declaration. Both private and public members may be declared static. The following class for a mock soda vending machine declares a static data member, `mPrice`, and a static member function `SetPrice(...)`:

```
// SODA.H

class SODA {     // Soda vending machine

  public:

    static void SetPrice(int price);

    SODA();
    void SellSoda();
    int GetDayTotal();

  private:

    static int mPrice;
    int mDayTotal;
};
```

This example demonstrates one of the more obvious uses of static members: defining a constant or a variable that has to be shared by all instances of the class, in this example the price of a can of soda.

A static data member <u>cannot</u> be initialized inside the class definition or in the constructor, because the constructor is called for every instance of the class. Instead, it is initialized separately in the source file, as follows:

```
// SODA.CPP

#include "soda.h"

int SODA::mPrice = 60;

void SODA::SetPrice(int price)
{
    mPrice = price;
}

SODA::SODA() : mDayTotal(0)
{}

void SODA::SellSoda()
{
    mDayTotal += mPrice;
}

int SODA::GetDayTotal()
{
    return mDayTotal;
}
```

This is how this class works in a test program:

```cpp
// TEST.CPP

#include <iostream.h>
#include <iomanip.h>
#include "soda.h"

int main()

{
    SODA machine1, machine2;

    SODA::SetPrice(75); // Sets the price for all machines (cents)

    int can;
    for (can = 0;   can < 100;   can++)
        machine1.SellSoda();
    for (can = 0;   can < 50;   can++)
        machine2.SellSoda();

    double dollars =
        .01 * machine1.GetDayTotal() +
        .01 * machine2.GetDayTotal();

    cout << setprecision(2)
         << setiosflags(ios::fixed | ios::showpoint)
         << "Day's sales: $" << dollars << endl;

    return 0;
}
```

A public static member can be accessed through any instance of the class. We could write:

```cpp
// TEST.CPP

    ...
int main()

{
    SODA machine1, machine2;

    machine1.SetPrice(75);
    ...
}
```

This usage would be misleading, though, because it would suggest that the price was set only for machine1 and would obscure the fact that the same price had been set for all "machines." That is why we wrote:

```cpp
SODA::SetPrice(75);
```

Now suppose we want to count total sales for all active soda machines automatically. We can add a static member, say, mGrandTotal, to the SODA class and increment it for every sale. At the end it will contain the total of all sales from all machines:

```
// SODA.H

class SODA {     // Soda vending machine

  public:

    static int mGrandTotal;
    ...
};

// SODA.CPP

#include "soda.h"

...
int SODA::mGrandTotal = 0;

...

void SODA::SellSoda()
{
    mDayTotal += mPrice;
    mGrandTotal += mPrice;
}
...

// TEST.CPP

...
int main()

{
    ...
    cout << "Total for all machines " <<
        << .01 * SODA::mGrandTotal << endl;
    ...
}
```

⌘   ⌘   ⌘

A less obvious use of static members is for allocating some temporary shared work space, for example a large array, especially for use in a recursive member function. Static members may also be used for more esoteric tasks related to the management of the class as a whole. Suppose we want to count all currently existing instances of a class. This can be done with a static counter:

```cpp
// SOMECLASS.H

class SOMECLASS {

  private:

    static int nObjects;
    ...
  public:

    static int NumberOfObjects() {return nObjects;}

    SOMECLASS() {       // Constructor
        nObjects++;
        ...
    }

    ~SOMECLASS() {      // Destructor
        ...
        nObjects--;
    }
    ...
};


// SOMECLASS.CPP

int SOMECLASS::nObjects = 0;
...

// TEST.CPP

#include <iostream.h>

int main()

{
    SOMECLASS object1, object2;

    cout << SOMECLASS::NumberOfObjects() << " objects\n";
                        // Output: "2 objects"

    if (SOMECLASS::NumberOfObjects() == 2) {
        SOMECLASS object3;
        cout << SOMECLASS::NumberOfObjects() << " objects\n";
                            // Output: "3 objects"
    }

    cout << SOMECLASS::NumberOfObjects() << " objects\n";
                        // Output: "2 objects"
    return 0;
}
```

21.9.   Efficiency and Design Considerations

In C++ the syntax for using user-defined class types is often the same as for built-in data types. This convenience and simplicity may be deceptive, because short code may actually hide a lot of activity. An innocent-looking declaration or `return` statement may trigger a call to a complicated constructor. The same thing may happen when an automatic cast is implied in an expression or a function call.

As we have seen, a class variable declared within a loop calls its constructor and destructor on every pass through the loop.

Some C++ programmers enjoy simplifying the interfaces to their classes. They may use many overloaded member functions and operators with many default arguments. To some extent, this defeats the use of function prototypes for argument checking in function calls.

Overloaded operators may also deceive the class user because a simple + or = may have a lot of code hidden behind it.

Suppose you want to read lines from a file and display them, adding five stars in front of each line. You code a trivial function:

```
apstring AddStars(const apstring &line)

{
    return "*****" + line;
}
```

Then you call it from your main program:

```
int main()
{
    apstring line;
    ...
    while (getline (file, line))
        cout << AddStars(line) << endl;
    ...
}
```

This style of programming is very tempting because it produces short and clear code; it is fine as long as you are dealing with short strings, or perform the operation only once, or if performance is not an issue. But if your task is to sort a large text file, this kind of "neat" code will quickly turn your quicksort algorithm into a "slowsort" program.

Consider what happens in the `AddStars(...)` function.   First it calls the constructor `apstring(const char *)` in order to convert `"*****"` into an `apstring` object. This is necessary if your `apstring` class does not provide an overloaded form of the + operator that can handle `char*` arguments directly. This constructor creates a temporary `apstring` object and copies `"*****"` into its character buffer. Then the + operator kicks in. It creates another temporary `apstring` object, with a buffer large enough to contain the concatenated strings, and copies characters from both strings into it. We are lucky if the + operator is coded efficiently. In a "quick and dirty" implementation the + operator may call other operators (e.g., `=`, `+=`), which, in turn, copy the strings several times. Finally, the `return` statement in `AddStars(...)` calls the `apstring` copy constructor, which copies the `apstring` object (and its character buffer) once more.
In this example, we can simply avoid the + operator:

```
while (getline (file, line))
    cout << "*****" << line << endl;
```

In a real-world project we might have to re-examine the `apstring` class to see if we should add new features or re-implement the `apstring` class to make it more efficient. If performance is critical, we might have to do without `apstring` altogether and instead write low-level code based on built-in arrays and null-terminated strings.

21.10.   Summary

It is desirable that user-defined types in C++ behave similarly to built-in types. In particular, a well-defined C++ class has to support simple declarations, assignments and initializations. This is achieved by defining a default constructor, a copy constructor, and an overloaded assignment operator for your class. These "canonical" features are especially important when working with templated classes such as `apvector` and `apmatrix`, because these classes expect their elements to have the appropriate copy constructor and assignment operator.

Sometimes it is also convenient to have appropriate arithmetic operators and stream I/O operators for user-defined types. These operators are implemented as overloaded class members or free-standing overloaded operators.

A C++ programmer can declare some functions and classes friends to his class. Friend functions and all member functions in friend classes have access to all private members of the class. One group of useful friend functions are overloaded free-standing operators, such as << and >> for stream I/O. Another useful friend is an iterator class, which works together with a class that contains a list and helps implement iterations over the elements of the list.

Static data members share the same memory for all instances of the class. They may be used for representing constants or variables common to all class objects, for temporary work buffers, or for more esoteric class management tasks such as counting the number of existing instances of a class. Static member functions manipulate static data members of the class.

If performance is important, you must have a fairly good understanding of your own classes and of the standard classes that you are using in your project. C++ is deceptive: it may hide a lot of processing and many implicit calls to constructors behind very concise code.

22

Trees

22.1. Discussion

A *tree* is a branching hierarchical structure in which each element except the top one has a link to exactly one element higher in the hierarchy called its *parent* (Figure 22-1). The elements of a tree structure are referred to as *nodes*. The top node in the structure is called the *root* of the tree. Any node in the tree may be connected to one or more nodes lower in the hierarchy, called its *children*. The nodes that have no children are called *leaves*. There is exactly one path from the root to any node. The intermediate nodes in this path are referred to as the node's *ancestors* (i.e., its parent, the parent of its parent, etc.). Trees may not have circular paths.

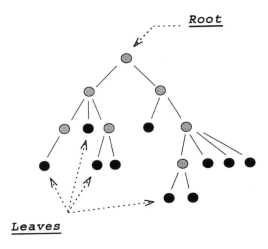

Figure 22-1. A tree structure.

As you can see, computer books normally show trees "growing" down, with the root shown on top. This convention probably reflects the fact that we read from the top of the page down and also process trees starting from the root. Trees may be used for representing branching systems or processes, such as organizational charts, game strategies (Figure 22-2), diagnostic procedures, and other hierarchies of objects. Figure C-1 in Appendix C, for example, shows the inheritance tree of the derived stream I/O classes in C++.

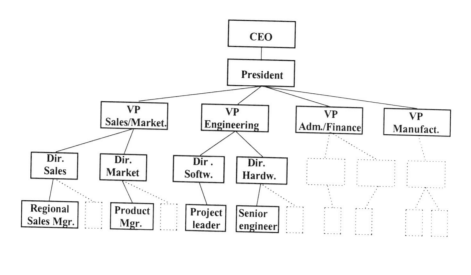

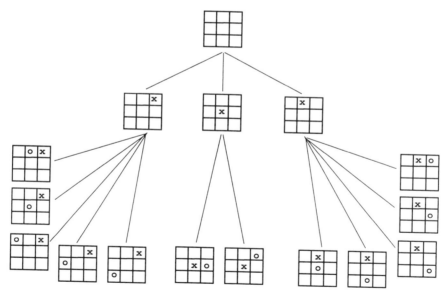

Figure 22-2. Common uses of tree structures.

All nodes in a tree can be arranged in layers with the root at level 0, its children at level 1, their children at level 2, and so on. The level of a node is equal to the length of the path from the root to that node. The total number of levels is called the **height** or the **depth** of the tree (Figure 22-3).

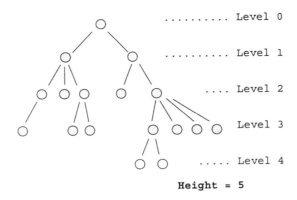

Figure 22-3. Arrangement of tree nodes in levels.

One important property of trees is that we can arrange a relatively large number of elements in a relatively **shallow** (having a small number of levels) tree. For example, if each node in a tree (except the last level) has two children, a tree with h levels contains $2^h - 1$ nodes (Figure 22-4). Such a tree with 20 levels contains over one million nodes. This property may be utilized for quick searching, data retrieval, decision trees, and similar applications where, instead of going through the whole list and examining all the elements, we can go down the tree and examine just a few. (In strategy games, this property works exactly in reverse and becomes a major stumbling block: if we consider all the possible responses to a given move, then all the responses to those responses, etc., the tree of possible game paths grows so fast that it is not feasible to plan ahead beyond a few moves.)

A list can be viewed as a special case of a tree where the first node is the root, the last node is the only leaf, and all other nodes have exactly one parent and one child. A list has only one node at each level. If a tree degenerates into a near-linear shape with only a few nodes at each level, its advantages for representing a large number of elements in a shallow structure are lost.

A tree is an inherently recursive structure, because each node in a tree can itself be viewed as the root of a smaller tree (Figure 22-5). In computer applications, trees are normally represented in such a way that each node "knows" where to find all its children. In the linked representation, for example, each node, in addition to some information, holds the list of pointers to its children. Knowing just the root, we can find all the elements of the tree; and given any node we can find all the nodes in its subtree.

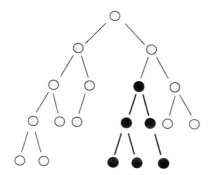

	Tree Height	Total Nodes
· · · · · · · · · ·	1	1
· · · · · · ·	2	3
· · · · ·	3	7
· · · ·	4	15
	...	...
	h	$2^h - 1$

Figure 22-4. A shallow tree can hold many nodes.

Figure 22-5. Each node in a tree is a root of its own subtree.

The recursive branching structure of trees suggests the use of recursive procedures for dealing with them. The following function, for example, allows us to "visit" each node of a tree, a process known as tree ***traversal***:

```
void Traverse (NODE *root)

{
    // Base case: root == 0, the tree is empty -- do nothing
    // Recursive case: tree is not empty
    if (root != 0) {
        Visit(root);
        for (... <each child of the root>)
            Traverse (<that child's subtree>);
    }
}
```

This function first "visits" the root of the tree, then, for each child of the root, calls itself recursively to traverse that child's tree. The recursion stops when it reaches a leaf: all its children's trees are empty. Due to the branching nature of the process, an iterative implementation of this function would require your own stack and would be quite cumbersome. In this example, the recursive implementation may actually be slightly more efficient in terms of the processing time, and does not take too much space on the system stack because the depth of recursion is the same as the depth of the tree, which is normally a relatively small number. The major advantage of a recursive procedure is that it yields clear and concise code.

A tree in which each node has no more than two children is called a **binary tree**. The children of a node are referred to as the **left** child and the **right** child. In the following sections we will deal exclusively with binary trees. We will see how a binary tree can be used as a **binary search tree** and as a **heap**.

22.2. Binary Search Trees

A binary search tree (BST) is a structure for holding a set of ordered data elements in such a way that it is easy to find any specified element and easy to insert and delete elements. As we saw in Part 1 (Section 9.3), if we have a sorted array of elements, the "divide and conquer" binary search algorithm allows us to find any element in the array quickly. We take the middle element of the array, compare it with the target value and, if they are not equal, continue searching either in the left or the right half of the array, depending on the comparison result. This process takes at most $\log_2 n$ operations for an array of n elements. Unfortunately, inserting elements into the array or deleting them from the array is not easy — we may need to shift large blocks of data in memory. The linked list structure, on the other hand, allows us to insert and delete nodes easily, but there is no quick search method because there is no way of getting to the middle of the list easily. Binary search trees combine the benefits of arrays for quick searching and the benefits of linked lists for inserting and deleting elements.

As the name implies, a binary search tree is a kind of a binary tree: each node has no more than two children. The children are called the *left* and *right child*, and the subtrees that "grow" from them are called *left* and *right subtrees*. The tree's nodes contain some data elements for which a relation of order is defined; that is, for any two elements we can say whether the first one is greater, equal, or smaller than the second. The elements may be numbers, alphabetized strings, some database record index keys, and so on. Sometimes we informally say that one node is greater or smaller than another, actually meaning that that relationship applies to the data elements they contain.

What makes this tree a <u>binary search tree</u> is the following special property: for any node, the element in the node is larger than all elements in this node's left subtree and smaller than all elements in this node's right subtree (Figure 22-6).

A binary search tree is specifically designed to support the "divide and conquer" method. Suppose we need to find a target element. First, we compare the target to the root. If they are equal, the element is found. If the target is smaller, we continue the search in the left subtree. If larger, we go to the right subtree. We will find the target element (or assert that it is not in the tree) after a number of steps which never exceeds the number of levels in the tree. If our tree is rather "bushy," with intermediate levels filled to near capacity with nodes, the number of steps required will be close to $\log_2 n$, where n is the total number of nodes.

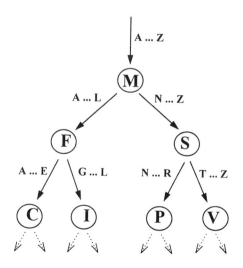

Figure 22-6. The ordering property of a binary search tree.

In a binary search tree, it is also easy to find the smallest and the largest element. Starting at the root, if we always go left for as long as possible, we come to the node containing the smallest element. If we always keep to the right, we come to the node containing the largest element (Figure 22-7). The smallest node, by definition, cannot have a left child, and the largest node cannot have a right child.

⌘   ⌘   ⌘

In this section we implement a binary search tree as a linked structure and discuss the operations for finding, inserting and removing a node. We also discuss different ways to traverse a binary tree. Although a binary search tree could be implemented as a C++ class, we have chosen not to do this for technical reasons that are explained later in this chapter.

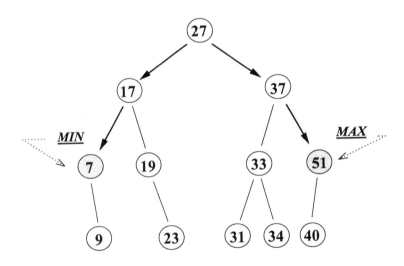

Figure 22-7. Location of the smallest and the largest elements in a BST.

The easiest way to access a binary tree is through one pointer to its root node. But first we have to define a structure for each node:

```
struct TREENODE {
    SOMETYPE data;
    TREENODE *left;
    TREENODE *right;
};
```

SOMETYPE is the data type of the information stored in nodes. We will use apstring in our examples.

Note the self-referential property of this definition: the TREENODE structure contains two pointers to structures of the same type, left and right, which represent its children. A null value indicates that there is no corresponding child.

Let us call a pointer to the root node of the tree root:

```
TREENODE *root;
```

An empty tree can be declared simply as a root pointer equal to null:

```
TREENODE *root = 0;          // Declare an empty tree.
```

root has a dual role: it points to the root node, and it also points to the whole tree. This is especially convenient for recursive treatment, because a subtree can be addressed directly as its root node. For example, the left subtree of the tree root can be addressed simply as root->left. A null value in left or right means that the corresponding subtree is empty.

In the linked implementation new nodes of the tree will be dynamically allocated using the new operator, so the tree must be explicitly destroyed at the end. For that purpose we need the Destroy() function:

```
void Destroy(TREENODE *root);
```

The find, insert, and remove operations can be implemented as the following functions:

```
TREENODE *Find(TREENODE *root, const apstring &data);
bool Insert(TREENODE* &root, const apstring &data);
bool Remove(TREENODE* &root, const apstring &data);
```

Note that the Insert(...) and Remove(...) functions may change the root of the tree, so root is passed to them by reference.

For the binary search tree, we assume that relational operators (<, <=, ==, etc.) are defined for information elements stored in nodes. We also assume that the assignment operator works. The apstring type meets these requirements.

The above definitions are collected in the header file TREE.H:

TREE.H

```
// TREE.H

#ifndef _TREE_H_
#define _TREE_H_

#include "apstring.h"

struct TREENODE {
    apstring data;
    TREENODE *left;
    TREENODE *right;
};

void Destroy(TREENODE *root);
TREENODE *Find(TREENODE *root, const apstring &target);
bool Insert(TREENODE* &root, const apstring &data);
bool Remove(TREENODE* &root, const apstring &data);

#endif // _TREE_H_
```

22.3. BST's Destroy, Find, and Insert Functions

These functions are implemented recursively here. We will also discuss an iterative implementation of Find(...).

The first step in a recursive implementation is to ascertain that the tree is not empty (i.e., root != 0). This is very important because it is the base case (or, as some people say, the *stopping* case) in a recursive function. The recursion stops when we reach a null pointer in the tree.

Let us begin by looking at the Destroy(...) function, which is the shortest:

```
// TREE.CPP

#include "tree.h"

void Destroy(TREENODE *root)

{
    // Base case 0: the tree is empty -- do nothing;
    if (root) {  // Recursive case:
        Destroy(root->left);
        Destroy(root->right);
        delete root;
    }
}
```

The best way to understand how this function works is to prove its correctness using the method of mathematical induction, explained in Section 19.5. In the base case of an empty tree, there is nothing to do, so the function works. Let us assume (inductive hypothesis) that this function works for any tree of depth less than some integer h greater or equal to 1. Based on that assumption, let us prove that it also works for any tree of the depth h. Suppose our tree has the depth h. Then left and right subtrees both have depths smaller than h. Therefore, by the induction hypothesis,

```
        ...
        Destroy(root->left);
        ...
```

correctly deletes all nodes in the left subtree, and

```
        ...
        Destroy(root->right);
        ...
```

correctly deletes all nodes in the right subtree.

Finally,

```
        ...
        delete root;
        ...
```

deletes the root node. So the function correctly deletes all nodes in the tree. Mathematical induction shows that this function works for a binary tree of any depth.

Unfolding this recursive function in order to see "exactly how it works" (e.g., in what order it actually removes the nodes) may be a good exercise... in frustration. What is important, though, is that at each recursive step we deal with a tree of smaller depth, so the maximum depth of recursion is equal to the depth of the tree (usually a reasonably small number), and not the total number of nodes in the tree (which may be a very large number).

⌘   ⌘   ⌘

In general, recursive functions for dealing with trees work in the following way. The first step (base case 0) is to check whether the tree is empty. Another base case is needed when we are looking for a target node and find it right at the root of the tree. The rest of the cases are recursive: we apply the same function to the left or right subtree, or both.

If we are looking for a target in a binary search tree, we go left if the target is smaller than the data at the root of the tree and right otherwise. Finally, at some depth of recursion, we find the correct node. This node is at the root of some subtree of the original tree, but at that level of recursion <u>it appears to us</u> at the root of the tree currently being considered.

The `Find(...)` function, which returns the pointer to a node that contains a data element equal to the target value, is a good example:

TREE.CPP

```
TREENODE *Find(TREENODE *root, const apstring &target)

// Finds the node such that node->data == target.
// Returns the pointer to the found node, or 0 if not found.

{
    if (!root)      // Base case 0: the tree is empty.
        return 0;

    if (target == root->data)
        return root;

    else if (target < root->data)           // Recursive case: search
        return Find(root->left, target);    //    left subtree.

    else // if (target > root->data)         // Recursive case: search
        return Find(root->right, target);    //    right subtree.
}
```

In this function we do not visit all the elements of the tree, but recursively build a path from the root to the element we are looking for. The branching is conditional:

at every node we either go left or right, but not both. So the process is essentially linear. This suggests that there must be a simple iterative solution as well. The iterative version is, indeed, as short as the recursive one:

TREE.CPP

```
TREENODE *Find(TREENODE *root, const apstring &target)

// *** Iterative version ***

{
    while (root && target != root->data) {
        if (target < root->data)
            root = root->left;
        else // if (target > root->data)
            root = root->right;
    }
    return root;
}
```

The iterative version of Find(...) is preferable to the recursive one, because it is more efficient and equally clear.

⌘ ⌘ ⌘

In the Insert(...) function, the new node is always inserted as a leaf. We go all the way down the tree to find an empty slot in the proper place and insert the new node there. Note that root is passed to the Insert(...) function by reference, so the variable that we pass down the line is actually a reference to a pointer to a node.

TREE.CPP

```
bool Insert(TREENODE* &root, const apstring &data)

// Creates a new node with node->data = data and inserts
//   it into the proper place in the tree.
// Returns true if successful, false if cannot
//    allocate a new node.

{
    if (!root) { // Base case 0: the tree is empty.

        // Allocate a new node and set the root
        //    equal to the new node:

        TREENODE *newnode = new TREENODE;
```

Continued

```
        if (!newnode)
            return false;
        newnode->data = data;
        newnode->left = 0;
        newnode->right = 0;
        root = newnode;
        return true;
    }

    if (data == root->data) // Base case: the element is already
                            //    in the tree.
        return true;        //    (Another version might report an error)

    else if (data < root->data)        // Recursive case: insert
        return Insert(root->left, data);  //    into the left subtree

    else // if (data > root->data)     // Recursive case: insert
        return Insert(root->right, data); //    into the right subtree
}
```

Paradoxically, it is easier to write this code than to understand why it works. One may wonder how a new node can be appended to the tree without ever explicitly mentioning its parent. The explanation is that the root of the tree is passed to `Insert(...)` by reference. `root->left` and `root->right` are also passed by reference in the recursive calls. At the bottom of the recursion when we finally come to the appropriate empty slot, `root` actually <u>refers</u> to a pointer — the `left` or `right` pointer — of some parent. The <u>value</u> of that pointer is null. The statement

```
        root = newnode;
```

replaces null with `newnode`.

22.4.   BST's Remove Function

The `Remove(...)` function is more involved because it requires rearranging the nodes in the tree. First we find the node we want to remove. There are two possibilities: either the node has no more than one child, or the node has both children.

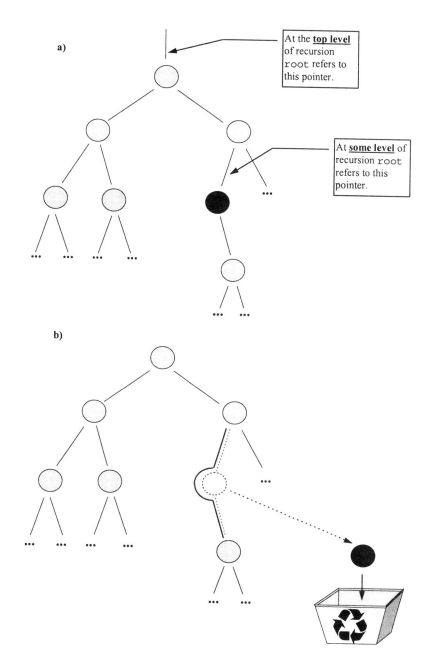

a)

At the **top level** of recursion root refers to this pointer.

At **some level** of recursion root refers to this pointer.

b)

Figure 22-8. Removing a node with only one child from a binary search tree.

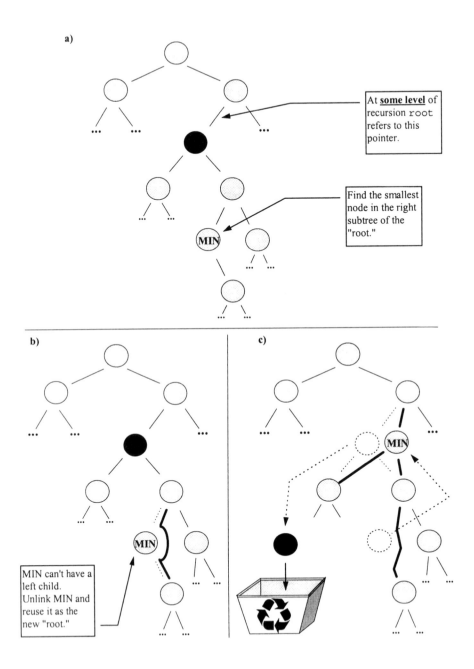

Figure 22-9. Removing a node with two children.

In the first case, we can rearrange the pointers to bypass the node by appending its only child directly to the removed node's parent (Figure 22-8). As an exercise, you can prove that the order property of the binary search tree still holds.

The second case — when both the node's children are present — requires some extra work. Our approach here is to replace the node with the smallest element of its right subtree (the same would work for the largest element of its left subtree). The order property of the binary search tree will still hold because the new node, coming from the right subtree, is larger than any node in the left subtree. And since it is the smallest node in the right subtree, it is smaller than all remaining nodes there.

As we mentioned earlier, we will find the node containing the smallest element of any tree by starting at the root and going left for as long as possible (see Figure 22-7). This node does not have a left child, so we can easily unlink it from the tree. We can put this node in place of the removed node to fill the gap (Figure 22-9). The method is implemented in the following recursive code:

```
                                                    │ TREE.CPP        💾 │
───────────────────────────────────────────────────┘─────────────────────└──
bool Remove(TREENODE* &root, const apstring &data)

// Removes the node whose data element is equal to data.
// Returns true if successful, false if cannot
//    find the node.

{
    if (!root) // Base case 0: the tree is empty.
        return false;

    if (data == root->data) {
        // Base case:
        //    found the node. root refers to
        //    the pointer to the node to be removed...

        // Case 1: root has no more than one child. Replace root
        //    pointer with the pointer to that child.
        //    That unlinks the root node from the tree.
        //    Then delete the node.

        // First save root -- it points to the
        //    node to be removed:

        TREENODE *oldroot = root;
```

Continued ✑

```
        if (root->left == 0)          // No left child
            root = root->right;
        else if (root->right == 0) // No right child
            root = root->left;
        if (oldroot != root) {        // If one of the above...
            delete oldroot;
            return true;
        }

        // Case 2: root has both children.
        //    Find the smallest element
        //    in the right subtree.  Unlink that element and
        //    make it the new root.

        // First find the smallest element in the right subtree.
        //    To do that, keep going left as long as possible.
        //    Also keep track of its parent

        TREENODE *parent = root;
        TREENODE *next = root->right;
        while (next->left) {
            parent = next;
            next = next->left;
        }

        // Unlink this node from the tree (it doesn't have
        //    a left child, so we can connect its right child to its
        //    parent)

        if (parent == root)
            root->right = next->right;
        else
            parent->left = next->right;

        // Make this element the new root

        next->left = root->left;
        next->right = root->right;
        delete root;
        root = next;

        return true;
    }

    else if (data < root->data)        // Recursive case: remove
        return Remove(root->left, data);   //    from the left subtree

    else // if (data > root->data)         // Recursive case: remove
        return Remove(root->right, data);  //    from the right subtree

}
```

22.5. Binary Tree Traversals

The process of "visiting" (performing some operation on) each node of a tree is called *tree traversal*. The purpose of traversal is to process each node once. Traversal by itself is a very simple recursive procedure.

Three commonly used ways to traverse a tree are called *preorder, postorder*, and *inorder*. They differ in the sequence in which the nodes are visited. In the code below, the Visit (...) function just prints out the node's data:

```
// TEST.CPP

#include <iostream.h>
#include "tree.h"

inline void Visit (TREENODE *node)

{
    cout << node->data << ' ';
}

void TraversePreOrder(TREENODE *root)

{
    if (!root) return;
    Visit(root);
    TraversePreOrder(root->left);
    TraversePreOrder(root->right);
}

void TraversePostOrder(TREENODE *root)

{
    if (!root) return;
    TraversePostOrder(root->left);
    TraversePostOrder(root->right);
    Visit(root);
}

void TraverseInOrder(TREENODE *root)

{
    if (!root) return;
    TraverseInOrder(root->left);
    Visit(root);
    TraverseInOrder(root->right);
}
```

TESTTREE.CPP

In preorder traversal, we visit the root first, then process the left and right subtrees. In postorder traversal we process the subtrees first, then visit the root. Finally, in inorder traversal, we process the left subtree, visit the root, then process the right subtree. As an exercise, prove (using mathematical induction) that during an inorder traversal of a binary search tree, the data elements will be visited in ascending order.

The Visit(...) function depends on what we want to do with the nodes. We do not know in advance what "visiting" a node might entail. This is discussed further in relation to implementing the "Tree" ADT as a class in the next section.

In the following test program we start with an empty binary search tree, insert a few elements, and then traverse the tree in preorder, postorder and inorder:

TESTTREE.CPP

```cpp
int main()
{
    TREENODE *root = 0;

    Insert(root, "Mexico City");
    Insert(root, "Munich");
    Insert(root, "Montreal");
    Insert(root, "Moscow");
    Insert(root, "Los Angeles");
    Insert(root, "Seoul");
    Insert(root, "Barcelona");
    Insert(root, "Atlanta");
    Insert(root, "Sydney");

    cout << "Preorder:\n";
    TraversePreOrder(root);
    cout << "\n\n";

    cout << "Postorder:\n";
    TraversePostOrder(root);
    cout << "\n\n";

    cout << "Inorder:\n";
    TraverseInOrder(root);
    cout << "\n\n";

    Destroy(root);
    return 0;
}
```

The program builds the following binary search tree:

```
                  Mexico City
                 /          \
                /            \
        Los Angeles       Munich
             /            /      \
       Barcelona    Montreal    Seoul
          /              \          \
     Atlanta           Moscow      Sydney
```

It produces the following output:

```
Preorder:
Mexico City Los Angeles Barcelona Atlanta Munich Montreal Moscow Seoul Sydney

Postorder:
Atlanta Barcelona Los Angeles Moscow Montreal Sydney Seoul Munich Mexico City

Inorder:
Atlanta Barcelona Los Angeles Mexico City Montreal Moscow Munich Seoul Sydney
```

The preorder traversal reaches the root first; the postorder, last. The inorder traversal, as expected, produces the output sorted (alphabetically) in ascending order.

The shape of the tree depends on the order in which the elements are inserted. If we start with the largest or smallest element it will be placed in the root and one entire subtree will remain empty. In real applications, the order of inserting elements may be randomized. There are also special algorithms for *balancing* a binary search tree, which make the tree and its subtrees as symmetrical as possible. These issues are outside the scope of this book.

22.6.   Implementing Tree as a Class

The tree structure can be implemented as a class. The first approach would be simply to convert the `TREENODE` structure into a class and to make `Find(…)`, `Insert(…)`, and `Remove(…)` its member functions. `Insert(…)` and `Remove(…)` cannot pass the class object by reference, but we could get around that by making them return the new root pointer. Still, this would be a somewhat unusual class. The user would address the class instances only through pointers, and the new instances would be created only in member functions, so the constructor would be declared `private`. The destructor would do nothing, but we would have to use a recursive `Destroy(…)` member function:

```
TREENODE::~TREENODE()

{
    if (this) {
        left->Destroy();
        right->Destroy();
        delete this;
    }
}
```

(For an explanation of this see Chapter 21.)

A more conservative approach is to encapsulate the root node in a new class:

```
class TREE {

    . . .
   private:

    TREENODE *mRoot;
    . . .
};
```

The difficulty here is that the member functions Find(...), Insert(...), etc., do not take root as an argument because it is a member, but their recursive versions should. We would need recursive "helper" functions to actually do the finding and inserting:

```
TREENODE *TREE::Find(const apstring &data)
{
    return RecursiveFind(mRoot, data);
}
```

This is a bit cumbersome.

The biggest hurdle in both approaches is traversals. We have seen that the traversal code itself takes three lines, but how would the class know what the "visit" procedure is? With linked lists, this problem can be solved using *iterators* (see Section 21.7). With trees it is much easier to implement traversals recursively than iteratively, but in a recursive implementation iterators do not apply. We can include various "visit" functions inside the class, but then it will lose its generality. We could also leave traversals outside the class and make root public or provide an access function for it, but then the whole tree would become accessible outside the class, which would defeat the purpose of the class.

It is also possible to pass the "visit" function to the `Traverse(...)` member functions as an argument (a ***callback*** function). That would retain some level of generality for the class. This approach takes us into unexplored territory, but you can make it work as an exercise. You can use the following definitions:

TREE_CLS.CPP

```
// TREE.H
// ======

#ifndef _TREE_H_
#define _TREE_H_

#include "apstring.h"

struct TREENODE {
    apstring data;
    TREENODE *left;
    TREENODE *right;
};

typedef void CALLBACK(TREENODE *node);
    // Defines the CALLBACK data type as a function which takes one
    //    argument of the type TREENODE *...

class TREE {

  public:

    TREE() {        // Default constructor
        mRoot = 0;
    }

    bool Insert(const apstring &data) {
        return RecursiveInsert(mRoot, data);
    }

    void TraverseInOrder(CALLBACK Visit) {
        RecursiveTraverseInOrder(mRoot, Visit);
    }
    ...
    ~TREE() {
        Destroy(mRoot);
    }

  private:
```

Continued

```
    TREENODE *mRoot;

    // recursive "helper" functions:
    bool RecursiveInsert(TREENODE* &root, const apstring &data);
    void RecursiveTraverseInOrder(TREENODE *root, CALLBACK Visit);
    ...
    void Destroy(TREENODE *root);

};

#endif // _TREE_H_


// TREE.CPP
// ========

#include "tree.h"

bool TREE::RecursiveInsert(TREENODE* &root, const apstring &data)

{
    ...
}

void TREE::RecursiveTraverseInOrder(TREENODE *root, CALLBACK Visit)

{
    if (!root) return;
    RecursiveTraverseInOrder(root->left, Visit);
    Visit(root);
    RecursiveTraverseInOrder(root->right, Visit);
}

...

void TREE::Destroy(TREENODE *root)

{
    if (root) {
        Destroy(root->left);
        Destroy(root->right);
        delete root;
    }
}
```

Continued ☞

```
// TEST.CPP
// ========

#include <iostream.h>
#include "tree.h"

static void Visit (TREENODE *node)

{
    cout << node->data << ' ';
}

int main()

{
    TREE tree;

    tree.Insert("Mexico City");
    ...
    tree.Insert("Sydney");

    cout << "Inorder:\n";
    tree.TraverseInOrder(Visit);
    cout << endl;
    return 0;
}
```

22.7.   *Lab:* Morse Code

Morse Hall, the Mathematics Department building at Phillips Academy, Andover, Massachusetts, is named after Samuel F. B. Morse, who graduated from the academy in 1805.

In 1838, Samuel Morse devised a signaling code for use with his electromagnetic telegraph. The code used two basic signaling elements: the "dot," a short-duration electric current, and the "dash," a longer-duration signal. The signals lowered an ink pen mounted on a special arm, which left dots and dashes on the strip of paper moving beneath. Morse's code gained wide acceptance and, in its international form, is still in use. (Samuel Morse also achieved distinction as an artist, particularly as a painter of miniatures, and between 1826 and 1845 served as the first president of the National Academy of Design.)

In this project, we will simulate a telegraph station that can encode messages from text to Morse code and decode the Morse code back to text. The encoding is accomplished simply by looking up a symbol in a list and copying its Morse code into the output string. The decoding is implemented with the help of a binary "decoding" tree. Morse code for each letter represents a path from the root of the tree to some node: a "dot" means go left, and a "dash" means go right. The node at the end of the path contains the symbol corresponding to the code.

The station is implemented as a class TELEGRAPH defined in the MORSE.H header file. The class contains two static data members: mHead is a pointer to the linked list of Morse codes for encoding, and mRoot is the pointer to the decoding tree. The static member function Open() builds the list and the tree and Close() destroys them. Encode(...) and Decode(...) convert text to Morse code and vice versa. Symbols are separated in the Morse code string by one space and words by two spaces.

Fill in the blanks and test the program:

```
                                                          ┌──────────────────────────┐
                                                          │  MORSE.H          💾     │
                                                          └──────────────────────────┘
// MORSE.H

#ifndef _MORSE_H_
#define _MORSE_H_

#include "apstring.h"
#include "apvector.h"

struct LNODE {                  // Node of the Morse Code encoding list
    char symbol;
    apstring code;
    LNODE *next;

    LNODE(char c, const apstring &str)
        : symbol(c), code(str), next(0) {}      // Constructor
};

struct TNODE {                  // Node of the Morse Code decoding tree
    char symbol;
    TNODE *left;
    TNODE *right;

    TNODE() : symbol('*'), left(0), right(0) {}  // Constructor
};
```

Continued

```
class TELEGRAPH {

    // This is an unusual class: it has only static data members--
    //    mHead, the head of the encoding list, and mRoot, the root
    //    of the decoding tree.  These list and tree are the same for all
    //    class instances.
    //
    //    Such class doesn't need a constructor or destructor because they
    //    wouldn't be able to deal with static members, anyway.  Instead
    //    the list and the tree are initialized in the static member
    //    function Open() and destroyed in the static function Close().

  public:

    static void Open();
    static void Close();

    void Encode(const apstring &text, apstring &morse);
    void Decode(const apstring &morse, apstring &text);

  private:

    static void RecursiveDestroy(TNODE *root);
    static void Insert(char symbol, const apstring &morsecode);

    static LNODE *mHead;        // The head of the decoding list.
    static TNODE *mRoot;        // The root of the decoding tree.
};

#endif _MORSE_H_
```

```
                                              ┌─────────────────────────┐
                                              │  MORSE.CPP          💾  │
                                              └─────────────────────────┘
// MORSE.CPP

#include <ctype.h>
#include "morse.h"

static const char DOT = '.';
static const char DASH = '-';

LNODE *TELEGRAPH::mHead = 0;
TNODE *TELEGRAPH::mRoot = 0;


//*************************************************************
```

Continued ➪

```
void TELEGRAPH::Open()

// Builds the encoding list and decoding tree for TELEGRAPH.

{
    // Create the mHead node:
    mHead = new LNODE(' ', "");   // A space char is encoded as
                                  //    the empty string.

    // Create the mRoot node:

    mRoot = new TNODE;
    if (!mRoot) return;
    mRoot->symbol = ' ';

    // Add codes to the encoding list and decoding tree:

    Insert ('A', ".-");
    ... ( in the file on disk)
    Insert ('Z', "--..");
    Insert ('0', "-----");
    ...
    Insert ('9', "----.");
    ...
    Insert ('?', "..--..");
}

void TELEGRAPH::Close()

// Destroys the encoding list.
// Destroys the decoding tree by calling the recursive helper function.

{
    // Destroy the encoding list:
    ...
    ...

    // Destroy the decoding tree:
    RecursiveDestroy(mRoot);
    mRoot = 0;
}

//*****************************************************************

void TELEGRAPH::RecursiveDestroy(TNODE *root)

{
    ...
    ...
}
```

Continued ☞

```
void TELEGRAPH::Insert (char symbol, const apstring &morsecode)

// Inserts a symbol and its Morse code into the encoding list
//    and decoding tree.
//    Each Morse code character will correspond to a path in the tree
//    from the root to a node: at a "dot" go left, at a "dash" go
//    right.  The node at the end of the path holds the symbol
//    for that character.

{
    // Append a new node at the end of the encoding list:

    LNODE *lnode;

    lnode = mHead;
    while (lnode->next)
        lnode = lnode->next;
    lnode->next = new LNODE(symbol, morsecode);

    // Insert a new node into the decoding tree:

    int i, len = morsecode.length();
    TNODE *tnode = mRoot;

    for (i = 0;   i < len;   i++) {
        if (morsecode[i] == DOT) {
            ...
            ...
        }
        else { // if (morsecode[i] == DASH)
            ...
            ...
        }
    }
    tnode->symbol = symbol;
}

//*************************************************************

void TELEGRAPH::Encode(const apstring &text, apstring &morse)

// Converts text into Morse code.

{
    int i, len = text.length();
    LNODE *lnode;
    char ch;

    morse = "";                              // Make the morse string empty;

    for (i = 0;   i < len;   i++) {
        ch = toupper(text[i]);
```

Continued ☞

```
            // Find this symbol in the encoding list;
            //   (skip this symbol if not found):
            for (lnode = mHead;  lnode;  lnode = lnode->next)
                if (lnode->symbol == ch)
                    break;

            // Append the code to the morse string
            //   (add one space to separate letters):
            if (lnode)
                morse += lnode->code + ' ';
/*
    The above statement looks neat, but it may be atrociously
    inefficient.  We start with an empty string and may end up
    with a string of considerable length.  Each time += is executed,
    the string buffer may be reallocated and the whole string will
    be copied into the new buffer.  This is repeated for every
    character in the text string.  To avoid such situations we
    could add a constructor to the apstring class that would
    build an empty string but allocate a large buffer for future
    expansion.  We could also add the space character to
    the codes that we place into the encoding list in the Insert()
    function instead of executing + every time here:

    (e.g. lnode->next = new LNODE(symbol, morsecode + ' ');)

    Alternatively, we could use null-terminated strings to handle
    concatenation more efficiently.
*/
    }
}


void TELEGRAPH::Decode(const apstring &morse, apstring &text)

// Converts Morse code into text.

{
    TNODE *tnode;
    int i, len = morse.length();

    text = "";                              // Make the text string empty;

    tnode = mRoot;

    // For each char in the encoded message (can be
    //   a dot, a dash, or a space):
```

Continued

```
    for (i = 0;   i < len;   i++) {
        // Go down the tree as long as you get dots or dashes.
        //   When you encounter a space, take the symbol from
        //   the node, add it to the text string, and return
        // to the mRoot.
            ...
            ...
        }
    }
}
```

TSTMORSE.CPP

```
// TSTMORSE.CPP

// This program tests the TELEGRAPH class. It prompts the user for a
//   "telegram", encodes it in Morse code, "sends" the telegram,
//   decodes the Morse code message and displays it.

#include <iostream.h>
#include <string.h>
#include "morse.h"

int main()

{
    TELEGRAPH station;
    apstring text, morse;

    TELEGRAPH::Open();

    cout << "\nEnter telegram ==> ";
    getline(cin, text);
    cout << "\nSending >>>  ";
    station.Encode(text, morse);
    cout << morse;
    cout << "  >>> Received\n\n";
    station.Decode(morse, text);
    cout << text << endl;

    TELEGRAPH::Close();
    return 0;
}
```

22.8.   *Programming Project:* e-Mail Revisited

This project builds upon the toy e-mail system developed in the Section 20.5 lab exercise. One of that system's flaws was that subscribers were kept in an array, which made it cumbersome to add or delete subscribers or search the list. A binary search tree structure is much more appropriate for a system with a large number of subscribers. Modify the system by adding the following features:

1. Change the structure to keep subscribers in a binary search tree instead of an array.

2. Add a password check at login and allow subscribers to change their password.

3. Keep track of the number of unread messages in each mailbox and report it at login.

4. Do not add subscribers automatically. Designate a special subscriber, SysOp, who, in addition to the usual mail commands, will have system privileges for adding and deleting subscribers. Make SysOp assign default passwords to new subscribers. Have SysOp log into the system just like any other subscriber, but make her name "SYSOP" and give her some additional functions to choose from her menu.

For "extra credit":

5. For billing purposes, keep track of the total number of messages sent by each subscriber. Allow SysOp to run a "billing cycle" in which she reports the charges for each subscriber (for instance, you can charge $.20 for each sent message, making all received messages and the first 3 sent messages free) and zero out the sent-message counter.

6. Save/read the whole system (the subscribers' tree and their mailboxes) to/from a file; (Optional: encrypt the passwords in the file). See below for a hint on how to save a tree in a file.

Prepare a report on testing, including your testing strategy and results.

Saving a Binary Tree in a File:

You can save a binary tree in a file and load it from a file using recursive functions. You can use some markers, such as [and], to separate the tree (and all its subtrees) from the rest of the file. The recursive functions are called from small, non-recursive functions that open and close the file with the given name:

```
// TREE.H

struct TREENODE {
    apstring data;
    TREENODE *left;
    TREENODE *right;
};

...
```

TREEFILE.CPP

```
// TREEFILE.CPP

#include <iostream.h>
#include <fstream.h>
#include "tree.h"

static void RecursiveSave (ofstream &file, TREENODE *root);
static void RecursiveLoad (ifstream &file, TREENODE* &root);

//*************************************************************

void SaveTree (const apstring &fileName, TREENODE *root)

// Opens a file for writing and saves the tree in it.

{
    ofstream file(fileName.c_str());
    if (!file) {
        cerr << "Cannot create " << fileName << endl;
        return;
    }
    RecursiveSave(file, root);
}

//*************************************************************
```

Continued ☞

```
void LoadTree (const apstring &fileName, TREENODE* &root)

// Opens a file for reading and loads the tree from it.
// If the file does not exist, returns null.

{
    ifstream file(fileName.c_str());
    if (!file) {
        cerr << "Cannot open " << fileName << endl;
        return;
    }
    RecursiveLoad(file, root);
}

//*************************************************************
//***          Recursive Save and Load functions          ***
//*************************************************************

static void RecursiveSave (ofstream &file, TREENODE *root)

// Recursive helper function -- called from SaveTree;
// Assumes that file is open for writing.

{
    file << "[";
    if (root) {
        file << endl;
        file << root->data << endl;
        RecursiveSave (file, root->left);
        RecursiveSave (file, root->right);
    }
    file << "]\n";  // An empty tree is saved as one line: []
}

//*************************************************************

static void RecursiveLoad (ifstream &file, TREENODE* &root)

// Recursive helper function -- called from LoadTree.
// Assumes that file is open for reading and that the tree is empty.

{
    apstring line;

    if (root != 0)
        return;

    // Skip all lines before the first '[':
    while (getline(file, line))
        if (line.length() > 0 && line[0] == '[')
            break;
```

Continued ☞

```
        if (line.length() >= 2 && line[1] == ']')
                                        // If the tree is empty...
            return;

        getline(file, line);          // Read the next line
        root = new TREENODE;
        root->data = line;
        root->left =
        root->right = 0;
        RecursiveLoad(file, root->left);
        RecursiveLoad(file, root->right);
        getline(file, line);            // Read the closing ']'
        if (line.length() < 1 || line[0] != ']')
            cerr << "Tree file format error: " << line << endl;
}
```

22.9.   Summary

A tree is a structure of connected nodes where each node, except one special root node, is connected to one parent node and may have one or more child nodes. Each node has a unique ascending path to the root. A tree is an inherently recursive structure because each node in a tree can be considered the root of its own tree, called a subtree. A binary tree is a tree where each node has no more than two children. These are referred to as the left and right children. In the linked representation, each node of a tree contains pointers to its child nodes. The nodes of a tree contain some data elements.

The nodes of a tree are arranged in layers: all nodes at the same level are connected to the root with a path of the same length. The number of levels in a tree is called its height or depth. One important property of trees is that they can hold a large number of elements in a relatively shallow structure. A full binary tree with h levels contains 2^h-1 elements.

A binary search tree is a binary tree whose data elements have some relation of order defined for them and are organized so that the data element in each node is larger than all the elements in the node's left subtree and smaller than all the elements in its right subtree. The binary search tree combines the benefits of an array for quick binary search and a linked list for easy element insertion and deletion.

Due to the recursive structure of trees, it is convenient to use recursive functions when working with them. This is especially true for the Destroy(...) function, which deletes all the nodes of a tree, and tree traversal functions that "visit" each node of the tree once. The `Find(...)` function, which finds a node with a target value, can be implemented recursively as well as with iterations.

Preorder tree traversal first visits the root of the tree, then processes its left and right subtrees; postorder traversal first processes the left and right subtrees, then visits the root; inorder traversal first processes the left subtree, then visits the root, then processes the right subtree.

The binary tree and binary search tree can be implemented as C++ classes after resolving some minor technical problems.

23

Expression Trees

23.1. Discussion

An algebraic expression with parentheses and defined precedence of operations is a nested structure which can be naturally represented by a binary tree, called an *expression tree*. A single binary operation can be represented as:

```
        operator
       /        \
   first        second
   operand      operand
```

For example, a + b can be represented as:

```
      +
     / \
    a   b
```

This is a building block for a binary tree. Each node of the expression tree contains a token, which can be an "operator" or an "operand." In a more general definition, an operator may be a unary or binary operator, or even any function of one or two arguments. For the sake of simplicity, we will consider only the binary arithmetic operators (+, −, *, /). An operand can be a variable or a number. The expression

$$(a + 1)(bc + 5 - c)$$

for example, is represented as:

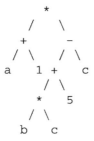

```
              *
           /     \
         +          -
        / \       /  \
       a   1     +     c
                / \
               *   5
              / \
             b   c
```

In an expression tree, operators are represented by nodes with children, and operands are represented by leaves.

The expression tree can be built recursively. For instance, if

$Expr = (Expr1) * (Expr2)$

then the expression tree for *Expr* will be:

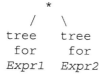

If an expression is given to us as a string of characters in the usual algebraic notation, a recursive *parsing* procedure can convert it into an expression tree. (*Parsing* is a general term that refers to converting text into some structured representation.) The parsing procedure may work along these lines:

```
Parsing an algebraic expression:
    If the expression is empty, do nothing.
    If the expression is a single operand, create one
        leaf node for that operand.
    If the entire expression is enclosed in
        parentheses, drop them and parse (recursive
        step) the expression inside.
    Otherwise, find the last operator of the lowest
        precedence order outside of any parentheses.
        Create a root node for that operator.  Parse
        (recursive step) the part of the expression to
        the left of that operator and append the
        resulting tree as the root's left subtree.
        Parse the part of the expression to the right
        of the operator and append the resulting tree
        as the root's right subtree.
```

23.2. Evaluating Expressions Represented by Trees

Expression *evaluation* means calculating the value of the expression for some given values of its variables. Recursion is the easiest way to implement an evaluation function for expression trees. If a node is an operand, we simply fetch its value; if it is an operator, we apply that operator to the results of evaluation of the left and right subtrees. Operands are represented by leaf nodes, operators by nodes with children:

```
inline bool IsLeaf(XNODE *node)

// Returns true if the node is a leaf.

{
    return (node && !node->left && !node->right);
}

inline bool IsOperator(XNODE *node)

// Returns true if the node is an operator.

{
    return (node && (node->left || node->right));
}
```

For demonstration purposes we will assume that operands and operators are represented by character strings in tree nodes:

```
struct XNODE {
    apstring token;      // Represents either an operator or an operand.
    XNODE *left;
    XNODE *right;
};
```

An expression evaluation function may look as follows:

```
double Eval(XNODE *root)

// Returns the value of the expression represented by
//   an expression tree.
// GetValue(...) and ApplyOperation(...) functions are
//   not defined here.

{
    double value;

    if (IsLeaf(root))                // root->token is an operand...
        value = GetValue(root->token);
    else                             // root->token is an operator...
        value = ApplyOperation(root->token,
                    Eval(root->left), Eval(root->right));
    return value;
}
```

Eval (...) calls the GetValue (...) function, which presumably converts a number into a double or gets the value of a variable, perhaps from some table of variables. ApplyOperation(op, x, y) returns the sum, product, etc., for x and y, depending on the operation specified in op.

As a lab exercise, you can add a constructor for the XNODE structure:

```
XNODE(const apstring &s, XNODE *lptr, XNODE *rptr);
```

This will help you initialize nodes. Then you can "hard code" the expression tree for

$$(a + 1)(bc + 5 - c)$$

directly into the program:

```
int main()

{
    /*

    Expression tree for the expression

        (a+1)(bc + 5 - c)
```

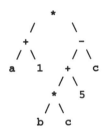

```
    */
    XNODE node1 ("b", 0, 0);    // Left and right pointers are set
                                // to null.
    XNODE node2 ("c", 0, 0);
    XNODE node3 ("*", &node1, &node2);
                                // Left and right pointers are set to
                                //   the addresses of node1 and node2.
    XNODE node4 ("5", 0, 0);
    XNODE node5 ("a", 0, 0);
    XNODE node6 ("1", 0, 0);
    XNODE node7 ("+", &node3, &node4);
    XNODE node8 ("c", 0, 0);
    XNODE node9 ("+", &node5, &node6);
    XNODE node10 ("-", &node7, &node8);
    XNODE node11 ("*", &node9, &node10);
    XNODE *root = &node11;      // root is set to the address of node11.
    ...
}
```

You can code the `GetValue(…)` and `ApplyOperation(…)` functions, prompt the user for the values of *a*, *b*, and *c*, and test your `Eval(…)` function.

23.3.   Prefix and Postfix Notations

An inorder traversal of an expression tree will print out the expression in a fully parenthesized form. We need some additional logic in the `PrintExprInOrder(…)` function for printing parentheses:

```
void PrintExprInOrder(XNODE *root)

// Prints out the expression in a fully parenthesized form
//    from an expression tree.

{
    if (root) {
        if (IsOperator(root->left)) cout << '(';
        PrintExprInOrder(root->left);
        if (IsOperator(root->left)) cout << ')';

        cout << ' ' << root->token << ' ';

        if (IsOperator(root->right)) cout << '(';
        PrintExprInOrder(root->right);
        if (IsOperator(root->right)) cout << ')';
    }
}

int main()

{
    ...
    cout << "Infix Notation:    ";
    PrintExprInOrder(root);
    cout << "\n\n";
    ...
}
```

The output will be:

```
Infix Notation:    ( a + 1 ) * ((( b * c ) + 5 ) - c )
...
```

This conventional algebraic notation is called ***infix notation***. In infix notation, the operator is placed between the operands:

Infix: $x + y$

There are two other ways to represent expressions which are not used in everyday life but are very useful in computer applications. They are called **prefix** and **postfix** notations. In prefix notation we place the operator <u>before</u> the operands, and in postfix notation we place it <u>after</u> the operands:

Prefix: $+ x y$
Postfix: $x y +$

Prefix and postfix notations are very convenient for evaluating expressions because they do not use parentheses and do not need to take into account the precedence of the operators. The order of operations can be uniquely reconstructed from the expression itself. For example, an expression in postfix notation

$$a \; 1 + b \; c * 5 + c - *$$

is evaluated in the following order:

$$(a \; 1 +) \, (((b \; c \, *) \, 5 +) \, c -) \, *$$

But there is no need to show parentheses because there is only one way of correctly placing them. We will show later in this section how to evaluate algebraic expressions written in prefix and postfix notations.

As you can guess, prefix and postfix notations for an algebraic expression can be generated by traversing the expression tree in preorder and postorder, respectively. If we add the preorder and postorder traversal functions to our program —

```
void PrintExprPreOrder(XNODE *root)

// Prints out an expression in prefix notation.

{
    if (root) {
        cout << root->token << ' ';
        PrintExprPreOrder(root->left);
        PrintExprPreOrder(root->right);
    }
}
```

```
    void PrintExprPostOrder(XNODE *root)

    // Prints out an expression in postfix notation.

    {
        if (root) {
            PrintExprPostOrder(root->left);
            PrintExprPostOrder(root->right);
            cout << root->token << ' ';
        }
    }

    . . .

    int main()

    {
        . . .

        cout << "Prefix Notation:   ";
        PrintExprPreOrder(root);
        cout << "\n\n";

        cout << "Postfix Notation: ";
        PrintExprPostOrder(root);
        cout << "\n\n";

        . . .
    }
```

— the output will be:

```
. . .

Prefix Notation:   * + a 1 - + * b c 5 c

Postfix Notation: a 1 + b c * 5 + c - *
```

We would like to stress, again, that both prefix and postfix notations unambiguously represent the original expression without any parentheses! We will see shortly that we can go back and reconstruct the expression tree from either of them.

Prefix notation is also called **Polish notation** after the Polish mathematician, Łukasiewicz, who invented it, and postfix notation is sometimes called **reverse Polish notation (RPN)**.

As opposed to conventional infix notation, which requires recursive evaluation of subtrees, the prefix and postfix notations allow us to evaluate an algebraic expression in a single sequential swipe. In postfix notation we proceed from left to right. The algorithm uses a temporary stack for holding unused operands and intermediate results:

```
To evaluate an expression in postfix notation:
   Going from left to right, consider the next token:
      If it is an operand: push its value on the stack.
      If it is an operator: pop the second operand,
         pop the first operand, perform the operation,
         push the result on the stack.
```

If the initial expression was valid, we will be left at the end with one value on the stack — the evaluation result.

Taking, again,

$$a\ 1 + b\ c * 5 + c - *$$

as an example, let us see the evolution of the stack (the elements under each token represent the stack contents after the program encounters that token).

a	1	+	b	c	*	5	+	c	-		*
				c		5		c			
	1		b	b	bc	bc	bc+5	bc+5	bc+5-c		
a	a	a+1	a+1	a+1	a+1	a+1	a+1	a+1	a+1		(a+1)(bc+5-c)

To evaluate an expression given in prefix notation, we do essentially the same thing, only going from right to left.

```
To evaluate an expression in prefix notation:
   Going from right to left, consider the next token:
      If it is an operand: push its value on the stack.
      If it is an operator: pop the first operand,
         pop the second operand, perform the operation,
         push the result on the stack.
```

You may find it peculiar that the operands appear in the same order in the infix, postfix, and prefix notations — only the position of the operators is different. This is a good test for converting one notation into another manually.

A manual procedure for short expressions does not have to follow the above formal algorithms: after some practice, triplets of operators with corresponding operands can be spotted immediately and replaced with their calculated results or parenthesized infix equivalents.

Very similar procedures can be used to reconstruct the expression tree from an expression in postfix or prefix notation. Instead of numbers, we push pointers to nodes on stack; instead of performing an operation, we link the operator node to the nodes of the operands.

```
To build the expression tree from a postfix expression:
   Going from left to right, take the next token:
      Create a new node for the token.
      If it is an operand: set the left and right children
         to null and push the pointer to the new node on
         the stack.
      If it is an operator: pop a pointer from the stack and
         set the new node's right child to it.
         Pop another pointer from the stack and set the
         new node's left child to it.
         Push the pointer to the new node on the stack.
```

At the end, the pointer to the root of the tree will be the only remaining element on the stack.

Finally, if we want to convert an expression from postfix notation into prefix notation, we can reconstruct the expression tree using the above procedure and then traverse the tree in preorder.

23.4.   Summary

Binary trees are a natural way to represent algebraic expressions. Leaf nodes represent operands, and other nodes represent operators. To build an expression tree from an ordinary algebraic expression we need to parse the expression. Parsing refers to the process of converting text to some more structured form. A parsing routine may be implemented as a recursive function.

You can print out the original expression in the conventional parenthesized form, called infix notation, through an inorder traversal of the expression tree. Preorder and postorder traversals convert the expression into prefix notation and postfix notation, respectively. In prefix notation the operation sign is placed before the two operands, and in postfix notation the operation sign is placed after the two operands. Postfix notation is also called reverse Polish notation, or RPN.

Postfix notation is very convenient for representing expressions without parentheses and without regard to the precedence of the operators. A postfix expression can be evaluated in one sequential swipe from left to right with the help of a stack that holds unused operands and intermediate results. A similar procedure can be used to reconstruct the expression tree from a postfix expression. The same applies to prefix expressions, but they have to be processed from right to left.

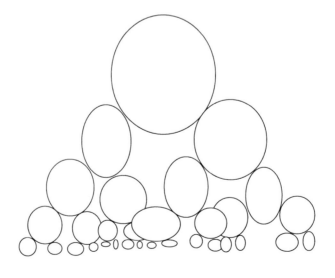

24

Heaps

24.1. Discussion

In some applications it is important to maintain a large set of elements that are ranked in some way and to have quick access to the highest-ranked element. A structure that supports this functionality is the ***priority queue***.

Consider, for example, a credit card authorization processing system in which pending transactions are phoned from merchants to the bank's central office for authorization. In addition to checking available credit limits, the system may run all its transactions through a special fraud detection module that ranks them according to the likelihood of fraud. All the transactions that receive a significant fraud score may be inserted into a priority queue, ranked by their score, for review by specially trained operators.

One obvious way of implementing a priority queue is to keep all the elements in a list in order of their rank. The element of the highest rank would be the last element in the list. This would be very convenient for accessing and removing that element, but to insert a new element, you would need to scan through the list until you found the spot corresponding to its rank. If the list were long, this could take considerable time. In an application where elements are frequently inserted and removed, the insert operation would create a bottleneck that would offset the advantage of instantaneous removal.

You may recall from previous chapters that binary search trees allow us to combine the advantages of quick binary search with relatively quick insertion and removal of elements. Binary trees of another type, called ***heaps***, help us implement the priority queue in such a way that both insertion and removal of elements is quick. In a heap, the largest element is in its root, and each node holds the largest element of the tree rooted in it. Insertion or removal of an element takes a number of steps less than or equal to the height of the tree, which is only $\log_2 n$ for a tree with n nodes. For a tree with a million nodes, we would have to run through at most 20 steps, as opposed to the average of half a million steps in a sequential list implementation.

The algorithm for quick insertion of elements into a heap requires going from a node to its parent. In the linked representation of a tree, we could add to the node structure a pointer to the node's parent. A more efficient way of implementing heaps, however, is based on non-linked representation of binary trees. In this method, all nodes are stored in an array in a certain order so that for each node it is easy to find its children and its parent.

24.2.   Binary Trees: Non-Linked Representation

A binary tree is called *full* if all its levels are filled with nodes. A binary tree is called *complete* if it has no gaps on any level. The last level may have some leaves missing on the right, but every node except the last must have a node after it. Figure 24-1 shows the shapes of a complete tree and a full tree. A full tree with h levels has 2^h-1 nodes. The number of nodes in its last level is 2^{h-1}.

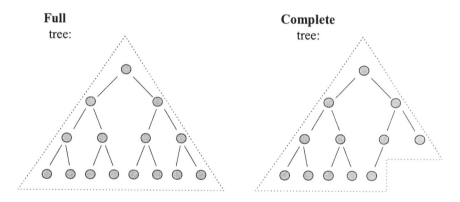

Figure 24-1. The shapes of *full* and *complete* trees.

If we have a complete tree, we can number all its nodes starting from 1 at the root, then proceeding from left to right at each consecutive level (Figure 24-2). Since the tree is complete, there are no gaps between its nodes, so a node's number tells us exactly where in the tree we can find it. In a full tree, each level contains twice as many nodes as the preceding level. The left and right children of the i-th node, if they are present, have the numbers $2i$ and $2i+1$, and its parent has the number $i/2$ (truncated to an integer).

We have numbered all the nodes of a complete tree with n nodes from 1 to n in such a way that knowing the number of a node lets us easily find the numbers of its left and right child and its parent. This property allows us to store a complete tree in an array where the element x[i] corresponds to node number i (Figure 24-3). This is one of a few cases where it is convenient to count the elements starting from 1, as opposed to the C++ convention of indexing the elements of an array starting from 0. In the C++ implementation it is convenient either to leave the first element of the array (x[0]) unused or to use it for some other purpose, such as for holding some additional information about the tree.

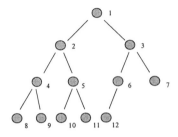

Figure 24-2. Numbering of the nodes in a complete tree.

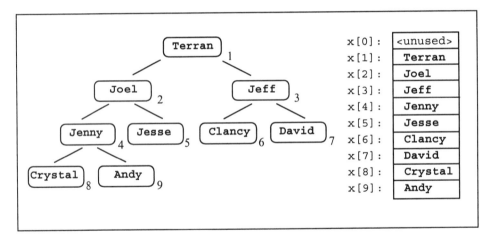

Figure 24-3. Representation of a complete binary tree in an array.

24.3.   Implementation of a Heap

A *heap* is a complete binary tree in which nodes hold some ranked data elements, and the element in each node is ranked at least as high as all the elements in its subtrees. In a heap, the rank of the element in the root node is the highest. Unlike binary search trees, heaps are allowed to have more than one element of the same rank and elements in the left subtree do not have to be ranked lower than elements in the right subtree. We can also consider heaps with reverse ordering where the element of the lowest rank is in the root and the rank of each node is not higher than ranks of all the nodes in its subtrees. These are often called *inverted* or *minimum* heaps.

The best way to implement a heap is through the array representation of a binary tree, where the element x[1] of the array corresponds to the root of the heap (Figure 24-4). The array may contain data elements, records, database access keys, pointers to strings, or pointers to data records. We have to specify some way of ranking these data elements.

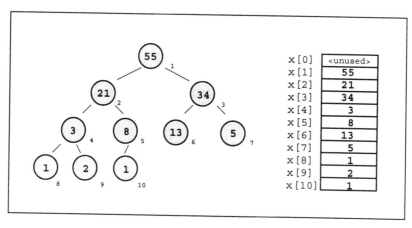

Figure 24-4. A heap of numbers, stored in an array.

In the following code the HEAP class is implemented as a templated class with elements of itemType for which the assignment and <= operators make sense. The heap array is implemented as a dynamically allocated array of the specified size. HEAP.H defines the class:

```
                                              ┌─────────────────────────┬──────┐
                                              │  HEAP.H              💾 │
                                              ├─────────────────────────┴──────┤
// HEAP.H

// Heap template class
// Author: Q. Prior

#ifndef _HEAP_H_
#define _HEAP_H_

#include "apvector.h"

template <class itemType>
class HEAP {

  private:

    int mSize;                  // Maximum size
    int mNodes;                 // Current number of nodes
    apvector<itemType> mBuffer; // Array of heap elements

  public:

    HEAP (int size = 1024);   // Constructor
    ~HEAP();
    bool isEmpty();
    bool isFull();
    bool Insert(const itemType &x);
    bool Remove(itemType &x);
};

  . . .

#endif // _HEAP_H_
```

The HEAP constructor uses an initializer list to set up a buffer of the specified size.
It sets the number of nodes to 0 for an empty heap:

```
                                                    ┌─────────────────────┐
                                                    │ HEAP.H        [💾] │
────────────────────────────────────────────────┤─────────────────────┤──
template <class itemType>
HEAP<itemType>::HEAP(int size)

// Constructor: builds a heap of size "size".

        : mNodes(0), mSize(size), mBuffer(size + 1)
        // Buffer is size+1 because the first element is not used.
{}

template <class itemType>
HEAP<itemType>::~HEAP()

// Destructor.

{}

//****************************************************************

template <class itemType>
bool HEAP<itemType>::isEmpty()

{
    return mNodes == 0;
}

template <class itemType>
bool HEAP<itemType>::isFull()
{
    return mNodes == mSize;
}
```

The heap `Insert(...)` function has to add an element to a heap while preserving the ordering property of its elements and at the same time making sure that the heap remains a complete tree. This requires some rearranging of nodes, but, fortunately, we do not have to move around all the nodes. We can visualize the insert operation as first appending a new element at the end of the heap, then moving it up from level to level by swapping it with its parent until it reaches the right place. The "last" element of the heap is the last element in its array representation, which is the rightmost occupied node of the bottom level of the tree. The procedure that adjusts the order of nodes in the heap by moving an element up the heap is called the "Reheap Up" procedure. In reality, when we insert a new element into a heap, there is no need to add it to the heap first and then physically swap it from level to level. Instead, we can move the element up "logically" by creating a vacancy for it in the heap and then inserting it into the right spot (Figure 24-5).

```
                                                    ┌─────────────────┐
                                                    │ HEAP.H       💾 │
─────────────────────────────────────────────────────┘                 └───
template <class itemType>
bool HEAP<itemType>::Insert(const itemType &x)

// Inserts x into the heap.
// Returns true if successful, false if the heap is full.

{
    if (isFull())
        return false;

    mNodes++;  // The last node of the heap is now vacant.

    // Starting from the (vacant) last node, go from node i to
    //    its parent iParent and, as long as the parent is
    //    smaller than x, move the parent down:

    int i = mNodes;
    int iParent;

    while (i > 1) {
        iParent = i/2;
        if (x <= mBuffer[iParent])
            break;
        mBuffer[i] = mBuffer[iParent]; // Move the parent down;
        i = iParent;                   // mBuffer[i] is now vacant.
    }

    // Insert x into the created vacancy:
    mBuffer[i] = x;

    return true;
}
```

The heap Remove (...) function is similar. We always remove an element from the root of the heap. After that the heap needs some adjustment to preserve its ordering property and to keep it a complete tree. We can visualize this procedure as first placing the last element of the heap into its root, then moving it down from level to level, swapping it with its larger child until it falls into place. This is called the "Reheap Down" procedure. Again, the swapping is done "logically" by simply moving the vacant spot down the heap before the last element of the heap is put into it (Figure 24-6).

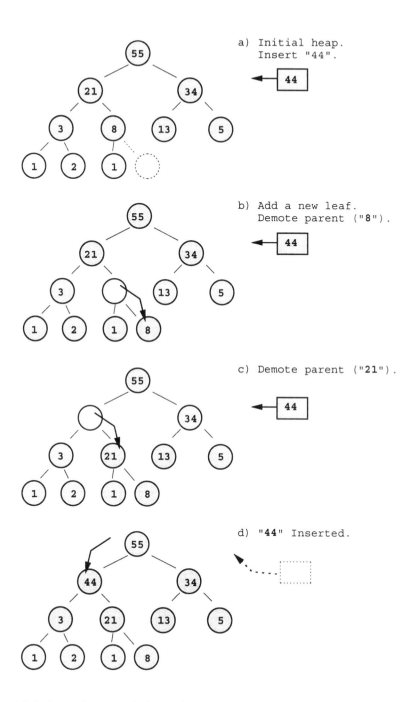

a) Initial heap.
   Insert "44".

b) Add a new leaf.
   Demote parent ("8").

c) Demote parent ("21").

d) "44" Inserted.

Figure 24-5. Inserting a node into a heap.

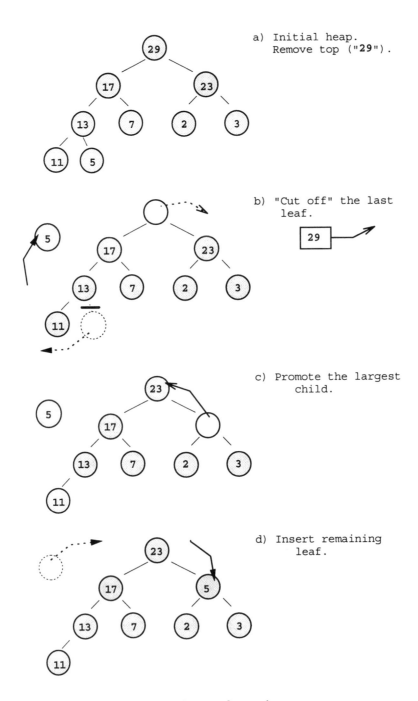

a) Initial heap.
   Remove top ("**29**").

b) "Cut off" the last
   leaf.

c) Promote the largest
   child.

d) Insert remaining
   leaf.

Figure 24-6. Removing the top element from a heap.

```
template <class itemType>
bool HEAP<itemType>::Remove(itemType &x)

// Removes the largest element (from the root of the heap).
// Returns true if successful, false if the heap is empty.

{
    if (isEmpty())
        return false;

    // Retrieve the top element:

    x = mBuffer[1];

    // Starting from the vacant root, go from node iParent to its
    //    larger child i and, as long as that child
    //    is greater than the last element of the heap,
    //    move that child up:

    int iParent = 1;        // root
    int i = 2;              // its left child

    while (i <= mNodes) {
        // Set i to the right child, i+1, if it
        //    exists and is larger:
        if (i < mNodes && mBuffer[i] < mBuffer[i+1]) i++;

        // Compare with the last node:
        if (mBuffer[i] <= mBuffer[mNodes]) break;

        mBuffer[iParent] = mBuffer[i];    // Move the child up;
        iParent = i;                      // mBuffer[iParent] is now vacant.
        i *= 2;                           // i is set to its left child
    }

    // Move the last element into the created vacancy:
    if (mNodes > 1)
        mBuffer[iParent] = mBuffer[mNodes];
    mNodes--;

    return true;
}
```

24.4. *Programming Project:* Stock Exchange

A stock exchange is an organization for trading shares in publicly owned companies. In the OTC ("Over the Counter") system, stocks are traded electronically through a vast network of dealers in securities connected to a computer network. There is no physical "stock exchange" location. The system keeps track of "buy" and "sell" orders placed by customers through their brokers and automatically executes orders when the highest "bid price" (order to buy shares at a certain price) meets the lowest "ask price" (offer to sell shares for a certain minimum price). There are also "market" orders to buy or sell shares at the current "bid" or "ask" price. With the advent of modern technology, some electronic brokerages let customers place their own orders through their personal computers over a modem or computer network.

Shares are normally sold in units of 100. The stocks are identified by their trading symbols, all capital letters. For example, Microsoft is "MSFT" and Intel is "INTC."

In this project you will implement a toy OTC system for trading in a dozen stocks. The system will maintain a list of all active buy and sell orders for each stock. In your system a customer can log in, give his or her name, request quotes (current prices) and place orders. An order holds the name of the customer, a buy or sell indicator, the stock symbol, the number of shares, and a price limit (or "market"). Your system does not have to keep track of the availability of money or shares on "customer" accounts.

Stock prices are traditionally quoted in dollars and fractions of 1/2, 1/4, 1/8, etc. For example, "52 1/2" means $52.50, and "38 7/8" means $38.87. But there is some talk about switching to the decimal system. For the sake of simplicity, your system may use dollars and cents.

Your system should keep all buy orders for each stock in a priority queue ranked by the bid price, and all sell orders in an inverted priority queue with the smallest "ask" price order on top. The priority queues may be implemented using the templated class HEAP. After a new order comes in, the system checks if it can be executed and, if so, executes it and reports to both parties as follows:

```
Sharon K.:                                                    ⌨
You sold 2000 of  MSFT at $84.37.
Commission $19.95.
Total proceeds $168720.05.

Bill M.:
You bought 2000 of  MSFT at $84.37.
Commission $19.95.
Total due $168759.95.
```

The system executes a "market" buy order at the price of the lowest ask and a "market" sell order at the price of the highest bid. Normally they can be executed immediately as they arrive. In the unlikely event that there is only a "market" sell and a "market" buy, execute them at the last sale price.

Your system should keep track of the day's "high" and "low" prices and the last sale price for each stock and be able to quote them to customers on demand. The quote should also contain the current (highest) bid and (lowest) ask and the number of shares in them. For example:

```
MSFT                                                          ⌨
Hi:  89.50    Lo: 82.87      Last: 84.37
Bid  82.87    Bid size  2000
Ask  84.00    Ask size  1000
```

In your system all orders will be "partial" orders. This means that if an order cannot be executed for the total number of shares requested in it, the maximum possible number of shares will change hands and a partial order for the remaining shares will still be active. For bid and ask quotes and partial orders you will need to add a function that "peeks" at the top of the heap without removing an element from it.

In addition to the source code and a working program, develop a plan for testing your program.

24.5. Summary

A binary tree is called complete if all its levels are completely filled with nodes without gaps up to the last level, which may have nodes missing on the right. A heap is a complete binary tree that holds some ranked data elements in such a way that the root holds an element of the highest rank and each node holds an element ranked not lower than all elements in its subtree. A heap is allowed to have several elements of the same rank. The heap structure is an efficient way of implementing a priority queue in which we can insert elements at any rank but remove the element of the highest rank. The heap allows us to insert or remove an element in $\log_2 n$ steps, where n is the total number of elements in the priority queue.

The best way of implementing a heap is through the non-linked representation of a complete binary tree. In this implementation the tree nodes are represented by the elements in an array. If x is the array, the root corresponds to x[1]; then follow the nodes in each consecutive level from left to right. In the C++ implementation, x[0] is not used. With this numbering of nodes, the children of the node x[i] can be found in x[2i] and x[2i+1], and the parent of x[i] is in x[i/2].

The Insert and Remove functions insert and remove a heap element, respectively. They have to rearrange a number of nodes in the heap to preserve the ordering property and to keep the tree complete. The process involves no more than one node at each level and therefore requires a number of steps no greater than the depth of the tree. These functions can be implemented in concise iterative code.

25

Analysis of Algorithms

25.1.   Discussion

Kevin writes, on average, one line of code per minute. Kevin's computer executes one million instructions per second. If an average line of code compiles into five instructions and Kevin's program ran for seven minutes, how long did it take Kevin to write the program?

Fortunately, the answer to this problem is <u>not</u> 160 years. The catch is that the same instruction may be executed many times. Kevin's program probably implements one or several algorithms that let him describe a large number of operations using a relatively small number of program statements.

Understanding, devising, and implementing algorithms are the key programming skills. Yet it is not easy to give a formal definition of what an algorithm is. We have presented a few examples of algorithms in Part 1 (Chapter 9). We know that an algorithm is a method, described in more or less formal notation, of getting from some initial state to some desired final state in a finite number of steps, but rigorous formalization of this concept would eventually lead us to a precise abstract model of a "machine" that performs computations.

To make our discussion more concrete, let us consider two tasks that are often used to illustrate the concept of an algorithm in a rather pure form. These tasks are *searching* (that is, finding an element with a target value in a list of values), and *sorting* (arranging the elements of a list in ascending or descending order). We have discussed examples of searching and sorting algorithms in Part 1 (Chapter 9). For a searching algorithm, the initial state is described by a list of values and a target value, and the final state is described by the found location of the target value in the list or the assertion that it is not in the list. For a sorting algorithm, the initial state is a list of values and the final state is the list rearranged in ascending or descending order.

The first property of algorithms, as we have already mentioned, is that they often use <u>iterations</u> (or recursion, which is a form of iteration implemented at the system level). This property makes an algorithm different from a straightforward cookbook recipe, which typically has the same number of instructions as there are steps executed by the cook. (That would not be very useful for computers that can execute millions of instructions per second.) Like a recipe, an algorithm describes all the necessary intermediate steps for getting from the initial state to the final state; however, it often includes instructions to repeat certain sequences of steps a number of times.

Another property of an algorithm is <u>generality</u>. The same algorithm applies to a whole set of initial states and produces corresponding final states for each of them. For example, a sorting algorithm must be applicable to any list regardless of the values of its elements. Moreover, an algorithm must also be independent of the *size* of the task. The concept of the size of a task is hard to formalize, too. It applies when the domain of all the initial states can be parameterized by a positive integer which is in some way related to the total number of steps necessary to do the task. The size can describe the length of a list, the dimensions of a multidimensional array, and so on. For example, the number of elements in the list determines the size of a list-sorting task. In finding an element in a binary search tree with n nodes, the size is the total number of nodes. In an iterative or recursive procedure for finding n-factorial or the n-th Fibonacci number, n is the size. The generality of an algorithm assures that the same algorithm applies to different sizes of the same general task.

When we study algorithms, it is useful to assume a certain level of <u>abstraction</u> and ignore extraneous details. For example, the same sorting algorithm applies to any type of elements for which there is a relation of order. It does not matter whether the elements are integers, floating point numbers, or some records that have to be sorted by some key. What is important for sorting is that for any two elements we can say whether the first is less than, equal to, or greater than the second, and that the elements of a list can swap places. The <u>abstract formulation</u> of algorithms allows us to talk about algorithms for searching, sorting, tree traversal, and so on, without referring to specific data types and other details. It also lets us study the properties and efficiency of algorithms in an abstract, theoretical way.

Algorithms are often analyzed in terms of their time efficiency and space requirements. These are the concerns of a branch of computer science called *computational complexity* or *operations research*. In this book we concentrate on <u>time efficiency</u>. One obvious way to measure the time efficiency of an algorithm is to implement it in a computer program, run that program on various sets of input data, and measure the running time. Computer practitioners call this type of measurement a benchmark. It may seem that benchmarks leave little room for theory, but that first impression is incorrect. Benchmarks depend on the details of implementation, such as the actual code, the programming language and optimizing capabilities of the compiler, the CPU speed and other hardware characteristics, and so on. It turns out it is possible to study efficiency of algorithms excluding all these practical matters. Such an abstract, theoretical approach is not only useful for discussing and comparing algorithms, but also ultimately leads to very concrete improved solutions to practical problems.

The theoretical study of algorithms relies on an abstract model of a computer as a device with some defined capabilities, such as the capability to perform arithmetic operations and to store and retrieve data elements in memory. The abstract model disregards specific features of a particular computer system, such as the CPU speed or RAM size. The abstract approach requires two simplifications. First, we have to stop measuring performance in real time (which depends on CPU speed, etc.). Nor do we measure it in terms of the number of required program instructions or statements (which depends on the language, compiler, implementation, etc.). Instead, we discuss performance in terms of some abstract "steps" that are necessary to complete the task. What constitutes a "step" depends on the nature of the task. In a searching task, for example, we may define one step as one comparison between the target value and a data element in the list. In calculating a Fibonacci number iteratively, one step may be defined as one addition. The total number of required steps may depend on the size of the task, but it is assumed that each step takes the same amount of time. With this approach we cannot say how long a particular implementation of an algorithm might run on a particular computer system, but we can <u>compare</u> different algorithms that accomplish the same task.

The second simplification is that our theoretical analysis applies only when the task size is a large number. Let us denote the total number of steps that an algorithm requires to complete the task as $T(n)$. $T(n)$ is some function of the task size n. The theoretical approach focuses on the behavior of $T(n)$ for large n, which is called *asymptotic behavior*. In the following section we will see why knowing the asymptotic behavior of an algorithm is important and how it can be expressed in formal mathematical terms.

25.2.   Asymptotics: Big-O Notation

As a starting point for our discussion, let us compare two searching algorithms, sequential search and binary search. We will assume that the elements in the array are arranged in ascending order.

In the sequential search algorithm we simply try to match the target value against each array value in turn until we find a match or finish scanning the whole array. If the array contains n elements, the maximum possible number of "steps" (comparisons with the target) will be

$$T(n) = n$$

This is "the worst case." If we assume that the target is randomly chosen from the values in the array, on average we will need to examine only half of the elements, so

$$T_{\text{avg}}(n) = n / 2$$

Suppose this algorithm is implemented as follows:

```
for (int i = 0;   i < n;   i++)
    if (a[i] == target) break;
```

The total running time includes the initialization and several iterations through the loop. In this example, the initialization is simply setting i equal to 0. Assuming that the average number of iterations is $n/2$, the average time may be expressed as:

$$t(n) = t_{\text{init}} + t_{\text{iter}}\, n / 2$$

where t_{init} is initialization time, and t_{iter} is the time required for each iteration. In other words, the average time is some linear function of n:

$$t(n) = An + B$$

As n increases, An also increases, and the relative contribution of the constant term B eventually becomes negligible as compared to the linear term An, even if A is small and B is large. Mathematically, this means that the ratio

$$\frac{t(n)}{An} = \frac{An + B}{An} = 1 + \frac{B}{An}$$

becomes very close to 1 as n increases without bound.

Therefore, <u>for a large n</u> we can drop the constant term and say that the average time is approximately An. That means that the average time for the sequential search algorithm ***grows linearly*** with n (Figure 25-1 (a)).

Now let us consider the binary search algorithm applied to the same task. For this algorithm it is important that the elements be arranged in ascending order. We compare the target with the middle element in the array. If it is smaller, we continue searching in the left half, and if it is larger, in the right half. For $n=3$, if we are lucky, we find the element on the first try; in the worst case we need 2 comparisons. For $n=7$, we first try a[3] and then, if it does not match the target, continue with a[0]...a[2] or a[4]...a[6]. In the worst case we need 3 comparisons. In general, if n is between 2^{h-1} and 2^h-1, the worst case will require h comparisons. Thus, the number of comparisons in the worst case is

$$T(n) = \log_2 n + 1 \text{ (truncated to an integer).}$$

For an element randomly chosen from the values in the array, the average number of steps in a binary search is (approximately, for large n) only one less than the worst case.

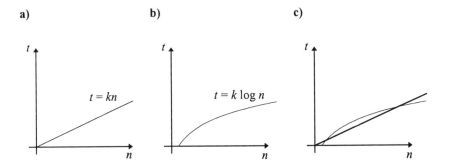

Figure 25-1.   (a) Linear growth; (b) logarithmic growth;
(c) log growth is slower.

Let us assume that the algorithm is implemented as follows:

```
...
int location = -1;
int left = 0, right = n-1, middle;

while (left <= right) {
    middle = (left + right) / 2;
    if (target > a[middle])
        left = middle + 1;
    else if (target < a[middle])
        right = middle - 1;
    else {
        // if (target == a[middle])
        location = middle;
        break;
    }
}
```

Again, the total time consists of the initialization time and the average number of iterations through the loop:

$$t(n) = t_{\text{init}} + t_{\text{iter}} \log_2 n$$

Following the same reasoning as for the sequential search, we conclude that the execution time of the binary search is, for large n, approximately proportional to the logarithm of n:

$$t(n) = C \log_2 n$$

The coefficient C is determined by the time spent in one iteration through the loop. Figure 25-1 (b) shows the general shape of this curve. $\log_2 n$ approaches infinity as n increases, but it does so more slowly than the linear growth of a straight line.

Note that "one step" in the sequential search is not exactly the same as "one step" in the binary search, because besides comparing the elements, we also need to modify some variables and control the iterations. Thus, the coefficients A and C may be different; for example, C may be larger than A. For some small n, a sequential search may potentially run faster than a binary search. But, no matter what the ratio of A to C, the linear curve eventually overtakes the logarithmic curve for large enough n (Figure 25-1 (c)).

In other words, asymptotically, binary search is faster than sequential search. Moreover, it is not just 5 times faster or 100 times faster. It is faster in principle: you can run sequential search on the fastest computer and binary search for the same task on the slowest computer, and still, if n is large enough, binary search will finish first.

This is an important theoretical result of our comparison of the two searching algorithms. The difference in their asymptotic behavior provides an important new way of looking at their performance.   Binary search time grows logarithmically and sequential search time linearly, so no matter what specific coefficients of the growth functions we use, linear time eventually surpasses logarithmic time.

In this context it makes sense to talk about the order of growth that characterizes the asymptotic behavior of a function, ignoring the particular constant coefficients. For example, $f(n) = n$ has higher order of growth than $g(n) = \log_2 n$, which means that for any positive constant C

$$n > C \log_2 n$$

when n is large enough. Two functions that differ only by a constant factor have the same order of growth.

The following definition of the *big-O* (order of growth) notation helps us formalize this terminology and refine our ideas about the order of growth. "Big-O" is defined as follows:

Given two functions $t(n)$ and $g(n)$, we say that

$$t(n) = O(g(n))$$

if there exist a positive constant A and some number N such that

$$t(n) \leq A\ g(n)$$

for all $n > N$.

The big-O definition basically means that $t(n)$ asymptotically (for large enough n) grows <u>not faster than</u> $g(n)$ (give or take a constant factor). In other words, the order of growth of $t(n)$ is not larger than $g(n)$.

So, in terms of order of growth, $f = O(g)$ is like "$f \leq g$." In practice, when the performance of algorithms is stated in terms of big-O, it usually refers to the "tightest" possible upper bound. In this book, we have chosen to follow the widely accepted practice of using big-O in the sense of "growth of $f = g$." For example, in our analysis of the two searching algorithms we say that both the worst and average time is $O(n)$ for the sequential search and $O(\log_2 n)$ for the binary search.

⌘   ⌘   ⌘

One set of functions that are often used for describing the order of growth are, naturally, powers of n:

$$1,\ n,\ n^2,\ n^3,\ ...$$

The order of growth for n^k is higher than n^{k-1}.

If a function is a sum of several terms, its order of growth is determined by the fastest growing term. In particular, if we have a polynomial

$$p(n) = a_k n^k + a_{k-1} n^{k-1} + ... + a_1 n + a_0$$

its growth is of the order n^k:

$$p(n) = O(n^k)$$

Thus, any second degree polynomial is $O(n^2)$. This is called *quadratic* growth.

Let us consider a common example of code that requires $O(n^2)$ operations. Suppose we have two nested loops:

```
... // set up the outer loop
for (i = 1;   i < n;   i++) {
    ... // set up the inner loop
    for (j = 0;   j < i;   j++) {
        ... // do something
    }
}
```

This kind of code may be used for finding duplicates in an array or in a simple sorting method (e.g., the selection sort explained in Part 1 and in Section 27.2.1), or in some operations on matrices (e.g., transposing a matrix by flipping an n by n 2-D array symmetrically over its diagonal).

The outer loop runs for i from 1 to $n-1$, a total of $n-1$ times, and the inner loop runs for j from 0 to $i-1$, a total of i times. The code inside the inner loop will, therefore, execute a total of

$$1 + 2 + ... + (n-1)$$

iterations. Since this sequence is an arithmetic progression, its sum can be found by taking the total number of terms and multiplying it by the average of the first and the last term:

$$1 + 2 + ... + (n-1) = (n-1)\frac{1 + (n-1)}{2} = \frac{(n-1)n}{2}$$

If the setup time for the outer loop is t_{setup1}, the setup time for the inner loop is t_{setup2}, and the time inside the inner loop is t_{iter}, the total time for this code can be expressed as

$$t(n) = t_{setup1} + t_{setup2}(n-1) + t_{iter}\frac{(n-1)n}{2}$$

This is a second degree polynomial of n:

$$t(n) = \frac{t_{iter}}{2}n^2 + (t_{setup2} - \frac{t_{iter}}{2})n + (t_{setup1} - t_{setup2})$$

Therefore,

$$t(n) = O(n^2)$$

⌘   ⌘   ⌘

As we know from the Change of Base Theorem, for any $a, b > 0$, and $a, b \neq 1$

$$\log_b n = \frac{\log_a n}{\log_a b}$$

Therefore,

$$\log_a n = C \log_b n$$

where C is a constant equal to $\log_a b$.

Since functions that differ only by a constant factor have the same order of growth, $O(\log_2 n)$ is the same as $O(\log n)$. Therefore, when we talk about logarithmic growth, the base of the logarithm is not important, and we can say simply $O(\log n)$.

⌘   ⌘   ⌘

The time efficiency of almost all of the algorithms discussed in this book can be characterized by only a few growth rate functions:

I. $O(1)$ — *constant time*. This means that the algorithm requires the same fixed number of steps regardless of the size of the task.

Examples (assuming a reasonable implementation of the task):

    A.   Push and Pop operations for a stack (containing n elements);
    B.   Insert and Remove operations for a queue.

II. $O(n)$ — *linear time*. This means that the algorithm requires a number of steps proportional to the size of the task.

Examples (assuming a reasonable implementation of the task):

    A.   Traversal of a list (a linked list or an array) with n elements;
    B.   Finding the maximum or minimum element in a list, or sequential search in an unsorted list of n elements;
    C.   Traversal of a tree with n nodes;
    D.   Calculating iteratively n-factorial; finding iteratively the n-th Fibonacci number.

III. $O(n^2)$ — *quadratic time.* The number of operations is proportional to the size of the task squared.

Examples:

    A.   Some more simplistic sorting algorithms, for instance a selection sort of n elements;
    B.   Comparing two two-dimensional arrays of size n by n;
    C.   Finding duplicates in an unsorted list of n elements (implemented with two nested loops).

IV. $O(\log n)$ — *logarithmic time.*

Examples:

    A.   Binary search in a sorted list of n elements;
    B.   Insert and Find operations for a binary search tree with n nodes;
    C.   Insert and Remove operations for a heap with n nodes.

V. $O(n \log n)$ — *"n log n" time.*

Examples:

    A.   More advanced sorting algorithms — quicksort, mergesort, etc. — explained in Section 27.3.

VI. $O(a^n)$ $(a > 1)$ — *exponential time.*

Examples:

    A.   Recursive Fibonacci implementation ($a \geq 3/2$; see Section 19.5);
    B.   Towers of Hanoi ($a = 2$; See Lab 19.6).
    C.   Generating all permutations of n symbols.

The best time in the above list is obviously constant time, and the worst is exponential time which, as we have seen, quickly overwhelms even the fastest computers even for relatively small n. **Polynomial** growth (linear, quadratic, cubic, etc.) is considered manageable as compared to exponential growth.

Figure 25-2 shows the asymptotic behavior of the functions from the above list. Using the "<" sign informally, we can say that

$$O(1) < O(\log n) < O(n) < O(n \log n) < O(n^2) < O(n^3) < O(a^n)$$

The slow asymptotic growth of $\log_2 n$ (in comparison to linear growth) is especially dramatic. The thousand-fold increase in the size of a task results in only a fixed, fairly small increment in the required number of operations. Consider the following:

$$\log_2 1000 \approx 10; \quad \log_2 10^6 \approx 20; \quad \log_2 10^9 \approx 30; \quad ... \text{ etc.}$$

This property is used in many efficient "divide and conquer" algorithms such as binary search and is the basis for using binary search trees and heaps. For example, binary search in an array of one million elements would take at most twenty steps.

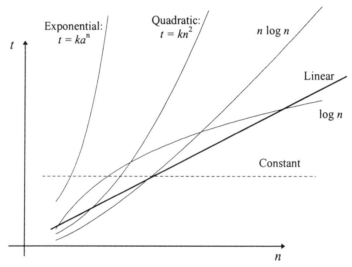

Figure 25-2. Rates of growth.

25.3. Summary

The efficiency of algorithms is usually expressed in terms of asymptotic growth as the size of the task increases toward infinity. The size of a task is basically an intuitive notion: it reflects the number of elements involved or other similar parameters. The asymptotic growth may be expressed using "big-O" notation, which gives an upper bound for the order of growth. In practice, the big-O estimate is usually expressed in terms of the "tightest" possible upper bound.

The most common orders of growth (in increasing order) are

$O(1)$ — constant;
$O(\log n)$ — logarithmic;
$O(n)$ — linear;
$O(n \log n)$ — "n log n";
$O(n^2)$ — quadratic;
$O(a^n)$ — exponential.

Logarithmic growth is dramatically slower than linear growth. This explains the efficiency of "divide and conquer" algorithms, such as binary search, and of binary search trees and heaps. Discovering an $O(\log n)$ algorithm instead of an $O(n)$ algorithm or an $O(n \log n)$ instead of $O(n^2)$ algorithm for some task is justifiably viewed as a breakthrough in time efficiency. Exponential growth is unmanageable: it quickly puts the task out of reach of existing computers, even for tasks of rather small size.

26

Searching and Hashing

26.1. Discussion

Searching, hashing, and *sorting* are vast and important subjects. At the practical level they are important because that is what many large computer systems do much of the time. At the theoretical level they help to distill the general properties and interesting theoretical questions about algorithms and data structures and offer rich material on which to study and compare them. At the junction of the theoretical and practical considerations there is a lot of room for original designs and ingenious solutions to various problems.

In this chapter we focus on searching and hashing. Searching tasks in computer applications range from finding a particular character in a string of a dozen characters to finding a record in a database of 100 million records. In an abstract formulation, searching is a task that involves a set of data elements represented in some way in computer memory. Each element includes a *key* which can be tested for an exact match against a target value. A successful search finds the element with a matching key and returns its location or some information associated with it: a value, a record, or the address of a record.

Searching refers to tasks where matching the keys against a specified target is straightforward and unambiguous. If, by comparison, we had to deal with a database of fingerprints and needed to find the best match for a given specimen, that application would fall into the category of *pattern recognition* rather than searching. It would also be likely to require the intervention of some human experts.

The key depends on the application and may be a number, a string of characters, a date, etc. In a database of taxpayers, for example, the key may be the taxpayer's social security number. In a database of bank customers, the key may be the account number. In situations where we search for a character in a string or a number in a list, the value itself serves as a key. A key may consist of several elements, for instance a person's last name and first name. The main key is called the *primary key* and additional keys are called *secondary keys*. If a match is found in primary keys, the search program examines secondary keys. From an abstract point of view, however, the division into primary and secondary keys and other details of the matching procedure are not important.

Searching of ordered lists relies on some relation of order defined for the keys, so that two keys can be compared not only in terms of an exact match, but also in terms of which key is larger or smaller.

In large database systems the actual data files reside in mass storage and the search is performed not on actual records but on some *index,* a data structure that links the key with the record's location in storage. Sometimes the same file may have several indices, depending on its use. For example, the customers of a telephone company may be indexed by telephone number for billing inquiries and by name for directory assistance.

Data organization and the choice of a search method depend on many factors: the number of elements, the range of values for keys, how often data elements are inserted or removed, how much we know about the frequency of access for various keys, etc. At one extreme, the data may be organized in such a way that we know exactly where to find each key. The key is used as an index in a *lookup* table; we go directly there and fetch the required data — no search is needed. At the other extreme is the situation where the elements are stored randomly, and the only solution is to examine them one by one until we find a match or have checked all elements — a *sequential search*. Between these two extremes are *hashing* methods, which build on the lookup table idea; *binary search* methods, which rely on the ordered arrangement of elements; and other variations. In the following sections we consider sequential and binary search, lookup tables, and hashing.

26.2. Sequential and Binary Search

The theoretical efficiency of a searching algorithm is expressed as the number of comparisons necessary to find a match in the worst case and on average.

Sequential search has to be used when the data elements are stored in a list in random order. Its running time is $O(n)$, where n is the number of elements. The worst case requires n comparisons, and an average search requires $n/2$ comparisons. In some instances, the performance of a sequential search may be greatly improved if some target key values that occur much more frequently than others are placed closer to the beginning of the list.

As we have seen in Part 1 (Chapter 9), binary search is generally a much more efficient method, requiring only $(\log_2 n) + 1$ (truncated to an integer) comparisons in the worst case. It is a $O(\log n)$ algorithm: the average number of comparisons is approximately $\log_2 n$, only one less than the worst case (for large n).

This method applies only if the data elements are stored in an array in ascending or descending order. If elements are inserted or removed frequently, the cost associated with maintaining the array in order may outweigh the advantages of a binary search.

In the following code, the `BinarySearch(...)` function is implemented as a template function for an array of elements of SOMETYPE arranged in ascending order. The function assumes that the ==, <, and > operators are defined for SOMETYPE:

SORTS.CPP

```
template <class SOMETYPE>
int BinarySearch (const apvector<SOMETYPE> &v, SOMETYPE target)

// Performs binary search in the array v.
//    The elements in the array must be arranged in
//    ascending order.
//    Looks for a value equal to target.
//    (the ==, < and > operators as well as assignment must be
//    defined for SOMETYPE.)
// Returns: the location of target in v, if found; -1 otherwise.

{
    int location = -1, n = v.length();
    int left = 0, right = n-1, middle;

    while (left <= right) {
        middle = (left + right) / 2;
        if (target > v[middle])
            left = middle + 1;
        else if (target < v[middle])
            right = middle - 1;
        else {
            // if (target == v[middle])
            location = middle;
            break;
        }
    }
    return location;
}
```

If the target value is not found in the middle of the array, the search range in the array shrinks to its left or right half, depending on the comparison result between the target and the middle element. A binary search requires direct access to the middle element and cannot be used with a linked list representation. As we saw in Section 22.2, a linked structure that supports a method analogous to binary search is the binary search tree.

⌘   ⌘   ⌘

A variation of the method, called the ***interpolation search***, is based on the assumption that the array contains a uniform distribution of values. The interpolation search works only for numeric types (or types that can be linearly mapped into numbers, such as characters in ASCII code). Instead of selecting the next trial element in the middle of the array, we can try to guess the location of the target value using linear interpolation based on the values at the two ends of the array:

```
    ...
    middle = (right * (target - v[left]) +
            left * (v[right] - target)) / (v[right] - v[left]);
    ...
```

We mention the interpolation search only because it supports our intuition: when we need to look up a word in a dictionary and the word starts with a "Y", we open the dictionary not in the middle but closer to the end. In computer programs an interpolation search may save a couple of comparisons, but it will probably waste more time computing the interpolation formula. Our first comparison must also check separately that `target` falls into the range between `v[left]` and `v[right]`.

26.3.   Lookup Tables

Lookup tables <u>do not</u> implement a search method but rather a method to <u>avoid</u> searching. The idea is to represent a data set in such a way that we know exactly where to find a particular element. The element's key or value is converted either directly or through some simple formula into an integer, which is used as an index to a special lookup table. The table may contain some associated data values, pointers, or addresses of records. The mapping from all valid keys to the computed indices must be unambiguous, so that we can go directly to the corresponding lookup table entry and fetch the data. The time of the data access is "instantaneous" (constant, $O(1)$), but some space may be wasted if not all lookup table entries are used.

Suppose, for example, that an application such as entering shipping orders needs to use a database of postal zip codes which would quickly find the town or locality with a given zip. Suppose we are dealing with 5-digit zip codes, so there are no more than 100,000 possible zip values — from 00000 to 99999. Actually, only a fraction of the 5-digit numbers represent a valid zip code. But in this application it may be important to make the zip code lookup as quick as possible. This can be accomplished using a table with 100,000 entries. The 5-digit zip will be used directly as an index into the table. Those entries in the table that correspond to a valid zip code will point to the corresponding record containing the locality name; all the other entries will remain unused.

Lookup tables may waste some space, but they also save a little space because the key values do not have to be stored with data elements. Instead, the value of the key is implicit in the element's location in the lookup table. .

Lookup tables are useful for many other tasks, such as data compression or translating one symbolic notation into another. In graphics applications and in hardware, for example, a "logical" color code (usually some number, say, between 0 and 255) can be converted into an actual screen color by fetching its red, green, and blue components from three lookup tables.

Another common use is for tabulating functions when we need to speed up time-critical computations. The function argument is translated into an integer index which is used to fetch the function value from its lookup table. In some cases, when the function argument may have only a small number of integer values, the lookup table may actually take less space than the code that would be needed to implement the function! If, for example, we need to compute 3^n repeatedly for $n = 0,...,9$, the most efficient way, in terms of both time and space, is to use a lookup table of 10 values.

In another example, an imaging application may need to count quickly the number of "black" pixels (picture elements) in a scan line. In a large black and white image, pixels can be packed eight per byte to save space. The task then needs a function which finds the number of set bits in a byte. This function can easily do the job by testing individual bits in a byte, but a lookup table with 256 elements which holds the bit counts for all possible values of a byte (0-255) may be a more efficient solution.

26.4. *Lab:* Cryptography

The purpose of this lab is to master the use of lookup tables and distributions, the two techniques that lead to a better understanding of *hashing*.

In the following example, both the input and output values are the letters 'a' through 'z'. A lookup table of 26 entries is used to translate one letter into another:

```
#include <ctype.h>
#include "apvector.h"

// A lookup table for writing encoded messages.
static apvector<char> lookup(26);

char Encode(char c)

// Translates c through the lookup table. Changes only letters
//   and preserves the upper and lower case.

{
    char newC = c;
    char lowC = tolower(c);
    int i;

    if (lowC >= 'a' && lowC <= 'z') {
        i = lowC - 'a';
        newC = lookup[i];
        if (isupper(c))
            newC = toupper(newC);
    }

    return newC;
}
```

The above function uses the fact that lowercase letters have consecutive ASCII codes and converts a character between 'a' and 'z' into an integer index between 0 and 25 simply by subtracting 'a'. The encoded character is fetched directly from the lookup table — no search is performed, and no long `switch` statement is needed.

A distribution of data values in a list can be represented as an array of counters. To build a distribution we first zero out all the counters. Then we scan through the list <u>once</u>. For each value in the list, we calculate the index into the array of counters based on that value (or, in a more general case, the range of values in which it falls), and increment the counter with that index.

In this lab, you will receive two short text passages in two separate files, SAMPLE.TXT and SECRET.TXT. The text in SECRET.TXT has been encrypted using a simple substitution cipher: each letter is represented by some other letter. To break the code quickly, you can analyze and compare the frequencies of occurrence of letters of the alphabet in the sample text and the encrypted text. Write a program that will calculate the distribution of frequencies of the letters in any text file. Keep track of the total number of letters in the file, and scale your output table to some reasonable units, such as occurrences per 1000 letters. Run

this program on SAMPLE.TXT and SECRET.TXT.   Compare manually the
distributions and come up with some guesses for possible meanings of encrypted
letters. (If you want to use a more advanced method and less guessing, you can
also calculate a two-dimensional distribution for occurrences of all combinations
of two letters as well as a letter and a space.)

Write another program (or modify the first one) for decoding the secret text
interactively.   Read the whole file into a buffer and use a lookup table for
translating the encoded letters into their actual values. Your Decode(...) function
can be exactly the same as the Encode(...) function above.   We called it
Encode(...) because we used it to create the encoded text. Initially all the entries
in your lookup table should be set to a special character that indicates an unknown
letter. For example:

```
    static apvector<char> lookup(26, '-');      // All unknown
```

When your program displays the secret text for the first time, all you can see is
dashes in place of letters. The program should help you use trial and error to
decode the text. Have it prompt you to enter a code letter and its guessed
meaning, substitute the letter into the lookup table, and display the unknown text
with all the guessed letters filled in. The Substitute(...) function may look as
follows:

```
void Substitute(char codeletter, char guess)
{
    int i;

    codeletter = tolower(codeletter);
    if (codeletter >= 'a' && codeletter <= 'z') {
        i = codeletter - 'a';
        lookup[i] = tolower(guess);
    }
}
```

**The text buffer never changes — only the lookup table should change as
you try different substitutions.**

When the secret text is decoded, save it in an output file.

You can combine all these operations in one interactive program. Your program
may show a menu and execute commands:

```
Commands:
    R <file name> -- Read secret or plain text from a file
    C             -- Calculate frequencies of letters
    A             -- Display text from the original file
    S <codeltr> <guess>
                  -- Substitute your guess for a code letter
    D             -- Display partially decoded text
    W <file name> -- Write text to a file
    Q             -- Quit
```

26.5. Hashing

The *hashing* technique builds on the lookup table concept. In a lookup table, a key is either used directly or converted through a very simple formula into an integer index. There is a one-to-one correspondence between the key values and indices of elements in the lookup table. This method is not practical, however, when the range of possible key values is large. It is also wasteful when the mapping from keys to integer indices is very sparse — many lookup table entries remain unused.

We can avoid these problems by using a better system of mapping from keys to integer indices in the table. The purpose of the mapping is to map all possible key values into a narrower range of indices and to cover that range more uniformly. Such a transformation is called a *hash function*; a table used with it is a *hash table*.

The price of hashing is that we lose the one-to-one correspondence between the keys and the table entries: two different keys may be mapped into the same location in the hash table. Thus when we try inserting a new element into the table, the slot may be already occupied. These situations are called *collisions*. We have to devise some method of dealing with them. When we retrieve an element, we have to verify that its key indeed matches the target, therefore the key must be explicitly stored in the table with the rest of the record.

The design of a hash table thus hinges upon successful handling of two problems: how to choose a good hash function and how to handle collisions. There is room for ingenious solutions for both.

A good hash function must have the following properties:

1. It must be easy to calculate;
2. It must map all possible values of keys onto a range that is not too large;
3. It must cover that range uniformly and minimize collisions.

To devise such a function, we can try some "random" things akin to transformations used for generating random numbers in a specified range. If the key is a string of characters, we can use some numeric codes (e.g. ASCII codes) for them. We then chop the key into pieces and combine them together using bitwise or arithmetic operations — hence the term "hashing." The result must be an integer in the range from 0 to `tableSize-1`.

Overly simplistic hash functions, such as simply truncating the key or converting it modulo the table size —

```
Hash(target.key) { return target.key % tableSize;}
```

— may create unexpected clusters of collisions resulting from some peculiar clustering in the data. Fortunately, we can evaluate our hash function on some simulated and real data before using it in an application.

⌘   ⌘   ⌘

There are two principal approaches to resolving collisions. In the first approach, each entry in the hash table is itself implemented as a structure that can hold more than one element. This approach is called ***chaining*** and the table entry is referred to as a ***bucket***. A bucket may be implemented as a linked list, a sorted array, or even a binary search tree (Figure 26-1). This approach works well for densely populated hash tables.

The second approach to resolving collisions is by storing the colliding element in a different slot of the same hash table. This approach is known as ***probing***. We calculate the index into the table using the hash function as usual. If the slot is already occupied, we use some ***probing function*** to convert that index into a new index, and repeat this step until we find a vacant slot.

```
    . . .
    int index = Hash(target.key);
    while (!isEmpty(hashTable[index]))
        index = Probe(index);
    hashTable[index] = target;
    . . .
```

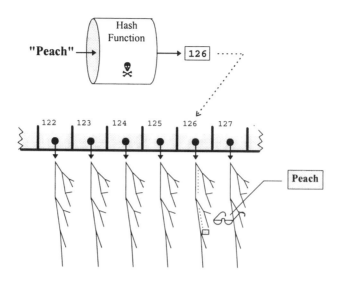

Figure 26-1. Resolving collisions in a hash table by chaining.

The same probing function, of course, must be used for finding an element:

```
int index = Hash(target.key);
while (!isEmpty(hashTable[index]) &&
       !Match(hashTable[index].key, target.key))
    index = Probe(index);
target = hashTable[index];
...
```

The simplest form of the probing function is to increment the index by one or by some fixed number:

```
inline int Probe(index) { return (index + INCR) % tableSize; }
```

This is called *linear probing* (see Figure 26-2). After the table has been in use for a while, linear probing may degrade the uniform distribution of the hash table population — a condition called *clustering*. In so-called *quadratic probing*, the sequence of examined slots is

```
index, index+1, index+4, index+9, ...
```

This can be implemented as:

```
...
int index = Hash(target.key);
int incr = 1;
while (!isEmpty(hashTable[index])) {
    index = (index + incr) % tableSize;
    incr += 2;
}
...
```

In more elaborate probing schemes, the next location may depend not only on the consecutive number of the attempt, but also on the value of the key. In addition, some *rehashing* function may be used instead of `% tableSize`:

```
...
int index = Hash(target.key);
int attempt = 1;
while (!isEmpty(hashTable[index]))
    index = Rehash(index, hashTable[index].key, attempt++);
...
```

Probing should be used only with relatively sparsely populated hash tables so that probing sequences are kept short. The sequence of probing attempts required to insert an element is repeated each time we search for that element.

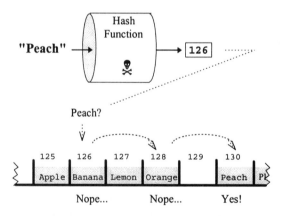

Figure 26-2. Resolving collisions in a hash table by linear probing.

As we can see, the performance of a search in a hash table varies with the details of implementation. In the best case, the data access is instantaneous, $O(1)$. But with many collisions, the performance may deteriorate. A badly designed hash table may result in all the elements clustered in just a few buckets or in very long probing sequences, and the number of comparisons may become as high as $O(n)$.

26.6. Summary

Sequential search is a universally applicable search method, but it is an $O(n)$ method which requires $n/2$ comparisons on average and n comparisons in the worst case. Binary search is much more efficient, with $O(\log_2 n)$ comparisons in the worst case, but it requires keeping the data in a sorted array.

Lookup tables have limited applicability. They can be used when the keys can be easily mapped onto integers from a relatively narrow range. Lookup tables provide constant access time, $O(1)$, but may waste considerable space.

In the hashing approach, the key is converted by some hashing function into an integer which is used as the index into a hash table. The performance and space requirements for hash tables may vary widely depending on implementation. In the best scenario, a hash table provides constant access time, $O(1)$, but with a lot of collisions the performance may deteriorate. One disadvantage of hash tables over a binary search tree or a sorted list is the difficulty of quickly traversing the table in ascending order of keys. This may be a serious consideration in some applications.

Practical solutions for the best data organization and most efficient search and retrieval methods often rely on some combination of methods.

27

Sorting

27.1. Discussion

To *sort* means to arrange a list of data elements in ascending or descending order. The data elements may be simply numeric values or some records ordered by keys for which an order relation has been defined.

In addition to preparing a data set for easier access (e.g., binary search), sorting has many other applications. One example is matching two data sets. Suppose we want to merge two large mailing lists and eliminate the duplicates. This task is straightforward when the lists are sorted by name and address but may be unmanageable otherwise.   Another application may be simply presenting information to a user in an ordered manner. A list of the user's files on a personal computer, for example, may be sorted by name, date, or size. A word processor uses sorting for the automatic creation of an index or a bibliography for a book. In large business systems millions of transactions (e.g., bank checks or credit card charges) are sorted daily before they are posted to customer accounts or forwarded to other payers.

In the real world, the efficiency of sorting methods depends on the nature and volume of data, in particular whether the whole set of data fits into memory and whether the order of data elements is totally random or nearly sorted. In this book we discuss different sorting algorithms only from the point of view of their theoretical efficiency. In this simplified view, sorting algorithms fall into two broad categories: more simplistic algorithms with $O(n^2)$ time, and more efficient methods with $O(n \log n)$ time.   The former are represented by the so-called *selection sort*, *insertion sort*, and *bubble sort* algorithms.   The latter include *mergesort*, *quicksort*, and *heapsort*.

All the programming examples in this section implement sorting an array v of n elements into ascending order. The elements have the type SOMETYPE for which the operators `<`, `>=`, etc., are defined. We also assume that a Swap (...) function is defined for two SOMETYPE elements:

```
template <class SOMETYPE>
inline void Swap(SOMETYPE &x, SOMETYPE &y)

{
    SOMETYPE temp = x;   x = y;   y = temp;
}
```

In real applications, instead of large records or strings, the array may contain only pointers to them. Pointers can still access the values or keys efficiently, but swapping is faster because only the pointers swap places (Figure 27-1). In the following sections, however, we will ignore these important details in order to focus more closely on the main ideas of various sorting algorithms.

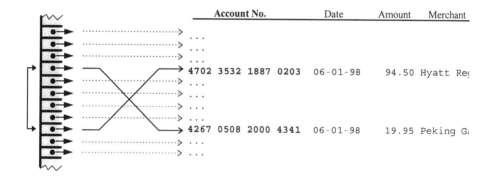

Figure 27-1. Sorting large records through pointers.

27.2. $O(n^2)$ Sorts

27.2.1.   Selection Sort

The method of selection sort is to find the largest element in the array and swap it with the last element, then continue the process for the first $n-1$ elements:

SORTS.CPP

```
template <class SOMETYPE>
void SelectionSort (apvector<SOMETYPE> &v)

{
    int i, iMax, n = v.length();

    while (n > 1) {

        // Find the largest element:
        for (iMax = 0, i = 1;   i < n;   i++)
            if (v[i] > v[iMax]) iMax = i;

        // Swap it with the last element:
        Swap(v[iMax], v[n-1]);

        n--;
    }
}
```

Selection sort is the slowest and the most predictable of all: it always takes $n(n-1)/2$ comparisons and $3(n-1)$ moves (counting each swap as 3 moves).

27.2.2.   Insertion Sort

In an insertion sort, we keep the beginning of the array sorted. Initially the "sorted" part is just the first element, v[0]. When the first $i-1$ elements are in order, we insert the i-th element among them in the right place, thus making sure that the first i elements become ordered. The process continues until we process the last element in the array:

SORTS.CPP

```
template <class SOMETYPE>
void InsertionSort (apvector<SOMETYPE> &v)

{
    int i, j, n = v.length();
    SOMETYPE vCurrent;

    for (i = 1;   i < n;   i++) {

        // Save the current element:
        vCurrent = v[i];

        // Find location j where it should be inserted
        //   among the first i-1 elements:
        for (j = 0;   j < i;   j++)
            if (v[j] >= vCurrent)
                break;

        // Shift all elements between j and i one place to the right:
        for (int k = i-1;   k >= j;   k--)
            v[k+1] = v[k];

        // Insert saved element where it belongs:
        v[j] = vCurrent;
    }
}
```

This method works better for linked lists, because inserting an element into an array may require a lot of moves. In the worst case, this algorithm takes $n(n{-}1)/2$ comparisons, but in the best case it takes only $n{-}1$ comparisons. On average, for a random list, an insertion sort takes $(n^2{+}n{-}2)/4$ or $n^2/4 + O(n)$ comparisons.

Interestingly, the <u>worst</u> case (in terms of the number of comparisons) happens when the list is <u>already sorted</u>! The <u>best</u> case happens when the list is <u>sorted in reverse order</u>. The reason for this peculiar behavior is that the above code traverses the list from the beginning forward in order to insert the element. If we are dealing with a singly linked list, that is our only option. For a doubly linked list or an array, however, we can traverse it backwards, starting at the end. This simplifies the code and makes the algorithm's behavior more intuitive:

```
                                                    ┌─────────────────┐
                                                    │ SORTS.CPP    💾 │
─ ─ ─ ─ ─ ─ ─ ─ ─ ─ ─ ─ ─ ─ ─ ─ ─ ─ ─ ─ ─ ─ ─ ─ ─ ─ ─ ─ ─ ─ ─ ─ ─ ─ ─ ─ ─

template <class SOMETYPE>
void InsertionSort2 (apvector<SOMETYPE> &v)

// A variation of insertion sort
//   with scanning the sublist backwards from i-1 down to 0

{
    int i, j, n = v.length();
    SOMETYPE vCurrent;

    for (i = 1;   i < n;   i++) {

        // Save the current element:
        vCurrent = v[i];

        // Going backwards from v[i-1], shift elements to the
        //   right until you find an element v[j] <= vCurrent:
        for (j = i-1;   j >= 0;  j--) {
            if (v[j] <= vCurrent)
                break;
            v[j+1]   = v[j];
        }

        // Insert saved element after v[j]:
        v[j+1] = vCurrent;

    }
}
```

In this modified version, the best case is when the array is already sorted. Then it takes only $n-1$ comparisons and $2(n-1)$ moves; in other words, the algorithm works in $O(n)$ (i.e., linear) time. In fact, this is an efficient method for fixing minor disorder in a nearly sorted array. The average case is still about $n^2/4$ comparisons and about the same number of moves, so it remains an $O(n^2)$ algorithm.

27.2.3. Bubble Sort

The idea of bubble sort is to traverse the array swapping all the pairs of adjacent elements that are out of order. At the end of the first pass the largest element "bubbles up" to the end of the array. At the same time we get a chance to check whether all the elements are already in the right order. Then the process continues for the first $n-1$ elements. In this algorithm it makes sense to take advantage of the opportunity to quit early when the array is already sorted:

SORTS.CPP

```
template <class SOMETYPE>
void BubbleSort (apvector<SOMETYPE> &v)

// Quits early when the array is confirmed to be in order.

{
    int i, n = v.length(), disorder = n;

    while (disorder) {

        disorder = 0;

        // Bubble up and mark any disorder:
        //    (When n becomes 1, the "for" loop is not
        //     executed, "disorder" remains 0, and the "while"
        //     loop is broken.)

        for (i = 1;   i < n;   i++) {
            if (v[i] < v[i-1]) {
                Swap(v[i], v[i-1]);
                disorder++;
            }
        }
        n--;
    }
}
```

In the worst case (when the array is in reverse order) bubble sort takes $n(n-1)/2$ comparisons and as many swaps. In the best case, when the array is already sorted, the algorithm requires only $n-1$ comparisons, so bubble sort can verify that the array is in order and fix a couple of swapped elements in linear time.

27.3. $O(n \log n)$ Sorts

Our experience with binary search trees and heaps suggests that there must be more efficient sorting methods than $O(n^2)$. After all, it takes an average of only $O(\log n)$ comparisons to insert an element into a binary search tree, and we know that inorder traversal of the tree produces all the elements in ascending order. So if we put all the elements from our list into a "magic box," a binary search tree, we can pull them out in ascending order in just $O(n \log n)$ steps. The same applies to heaps: we can put all the elements from our list into a heap and then pull them out one by one from the top of the heap in descending order. These ideas are the basis for two sorting algorithms, **treesort** and **heapsort**, discussed later in this section. In any case, all $O(n \log n)$ sorting algorithms are based on the general "divide and conquer" principle, of which **mergesort** is the most direct illustration.

27.3.1. Mergesort

If we have two sorted arrays, we can combine or *merge* them into one sorted array in linear time, that is, in $O(n)$ comparisons and moves where n is the total number of elements. This fact is the basis of a sorting method called *mergesort*, which is best described in recursive terms.

<u>To sort an array:</u>
```
  1. Split it into two equal (or almost equal) halves;
  2. Sort the first half;
  3. Sort the second half;
  4. Merge the two halves.
```

The base case occurs when the array has only one element. For better performance, we can treat an array of two elements as another base case.

One problem with mergesort is that merging two arrays requires a temporary working space at least the size of the combined array. (This is not true for linked lists, but linked lists need extra memory to store link pointers.) Fortunately, there are no nested calls to the `Merge(...)` function, so we can use one work array created <u>outside</u> of the `Merge(...)` function and reuse the same memory for all `Merge(...)` calls.

It is convenient to collect all the related mergesort definitions into one MERGESORT class:

```
                                            ┌─────────────────────┐
                                            │ SORTS.CPP      [💾]  │
┌───────────────────────────────────────────                    ──┐
// MERGESRT.H

template <class SOMETYPE>
class MERGESORT {

  public:

    void Sort (apvector<SOMETYPE> &v);

  private:
```

Continued ✒

```
    apvector<SOMETYPE> work;

     void RecursiveSort(apvector<SOMETYPE> &v, int i1, int i2);
    void Merge(apvector<SOMETYPE> &v, int i1, int m, int i2);
};

//****************************************************************

template <class SOMETYPE>
void MERGESORT<SOMETYPE>::Sort (apvector<SOMETYPE> &v)

// Sorts array v in ascending order.

{
    int n = v.length();
    work.resize(n);
    RecursiveSort(v, 0, n-1);
    work.resize(0);
}

template <class SOMETYPE>
void MERGESORT<SOMETYPE>::RecursiveSort (apvector<SOMETYPE> &v,
                                              int i1, int i2)

// Sorts elements of v between i1 and i2 in ascending order.

{
    int m;

    if (i2 - i1 <= 1) {           // Base case:
        if (i2 - i1 == 1 && v[i2] < v[i1])
            Swap(v[i2], v[i1]);
    }
    else {                        // Recursive case:
        m = (i2 + i1) / 2;
        RecursiveSort(v, i1, m);
        RecursiveSort(v, m + 1, i2);
        Merge(v, i1, m, i2);
    }
}

//****************************************************************
```

Continued

```
template <class SOMETYPE>
void MERGESORT<SOMETYPE>::
        Merge(apvector<SOMETYPE> &v, int i1, int m, int i2)

// Merges sorted segments of the array v between i1 and m
//   and between m+1 and i2 into one sorted segment between i1 and i2.

{
    int j1 = i1, j2 = m + 1, j;

    // Merge two arrays into the work array:
    for (j = i1;   j <= i2;   j++) {
        if (j1 <= m && j2 <= i2) {
            if (v[j1] < v[j2])
                work[j] = v[j1++];
            else
                work[j] = v[j2++];
        }
        else if (j1 <= m)
            work[j] = v[j1++];
        else // if (j2 <= i2)
            work[j] = v[j2++];
    }

    // Copy work back to v:
    for (j = i1;   j <= i2;   j++)
        v[j] = work[j];
}
```

This class may be used as follows:

```
...
#include "mergesrt.h"
...

int main()

{
    apvector<int> array(100);
    MERGESORT<int> mergesort;
    ...
    mergesort.Sort(array);
    ...
}
```

Mergesort never takes more than $n \log_2 n - n + 1$ comparisons, so it is an $O(n \log n)$ algorithm. Its performance is virtually the same for the best case (presorted array) and the worst case.

27.3.2. Quicksort

Quicksort was invented by C.A.R. Hoare.[*] Although its performance is less predictable than mergesort's, it averages a faster time for random arrays than other methods and requires no temporary work space.

The main idea of the algorithm is to split the array into left and right parts in such a way that all the elements in the right part are larger than all the elements in the left part, then sort each part (recursively) to produce a sorted array. Obviously, we have to rearrange the elements of the array to achieve the desired partitioning. First we chose an element for a "pivot." A simple procedure that works in linear time allows us to find a new place for the pivot and rearrange other elements so that all the elements to the left of the pivot are less than or equal to the pivot, and all the elements to the right of the pivot are greater than or equal to the pivot. This is reminiscent of binary search trees, in which all the elements of the left subtree are less than or equal to the root, and all the elements of the right subtree are greater than or equal to the root.

The partitioning procedure works as follows. We keep track of two indices, j1 and j2. Initially j1 is set to the index of the first element and j2 is set to the index of the last element of the array. If v[j1] is less than or equal to the pivot, v[j1] is already on the correct (left) side — we leave it alone and <u>increment</u> j1. Otherwise, if v[j2] is greater or equal to the pivot, v[j2] is already on the correct (right) side — we <u>decrement</u> j2. The only remaining possibility is that both v[j1] and v[j2] are on the wrong sides. Then we <u>swap</u> them and advance both j1 and j2. The process continues until j1 and j2 converge and overlap. The place where they converge marks the new pivot location. The final step is to actually place the pivot into its new location. This is necessary because we want to exclude the pivot element from future sorting, thus reducing the size of the recursive task. We swap the pivot with either v[j1] or v[j2], depending on which side of the array it comes from.

In random arrays, the choice of the pivot element is not very important. It is acceptable to take the first element of the array as a pivot. Our implementation, presented below, is more general. The first line in the Split(...) function —

```
int p = ...
```

— determines which element is chosen as the pivot. In our code it is set to the middle element, but the rest of the code would work with any other formula.

---

[*] C.A.R. Hoare. Quicksort. *Comp. J.*, Vol. 5, No. 1 (1962), pp. 10-15.

For best performance we want to split the array into parts of nearly equal sizes. If the pivot happens to be the smallest or the largest element of the array, however, the split is not much of a split: one of the parts is simply empty. If this happens repeatedly, quicksort degenerates into a slow recursive version of selection sort. This is the case, for example, when the array is initially sorted, and we always choose the first element as the pivot. It may be worthwhile to explore better ways of choosing the pivot. For example, we may examine several elements of the array (e.g. first, last, and middle) and chose the <u>median</u> element (i.e. the element whose <u>value</u> falls in the middle of the others) as the pivot.

In the code below, the quicksort algorithm is implemented as a class QUICKSORT. The private Split (...) function partitions the array and returns the new location of the pivot. The RecursiveSort (...) function first calls Split (...), then calls itself recursively to sort the left and right parts. The pivot is excluded from future sorting, so both parts are smaller than the initial array. This reduces the size of the task and assures that recursion eventually stops. The base case is when the number of elements left to sort is 0 or 1. For improved performance, we have also added another base case, when there are only two elements.

SORTS.CPP

```
// QUICKSRT.H

template <class SOMETYPE>
class QUICKSORT {

  public:

    void Sort (apvector<SOMETYPE> &v);

  private:

    void RecursiveSort(apvector<SOMETYPE> &v, int i1, int i2);
    int Split(apvector<SOMETYPE> &v, int i1, int i2);
        // Returns the new location of the pivot element.

};

//***************************************************************
```

Continued

```
template <class SOMETYPE>
void QUICKSORT<SOMETYPE>::Sort (apvector<SOMETYPE> &v)

// Sorts array v in ascending order.

{
    int n = v.length();
    RecursiveSort(v, 0, n-1);
}

template <class SOMETYPE>
void QUICKSORT<SOMETYPE>::RecursiveSort (apvector<SOMETYPE> &v,
                                                int i1, int i2)

// Sorts elements of v between i1 and i2 in ascending order.

{
    int p;

    if (i2 - i1 <= 1) {   // Base case:
        if (i2 - i1 == 1 && v[i2] < v[i1])
            Swap(v[i2], v[i1]);
    }
    else {            // Recursive case:
        p = Split(v, i1, i2);
        RecursiveSort(v, i1, p-1);
        RecursiveSort(v, p+1, i2);
    }
}

//***************************************************************

template <class SOMETYPE>
int QUICKSORT<SOMETYPE>::Split(apvector<SOMETYPE> &v, int i1, int i2)

// Takes one of the values (here v[(i2+i1)/2]) as "pivot"
//    and splits the segment of the array v between i1 and i2
//    into two parts so that:
//       v[p] == pivot
//       v[j] <= pivot for j < p
//       v[j] >= pivot for j > p
// Returns p;

{
    int p = (i2 + i1) / 2;  // In this version the "pivot" value is the
                            //    middle element

    SOMETYPE pivot = v[p];

    int j1 = i1, j2 = i2;
```

Continued ☞

```
    // Increment j1 if v[j1] <= pivot; decrement j2 if v[j2] >= pivot;
    //   otherwise swap v[j1] and v[j2] and advance both j1 and j2:
    while (j1 <= j2) {
        if (v[j1] <= pivot)
            j1++;
        else if (v[j2] >= pivot)
            j2--;
        else {
            Swap(v[j1], v[j2]);
            j1++;
            j2--;
        }
    }

    // Now v[j1] and v[j2] are adjacent elements; j1 > j2.
    //   Swap v[j1] or v[j2] with the pivot, making sure that
    //   the swapped element remains on the same side of the pair:
    if (p < j2) {
        Swap(v[p], v[j2]);
        p = j2;
    }
    else if (p > j1) {
        Swap(v[p], v[j1]);
        p = j1;
    }
    return p;
}
```

On average, quicksort works in $O(n \log n)$ time, and, according to some published benchmarks, beats mergesort almost by a factor of two.

As we have mentioned earlier, when the partitions are very uneven, quicksort can degenerate into slow $O(n^2)$-time performance. This situation creates another pitfall: if we are not careful, the depth of recursion may become $O(n)$ instead of $O(\log n)$, and the function may overflow the system stack for a large array.

This is one of the finer points of recursive programming. Fortunately, there is a good solution. In quicksort, the last call to `RecursiveSort(...)` is actually a case of **tail recursion** (see Section 19.4). Therefore it can be easily replaced with iteration. The trick is that the maximum depth of recursion may differ dramatically depending on which part of the array we handle recursively and which part iteratively. The safe way is to process the <u>shorter</u> part of the array recursively. This assures that the maximum depth of recursion never exceeds $\log_2 n$ frames. Thus, for "real world" use, the `RecursiveSort(...)` function in quicksort should be rewritten like this:

```
                                                    ┌─────────────────────┐
                                                    │ SORTS.CPP      [💾] │
──────────────────────────────────────────────────┤─────────────────────├──
template <class SOMETYPE>
void QUICKSORT<SOMETYPE>::RecursiveSort (apvector<SOMETYPE> &v,
                                              int i1, int i2)

// Modified to assure the maximum recursion depth is O(log n).

{
    int p, m;

    while (i2 - i1 >= 1) {
        if (i2 - i1 == 1) { // Base case
            if (v[i2] < v[i1])
                Swap(v[i2], v[i1]);
            break;
        }
        else {  // Recursive case
            p = Split(v, i1, i2);
            m = (i2 + i1) / 2;
            if (p > m) {
                RecursiveSort(v, p+1, i2);
                                    // Process recursively the
                                    //    right part
                i2 = p-1;           // Continue iteratively with
                                    //    the left part
            }
            else {
                RecursiveSort(v, i1, p-1);
                                    // Process recursively the
                                    //    left part
                i1 = p+1;           // Continue iteratively with
                                    //    the right part
            }
        }
    }
}
──────────────────────────────────────────────────────────────────────────
```

The same principle applies when we implement quicksort without recursion by
using our own stack. We can process one part of the array immediately while
saving the address and the length of the other part on the stack. To reduce the risk
of stack overflow, we have to push the <u>longer</u> part on the stack and process the
<u>shorter</u> part immediately.

27.3.3. Treesort and Heapsort

The idea of the ***treesort*** is simply to use a binary search tree for sorting. We start with an empty binary search tree and insert all the elements of our array into the tree one by one. (We are using a generalized "binary search tree" which allows duplicate index values, and we do not really use it for searching.) Then we traverse the tree in order, retrieve the elements in ascending order, and place them back into the array.

This method takes an average of $O(n \log n)$ comparisons, but it can degenerate into $O(n^2)$ comparisons, particularly when the initial array is already sorted. Treesort requires additional space for building the tree. In general, there is little to recommend this obvious method, especially in comparison with quicksort and ***heapsort***.

Heapsort, proposed by J. Williams,[*] takes advantage of the array representation of heaps and the $O(\log n)$ time it takes to insert an element into a heap and remove the largest element from the top of a heap. Heapsort can be performed within the original array without using additional space.

As we know (Chapter 24), a heap is a complete binary tree in which the root of the tree contains the largest element and each node contains the largest element of the tree growing from that node. A heap can be represented as an array; for the sake of convenience when using heaps, we index the elements of the array starting from 1 rather than 0. The element with the index 0 is not used. The "Reheap" procedure fixes a heap in which all elements are in order except the root. For the heapsort, it is actually more efficient not to build the heap from scratch but to fix the original array. This can be accomplished by applying the Reheap procedure to all nodes that have children, starting at the lowest level and proceeding towards the root. In the second phase of the algorithm we remove the elements one by one from the top of the heap and store them in reverse order starting at the end of the array. To do that, we swap the root (the first element) with the last element, decrement the size of the array, and apply the same Reheap procedure to fix the heap.

In the following code, heapsort is implemented as a class HEAPSORT:

---

[*] J.W.J. Williams. Heapsort (Algorithm 232). *Comm. ACM*, Vol. 7, No. 6 (1964), pp. 347-48.

```
                                               ┌─────────────────────────┐
                                               │  SORTS.CPP          💾  │
─ ─ ─ ─ ─ ─ ─ ─ ─ ─ ─ ─ ─ ─ ─ ─ ─ ─ ─ ─ ─ ─ ─ └─────────────────────────┘ ─ ─
// HEAPSORT.H

template <class SOMETYPE>
class HEAPSORT {

  public:

    void Sort(apvector<SOMETYPE> &v);
        // Sorts elements v[1] through v[n].  v[0] is not used.

  private:

    void Reheap(apvector<SOMETYPE> &v, int i, int n);

};

//***************************************************************

template <class SOMETYPE>
void HEAPSORT<SOMETYPE>::Reheap(apvector<SOMETYPE> &v, int i, int n)

//  Fixes the (sub)heap rooted at the node v[i], assuming that
//     all the nodes below it (all its descendants) already
//     satisfy the heap ordering property.
//  n is the largest possible index of an element in the heap:
//     v[j] is not in the heap when j > n (v[0] is unused).

{
    SOMETYPE x = v[i];   // Save the root value.

    int iParent = i;
    i *= 2;                 // Set i to left child.
    while (i <= n) {
        // Set i to the right child, if it is larger:
        if (i < n && v[i] < v[i+1])
            i++;

        if (v[i] <= x)
            break;

        v[iParent] = v[i];      // Move the child up
        iParent = i;            // v[iParent] is now vacant
        i *= 2;                 // i set to its left child
    }
    v[iParent] = x;
}

//***************************************************************
```

Continued ✏️➔

```
template <class SOMETYPE>
void HEAPSORT<SOMETYPE>::Sort(apvector<SOMETYPE> &v)

// Sorts elements v[1] through v[n] in ascending order
//    (v[0] is not used).

{
    int i, n = v.length() - 1;
    SOMETYPE x;

    // Fix heaps rooted in all nodes with children, going
    //    from the lowest-rightmost such node and proceeding
    //    left and up to the root.  v[i] is a leaf for any i > n/2,
    //    and v[n/2] is the parent of v[n], and therefore not a leaf.
    //    So we start with v[n/2].

    for (i = n/2;   i >= 1;   i--)
        Reheap(v, i, n);

    // Remove elements from the top of the heap and store them
    //    in reverse order starting from the end of the array:
    while (n > 1) {
        Swap(v[1], v[n]);
        n--;
        Reheap(v, 1, n);
    }
}
```

27.4.   Radix Sort

Is it possible to sort faster than in $O(n \log n)$ time?   In general, a theoretically proven result is that any sort based on a comparison of keys will take, on average, at least $O(n \log n)$ comparisons.   It is also true that for <u>searching</u> methods based on comparison of keys, the best time is $O(\log n)$.   And yet, lookup tables and hash tables allow us to do better. These techniques, which tie the location of data elements to the values of their keys, let us find data in constant time, $O(1)$. Similar strategies can be applied to sorting.

Let us start with a simple case where we have a large list of data elements but all their keys have values from a small set; for example, integers between 0 and 9. Let us apply the lookup or hashing idea to this situation.   We can create 10 buckets, corresponding to the 10 possible key values.   In one pass through the data we add each element to the appropriate bucket.   Then we scan through the ten buckets in ascending order and collect all the elements together.   The result will be the list sorted in the ascending order.   It is easier to implement this method for linked lists, because combining the buckets into one list means changing only ten pointers.   The time of this method is $O(n)$ because we handle each element once.

Now let us assume that all the keys are integers in the range between 0 and 99999. Suppose memory limitations do not allow us to have 100000 buckets. The radix sort technique lets us sort the list one digit at a time: we can complete the task with only 10 buckets, but we will need five passes through the data. We have to make sure that the buckets preserve the order of inserted elements; for instance, each bucket can be a list with the elements inserted at the end. We start with the <u>least</u> significant digit in the key and distribute the data elements into buckets based on that digit. When we are done, we scan all the buckets in ascending order and collect the data into one list. We then take the second digit (the tens digit) and repeat the process. We have to make as many passes through the data as there are digits in the key. After the last pass, the list is sorted.

The radix sort works like magic! (In fact it can be conveniently demonstrated on a deck of 16 cards of four suits and four ranks.) There is also a mathematical proof of its correctness, of course. The method works for data with any keys that permit positional representation. For integers, using hexadecimal digits or whole bytes is actually more appropriate than decimal digits. A program that sorts words in lexicographic order can perform a radix sort with a bucket for each letter or symbol. In the latter case, we have to pad all the words with blanks to the maximum length and start sorting from the last character position.

A radix sort takes $O(n)$ time, but the constant coefficient depends on the number of positions in the key. We have to remember that $\log_2 n$ grows rather slowly, so if your key has ten positions and you are sorting less than 1000 items, you would probably do better with conventional $O(n \log n)$ algorithms. Also, the radix sort is not very practical for arrays because it requires a lot of extra space and a lot of moves. It makes more sense for linked lists, because it is easy to unlink an element and link it to the end of a bucket list and then collect all the bucket lists back into one list. The implementation and proof of correctness for the radix sort is left for a lab exercise.

27.5. Summary

In addition to their utility in building computer applications, sorting algorithms provide a fertile field for formulating and studying general properties of algorithms and comparing their efficiency.

Selection sort:
> While n is greater than 2: find the largest element, swap it with the last element of the array, decrement n. $O(n^2)$ comparisons.

Insertion sort:

Starting at $i=2$, for each element v[i] find its place in order among the first $i-1$ elements, shift the required number of elements to the right to make room, and insert v[i]. $O(n^2)$ comparisons, but can be $O(n)$ for a nearly sorted array.

Bubble sort:

While any elements are out of order: traverse the array from the beginning to n, swapping all pairs of adjacent elements that are out of order; then decrement n. $O(n^2)$ comparisons, but can be $O(n)$ for a nearly sorted array.

Mergesort:

Split the array into two halves. (Recursively) sort the first half and the second half, then merge the two sorted halves. $O(n \log n)$ comparisons; needs a temporary work space of n elements.

Quicksort:

Choose a "pivot" element. Running from both ends of the array and swapping the elements if necessary, find a new place for the pivot and rearrange the elements so that all the elements to the left of the pivot are less than or equal to the pivot, and all the elements to the right of the pivot are greater than or equal to the pivot. (Recursively) sort the left part and the right part, excluding the pivot itself. $O(n \log n)$ comparisons, on average, with very good benchmarks, but may sometimes degenerate into $O(n^2)$ time.

Heapsort:

First: pretend that your array represents a heap and, to fix the order of elements, repeat the "Reheap" procedure for all elements, skipping the leaves and going from the bottom up. Second: while n is greater than 1: swap the top element with the last element of the array, decrement n, and perform Reheap for the root (first element). $O(n \log n)$ comparisons.

Radix sort:

Starting from the least significant digit (or the rightmost letter) in the key: distribute all elements into buckets that correspond to possible values of that digit (or letter) using a FIFO method. Scan all the buckets in ascending order and collect them back into one list. Repeat for each position in the key. $O(n) \cdot d$ operations, where d is the number of positions in the key. More appropriate for linked lists.

There are many more sorting algorithms and variations of the above algorithms, but the methods described here cover a representative basic set that has become standard in college computer science curricula over the years.

28

Inheritance

28.1.   Discussion

In conventional programming a program is thought of as a set of procedures applied to some data structures. By comparison, in the realm of Object-Oriented Programming (OOP), a program is thought of as a set of actively interacting objects. In C++, objects are represented as instances of classes. An object can be a variable of some class type declared directly or addressed through a pointer returned by the `new` operator. One of the most difficult tasks in object-oriented software design is to define the objects and their relationships.

OOP languages explicitly support one common type of relationship, the hierarchical taxonomy. Taxonomy is a system of classification in which an object can be defined as a special case, "a kind of" another object. In Linnaeus' zoological taxonomy, for example, a person is a kind of primate which is a kind of mammal which is a kind of animal. Taxonomies have been one of the main ways of thinking in natural science for centuries, and they undoubtedly reflect the inclination of the human mind toward descriptive hierarchies. In software, ideas of hierarchical classification can be traced to Artificial Intelligence, a branch of computer science that strives to model intelligent systems and rational behaviors. AI uses taxonomies to create formal representations of some aspects of the real world.

In object-oriented programming languages, an object can be formally declared to be "a kind of" another object. This feature is called *inheritance.* **In C++, if class D inherits from class B, all members of B, both data and functions, become members of D. B is referred to as the** *base* **class and D is referred to as the** *derived* **class.**

The derived class may include additional data members and member functions and can redefine some of the member functions inherited from the base class. The derived class itself may serve as a base class for the next derivation, and so on. In this way, we can build a hierarchy of classes, each derived from some class of a previous level. The inheritance proceeds from more general, abstract classes to more specialized classes. Figure C-1 in Appendix C shows the C++ hierarchy for the standard stream I/O classes. Defining class hierarchies brings some order into the multitude of all the defined classes in a project.

> **On a more practical level, inheritance can also be viewed as a convenient tool for reusing code. A derived class may have all the functionality of the base class with some data members added and some member functions tweaked for slightly different functionality.**

The syntax for defining a derived class, which we will explain in greater detail later in this chapter, is as follows:

```
class D : public B {
    ...     // Additional members for the derived class D.
};
```

The base class B must be defined (or `#include`-ed) above the derived class D.

Inheritance is a fairly simple concept, but its implementation in a specific programming language poses many questions and challenges to language designers:

- What is the difference between inheritance and embedding the base class as a member, and how is it implemented syntactically?
- Should private members of the base class be accessible within the derived class?
- If a function is redefined in the derived class, is it possible to call the original function of the base class from the derived class functions?
- How do the constructors interact? How can the constructor of a derived class pass arguments to the constructor of the base class?
- Can the variables of the base class type be assigned values of the derived class type, and vice versa? Can pointers of the base class type point to objects of the derived class type?
- How can an object always know to call the appropriate member function, even if it is accessed through a pointer of another type?

In the following sections we will examine these questions and the way C++ handles them.

28.2.   Inheritance vs. Embedding

At the outset, we have to make a clear semantic and syntactic distinction between inheritance and embedding and provide some guidelines for their use.

As we know, a class may include as one of its members another class:

```
class D {
    ...
    class B;
    ...
};
```

This structure represents a relationship of a part to a whole, or inclusion: D "has a" B. Inheritance, on the other hand, represents a relationship of specialization: D "is a kind of" B. Each of these relationships has its proper place in object-oriented design.

Let us consider, for example, a class RECT which describes a rectangle through its upper left corner, width and height. It has an embedded member class, POINT — its upper left corner — together with integer members width and height:

```
class POINT {
    ...
    int x;
    int y;
    ...
    void MoveTo(int ax, int ay);
    ...
};

class RECT {
    ...
    POINT ulCorner;
    int width;
    int height;
    ...
    void MoveTo(int ax, int ay);
    ...
};
```

RECT is not "a kind of" POINT, so it would be wrong to <u>derive</u> it from POINT. When POINT ulCorner is embedded into RECT, its data members and member functions have to be accessed through ulCorner. For example:

```
void RECT::MoveTo(int ax, int ay)

{
    ulCorner.x = ax; // works only if x and y are public in POINT
    ulCorner.y = ay;
}
```

or, better:

```
void RECT::MoveTo(int ax, int ay)

{
    ulCorner.MoveTo(ax, ay);
}
```

In the latter code fragment, RECT's MoveTo(...) function calls POINT's MoveTo(...) function. We have intentionally given them the same name to show that there is no conflict.

Embedding one class into another causes all kinds of problems with public and private members, but they can be worked out one way or another. Useful functions of the embedded class can be channeled through the corresponding functions of the encompassing class, like the MoveTo(...) function above. This is the prescribed way of laying out classes related to each other as a part to a whole.

A conceptually and stylistically <u>incorrect</u> but also effective method would be to derive RECT from POINT, the taxonomic relationship notwithstanding. Then we would write:

```
class RECT : public POINT {
    ...
    int width;
    int height;
    ...
};
```

In this case, RECT directly inherits x, y, and the MoveTo(...) function, so these members of POINT implicitly become members of RECT and there is no need to mention them explicitly in RECT's definition. Sooner or later, however, we will have to pay the price for (so to speak) cutting corners. The fact that the point is used as the upper left corner is not documented anywhere in the above RECT class definition. And what if we want to add another point, say the lower right corner?

In some situations, the temptation to derive from some general-purpose class — even though your class is not at all "a kind of" that class but simply wants to inherit some general functionality — is too great to resist. Suppose you need some uniform error handling capability in each of the classes of the graphics package you are working on. You would be tempted to write a class ERROR and derive each of your classes from it. This would be poor design from the OOP point of view. More elegantly, you could create an abstract base class GRAPHOBJECT and place it at the root of the hierarchy for all graphics classes. This class could provide error handling as well as some other very general functions related to graphics objects. As we will explain in Section 28.7, these functions can be pure virtual functions that have nothing but a prototype and an indicator that they will be redefined at the lower levels of the class hierarchy.

28.3. Member Access in Derived Classes

The next question that has to be answered is how encapsulation relates to inheritance and, in particular, whether a derived class should have access to the private members of its base class. In C++ a third type of member access is introduced as a compromise: the ***protected*** member. Protected members act just like private members with the only difference that they are directly accessible within all the derived classes at all levels of the class hierarchy. Private members remain inaccessible to derived classes.

For additional flexibility, C++ supports different types of inheritance. In this book we consider only ***public inheritance***, in which all three types of class members, private, protected, and public, retain their access type in the derived classes. This is by far the most often used type of inheritance. Public inheritance is indicated by the keyword public in the class derivation syntax:

```
class D : public B { // D derived from B through public inheritance
   ...
};
```

In ***private*** and ***protected inheritance***, protected and public members in the base class change their access properties in the derived classes.

Protected members should be used instead of private members in a class's definition if there is a chance that another class may be eventually derived from it, which is almost always the case.

In the following example, we derive a class FILLEDRECT from the class RECT. In addition to the RECT members, FILLEDRECT contains the color and fill pattern for its interior:

```
enum COLOR {BLACK, RED, GREEN, BLUE, WHITE};
enum FILL {EMPTY, HATCH, SOLID};

class POINT {

  protected: // Accessible only in classes derived from POINT

    int x;
    int y;

  public:    // Accessible everywhere

    ...
    int GetX() {return x;}
    int GetY() {return y;}
    ...
    void MoveTo (int ax, int ay) {x = ax; y = ay;}
    void MoveRel (int dx, int dy) {x += dx; y += dy;}
    ...
};

class RECT {

  protected: // Accessible only in classes derived from RECT

    POINT ulCorner;
    int width;
    int height;
    COLOR color;

  public:    // Accessible everywhere

    ...
    void MoveTo (int ax, int ay) {ulCorner.MoveTo(ax, ay);}
    void MoveRel (int dx, int dy) {ulCorner.MoveRel(dx, dy);}
    ...
};

class FILLEDRECT : public RECT {

  protected:

    // Implicitly includes all protected members from RECT:
    //    ulCorner, width, height, and color

    FILL fill;
    COLOR fillcolor;

  public:
```

Continued ☞

```
    // Implicitly includes all public members from RECT:
    //    MoveTo(), etc.

    ...
    void SetFillPattern(FILL f) {fill = f;}
    void SetFillColor(COLOR fc) {fillcolor = fc;}
    ...
};
```

The RECT members ulCorner, width, height, and color are directly accessible within the FILLEDRECT member functions. ulCorner members x and y are not directly accessible within RECT or FILLEDRECT, because they are not RECT members.   Nor are they accessible indirectly through ulCorner.x, ulCorner.y, because they are not public members in POINT. They can be accessed only through the ulCorner.GetX() and ulCorner.GetY() calls.

The x and y members of POINT in the above code are defined as <u>protected</u>, as opposed to <u>private</u>. This does not affect the RECT definition, but it may be useful in the future if we decide later to <u>derive</u> a new class from POINT, such as a class PIXEL.   Protected POINT members x and y will then be directly accessible to the PIXEL member functions:

```
class PIXEL : public POINT {

  protected:

    // Implicitly includes protected members of POINT: x and y

    int color;

  public:

    // Implicitly includes all public members of POINT
    ...
    void SetColor(int a_color);
    void Draw();
    ...
};
```

Member access privileges in derived classes in C++ may be confusing and lead to a lot of compiler errors and general frustration among beginners. Some might be even tempted to declare "everything public" and "forget about it." But this would violate encapsulation and could make life more difficult for programmers who "inherit" the task of maintaining your code.

28.4.   Redefining Member Functions

An important concept in object-oriented design is that objects represent active entities that themselves know how to implement a certain function. In the C++ implementation, it is desirable that different classes use the same name for a member function that performs a semantically similar task. Normally this does not cause any conflict, because a member function is called either by other member functions inside the same class or with an instance of that class.

Inheritance, however, slightly complicates the matter. It is sometimes necessary to modify an inherited member function for the derived class. For example, the RECT class may have a member function that draws a rectangle. The implementation below is based on some fictional graphics primitives (low-level graphics functions):

```
#include "graphics.h"

...

void RECT::Draw()

{
    SetPenColor(color);
    MovePenTo(ulCorner.GetX(), ulCorner.GetY());
    PenDown();
    MovePenRel(width, 0);
    MovePenRel(0, height);
    MovePenRel(-width, 0);
    MovePenRel(0, -height);
    PenUp();
}
```

The FILLEDRECT class also needs a function that draws a filled rectangle, and the object-oriented approach requires that it have the same name, Draw(). This function may first fill the interior of the rectangle and then draw its border:

```
void FILLEDRECT::Draw()

{
    SetPenFillPattern(fill);
    SetPenColor(fillcolor);
    DrawFilledBox(ulCorner.GetX(), ulCorner.GetY(), width, height);

    // Now call the Draw() function for the base class RECT
    //  in order to draw the border:

    ...
}
```

We would like to call the `Draw()` function for the base class, but we need some special syntax for it. If we said simply

```
Draw();
```

it would be interpreted as a recursive call to FILLEDRECT::Draw() — a bad error.

To distinguish the `Draw()` function for the base and derived classes we specify the class name before the function name:

```
void FILLEDRECT::Draw()

{

    SetPenFillPattern(fill);
    SetPenColor(fillcolor);
    DrawFilledBox(ulCorner.GetX(), ulCorner.GetY(), width, height);

    RECT::Draw();
}
```

A conflict is also possible between a member function name and a non-member free-standing function. Suppose our fictional graphics primitive MovePenRel (...) were called MoveRel (...) instead. That name would clash with the RECT class's member function MoveRel (...). To distinguish between the two, we would have to precede the free-standing function's name with the global scope prefix ::

```
void RECT::Draw()

{
    ::SetColor(color);
    ::MoveTo(ulCorner.GetX(), ulCorner.GetY());
    ::PenDown();
    ::MoveRel(width, 0);
    ::MoveRel(0, height);
    ::MoveRel(-width, 0);
    ::MoveRel(0, -height);
    ::PenUp();
}
```

We have also used :: with PenDown() and PenUp() for consistency and to emphasize that they are free-standing functions.

28.5. Base and Derived Class Constructors

A special case of function redefinition takes place with constructors. Before entering its own code, the constructor for the derived class automatically executes the constructor for the base class. By default, the compiler calls the base class constructor version that does not take any arguments. Consider the following example:

```
// GRAPHICS.H

...

class RECT {

  protected:

    POINT ulCorner;
    int width;
    int height;
    COLOR color;

  public:

    RECT ();      // Constructor with no arguments
    RECT (POINT ul, int w, int h, COLOR c = WHITE);
              // Constructor with initialization
    ...
};

class FILLEDRECT : public RECT {

  protected:

    FILL fill;
    COLOR fillcolor;

  public:

    FILLEDRECT ();     // Constructor with no arguments
    FILLEDRECT (POINT ul, int w, int h, COLOR c = WHITE,
        FILL f = SOLID, COLOR fc = BLACK);
              // Constructor with initialization
    ...
};
```

```
// GRAPHICS.CPP

...

RECT::RECT()                    // Constructor with no arguments

{
    ulCorner.MoveTo(0,0);
    width = 1000;
    height = 1000;
    color = WHITE;
}

FILLEDRECT::FILLEDRECT()        // Constructor with no arguments

{
    fill = SOLID;
    fillcolor = BLACK;
}

// TEST.CPP

...
int main()

{
    FILLEDRECT filledrect;
    ...
}
```

When a FILLEDRECT object is declared without arguments, the RECT constructor (the form without arguments) is called first. It sets ulCorner to (0,0), width and height to 1000, and color to WHITE. Then additional statements are executed in the FILLEDRECT constructor: fill is set to SOLID and fillcolor is set to BLACK. The call to the base class constructor is implicit and not shown anywhere in the code.

Suppose now we want to declare a FILLEDRECT object and initialize it with some arguments, as follows:

```
// TEST.CPP

...
int main()

{
    FILLEDRECT filledrect(POINT(0,0), 200, 100, BLUE, SOLID, RED);
    ...
}
```

In the FILLEDRECT class definition we have declared a special constructor with these arguments. However, we need to pass some of these arguments to the RECT constructor, which is called first. The syntax for doing this is the same as in an initializer list:

```
// Constructor for FILLEDRECT with arguments

FILLEDRECT::FILLEDRECT (POINT ul, int w, int h, COLOR c,
    FILL f, COLOR fc) : RECT(ul, w, h, c)

{
    fill = f;
    fillcolor = fc;
}
```

The statement

```
... : RECT(ul, w, h, c)
```

indicates that the appropriate form of the constructor for the base class should be called before entering the code for the FILLEDRECT constructor. Note that the RECT constructor is called implicitly. There is no syntax for an explicit call because there is no need to construct any additional object — the RECT object is simply a part of the FILLEDRECT object.

The destructors are executed in <u>reverse</u> order: the destructor for the derived class, after finishing its own code, automatically calls the destructor for the base class.

28.6. Assignments and Pointer Conversions

Is it valid to assign a variable of a derived class to a variable of the base class and vice versa? Can a pointer of the base class type point to an object of the derived class type and vice versa?

Consider the following code:

```
// TEST.CPP

#include "graphics.h"

int main() {

{
    RECT rect, *prect;
    FILLEDRECT filledrect, *pfilledrect;

    . . .
    rect = filledrect;          // Base set to derived -- OK!
    . . .                       //    (all members of rect can be copied
                                //     from the corresponding members of
                                //     filledrect)

    filledrect = rect;          // Derived set to base -- ERROR!
                                //    (values for additional members
                                //     fillpattern, fillcolor are
                                //     undefined)
    . . .
    prect = &filledrect;        // Automatic cast -- OK:
    prect->MoveTo(100,100)      //    all members addressed through prect
                                //    are defined in filledrect
    . . .
    pfilledrect = &rect;        // ERROR:
                                //    some members defined for filledrect
                                //    are undefined for rect
    pfillrect->                 //
        SetFillColor(c);        // This would assign c to a non-existing
                                //    member in rect

    . . .
}
}
```

The above code demonstrates that in C++ you can assign a variable of the derived type to a variable of the base type. C++ provides an automatic conversion from the derived type to the base type, because an object of the derived class has all the inherited elements of the base type, and it can assign these values to an object of the base type. The converse is not true. An attempt to assign an object of the base type to an object of the derived type normally generates a compiler error, because such assignments leave the additional members of the derived class (e.g., fillcolor, fillpattern) undefined. Figure 28-1 illustrates this situation. (The base-to-derived assignment becomes possible if a special constructor that assigns some default values to all additional members is provided for the derived class.)

Derived class: Base class:

FILLEDRECT   RECT

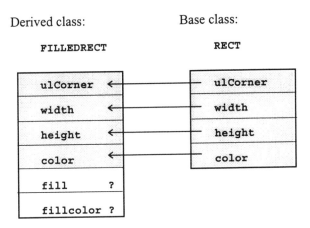

Figure 28-1. Assignment from a base class to the derived class is not allowed.

The same is true for pointers. A base class pointer can point to an object of the derived class because all members accessible with the base type pointer are defined in the derived class.

⌘   ⌘   ⌘

The automatic cast of pointers from the derived to the base class is an important feature for OOP, where it is desirable to be able to handle all the objects in a hierarchy uniformly. Suppose you want to create a list of several graphics objects to be displayed on the screen. You cannot just put all the objects into an array or a linked list, because the objects, represented by various classes (e.g. RECT, FILLEDRECT, CIRCLE), have different data types and sizes. A good solution is to derive all your graphics classes from some common abstract class, GRAPHOBJECT, and to keep your master list in the form of an <u>array</u> (or linked list) of <u>pointers</u> to GRAPHOBJECTs. For example:

```
// GRAPHICS.H

class GRAPHOBJECT {

  protected:

    apstring errormsg;
    ...

  public:

    ...
    void Draw();
    ...
};

...

class RECT : public GRAPHOBJECT {
    ...
};

class FILLEDRECT : public RECT {
    ...
};

class SQUARE : public RECT {
    ...
};

class CIRCLE : public GRAPHOBJECT {
    ...
};

...


// TEST.CPP

#include "graphics.h"

int main()

{
    GRAPHOBJECT *displayList[100];

    ...
    displayList[0] = new RECT(POINT(0,0), 100, 100, RED);
    displayList[1] = new FILLEDRECT(POINT(0,0), 100, 100, RED,
                                                    HATCH, BLUE);
    displayList[2] = new CIRCLE(POINT(50,50), 100);
    ...
}
```

28.7. Virtual Functions, Polymorphism

The example of a display list from the previous section poses a question: how can we display all its elements? The information about the specific types of objects in the list seems to be lost. One possible solution would be to include the graphics object type descriptor within the GRAPHOBJECT class definition. Then we could write one Draw() function with a big switch statement that would properly handle all the different types of graphics objects:

```
enum GTYPE {GPIXEL, GRECT, GFILLEDRECT, GCIRCLE, ...};

class GRAPHOBJECT {

  protected:

    GTYPE gtype;
    ...
};

void GRAPHOBJECT::Draw()

{
    switch (gtype) {
    ...
    }
}
```

This solution would be cumbersome and contrary to the spirit of OOP.

What we would like to be able to do is write something simple:

```
    ...
    for (int i = 0;   i < nObjects;   i++)
        displayList[i]->Draw();
    ...
```

Based on what we have learned so far, we would not expect this to work because the same Draw() function for the GRAPHOBJECT class would be called for every element in the list. This function knows nothing about rectangles or circles. But as we will see shortly, the addition of just one keyword, virtual, in the declaration of the function Draw() can make the above code work.

Each type of object in the list has its own Draw() function, and the appropriate function should be called for that object automatically. This feature is called *polymorphism* (from Greek: *poly* — many; *morphe* — form). Polymorphic behavior lets the same base type of pointers properly manipulate objects of different derived types. It is one of the key features in C++ and other object-oriented languages. In C++, polymorphism has to be implemented through pointers, because we cannot store objects of different types in the same list, but we can store the pointers of the same base class type.

Polymorphism requires in one way or another a run-time support feature called *run-time operator identification*. The address of a polymorphic function cannot be hard-coded in the compiled code. Instead, it has to be determined at run time. In the C++ run-time implementation, each class has a table of the addresses of its member functions and each object has a pointer to the table of its class. This is structurally similar to the object type descriptor and `switch` statement solution, but all the mechanics are handled by the compiler and kept hidden from the programmer.

C++ requires that functions that will be called in a polymorphic manner be declared with the keyword `virtual`. For example:

```
class GRAPHOBJECT {
    ...
  public:

    virtual void Draw();
    ...
};
```

This declaration assures that in the whole hierarchy of classes derived from GRAPHOBJECT, `Draw()` will be a virtual function. If a class has its own redefined version of `Draw()`, that version will be called; otherwise, a version higher in the hierarchy will be called. This will work whether the object is accessed through its own pointer type or the base type (or any type higher in the hierarchy). Moreover, GRAPHOBJECT does not even have to specify a body for `Draw()`. It can declare it as a *pure virtual function*:

```
class GRAPHOBJECT {
    ...
  public:

    ...
    virtual void Draw() = 0;  // Pure virtual function
    ...
};
```

A class with one or more pure virtual member functions is called an *abstract* class. It exists only to serve as a base class for deriving other classes. Objects of class types do not exist: the compiler will report an error if you try to actually declare or create an object with the type of an abstract class. Lower in the hierarchy we eventually define classes where all pure virtual functions are redefined into actual functions. These classes are called **concrete** classes.

Let us consider another example where polymorphism and virtual functions help us avoid duplication of code. This time we are concerned with the implementation of the derived class. Suppose we have a member function Stretch(...) in the RECT class which implements a "rubber box" — erases a rectangle, changes its size, and draws it again:

```
// GRAPHICS.H

...

class RECT {

  protected:

    POINT ulCorner;
    int width;
    int height;
    COLOR color;

  public:

    ...
    void Draw ();
    void Stretch (int dw, int dh);
    ...
};
```

There is a method of painting pixels on the screen in such a way that the new image is "xor'ed" (that is, added in binary arithmetic) to the screen. Drawing the image the second time in the same place erases the image and leaves no trace. This method can be used for drawing erasable objects.

Suppose a current "erasable" object is already on the screen. We may write a function that looks like this:

```
// GRAPHICS.CPP

...

void RECT::Stretch (int dw, int dh)

{
    Draw();         // Erase the current rectangle
    width += dw;
    height += dh;
    Draw();         // Draw the changed rectangle
}
```

We can use it as follows:

```
// TEST.CPP

...
int main()

{
    RECT rect;
    ...
    SetWriteMode(XOR_PUT);
    rect.Draw();
    for (int k = 0;   k < 100;   k++)
        rect.Stretch(10,10);
    ...
}
```

Now we might create a derived class, FILLEDRECT, which inherits the Stretch(...) function. But for some reason, the inherited function does not quite work. In desperation, we implement an exact replica of Stretch(...) as a FILLEDRECT member function — and this time, it works!

The mystery is explained by the differences in the Draw() function in the RECT and FILLEDRECT classes. The inherited version of Stretch(...) fails to call the correct version of Draw(), redefined for the FILLEDRECT class. An elegant remedy is to declare Draw() in RECT as a virtual function:

```
class RECT {

  public:

    ...
    virtual void Draw(); // Works when redefined in derived classes
    void Stretch (int dw, int dh);
    ...
};
```

Then `Draw()` acquires polymorphic behavior, the correct version is called in the inherited version of `Stretch(...)`, and there is no need to duplicate `Stretch(...)` in the `FILLEDRECT` class.

Polymorphism is a way to relax the strong type checking in C++ to support the OOP approach. It is a very powerful method for properly designed class hierarchies. Note that in case of ambiguities, you can precisely specify which version of the function you are referring to anywhere in your code by using its name with the class scope prefix. For example:

```
void FILLEDRECT::DrawBorder()

{
    RECT::Draw();
}
```

28.8.   Inheritance and Sound Software Design

As we explained earlier, inheritance helps bring some order to a multitude of classes by arranging them into neat hierarchies. As always, though, there is the danger of the generalizer's overkill: a programmer may enjoy creating an elaborate hierarchy of abstract and concrete classes only to achieve some modest functionality at the bottom. The general applicability of these classes may exist only in the mind of the creator.

Another danger is trying to take the ideal of clear semantic relations between classes too far. Often specialization among classes should be achieved by imposing constraints on their members, not by adding new members. For example, a square is "a kind of" rectangle whose width is equal to its height. What do we do with the `width` and `height` elements if we derive a class `SQUARE` from the class `RECT`? It seems more feasible to do the reverse derivation by adding the `height` element to the `SQUARE` class. These situations must be handled carefully on a case-by-case basis.

From a more practical point of view, inheritance offers a simple way of reusing existing classes by adding a few members and redefining some member functions. However, you should make sure that most of the members in the base class are useful for your derived class — otherwise, the inheritance may be unnecessary. Also always consider embedding as an alternative. It is sometimes quite difficult to decide between these two methods.

Another common use of inheritance is inheriting just the interface of a class. This can be convenient when different classes share the same set of public function names and their arguments, but like anything else, it can be taken too far. The apstack and apqueue classes, for example, both have functions for inserting and removing elements and checking for the empty condition. A programmer may be tempted to derive their interfaces from some abstract class SET, ignoring the fact that there are already conventional names for the stack functions, "push" and "pop," and conventional names for the queue functions, "enqueue" and "dequeue."

Finally, inheritance is a convenient vehicle for commercial delivery of reusable software components to developers. Software components are delivered in the form of class libraries, and developers, in addition to using the supplied classes directly, can derive their own classes from them.

28.9. Summary

Inheritance is a concept in object-oriented programming languages that supports taxonomic hierarchies of objects. In C++, inheritance is implemented through the capability of defining a new class which contains all the members of the base class. The new class is called a derived class. In the most common form of inheritance, public inheritance, public and protected members of the base class keep their status in the derived class and are accessible to the derived class member functions. Some member functions can be redefined in the derived class.

Inheritance is also a convenient tool for reusing classes by adding or modifying a few members, and for reusing a class's interface.

C++ allows a pointer of the base class type to point to any of the derived class objects. A program can call the member function appropriate to an object's class regardless of the type of pointer through which the object is accessed. This feature is known as polymorphism. Functions with polymorphic capability are declared with the keyword virtual and are called virtual functions.

Inheritance allows programmers to define elaborate hierarchies of classes with great ease. It should be used with care, though, to avoid unnecessarily complicated designs.

Appendix A: Bit-Wise Logical Operators

Besides representing a number or a character, a memory location can be used for various purposes simply as a set of bits. For example, individual bits in a byte can represent "flags" that identify the properties or current state of an object or program. Combinations of bits may represent "fields" packed into one `int` or `long` memory location. Individual bits may also represent pixels in an image, and bit patterns may be used in low-level routines for programming hardware registers.

Variables used as sets of bits can be declared as unsigned integral types. It makes sense to distinguish these variables from numeric and character variables by introducing special data type names for them. The following data type names have become rather common:

```
typedef unsigned char BYTE;
typedef unsigned short WORD;
typedef unsigned long DWORD;   // "double word"
```

A `BYTE` variable has eight bits. To make our discussion more concrete, let's assume that a `WORD` has two bytes (16 bits) and a `DWORD`, four bytes (32 bits). The individual bits are often referred to by their positions in a byte or a word, starting from 0 at the rightmost, least significant bit. For example, bits in a byte would be numbered from 0 through 7 (Figure A-1).

Bit 7 6 5 4 3 2 1 0

01001101

Figure A-1. The usual numbering of bits in a byte.

The easiest way to initialize variables that represent bit patterns in C++ is by using hexadecimal numbers. Recall that each hex digit corresponds to four bits, as follows:

```
Binary          Hex

0000             0
0001             1
0010             2
0011             3
0100             4
0101             5
0110             6
0111             7
1000             8
1001             9
1010             A
1011             B
1100             C
1101             D
1110             E
1111             F
```

C++ allows you to write a hex constant as a sequence of hex digits preceded by 0x. For example:

```
WORD flags = 0x8020;            // 1000 0000 0010 0000
WORD mask = 0xFFC0;             // 1111 1111 1100 0000
BYTE data_ready_bit 0x20;       // 0010 0000
```

A byte can be defined by two hex digits, a word by four hex digits, and a double word by eight hex digits.

It is useful to remember hex equivalents for the following bit patterns:

```
  Binary                      Hex

  00000000                    0x00  (or simply 0)

  00000001                    0x01
  00000010                    0x02
  00000100                    0x04
  00001000                    0x08
  00010000                    0x10
  00100000                    0x20
  01000000                    0x40
  10000000                    0x80

  11111111                    0xFF
  11110000                    0xF0
  00001111                    0x0F

  0000000000000001            0x0001
  . . .
  1000000000000000            0x8000
  1111111100000000            0xFF00
  0000000011111111            0x00FF
  1111111111111111            0xFFFF
```

⌘ ⌘ ⌘

C++ offers four bit-wise logical operators: the binary operators "and," "or," and "xor," and a unary operator "not." These operators take operands of integral types, but the values of individual bits in the result are determined by the values of corresponding bits (bits in the same positions) in the operands.

The "and" operator is denoted by the symbol '&'. In the & operation the resulting bit is 1 if and only if <u>both</u> corresponding bits in the two operands are 1.

For example:

```
    00010100 11100010
  & 11111111 00000000
    -----------------
    00010100 00000000
```

Or, in hex representation:

```
  0x14E2 & 0xFF00 = 0x1400
```

The "or" operator is denoted by the symbol ' | '. In the | operation the resulting bit is 1 if and only if <u>at least one</u> of the corresponding bits in the two operands is 1.

For example:

```
  00010100 00010001
| 00000000 00111111
  -----------------
  00010100 00111111
```

Or, in hex representation:

```
0x1411 | 0x003F = 0x143F
```

The "xor" operator is denoted by the symbol ' ^ '. In the ^ operation the resulting bit is 1 if and only if <u>exactly one</u> of the corresponding bits in the two operands is 1.

For example:

```
0x14F1 ^ 0x00FF = 0x140E
```

In other words, in the "xor" operator the resulting bit is set to 1 when the corresponding bits in the operands are <u>different</u>. "Xor" stands for "exclusive or."

The "not" operator is a unary operator. It is denoted by ' ~ '. In the ~ operation the resulting bit is set to 1 if the corresponding bit in the operand is 0 and to 0 if the corresponding bit in the operand is 1.

For example:

```
~0x0F01 = 0xF0FE
```

⌘   ⌘   ⌘

&, | and ^ have <u>lower</u> precedence than relational operators, including the == and != operators.

For example,

```
... (x & 0x0001 != 0)
```

is interpreted as:

```
... (x & (0x0001 != 0))
```

as opposed to the possibly intended:

```
... ((x & 0x0001) != 0)
```

This is a potential source of nasty bugs. It is always safer to use parentheses around binary bitwise operators.

The &, |, and ^ operators can be used in compound assignments. For example:

```
WORD flags = 0x0020;

flags |= 0x8000;        // Same as: flags = flags | 0x8000;
flags &= 0x00C0;        // Same as: flags = flags & 0x00C0;
```

⌘ ⌘ ⌘

The & operator can be used to test or reset a bit in a byte or word. For example:

```
BYTE flags = 0;
const BYTE data_ready_bit = 0x20;

...
if (flags & data_ready_bit) // Test the "data ready" bit
    ...
...
flags &= ~data_ready_bit;   // Reset the "data ready" bit (to 0)
```

& can be also used to "cut out" a field from a byte or word:

```
DWORD a = 0x802A0013;

lowbyte = a & 0x000000FF;
```

The | operator can be used to set a bit in a byte or word. For example:

```
flags |= data_ready_bit;    // Set "data ready" bit to 1
```

The `^=` operator is handy when you need to toggle a bit or a value. The following function calculates the alternating sum of numbers in an array and uses `^=` to toggle the sign flag:

```cpp
double AlternatingSum(const apvector<double> &x)

// Returns x[0] - x[1] + x[2] - x[3] + ... - (or +) x[n-1].

{
    int i, len = x.length();
    double sum = 0.;
    BYTE sign = 0;

    for (int i = 0;   i < len;   i++) {
        if (sign == 0)
            sum += x[i];
        else
            sum -= x[i];
        sign ^= 1;              // Toggle sign
    }
    return sum;
}
```

⌘ ⌘ ⌘

C++ also offers left and right shift operators. They use the same symbols, `<<` and `>>`, as the stream insertion and extraction operators. (In fact, the stream insertion and extraction operators are overloaded shift operators.) The format is illustrated below:

```cpp
WORD a, b, x, y;

...

x = a << 8;             // x = value in a, shifted left by 8 bits
y = b >> k;             // y = value in b, shifted right by k bits
```

Bits shifted out of the range are lost, and the new bits shifted into the range are set to 0. For example:

```cpp
0xFF11 << 1 = 0xFE22;
```

The shift operators can be used in compound assignments. The following function counts the number of set bits in a word and uses the `>>=` operator to shift the tested word:

```
int BitsInWord (WORD w)

// Returns the number of set bits in w.

{
    int count = 0;

    while (w) {
        if (w & 0x0001) count++;
        w >>= 1;
    }

    return count;
}
```

In the following example, an array of words represents pixels in one horizontal scan line in an image: 1 stands for black and 0 for white. The HorizBorders(...) function efficiently whites out all black pixels that are not on the border, that is, the ones with both a left and a right neighbor.

```
void HorizBorders(const apvector<WORD> &pix, apvector<WORD> &pixl)

// Eliminates inner pixels (that have both a left and a right
//   neighbor) in a horizontal scan line, represented by bits in
//   the pix array.  Places the result in pixl.

{
    WORD lword, rword;
    int i, n = pix.length();

    for (i = 0;  i < n;  i++) {
        lword = pix[i] >> 1;              // Left neighbors;
        if (i > 0)                        //    fix the leftmost bit
            lword |= pix[i-1] << 15;      //    from the previous word
        rword = pix[i] << 1;              // Right neighbors;
        if (i < n-1)                      //    fix the rightmost bit
            rword |= pix[i+1] << 15;      //    from the next word
        pixl[i] = pix[i] & ~(lword & rword);
    }
}
```

Bitwise operators and shifts are very economical — they are usually compiled into one CPU instruction.

Appendix B: Pointers and Arrays

There is a close relationship between arrays and pointers in C++. Suppose we have declared an array of 100 elements of the data type double:

```
double a[100];
```

The elements of the array can be referred to in the program as a[0] ... a[99]. When the program is compiled, the compiler does not save the addresses of all the elements, but only the address of the first element, a[0]. When the program needs to access any element, a[i], it <u>calculates</u> its address by adding i units to the address of a[0]. The number of bytes in each "unit" is, in our example, equal to the sizeof(double) (e.g., 8). In general, it is equal to the number of bytes required to store an element of the array.

The address of a[0] can be explicitly obtained using the & ("address of") operator: &a[0]. Since the data type of a[0] is double, the data type of &a[0] is, as usual, double* (pointer to double).

C++ allows us to use the name of the array a, without any subscript, as another name for &a[0].

The name a can be used as an rvalue of the type double*. It cannot be used as an lvalue, because it cannot be changed. We can assign this value to any double* variable. For example:

```
double a[100];
double *p;

p = a;   // Same as p = &a[0];
...
```

As long as p points to the first element of the array, *p becomes an alias for a[0]. In general, we can assign

```
p = &a[i];
```

Then *p becomes temporarily an alias for a[i].

⌘   ⌘   ⌘

C++ supports arithmetic operations on pointers that mimic calculations of addresses of array elements. In this pointer arithmetic, we can add an integer to a pointer or subtract an integer from a pointer. For convenience, the integer operand signifies "units" corresponding to the pointer's data type, not bytes.

For example, if we have

```
double a[100];
double *p;

p = &a[0];
```

then p+1 points to a[1], p+2 points to a[2], and so on. The actual difference in bytes between p+1 and p is sizeof(double) (e.g., 8).

If p is equal to a, then we can refer to a[1] as *(p+1) and, in general, to a[i] as *(p+i).

We can also increment and decrement a pointer using the ++ and -- operators.

In the expression *p++, the increment operator applies to the <u>pointer</u>, and <u>not to the value to which it points</u>. It means: take the value *p, then increment p, (<u>not</u> the dereferenced value *p).

The statement:	Is the same as:
x = *p++;	{ x = *p; p++; }

The relational operators <, >, <=, and >= can be applied to pointers that point to elements of the same array. For example:

```
...
char s[20], *p1, *p2;

p1 = &s[0];
p2 = &s[19];
while (p1 < p2) {
    ...
    p1++;
}
```

All of the above allows us to scan through an array using a pointer variable rather than subscripts. Instead of

```
for (i = 0;   i < 100;   i++)
    cout << a[i] << ' ';
```

we can write:

```
p = a;
for (i = 0;   i < 100;   i++) {
    cout << *p << ' ';
    p++;
}
```

Or, even more economically, utilizing all the shortcuts that C++ provides:

```
for (p = a, i = 0;   i < 100;   i++)
    cout << *p++ << ' ';
```

You may encounter this idiom in the code that deals with null-terminated strings:

```
char str[60], *s = str;
...
// Find the first '@':
while (*s && *s != '@') s++;
```

⌘ ⌘ ⌘

This relationship between arrays and pointers is reciprocal. Any pointer may be construed as pointing to the first element of <u>some</u> logical array, albeit undeclared. If p is a pointer, C++ allows us to write p[0] instead of *p, and in general, p[i] instead of *(p+i).

Consider the following example of a function that shifts the elements of an array to the left by 3 (starting at a[3]):

```
void ShiftLeftBy3(double a[], int size)

// Shifts elements:
//    a[0] = a[3];
//    a[1] = a[4];
//    ...
//    a[size-4] = a[size-1];

{
    double *p = a + 3;

    for (int i = 0;    i < size-3;    i++)
        a[i] = p[i];
}
```

**In view of the reciprocity between pointers and arrays, we have to
conclude that the most appropriate way of looking at the expression p[i]
is to think of [] as the "subscript" operator: we are applying the
operator [] to the operands p (of a particular pointer data type) and i
(an integer).**

We have to be a little careful, though. When we declare a pointer p, this by itself
does not declare any array. Before we start using p[i], we have to make sure that
p points to some element in an array declared elsewhere, and that p[i] is within
the range of that array.

In a nutshell, whether s is declared as an array or as a pointer, the following
expressions are equivalent:

Expression:	Is the same as:
s	&s[0]
s + i	&s[i]
*s	s[0]
*(s+i)	s[i]

If a is declared as an array, enough memory is reserved to hold the specified
number of elements, and a cannot be used as an lvalue (i.e., you cannot set a equal
to a new address). If p is declared as a pointer, the declaration by itself <u>does not</u>
reserve any memory to which p points; p can be used as an lvalue, and, in fact,
before p is used as a pointer, it must be set to some valid address (the address of
some variable or constant, or an array element).

⌘ ⌘ ⌘

The difference between an array and a pointer disappears completely within a function to which an array is passed as an argument. An array argument, a, is passed to a function as a pointer equal to the address of the first element of the array. The function declarations

```
... MyFunction (double a[], ...)
```

and

```
... MyFunction (double *a, ...)
```

are identical. The former simply emphasizes the fact that a points to the whole array, not just one variable.

Within the function, this array (or pointer) argument is <u>a copy</u> of the pointer passed from the calling code. That is why this pointer can be used as both an lvalue and an rvalue. For example, the following function copies one array into another:

```
void Copy (double a[], double b[], int size)

// Copies a[0] into b[0], ..., a[size-1] into b[size-1]

{
    for (int i = 0;   i < size;   i++)
        b[i] = a[i];
}
```

The same function can be written with pointers:

```
void Copy (double a[], double b[], int size)

// More obscure implementation with pointers:

{
    while (size-- > 0)   // Compare size with 0, then decrement it
        *b++ = *a++;
}
```

But there is no legitimate reason for using the latter version, and it may even seem obscure to some programmers.

In another example, consider the function AddElements (...), which returns the sum of an array's elements:

```
double AddElements (double a[], int size)

// Returns a[0] + ... + a[size-1]

{
    double sum = 0.;
    int i;

    for (i = 0;   i < size;   i++)
        sum += a[i];

    return sum;
}
```

Now, suppose we have an array of 100 elements:

```
...
double a[100];
...
```

We can call AddElements (...) to calculate, for instance, the sum of the first 80 and the sum of the last 20 elements of this array, as follows:

```
...
double sum1, sum2;
...
sum1 = AddElements(a, 80);        // sum1 = a[0] + ... + a[79]
sum2 = AddElements(a + 80, 20);  // sum2 = a[80] + ... + a[99]
// or, equally acceptable,
// sum2 = AddElements(&a[80], 20);
```

Appendix C: Stream I/O Classes

C++ stream I/O classes allow programs to handle files and input and output devices consistently. The classes are arranged into a hierarchy, with the base `ios` class at the root (Figure C-1). `ios` defines input or output stream abstraction and includes functions and constants that report and define the stream state.

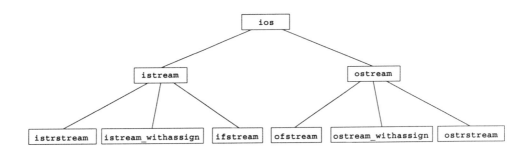

Figure C-1. C++ I/O classes hierarchy.

The public constants in the `ios` class are written with the `ios::` prefix. For example, in the following line:

```
cout.flags (ios::showpoint | ios::fixed);
```

`long flags(...)` is a member function of the `ios` class (inherited by `cout`) which sets the formatting attributes of the stream (represented as "flags," i.e., bits in a special data member that holds the formatting information).

`ios::showpoint` is a flag that tells the stream always to show the decimal point in the output of `float` and `double` types; `ios::fixed` tells the stream to show the fixed number of decimal places defined by the current precision setting, including the trailing zeroes. These two constants represent individual bits in the stream format variable and are combined by using the bit-wise "or" operator to set both flags. `flags(...)` returns the old values of flags and can be called without an argument just to read the current flag settings. For example:

```
cout << hex << cout.flags() << endl;
```

You can find a complete list of formatting flags in the compiler documentation or in the `iostream.h` file.

⌘   ⌘   ⌘

`ios` also provides output formatting through the use of manipulators, which are specialized functions usually used by "inserting" them into the stream. The most commonly used ones are:

```
endl                  — inserts end of the line
setw(d)               — sets output width to d
setprecision(d)       — sets decimal precision
dec                   — switches to decimal output
hex                   — switches to hex output
setfill(ch)           — defines a new fill character
                           (for padding between fields)
ends                  — inserts the null character '\0'
                           (used in output to strings)
```

To use manipulators with a parameter, `setw(...)`, `setprecision(...)`, `setfill(...)`, you need to include the `iomanip.h` header file into your source. `setprecision`, `setfill`, `dec`, and `hex` settings remain in effect until changed, but `setw` is reset to the default after the first output item.

For example:

```
#include <iostream.h>
#include <iomanip.h>

int main()

{
    double amt = 1.5;
    cout.flags(ios::showpoint | ios::fixed);
    cout << setprecision(2) << setfill('*');
    cout << "Amount " << setw(10) << amt << endl;
    cout << setw(10) << "Amount " << amt << endl;
    ...
}
```

would produce:

```
Amount ******1.50
***Amount 1.50
```

The `ios setf(...)` member function allows you to set a few format bits selectively while leaving other bits unchanged. For example,

```
    cout.setf(ios::left, ios::adjustfield);
```

tells the output stream to left-justify all output items within their width fields. If followed by

```
    cout << setfill('.') << setw(20) << "Preface" << 1 << endl;
```

it will produce

```
Preface.............1
```

Some compilers may not right-justify the value in the output field by default. Then you need to add the statement

```
    cout.setf(ios::right, ios::adjustfield);
```

to your program.

The `ios unsetf(...)` member function resets selectively the specified format bits while leaving other bits unchanged.

⌘   ⌘   ⌘

The `ios` class also provides functions for conditions and error checking:

```
int eof()  - returns true on the end-of-file condition
int bad()  - returns true if an invalid operation was attempted
int fail() - returns true if the operation failed or was invalid
int good() - returns true if none of the above
```

The overloaded `!` ("not") operator is simply a convenient shorthand for `fail()`.
For example:

```
ifstream file("myfile");
if (!file) {      // The same as:     if (file.fail())
    cout << "Cannot open myfile" << endl;
    ...
```

⌘ ⌘ ⌘

The file I/O classes `ifstream` and `ofstream` are derived from `istream` and `ostream` respectively and are defined in the `fstream.h` header file. In most compilers `fstream.h` also includes `iostream.h`. Each of these classes provides a default constructor as well as a constructor that takes a file name and an opening mode as arguments. The destructor closes the file. You can also use the `open(...)` member function to open a file explicitly and the `close()` function to close it explicitly.

```
class ifstream: public istream {

public:

    ifstream();
    ifstream(const char *filename, int mode = ios::in,
                             int prot = filebuf::openprot);
    void open(const char *filename, int mode = ios::in,
                             int prot = filebuf::openprot);
        //   modes:
        // ios::in -- default
        // ios::binary -- binary mode (the default is text mode)

    void close();
    ...
};
```

```
class ofstream: public ostream {

public:

    ofstream();
    ofstream(const char *filename, int mode = ios::out,
                            int prot = filebuf::openprot);
    void open(const char *filename, int mode = ios::out,
                            int prot = filebuf::openprot);
        // modes:
        // ios::out  -- default (truncate the file if it exists)
        // ios::app  -- always write at the end
        // ios::ate  -- start writing at the end
        // ios::nocreate -- fail if the file does not exist
        // ios::noreplace -- fail if the file already exists
        // ios::binary -- write in binary mode (i.e., with no
        //     formatting of any kind); the default is text mode

    void close();
    ...
};
```

In most situations you can simply use constructors to open files:

```
#include <fstream.h>
...
    // Declare and open myInp
    ifstream myFile("INPUT.DAT", ios::binary);
    if (!myFile)...

    // Declare and open myOutp
    ofstream myOutp = ofstream("OUTPUT.DAT", ios::binary | ios::app);
    if (!myOutp)...
```

⌘   ⌘   ⌘

Input streams (cin and files) provide the following member functions for input:

```
istream& operator>>(...) -  Extraction operator >>

int get()                -  Reads and returns one character

int peek()               -  Returns the next character but leaves
                              it in the stream
istream& get(char &c)    -  Reads a char into c

istream& get(char *s, int n, char delim = '\n')
                         -  Reads up to n-1 chars or until encounters
                              the delim char and places them into s;
                              appends a null char, leaves the delim
                              char in the stream
```

```
istream& getline(char *s, int n, char delim = '\n')
                        -  Same as above, but extracts the delim
                           char from the stream

istream& ignore(int n = 1, int delim = EOF)
                        -  Reads and discards up to n characters,
                           or up to and including the delim char

istream& read(char *s, int n)
                        -  Reads n chars into s (including
                           null chars). May read less than n chars
                           in case of eof or an error

int gcount()            -  Returns the number of chars actually read
                           in the last call to get(…), getline(…),
                           or read(…)
```

Extraction operator calls may use other read functions, so the result of gcount() becomes unpredictable after you use >>.

There are also versions of get(…), getline(…), and read(…) that put the result into an array of bytes (unsigned char*).

The input file streams also offer positioning functions:

```
long tellg()            - Tells the current position in the file

istream& seekg(long pos) - Moves to the new absolute position

istream& seekg(long offset, ios::seek_dir dir)
                        - Moves to a position relative to the
                          beginning (dir = ios::beg),
                          current position (dir = ios::cur), or
                          the end (dir = ios::end) of the file
```

The following code, for instance, reports the file size and then "rewinds" the file to the beginning:

```
#include <fstream.h>
...
    ifstream inpFile("MYFILE.DAT");
    inpFile.seekg(0, ios::end);    // Set file position to the end of file
    cout << inpFile.tellg() << " bytes.\n";
    inp.seekg(0);                  // Rewind
```

⌘   ⌘   ⌘

Output streams (`cout` and files) provide the following member functions for output:

```
ostream& operator<<(...) - Insertion operator <<

ostream& put(char c)      - Writes one char
ostream& write(char *s, int n)
                          - Writes n chars (including null chars)
                                to the output stream
```

The `write(...)` function is more useful for writing unformatted data into binary files. In the text mode it may append carriage return characters at the end of lines.

The `ostream` class also provides positioning functions similar to those for the input streams:

```
long tellp()
ostream& seekp(long pos)
ostream& seekp(long offset, ios::seek_dir dir)
```

⌘ ⌘ ⌘

`cout` is actually an instance of the classes `ostream_withassign`. This class includes an overloaded assignment operator, so you can assign an output file stream to `cout` and thus redirect all the standard output to a file:

```
...
ofstream file("TEMP.OUT");
cout = file;    // All standard output will now go to TEMP.OUT
...
```

The same applies to `cin`, which is an instance of `istream_withassign`.

Index